Understanding the Courses We Teach

Understanding the Courses We Teach

Local Perspectives on English Language Teaching

Edited by

John Murphy, Georgia State University

Patricia Byrd, Georgia State University

Ann Arbor

THE UNIVERSITY OF MICHIGAN PRESS

Copyright © by the University of Michigan 2001
All rights reserved
Published in the United States of America by
The University of Michigan Press
Manufactured in the United States of America
∞ Printed on acid-free paper

2004 2003 2002 2001   4 3 2 1

A CIP catalog record for this book is available from the British Library.

Library of Congress Cataloging-in-Publication Data

Murphy, John, 1952–
    Understanding the courses we teach : local perspectives on English language teaching / John Murphy, Patricia Byrd.
        p.   cm.
    Includes bibliographical references (p.   ).
    ISBN 0-472-09770-9 (cloth : acid-free paper) — ISBN 0-472-06770-2 (paper : acid-free paper)
    1. English language—Study and teaching—Foreign speakers.   I. Byrd, Patricia. II. Title.
PE1128.A2 M875   2001
428′.0071—dc21   2001001993

To the language teachers who contributed to this book and the learners who inspired them.

> I tramp a perpetual journey, (come listen all!)
> My signs are a rain-proof coat, good shoes,
>   and a staff cut from the woods,
> No friend of mine takes his ease in my chair,
> I have no chair, no church, no philosophy,
> I lead no man to a dinner-table, library, exchange,
> But each man and each woman of you I lead upon a knoll,
> My left hand hooking you round the waist,
> My right hand pointing to landscapes of continents
>   and the public road.
>
> Not I, not any one else can travel that road for you,
> You must travel it for yourself.
>
> It is not far, it is within reach,
> Perhaps you have been on it since you were born
>   and did not know,
> Perhaps it is everywhere on water and on land.
>
> —Walt Whitman, "Song of Myself"

Acknowledgments

We owe special thanks to our colleagues (Sharon Cavusgil, Joan Hilden-brand, Gayle Nelson, Debra Snell, Sara Weigle) and students (Mustafa Elsawy, Barbara Hegyesi, Jing Fang Liu, and Jonathan Smith) in the Department of Applied Linguistics and ESL of Georgia State University and to the editorial staff of the University of Michigan Press (Kelly Sippell, Nichole Argyres) for feedback and other generous forms of support while working on this book.

Contents

Part 1
Background

Chapter 1

A Time for Local Perspectives

John Murphy

My left hand hooking you round the waist,
My right hand pointing to landscapes of continents and the public road.
—Walt Whitman, "Song of Myself"

Teachers of English to speakers of other languages have interesting stories to share about the courses they offer. Some of the more compelling stories focus on a specific course and reveal details of a teacher's local approach to language instruction. In teachers' conversations with one another, such stories capture the imaginations of tens of thousands of language teachers all over the world. Unfortunately, far too few of our stories ever appear in written form. In this book, English language teachers share stories and understandings of the courses they teach.

Understanding the Courses We Teach (hereafter, the *Understanding* collection) provides opportunities to examine descriptions of 18 authentic English language courses as composed by individual, or a collaborative team of, classroom teachers. For too long, the field of English language teaching (ELT) has been dominated by generic discussions that fail to illustrate teachers' and learners' actual experiences within specific courses. Individual teachers' firsthand accounts rarely serve as centerpieces in professional development literatures. The *Understanding* collection is different. It begins with the assumption that current and prospective language teachers are interested in learning even more than they already know about what happens within other teachers' courses. One of the collection's distinctive features is the opportunity it provides to examine experienced teachers' understandings and explanations of their ways of offering language courses.

Anyone reading this book, already interested in the teaching of English to speakers of other languages, has the good fortune of being part of a worldwide cast. Some of the more visible members of the cast include current and prospective language teachers, language learners, program administrators, materials writers, teacher educators, curriculum developers, researchers, and publishers. In actual practice, distinctions between some of these roles and role relationships are difficult to maintain. Many ELT classroom teachers, for example, contribute to the profession as materials writers, curriculum developers, and program administrators. There are many English language teachers who are second language (L2) speakers of English and former ELT classroom learners. In some settings, learners play significant roles as contributors to the planning and development of language courses in which they participate. Thus, the roles that teachers, learners, and other cast members play within contemporary stories of ELT are varied and multidimensional.

One theme that permeates the *Understanding* collection may be stated concisely as follows: *all instances of English language teaching take place within particular sets of circumstances.* In contrast, most introductions to the field of ELT center on generic rather than local treatments of teaching. There are serious drawbacks to such generic discussions. In the real world of ELT, acts of teaching and learning are always situated within local settings. Particular sets of circumstances significantly impact plans for teaching as well as teachers' instructional insights, actions, and behaviors. Practicing teachers realize it is within particular settings that we learn to develop, hone, and revise not only our teaching skills but our understandings of instructional possibilities. Beginning and developing teachers can learn valuable lessons from accounts of how other teachers adapt their instructional plans, decisions, and behaviors to local conditions. Throughout the *Understanding* collection, we use the phrase *situated nature of language teaching* to call attention to the importance of local contexts in which ELT courses are offered. All of the collection's chapters celebrate this theme. Hereafter, phrases such as *local understandings and explanations, own ways of teaching,* and *personal ways of teaching* will signal an individual teacher's approach to ELT as focused on a specific language course and setting.

Here are some of the recurring terms and terminology featured throughout the book. Following widely accepted usage (see, e.g., Brown 1994a), we will be using the phrases/acronyms *English as a second language* (ESL) and *English language teaching* (ELT) in special ways. The ELT acronym will serve as a generic descriptor tied to the teaching of English to speakers of other languages in diverse parts of the world, in different kinds of settings, regardless of more specific sets of circumstances. We use the ESL acronym to signal the teaching of English as a *second* language (specifically) in countries such as Australia, most parts of Canada, Great Britain, New Zealand, the United States and other parts of the world where English is the major language of commerce and education. In places such as these, students of ESL teachers are likely to hear English being spoken on a regular basis in settings beyond the classroom. We reserve the phrase *English as a foreign language* (EFL) to indicate the teaching of English in regions of the world such as China, Egypt, Japan, Russia, Mexico, and Spain, where English is not the primary language of commerce and education. Such usage is parallel to the teaching of Chinese, Arabic, Japanese, Russian, or Spanish as a "foreign" language in secondary, college, and university classrooms in Australia, Canada, Great Britain, New Zealand, and the United States. As mentioned previously, the phrase *English language teaching* and its acronym, ELT, will be used for more general topics applicable to the teaching of either ESL or EFL.

Organization of the Book

The *Understanding* collection's first five chapters are background discussions setting the stage for the local perspectives on ELT featured in chapters 6 through 23. As signaled by the section titles in the table of contents, this series of 18 local-perspectives chapters is arranged in four thematic clusters: (*a*) general purposes instruction including workplace literacy, community-based ESL, and courses designed for recent immigrants in Australia, Canada, and the United States, (*b*) the teaching of English as a Foreign Language in Hong Kong and Japan, (*c*) university credit-bearing courses focused on the teaching of English for Academic Purposes in Canada and the United States, and (*d*) noncredit university-affiliated courses offered through Intensive English Programs. Each of the 18 local-perspectives chapters begins with a description of the instructional context for the targeted course. These descriptions and discussions of genuine teaching and learning experiences in language courses reveal details of the stories contributors have to share and illustrate that teachers' firsthand accounts have something valuable to offer. Rather than highlighting a skills focus for L2 teaching, an overarching instructional philosophy, or a favorite instructional technique, each chapter's centerpiece is an authentic course as offered by one of the contributor-teachers. The local-perspectives chapters are rich in descriptive details and narrative tones. They resonate with the contributors' personal investments in their own acts of teaching.

The purpose of this initial chapter is to introduce the *Understanding* collection's scope and purpose. Chapter 2 reviews theoretical underpinnings and intended purposes for the collection as a whole. It traces some of the historic and contemporary developments in the field that launched our interest in making the collection available. For those interested in contemporary theory to support English language instruction, the second chapter concludes with a synthesis, listing, and discussion of 14 general principles of ELT. Following this review of contemporary theory, the third chapter focuses on specific precursors to the *Understanding* collection's organizing schema and serves as a backdrop for the collection overall. Chapters 4 ("A Framework for Discussion—Part 1") and 5 ("A Framework for Discussion—Part 2") provide a unified discussion of a framework for organizing individual teachers' understandings and written discussions of specific courses they offer. We refer to the framework featured in chapters 4 and 5 as the "*Understanding* chapter framework" and present it as a conceptual lens for readers to refer to while examining the collection's remaining chapters. In chapters 6 through 23, contributor-teachers apply the framework in modified ways to discuss separate English language courses. Although chapters 6 through 23 are freestanding and can be read in any order, chapters 1 through 5 should be read before them and in sequence. Of these first five chapters, the fourth and fifth chapters are probably the most important since they establish necessary context and may serve as a conceptual lens for more clearly appreciating the rest of the collection.

As it appears throughout the rest of the book, the *Understanding* chapter framework is organized around contributors' responses to the 13 topics presented in table 1.1. Responses to topics 1–9 were required for inclusion in each of the local-perspectives chapters. However, decisions on how to sequence the topics and whether to include topics 10–13 were left to the discretion of each contributor. As mentioned earlier, each of the components of the *Understanding* chapter framework is elaborated in detail in chapters 4 and 5. The framework serves as a cohesive story structure tying together the various ways of teaching introduced throughout the collection. A point to bear in mind is that the chapter framework was intended to facilitate contributor-teachers' efforts as writers rather than constrain them. That is, we designed the framework to be flexible enough for contributors to discuss their understandings of ELT courses they offer in ways consistent with their own voices as writers, storytellers, and teachers.

The Contributors' Charge

In chapters 6 through 23 contributors discuss how they plan, organize, and set about teaching specific ELT courses. By focusing on individual teachers' written discussions of their instructional plans, decisions, and experiences, the *Understanding* collection reflects the wider field's continuing progres-

TABLE 1.1.   Framework for *Understanding* Chapters 6 through 23

Nine Required Topics for Discussion

1. What is the *setting* for the course?
2. What are the *theory, principles, or concepts* serving to support the teacher's way of offering the course?
3. What will students *be able to do* by the end of the course as a result of having participated in it successfully? (goals/objectives)
4. How is the course organized; what is the *overall design* of the course?
5. What *activity types* are featured prominently?
6. What roles do *learners* play?
7. What roles does *the teacher* play?
8. What types of *instructional materials* are included in the course? What are they like? How are they selected?
9. What are some *details of communication and interaction patterns* that have actually taken place within the course? (lesson particulars)

Four Optional Topics for Discussion

10. How are *affective considerations* addressed?
11. What roles do *culture* and cultural considerations play in the course?
12. How is learner *assessment* accomplished?
13. Is there *anything else* you would like other teachers to know?

sion away from generic to more specific treatments of language teaching (Brown 1993a, 1993b; Kumaravadivelu 1993, 1994a; Richards 1998, 1996). Through presentation of a range of different teachers' personal understandings and explanations of their work in whole courses, the collection complements other ELT professional development resources. Chapters 6 through 23 illustrate some of the ways in which English language teachers from different parts of the world (including Australia, Canada, China, Japan, and the United States) organize and implement authentic plans for teaching. Overall, the collection (1) highlights connections between theory and practice in contemporary teachers' perspectives on ELT, (2) provides a range of teachers' local approaches to some of the actual courses they offer, and, through provision of context-specific discussions, (3) supports other teachers' efforts to share their own understandings and explanations of ELT. Each of the local-perspectives chapters represents an opportunity to read about one teacher's way of teaching English to speakers of other languages. Since we asked contributors to suppress impulses to generalize beyond their own experiences within a single English language course, these chapters focus on context-specific themes. The clustering of chapters 6 through 23 into different areas of ELT is intended to make it easier to infer points of comparison and contrast across the various courses presented. As a complement to how chapters 6 through 23 are clustered in the collection, table 1.2 provides additional information on the courses that the contributors discuss.

Why should you take the time to examine individual teachers' local perspectives as presented here? Two reasons signal the path followed in this collection. First, the trajectory of the field suggests a pressing need for a collection of this kind. Over recent decades, the field of ELT has been inundated with broad discussions of teaching. Although many of them merit close examination, there are far too few illustrations of individual teachers' local perspectives on authentic courses. Of the illustrations that are available, even fewer are firsthand accounts. To fill this gap, the *Understanding* collection foregrounds individual teachers' local understandings and explanations of their own courses. A second reason is that current and prospective language teachers naturally are curious about other teachers' understandings and explanations of what they are trying to accomplish in language courses. If our instincts are right, many of the ELT stories appearing in the collection will resonate with potential connections to your current, or future, teaching.

As helpful as we believe their collective presentation to be, we realize that the contributors' stories included in this volume barely scratch the surface. They are indications of an even wider range of stories other teachers have to tell. In this respect, chapters 6 through 23 illustrate ways of sharing local understandings and explanations of ELT that other teacher-writers may be interested in exploring for themselves. If you are an English language teacher, the *Understanding* collection may serve to support your efforts as a teacher-writer interested in sharing with others your insights into one or more of the courses you offer. If you are a prospective teacher such efforts may seem somewhat distant from more immediate concerns. Over time, however, opportunities to teach, reflect on, synthesize, and learn even more about processes of English language teaching and learning are likely to shorten such distances.

Part of the plan for the *Understanding* collection is to enable readers to interact with some of the themes highlighted in the book through communications made possible by the Internet. To this aim, the final chapter, titled "Looking Forward: Connectivity through the Internet," introduces an Internet site tied to the collection. By accessing this site on the World Wide Web, readers have the option of using it to learn even more about individual chapters, gain access to additional information and resource materials, and interact with other readers—as well as the coeditors and some of the book's other contributors—via electronic communications. For example,

TABLE I.2. Additional Ways of Classifying Chapters 6 through 23

Chapter	Integrated Skills	List	Speak	Read	Write	Location	Other Information
6. Terdal, Ruhl, and Armstrong	●		○				Workplace/Literacy
7. Wilson-Keenan, Willett, and Solsken	●						Child age/Public school/Community involvement
8. Morgan	●		○	○		Canada	Citizenship/Recent immigrants/Critical theory
9. DeVillar and Jiang	●		○				Recent immigrants/Acculturation model
10. Burns and McPherson	●		○			Australia	Recent immigrants/National and local perspectives
11. Murphey		○	●			Japan	Postsecondary EFL/Oral fluency/"Fluency first"
12. Acton		○	●			Japan	Postsecondary EFL/Pronunciation/Focal stress
13. Robb				●		Japan	Postsecondary EFL/Extensive reading
14. Miller		●		○		China	ESP: English for engineers
15. Goodwin	●		○	○	○		EAP: Adjunct course/Video recorded lectures
16. Brinton	●			○	○		EAP: Sustained content
17. Mendelsohn	●		○	○		Canada	EAP: Credit bearing (9 credits), 2 semesters
18. Ferris	○			○	●		EAP: Summer term
19. Shih				●	●		EAP: Grammar/Editing
20. Janzen	○		○	○			IEP: Strategy instruction
21. Numrich	●			○			IEP: Theme based/Project work
22. Graham and Barone	○		●				ITAs: Academics professionals
23. Shetzer and Warschauer	○		○		●		Web based/Internet

Notes: Compare the classifications given here with those provided in the table of contents (part titles 2 through 5). ● signals a primary course focus; ○ signals secondary foci; "Location" indicated if other than United States.

while the book presents a unified bibliography at the end, the *Understanding* website **<http://www.gsu.edu/~wwwesl/understanding/>** features a listing of references cited in each chapter along with some additional suggestions for further reading. As will be explained in the final chapter, the collection's Internet site also makes it possible for teacher educators to arrange for students in teacher development courses to post responses to the collection's various prompts for discussion and reflection—as appearing in the book at the ends of chapters 6 through 23—on the World Wide Web. In addition, ELT teachers who are interested will be able to post their own course descriptions on the Internet site. For further discussion of the features and resources made available on the *Understanding* collection's Internet site, see chapter 24.

We trust that your experience in reading this book will illuminate ways of organizing and offering ELT courses. As indicated by its title, the collection is an opportunity to learn about local perspectives on ELT through contemporary teachers' course-specific accounts. We believe such opportunities to be all the more worthwhile when they remind us of some of the potentialities of our own efforts and experiences as language teachers. In the spirit of Walt Whitman's vision depicted at the beginning of this chapter, we hope the *Understanding* collection points to landscapes of possibilities for learning more about the teaching of English to speakers of other languages.

Chapter 2

Background and General Principles

John Murphy

General Good is the plea of the scoundrel hypocrite & flatterer.
—William Blake, *Jerusalem*

The *Understanding* collection illustrates a recent genre of professional development teacher resource material. To contextualize the collection's scope and purpose, we may compare it with five other genres. Historically, many introductions to ways and principles of second/foreign language teaching give attention to well-known global or "designer" methods of teaching such as Audio-Lingual Method, Comprehension Approaches, Counseling-Learning/Community Language Learning, Direct Method, Natural Approach, Rassias Method, Saint-Cloud (audiovisual) Method, Silent Way, Situational Language Teaching, (De)Suggestopedia, and Total Physical Response (for concise reviews see Brown 1994a, 1994b; Oller and Richard-Amato 1983; Larsen-Freeman 1986, 2000; Richards and Rodgers 1986; Stevick 1976, 1980). Illustrations of this first genre appear as whole volumes that introduce, survey, analyze, and/or critique global methods of L2 teaching. Such volumes were especially popular during the 1970s and 1980s, although the roots of several global methods reach considerably further back into the history of the field (Byrd, Forsyth, and Sherbahn 1996; Howatt 1984; Kelly 1969; Palmer 1917). Although currently out of favor in many circles, global methods serve as something more than historical curiosities. Many continue to be introduced in professional development programs and are likely to be familiar to contemporary English language teachers. However, as the following comments from Brown 1994b suggest, their impacts are, and are likely to remain, on the periphery of the field.

> These [global] methods . . . were touted as "innovative" and "revolutionary," especially when compared to [considerably earlier] Audiolingual or Grammar Translation methodology. Claims for their success, originating from their

> proprietary founders and proponents, were often overstated in the interest of attracting teachers to weekend workshops and seminars, to new books and tapes and videos, and, of course, to getting their learners to reach the zenith of their potential. These claims, often overstated and overgeneralized, led David Nunan (1989[c], 97) to refer to the methods of the day as "designer" methods, prescriptive, and ostensibly appropriate for all learners in all contexts. (95)

Even though several generations of teachers have explored them firsthand (Oprandy 1999), what today's teachers find useful with respect to principles and techniques of global methods tends to be tempered by greater awareness of teaching-learning possibilities. Shifting learner demographics, worldwide expansion of ELT over the past several decades, concern for cultural sensitivity, and clearer appreciation for language teachers' individual ways of envisioning their own instructional efforts increasingly have drawn attention to more context-specific and local concerns. Hence, this book is dedicated to presenting *local* rather than global ELT perspectives.

The scope and purpose of the *Understanding* collection may also be compared to a second genre of professional development materials. In comparison with discussions of global methods, these resources adopt a considerably broader view. Stepping well beyond descriptions and analyses of prepackaged designs for language teaching, examples of the second genre provide book-length discussions of contemporary theory-to-practice themes. They are sometimes called *MATESOL methods texts, foreign language methods texts,* or simply *methods texts* since their primary audiences are preservice teachers, less experienced teachers, and participants in introductory courses of applied linguistics. Examples such as Brown 1994a; Celce-Murcia 1991; Cross 1992; Gebhard 1996; Harmer 1991; Long and Richards 1987; Nunan 1991a, 1999; Omaggio 1993; Richard-Amato 1988; Scarcella and Oxford 1992; and Ur 1996 include state-of-the-art overviews focused on a range of topics central to the field. Typically, these topics include the teaching of listening, speaking, reading, writing, and grammar. Additional topics may be presented through whole chapter discussions of learner proficiency levels, language learning styles and strategies, communication patterns in classrooms, specific purposes instruction, sociopolitical concerns, ways of classroom management, lesson planning, needs assessment, testing and evaluation, and pathways of long-term professional development, among other themes.

Along with methods texts of the second genre, there are numerous professional development books treating in much greater depth each of the individual topics and themes mentioned previously. Such in-depth treatments take the form of whole books devoted to specific subtopics of the

TABLE 2.1.   Three Genres of Professional Development Resource Texts: Background to the *Understanding* Collection

Genre Type	Characteristics	Examples
1. Surveys of global methods	Introduce, survey, and/or critique global methods of second/foreign language teaching	Howatt 1984; Kelly 1969; Larsen-Freeman 1986; Oller and Richard-Amato 1983; Palmer 1917; Richards and Rodgers 1986; Stevick 1976, 1980
2. Methods texts	Broad-based introductions to the ELT field. These survey a wide range of interrelated instructional themes.	Brown 1994a; Celce-Murcia 1991; Cross 1992; Gebhard 1996; Harmer 1991; Long and Richards 1987; Nunan 1991a, 1999; Omaggio 1993; Richard-Amato 1988; Scarcella and Oxford 1992; Ur 1996
3. Topic-specific reference texts	Focused, in-depth, theory-to-practice discussions of sub-topics in the field of applied linguistics and ELT Book-length specialist discussions Largest and fastest-growing of the first three genres	Anderson 1999 on reading; Byrd 1995 on materials development; Byrd and Reid 1998a on grammar in the composition class; Carson and Leki 1993 on reading-writing connections; Ellis 1994 on SLA; Ferris and Hedgcock 1998 on writing; Flowerdew 1994 on academic listening; Hinkel 1999 on culture; Morley 1994a on speech-pronunciation; Nunan 1988 on syllabus design; Oxford 1990 on learning strategies; and Reid 1993 on writing, among many other examples

field. The entire Mendelsohn and Rubin 1995 collection, for example, focuses on theory and practice in the teaching of L2 listening, while Flowerdew 1994 reveals an even more specific focus on listening for academic purposes. Oxford 1990 is dedicated to in-depth discussion of language learning strategies, while Anderson 1999 and Aebersold and Field 1997 explore issues in the teaching of L2 reading. Grabe and Kaplan 1996 and Ferris and Hedgcock 1998 are two of the more recent books giving sustained attention to theory-practice in the teaching of L2 writing. Other book-length collections are devoted to such topics as L2 speaking, grammar, culture, and so forth. Since their treatments focus on specific topic areas and are sustained as entire book-length discussions, such resources represent yet a third resource genre. Table 2.1 summarizes each of the three resource genres outlined thus far.

Each of the resource genres listed in table 2.1 has contributed in important ways to the professional development of contemporary English language teachers. In recent decades, however, examples of the second and third genres have proven to be more useful than the first. Several introductory methods texts, as well as growing numbers of topic-specific collections, are worthy resources meriting teachers' careful reviews. Nevertheless, an underlying complication is shared by the first and second genres: for different reasons, both first genre surveys of global methods and second genre methods texts tend to foreground generic treatments of language instruction. They are less likely to present much in the way of context-specific considerations. Of the two genres, this tendency is easier to recognize in the first, since global methods by definition lack context specificity. Though theory-to-practice overviews representative of the second genre are, and should continue to be, required reading for all those interested in discussions of ELT, they too are similarly constrained. From another perspective, an undeniable strength of second genre methods texts is that within a single volume they include substantive treatments of a wide range of worthy instructional themes. While we acknowledge this strength, and it is a significant one, contemporary methods texts rarely succeed in discussing ELT in ways situated within clearly defined instructional settings. With few exceptions, similar critiques may be applied to third genre resources, as well. Since the *Understanding* collection features individual teachers' discussions of what they try to accomplish within clearly defined instructional contexts, it targets and begins to fill a gap in professional resource literatures. Fortunately, the *Understanding* collection does not stand alone. In addition to the three genres outlined thus far, at least two other ELT resource genres merit further consideration.

Two Additional Professional Development Resource Genres

Beginning in the mid-1980s and certainly continuing today, there has been a steady groundswell of interest in local perspectives on ELT. As signaled by growing numbers of journal articles and books, language instruction specialists value attention to local perspectives, encourage their continuing explorations, and seek ways of sharing individual teachers' local perspectives with wider audiences. ELT practitioners have always been interested in what other teachers do in language classrooms, but contemporary specialists are interested in local perspectives, as well. Examples of this surge in attention fall into categories such as classroom-oriented research (Chaudron 1988; Nunan 1989c), classroom interaction analysis (Ernst 1994; Fanselow 1987; Spada 1994), classroom ethnography (Hornberger 1994; van Lier

1988), action research (Wallace 1998; Nunan 1990), participatory action re-search (Auerbach 1994), and exploratory teaching (Allwright and Bailey 1991). Published scholarship in these areas supports the roles of teachers as course developers (Graves 1996), decision makers (Freeman 1998; Johnson 1992, 1994, 1999; Woods 1996, 1989), reflective teachers (Gebhard and Oprandy 1999; Richards and Lockhart 1994), and self-directed managers of teaching-learning phenomena (Nunan and Lamb 1996). As a profession, we owe a considerable debt to these and other specialists who explore the evolution of language courses along with the perceptions of participating teachers and learners. By focusing attention on the language classroom as the very heart of our profession, they expand interest in the value of local perspectives and illuminate ways in which local considerations fit within the field's broader contexts of teaching and learning.

Bailey and Nunan (1996), for example, present a series of research reports "conducted in the tradition of naturalistic inquiry" and "gathered in naturally occurring settings" within language courses worldwide (1). Contributors to their collection explore such topics as reticence and anxiety in language classrooms, processes of curriculum renewal, ELT classroom communication patterns, teacher decision making, and the socialization of teachers and learners. Serving as precursors to Bailey and Nunan's collection, Allwright and Bailey 1991 and Chaudron 1988 provide richly detailed discussions of classroom-centered research findings spanning recent decades.

Such resources support our belief that individual teachers' local perspectives on ELT illuminate themes affecting language teachers and learners worldwide. By examining language classroom research reports, we are better prepared to recognize ways in which local acts of teaching and learning reflect such broader concerns as (1) affective considerations, (2) the need for coherent structure and sequencing in language teaching, (3) teacher reasoning, (4) teacher decision making, (5) learner reasoning, (6) learner inputs, and (7) the participatory nature of language lessons. For those interested in precursors to published reports of local perspectives on whole ELT courses, Richards's (1989) article titled "Profile of an Effective Reading Teacher" is an early example of the genre. For his report, Richards implemented a case study methodology grounded by the experiences of one teacher working in a single ESL academic-preparatory reading course. The article focuses on one teacher's way of offering such a course and demonstrates that careful description and discussion of one teacher's approach to even a single course can illuminate the puzzling events, themes, and issues many teachers face (see also Allwright 1992). By illustrating the value of describing one ESL teacher's instructional approach, Richards's article signaled a direction for several of the classroom-oriented collections mentioned previously and prompted our own thinking about the possible content and structure of an *Understanding* collection.

In the early 1990s the TESOL International professional organization initiated publication of the first volumes of its New Ways series (e.g., Bailey and Savage 1994; Day 1993; Freeman and Cornwell 1993). Without any pejorative connotation intended, teacher resources of this genre may be characterized as classroom "activity-recipe" collections. They are quite different from the other professional development resources described up to this point. Though both welcomed and sorely needed, volumes of the New Ways series were relative latecomers to this resource tradition since similar series had been on the market for over a decade. Grellet 1981 is one of the earliest examples of the genre, while Hedge 1988, Klippel 1987, and Ur 1990 are some of its best-known exemplars. Publishers and teacher-authors outside of North America, especially in Great Britain and other parts of Europe, played prominent roles in the generation of such resources. Activity-recipe collections are designed for ELT teachers worldwide and provide opportunities for experienced teachers to describe and discuss favored classroom procedures. Book-length collections of this kind are highly practical contributions to the field and useful as both reference points and points of departure for teachers who (1) sometimes find it necessary to generate classroom activities of their own design and (2) at other times may find it useful to adapt, elaborate, extend, or individualize classroom activities described by others. An extensive number of activity-recipe collections are now available. Several dozen book-length examples were published during the latter half of the 1990s, and many more are sure to follow.

While their quality and diversity are impressive, descriptions of language classroom activity types, as typically represented in such collections, are limited in scope. The great majority depict options for teaching individual lessons and lesson segments but give much less attention to underlying theory. As will be emphasized in the second half of this chapter (and elsewhere in chaps. 6 through 23), an appreciation for underlying theory is essential for language teachers interested in continuing to grow, develop, and explore their own understandings and explanations of teaching. Although a few activity-recipe collections extend the scope of their discussions by describing more sustained thematic units that might span a series of separate classes or even weeks of class (e.g., Fried-Booth 1986), we know of none that focus on the development of whole courses. As useful as language classroom activity-recipe collections can be, their focus and scope are considerably less comprehensive than the kinds of discussions presented in chapters 6 through 23 of this collection.

Concurrent with the growing popularity of activity-recipe collections, several book-length discussions further expanded the tradition of documenting local perspectives on English language teaching. In addition to Bailey and Nunan 1996, other resources such as Graves 1996, Richards 1998, Richards and Lockhart 1994, and Plaister 1993 feature locally grounded discussions of teaching organized around course-focused investigations of curriculum design, cases, case studies,[1] action research, and exploratory teaching. Such collections continue to illuminate the multiple roles contemporary language teachers play as task designers, needs assessors, and reflective teachers. Not surprisingly, Richards 1998 is an especially accessible example of this genre. Extending some of the earlier premises of his work, Richards's edited collection provides numerous case studies that illustrate ways in which ELT teachers from around the world learn to identify and respond to some of the puzzling events they encounter within English language classrooms. We may now extend our previous listing of three types of precursors to the *Understanding* collection to include a total of five professional development resource genres, as shown in table 2.2.

Continuing to learn about, explore, and contribute to such traditions seems especially important to bear in mind as we prepare to examine individual teachers' understandings of ELT. Traditions of classroom-oriented research, cases and case studies, action research, reflective teaching, and exploratory teaching are likely to continue to play vital roles in the lives of English language teachers.

General Principles of English Language Learning and Teaching

While individual teachers' local understandings and explanations are the focus of the *Understanding* collection, there are a number of contemporary ELT principles that may help to establish a broader context for interpreting

---

1. Though sometimes confused, "cases" and "cases studies" are not the same thing. The former tend to be more open-ended and are designed to introduce unresolved themes in narrative form for purposes of discussion-learning (e.g., as part of in-service training or in teacher preparation seminar discussions). Case studies are more directly tied to research methodology. For more on this topic, see Johnson 1996a and Silverman and Welty 1992.

TABLE 2.2.   Five Genres of Professional Development Resource Texts: Background to the *Understanding* Collection

Genre Type	Characteristics	Examples
1. Surveys of global methods	See table 2.1	See table 2.1
2. Methods texts	See table 2.1	See table 2.1
3. Topic-specific reference texts	See table 2.1	See table 2.1
4. Activity-recipe collections	Descriptions of individual teachers' favored lesson activities, plans for teaching, instructional procedures	Bailey and Savage 1994; Day 1993; Hedge 1988; Klippel 1987; Nunan and Miller 1995; Rinvolucri 1984; Ur 1990
5. Collections designed to support teachers' local explorations of ELT	Discussions and illustrations of exploratory teaching, classroom-centered research, teacher-initiated investigations, action research, cases, and case studies	Allwright and Bailey 1991; Bailey and Nunan 1996; Fanselow 1987; Freeman 1998; Graves 1996; Johnson 1994, 1999; Nunan 1989c; Gebhard and Oprandy 1999; Plaister 1993; Richards 1998; Richards and Lockhart 1994; Wallace 1998

what contributors have to say about their courses in chapters 6 through 23. Grounded by the review of five professional resource genres introduced thus far, the next few pages present 14 principles to support English language learning and teaching in general. Though unanimity is impossible when it comes to underlying theory in any professional field, the 14 principles set forth in this section are widely recognized and, for the most part, noncontroversial. They reflect some of the best-supported insights into contemporary understanding of language learning and teaching.

Sources for generating the general principles were 11 influential discussions published in major forums. Most of them reflect earlier attempts to synthesize contemporary ELT principles. These sources include two ELT methods texts (Brown 1994a; Omaggio 1993), five journal article surveys of English language learning-teaching research (Kumaravadivelu 1994a; Larsen-Freeman 1991; Nunan 1991b; Oxford 1992; Pica 1994b), three classroom-focused syntheses of teaching-learning principles (Allwright and Bailey 1991; Mendelsohn 1992; Morley 1994a), and a plenary address from an international convention that synthesized research implications

TABLE 2.3. Sources for General ELT Principles

Abbreviation	Full Citation
A&B	Allwright, D., and K. Bailey, 1991. *Focus on the language classroom: An introduction to classroom research for language teachers.* New York: Cambridge University Press.
B	Brown, H. D. 1994a. Teaching by principles. In *Teaching by principles: An interactive approach to language pedagogy,* 15–31. Englewood Cliffs, NJ: Prentice-Hall Regents.
K	Kumaravadivelu, B. 1994a. The postmethod condition: (E)merging strategies for second/foreign language teaching. *TESOL Quarterly* 28 (1): 27–48.
L-F	Larsen-Freeman, D. 1991. Second language acquisition research: Staking out the territory. *TESOL Quarterly* 25 (2): 315–50.
Me	Mendelsohn, D. 1992. Making the speaking class a real learning experience: The keys to teaching spoken English. *TESL Canada Journal* 10 (1): 72–89.
Mo	Morley, J. 1994a. Multidimensional curriculum design for speech-pronunciation instruction. In J. Morley, ed., *Pronunciation pedagogy and theory: New views, new directions,* 64–91. Alexandria, VA: TESOL.
N1	Nunan, D. 1991b. Communicative tasks and the language curriculum. *TESOL Quarterly* 25 (2): 279–95.
N2	Nunan, D. 2000. Seven hypotheses about language learning and teaching. Audiotape 110-1524. Plenary Address, TESOL International Convention, Vancouver, Canada, March.
Om	Omaggio, A. C. 1993. *Teaching language in context: Proficiency-oriented instruction.* 2d ed. Boston, MA: Heinle and Heinle.
Ox	Oxford, R. 1992. Who are our students? A synthesis of foreign and second language research on individual differences with implications for instructional practice. *TESL Canada Journal* 9 (2): 30–49.
P	Pica, T. 1994b. Questions from the language classroom: Research perspectives. *TESOL Quarterly* 28 (1): 49–79.

for ELT (Nunan 2000). The next few pages present (1) a complete listing of these 11 sources (table 2.3), (2) a brief listing of the 14 principles (table 2.4), and, finally, (3) elaborated discussions of each principle. For ease of reference and unless otherwise indicated, sentences and phrases either quoted or paraphrased closely from one of the 11 sources will be followed by the first initial(s) of the writer-specialist's last name(s) (e.g., "A&B" for Allwright and Bailey 1991; "K" for Kumaravadivelu 1994a). Where more than

TABLE 2.4   Fourteen Principles to Support English Language Learning and Teaching

With respect to the process of learning either a second or a foreign language:

1. Learners rely on knowledge and experience they bring to the process (L-F; P).

2. Boredom stifles progress (B; Om; P).

3. Learners progress when they are ready to do so (L-F; P).

4. Motivation plays an essential role (B; Ox).

5. The process is purposeful (L-F).

6. Learners depend upon feedback from others (Me; P; A&B).

7. At times the process can be anxiety provoking (A&B; Me).

8. Learners require access to contextualized illustrations of language (K; B; N1).

9. The process is complex (L-F; A&B).

10. Classroom instruction may be structured to support activation of more diverse learning strategies (Ox; L-F).

11. Especially for adults, complete mastery of a new language may be impossible (L-F; B; Mo).

12. One's native language influences the process in significant ways (P; B; L-F).

13. Language and culture are inextricably interconnected (B; K; Om).

14. The process unfolds within social phenomena (L-F; Om).

one specialist's initial appears, the first initial signals the original source for the wording presented. Other initials listed signal that these specialists, in their publications listed in table 2.3, also discuss the principle set forth.

Expanded Discussion of the Principles

1. *Learners rely on knowledge and experience they bring to the process* of language learning (L-F; P). Few language teachers would take issue with the fact that the incorporation and enhancement of a learner's personal experiences within the learning process are important contributing elements to classroom learning (Om). Second language learning will be enhanced if course structures acknowledge that learners both transform and reinterpret whatever inputs are presented to them from the teacher, the textbook, and other instructional resources (N2). When a new topic or concept is introduced in the classroom, teachers should attempt to anchor it in students' existing background knowledge for it to be more easily associated with something they already know (B). Whenever possible, English language

learners need to be given opportunities to contribute their own ideas, experiences, and feelings to the learning process (N2).

2. *Boredom stifles progress.* For most students, "meaningful learning leads toward better long-term retention than rote learning" (B, 18; Om; P). Teachers can lessen potential for boredom and "capitalize on the power of meaningful learning by appealing to students' interests, academic goals," and plans for the future (B, 18). Classroom teachers play an essential role in this area since their enthusiasm (or lack of enthusiasm) for teaching can be contagious (Me). In language courses, students become very adept at noticing verbal, nonverbal, and deliberate as well as unintended cues from teachers. Whenever possible, learners need to perceive that teachers are invested, interested, and engaged in their own acts of teaching (P; K; Johnson 1999; Prabhu 1992). If requisite levels of enthusiasm and interest are missing on the part of the teacher, classrooms can become enervating places for language learners (Me).

3. *Learners progress* in language development *when they are ready to do so.* Several decades of research document that, ultimately, learners are the ones in charge of the second language acquisition (SLA) process (L-F; P; B). English language learning and teaching are more likely to succeed if course structures acknowledge that there are different routes to success and if teachers are conscientious in assisting learners to find their own ways (N2; Ox). Since the learning process is enhanced when teachers are attuned to learner readiness, teachers and course structures should feature opportunities *for learners* to (1) negotiate at least some aspects of their learning (N2) and (2) provide formative, in-process feedback to their teacher on what they perceive the quality of the course to be.

4. *Motivation plays an essential role* in success in language learning (B; Ox). We are all driven to "act, or 'behave,' by the anticipation of some sort of reward—tangible or intangible, short term or long term—that will ensue as a result of the behavior" (B, 19). To foster motivation, teachers can help students to appreciate more fully some of the advantages of learning their target language. For example, teachers might point out what learners "can do with English where they live and around the world, the prestige in being able to use English, the academic benefits of knowing English, jobs that require English," among other possibilities (B, 20). However, rewards for learning can emerge from internal as much as from external sources. In connection with language learning, "the most powerful rewards are those that are intrinsically motivated within the learner" (B, 20; A&B; Ox). Classroom learning will be enhanced if course structures leave room for students to pursue language learning behaviors stemming from their own wants,

desires, and needs (B; N1; N2). Because they are intrinsically motivating, opportunities for extemporaneous and creative language practice often enhance lesson possibilities (Om; B). Many teachers find efficient ways to gather information about learners early in the course, and periodically throughout the course, in order to design tasks and activities responsive to learners' expressed interests and preferences for language study. When handled well by teachers, such efforts are more likely to lead to the emergence of intrinsic motivation within learners.

5. *The process of language learning is purposeful* (L-F). Reflecting basic features of human perception and cognition, learners (especially adolescents and adults) naturally are curious and wonder why their teachers structure classroom experiences in particular ways. Classroom lessons carry greater potential for success if learners are able to recognize a meaningful purpose in what their teacher is asking them to do. To make instructional purposes easier to perceive, teachers can structure lessons in ways providing opportunities for using language in contexts, working with materials, and completing tasks learners are likely to encounter outside the classroom (N2; P; Om). It should be easily recognizable to learners that course contexts, materials, and tasks reflect purposes for which they will be using English in the real world. In addition, teachers should seek opportunities to discuss with learners at least some of the rationale underlying their instructional efforts.

6. *Learners depend upon feedback from others* (Me; P; A&B). Successful language development is partially a factor of noticing, and learning to utilize, both cognitive and affective feedback from other target language users (B; Om). Without appropriate and well-timed feedback, classrooms can become frustrating places to be (Me). Supportive feedback not only provides learners with a sense of how well they are doing in the course but facilitates continuing progress toward more intelligible language use in general. Though it is not clear how effective specific forms of cognitive feedback (such as explicit styles of error correction) might be (P; L-F), teachers need to explore a range of ways to encourage increased accuracy in speech and writing. Research indicates consistently that most teachers use a very limited repertoire for cuing learners in learning to recognize or modify their own errors (A&B; P; Me).

7. *At times the process can be anxiety provoking* (A&B; Me; Ox). Learners sometimes find language classrooms uncomfortable places to be. To the extent possible, instruction should be responsive to students' affective needs. Progress in language acquisition is unlikely to be sustained if, for whatever reason, learners begin to distance themselves from the kinds of

learning opportunities being provided (A&B). Yet affective responses to classroom events pose a complex array of issues. While too much anxiety may interfere, a learner's experiences with manageable levels of anxiety sometimes prompt improved performance and an enhancement of learning (A&B). In general, learners need to feel good about what they are trying to accomplish, and they need to experience requisite levels of self-confidence. They are more likely to learn if lessons feature manageable challenges, reasonable risks (B; Mo), and opportunities to realize they are capable of accomplishing whatever tasks are featured in the course. Teachers should learn to recognize and respond to signs of both the facilitating and debilitating degrees of anxiety that learners inevitably experience in language classrooms. Ultimately, language courses should provide opportunities for learners of English to become more self-sufficient, more autonomous, and less anxious (N1; N2).

8. *Learners require access to contextualized illustrations of language* (K; B; N1). As complements to learners' experiences using English in the outside world, language classrooms are places where preplanned contextual supports for learning may be featured prominently during lessons. In fact, a teacher's explicit provision of contextualized illustrations of language is one of the distinguishing features of instructed language learning (K). Classroom learning will be enhanced if the course engages learners with authentic samples of language along with appropriate scaffolding in the form of contextual supports. Though teachers explore many options for providing such scaffolding, an important way is to teach through the integration of language skills (K; B; N1; Om).

9. *The process of language learning is complex* (L-F; A&B), and most learners benefit from assistance in learning to live with its complexity. This principle applies to individuals as well as groups of classroom learners. In explorations over the past three decades, SLA research has confirmed that the process is dynamic (L-F; K; P; Ox), nonlinear (L-F; K; P), and inherently unstable (N2). For instruction to be successful, teachers need to realize that relationships between teaching and learning are asymmetrical (L-F; K). That is, students of English tend not to learn what teachers have to offer in simple linear or additive fashions (N2). Since language courses are comprised of people with varying needs, wants, strengths, values, moods, and personalities, both language teaching and language learning are complex undertakings. Plans for language courses need to reflect a teacher's realistic appraisal of the complex natures of learning and teaching. Classroom learning is enhanced when teachers, learners, and course features focus not only on language content but also on the process of language learning (N2).

Teachers should expect the members of any class to vary in their responses to whatever events are taking place during language lessons (L-F; Ox). Such variation reflects the underlying complexity of SLA experiences.

10. *Classroom instruction may be structured to support activation of more diverse learning strategies.* The potential benefit of strategy instruction represents one of the better-documented advantages classroom learning has over outside-of-the-classroom learning opportunities (Ox; Doughty 1991; L-F; Long 1983). Through guided instruction, learners can be made aware of an expanded array of strategic options for learning and using the target language (Ox). Language learning is enhanced when students are learning about, and learning to use, a wider repertoire of strategies (B). Within the context of ELT courses, teachers have opportunities to introduce learners to previously unfamiliar strategies for comprehending and producing English (K; Om). Through increased awareness, direct instruction, and teacher support, learners may begin to grow beyond what previously had been their "stylistic comfort zones" (Ox, 42) by investing time, effort, and attention in learning to explore strategic alternatives (B; K). While providing such instruction, teachers should take students' predispositions, cultural backgrounds, preferences, and more general learning styles into account (B; Om).

11. *Especially for adults, complete mastery of a new language may be impossible* (L-F; B; Mo; P). This observation is especially relevant in the area of speech-pronunciation, but it applies to other areas as well. Second language learning will be enhanced if instruction focuses on enhancing speech intelligibility rather than striving to attain unrealizable standards of nativelike speech (Mo). Therefore, teachers need to be both well informed and realistic in their appraisals of what legitimately can be expected of individual learners and groups of learners in language courses. Fortunately, complete mastery of English is an unnecessary goal for most language learners.

12. *One's native language influences the process of second language learning in significant ways* (P; B; L-F). A native language is a "significant system on which learners will rely to predict" some aspects of how English operates (B, 27). A native language system may have "both facilitating and interfering effects" (B, 27). In classrooms, the interfering effects of learners' native languages tend to be the most noticeable to teachers (B; L-F; P), while potential facilitating effects of a learner's native language tend to be underappreciated (B; L-F). A challenge for ELT teachers is to learn to recognize and more fully appreciate ways in which a learner's native language, and prior experiences with using language, may sometimes facilitate efforts in learning English.

13. Along with the significance of learners' native languages, we should also bear in mind that *language and culture are inextricably interconnected* (B; K; Om; P). When teaching a second language, we are also teaching "a complex system of cultural customs, values, and ways of thinking, feeling, and acting" (B, 25; K). Especially in connection with the role of the teacher, learners' roles, classroom management, and affective concerns, language teachers are continually learning to coordinate however many cultural systems learners bring to the course. Even more broadly, attention to the cultures represented by members of the class, along with the target language culture, can be featured during lessons as a basis for raising cultural awareness, fostering cross-cultural tolerance, and engendering mutual respect (K; Me; Om).

14. *The process unfolds within social phenomena* (L-F; Om). What happens inside a language classroom can be described as a coproduction between and among everyone involved, teacher and learners alike (A&B; K). In order to maximize learning opportunities during lessons, teachers sometimes need to shift gears in response to unplanned events (K; A&B). Johnson 1995 reminds us that the internal knowledge, values, beliefs, and predispositions of everyone present in the classroom merge with and help to shape events evolving during language lessons. Many teachers find ways to bring learners' internal knowledge, values, beliefs, and predispositions to the surface of classroom communications. In response to social dimensions of language learning, teachers might explore a range of alternative class configurations in order to provide supportive structures for learners to negotiate meanings with others and to use language for purposes of authentic communication (Om; P). A special characteristic of language lessons is that they provide opportunities for learners' uncertainties to become clarified by engaging learners in negotiations of meanings, participatory communications, and interactive language use (Om; B; P).

Conclusion

A consistent theme permeating the sources, issues, and general ELT principles cited in this chapter merits restating here. Teachers and learners who meet within contexts of an English language course influence each other, as well as teaching-learning processes within which they are participating, in significant ways. As part of whole course experiences and individual lesson events, language classrooms are matrices where a teacher's and learners' individual and collective values, beliefs, presuppositions, and behaviors interact in sometimes familiar and at other times surprising ways

(Allwright and Bailey 1991; Johnson 1995). A reason to take the time to learn about the various resource genres and ELT principles presented in this chapter is to help clarify what might be some of our own beliefs and values with respect to language learning and teaching—as a starting point for understanding language courses.

In addition to introducing a series of contemporary principles, chapter 2 has traced historical developments that contributed to our interest in making the *Understanding* collection available. The chapter began with a categorization of five professional development resource genres and ended with a listing of 14 principles of English language learning and teaching. The 14 principles were synthesized from contemporary examples of second genre methods texts, third genre topic-specific reference texts, and journal article surveys of second language learning and teaching principles. These efforts help set the stage for the depictions of individual teachers' local perspectives on English language teaching as featured in chapters 6 through 23. The next chapter focuses specifically on two primary sources that served as foundational supports for our way of organizing the *Understanding* collection.

Chapter 3

Precursors to the *Understanding* Collection

John Murphy

> For Art & Science cannot exist but in minutely organized Particulars.
> —William Blake, *Jerusalem*

The decision to anchor the *Understanding* collection with a unifying chapter framework (as will be presented in chaps. 4 and 5) reflects a synthesis of several different traditions in the modern era of English language teaching. What we adapted from first genre descriptions of global methods were strategies for generating and presenting discussions of teaching and for arranging the collection overall. This decision reaches back to first genre resources such as Larsen-Freeman 1986, Richards and Rodgers 1986, and Stevick 1980 and to even earlier discussions of applied linguistics (Anthony 1963; Clarke 1983; Richards 1983; Richards and Rodgers 1982; Stevick 1976). Building upon such traditions, we constructed the collection around a single framework for presenting teachers' understandings of their courses. Our reasoning was to encourage contributors to treat a range of topics posited by the historical development of the field as crucial to discussions of ELT. Now that chapters 6 through 23 are in place, we trust that the *Understanding* chapter framework will be useful as a conceptual lens for comparing and contrasting some of the local approaches to teaching presented by the contributors. Once familiar with the framework, readers may find it easier to compare contributors' understandings and explanations of even very different courses. While developing the framework, we heeded the advice of van Lier (1987a, 1987b) and Larsen-Freeman (1987) concerning potential dangers when working with any framework for describing approaches to ELT. A primary danger is that such frameworks might be applied too rigidly by either contributors or readers. We have taken care to design the *Understanding* chapter framework in keeping with historical and contemporary developments. Yet, the framework we present is no more than one way among many possible ways of sharing information and prompting meaningful discussion between classroom teachers and others interested in the field. In the end, it is what contributors and readers are able to accomplish while discovering their own ways of interacting with and moving beyond such frameworks that matters most. Just as there are many ways to go about teaching an L2, the contributors vary in how they envision their courses and work with the *Understanding* chapter framework.

Another tradition contributing to the genesis of this book acknowledges that at their source all facets of language instruction are rooted in teacher thinking, teacher cognition, or what Johnson (1999) refers to as the "robust reasoning" of language teachers (2).

> By robustness I mean the completeness of [teachers'] understanding of themselves, their students, and the classrooms and schools where they work, the flexibility with which they make use of these understandings, the complexity of their reasoning, and the range of instructional considerations they use as they carry out their professional activities. . . . [Robust reasoning] emerges when teachers engage in a continual process of "criss-crossing" their professional landscape, seeing and experiencing it from multiple perspectives, recognizing its inherent complexity, and considering the interconnectedness of its various components. Robust reasoning occurs when teachers are able to assemble and apply their knowledge of their professional landscape flexibly so that it can be used in different situations and for different purposes. (2)

As Johnson calls to our attention, there are alternative landscapes of experience that impact teachers' reasonings. Simultaneously, the very nature of our professional activities as teachers compels us to serve as participants within multiple dimensions of teaching and learning. Even within the context of a single lesson, affective, social, and behavioral dimensions of classroom events continuously influence a teacher's understandings and reasonings about instructional possibilities. Minimally, a teacher's management of whole courses, instructional units, entire lessons, and individual lesson segments depends upon her or his insights, beliefs, decisions, moods, and behaviors in interaction with comparably complex sets of language learners' insights, beliefs, decisions, moods, and behaviors. Such complexities are integral features of the situatedness of teaching and learning. They suggest diverse landscapes of possibilities.

Since diversity in understanding of teaching is to be expected, we have designed the collection's chapter framework to serve as the connective tissue for the volume overall. Access to the *Understanding* framework should make it easier to recognize points of convergence and divergence between teacher-contributors' alternative perspectives. Ultimately, as a reader and language teacher you will have to decide whether or not the framework is an asset serving to support the collection's purposes and your own interests. The *Understanding* collection will have met one of its purposes if you find the framework useful as a conceptual lens while examining chapters 6 through 23. With an eye toward the future (and as discussed in chap. 24), some readers may also find it useful for clarifying, describing, and sharing with others their own "robust reasonings" tied to particular language courses they either are, or one day may be, teaching.

A related theme underpinning the *Understanding* collection takes seriously Prabhu's (1992) call for language teachers to explore and share with others their local perspectives on teaching. Prabhu's position complements similar calls from a long line of L2 teacher development specialists (Allwright and Bailey 1991; Clarke 1984, 1994; Fanselow 1987; Freeman 1998; Gebhard and Oprandy 1999; Kumaravadivelu 1994a, 1994b; Murphy 1994; Palmer 1917; Politzer 1970; Richards 1996; Stevick 1976). These specialists remind all of us who are interested in continuing to grow and develop as language teachers how important it is to acknowledge, explore, and share with others some of the local understandings and explanations of our own work, especially those facets that may already be evolving into local approaches to teaching. Prabhu (1990) refers to what we call an individual teacher's "approach" as the individual's subjective understanding of language teaching. He proposes the phrase "[a teacher's] sense of plausibility" as a way of labeling a teacher's insights into classroom possibilities (172). Along with Richards (1996), the same writer places at center stage the importance of teachers' personal understandings of teaching practice and calls the wider field's attention to the vital role already being played by individual practitioners' understandings, instructional decisions, and teaching behaviors. The *Understanding* collection aims to build upon, bolster, and extend such understandings and traditions.

As will be elaborated in the next two chapters, we drew upon two primary sources while designing the *Understanding* collection's chapter framework. The first source is Richards and Rodgers' (1986) framework for the description and analysis of approaches and methods of L2 teaching, a framework based upon the work of Anthony (1963). These specialists examine alternative means for teaching an L2 at three levels of analysis: (1) *approach* (a theory of native language and a theory of the nature of language learning), (2) *design* (the general and specific objectives of the teaching method, a syllabus model, types of learning and teaching activities, learner roles, teacher roles, the role of instructional materials), and (3) *procedure* (classroom techniques, practices, and behaviors observed during acts of teaching).

The second source is a comparable framework designed for the description and analysis of L2 teaching methods first proposed by Larsen-Freeman (1986). As later reviewed by van Lier (1987a, 1987b) and further clarified by Larsen-Freeman (1987), this second framework includes six components: *introduction* (presents origin and rationale of a global method); *experience* (introduces detailed prose descriptions of the method in action that are based on a real, though idealized, lesson); *thinking about the experience* (presents observations and principles underpinning the lesson depicted in the experience section); *reviewing the principles* (discusses principles underpinning the method a second time as more elaborated answers to a series of 10 questions); *reviewing the techniques* (provides labels, descriptions, summaries, and discussion of specific teaching techniques associated with the global method); *conclusion* (summarizes basic principles once more along with suggestions for assessing their value). Larsen-Freeman's series of 10 questions included in the reviewing-the-principles component of her framework seemed closest to our vision for the *Understanding* chapter framework. Collectively, the 10 questions Larsen-Freeman presents serve as the cornerstone for her popular book. Going well beyond surface level descriptions, Larsen-Freeman uses her 10 questions to encourage teachers to probe beneath the level of observable classroom behaviors in order to reason in greater depth about conceptual underpinnings of language teaching. Larsen-Freeman's (1986, 1–3) 10 questions for reviewing the principles of second language teaching are presented here.[1]

1. What are the goals of teachers who use the method?
2. What is the role of the teacher? What is the role of the students?
3. What are some of the characteristics of the teaching/learning process?
4. What is the nature of student-teacher interaction? What is the nature of student-student interaction?
5. How are the feelings of students dealt with?
6. How is language viewed? How is culture viewed?
7. What areas of language are emphasized? What language skills are emphasized?
8. What is the role of the students' native languages?
9. How is evaluation accomplished?
10. How does the teacher respond to student errors?

---

1. From *Techniques and Principles in Language Teaching* by Diane Larsen-Freeman. © 1986 by Oxford University Press. Reproduced by permission of Oxford University Press.

There are several reasons to believe that a chapter structure synthesizing the Richards and Rodgers (1986) framework and Larsen-Freeman's 10 reviewing-the-principles questions meets our criteria of being readily accessible to practicing English language teachers. For several decades the "MATESOL Methods course" has served as the "primary vehicle for pedagogical instruction in a majority of TESOL teacher preparation programs" worldwide (Grosse 1991, 29). Though alternative teacher development structures are intriguing (see, e.g., Edge 1994; Freeman and Johnson 1998; Johnson 1996b; Richards 1994), the MATESOL Methods course is likely to continue as a "primary vehicle" for the foreseeable future. Through survey research, Grosse documented the 10 textbooks most commonly included as required reading materials in MATESOL Methods courses in the United States. Richards and Rodgers 1986 tops Grosse's list, and Larsen-Freeman 1986 is the third text listed. Both books are organized around their respective schemes. Further, Long and Richards 1987 is the second most popular text listed by Grosse (1991), and it features two chapters organized around the Richards and Rodgers 1986 framework. Though Grosse's contribution may seem somewhat dated today, her investigation took place during the teacher preparation years of thousands of contemporary English language teachers and teacher educators. More recently, Brown 1994a is a widely adopted MATESOL Methods text that devotes generous attention to the Richards and Rodgers scheme (Brown 1994a, see 47–72). Due to its continuing popularity in ELT circles worldwide, a revised and expanded edition of Richards and Rodgers 1986 is forthcoming (Ted Rodgers, personal communication, April 28, 1999). Similarly, a revised and expanded edition of Larsen-Freeman 1986 was published in the year 2000. Along with a few other sources, Larsen-Freeman 1986 and Richards and Rodgers 1986 served as our reference points while constructing the framework applied by contributors with varying degrees of modification throughout this book.

The framework generated for the *Understanding* collection is the result of synthesizing and adapting from the sources cited previously. With one difference: Our purpose was to construct a framework/conceptual lens that would be useful to other language teachers as they analyze particular courses. Rather than considering how a global method might work out in a classroom, we wanted a system for moving between the realities of an actual course and the theories, organizing strategies, and situational factors that have led to the particular course. That is, the system explored in this book is not about how external methods are applied in the classroom but rather about how a course for which a teacher is responsible grows out of a vast array of factors, only one of which might be an attempt to apply facets of a more widely recognized approach to language teaching. Prior to initiating the *Understanding* project, one of the coeditors published an earlier version of its chapter framework as an organizing scheme in two journal articles focused on descriptions of separate sections from different years of a single ELT course (see Murphy 1992, 1993). We shared reprints of each of these articles with potential contributors as illustrations of the kinds of context-specific discussions we were asking each of them to produce.

Conclusion

In these three preliminary chapters we have described the purposes and scope of the *Understanding* collection, discussed theory behind it, traced its development, and surveyed some of its precursors in professional literatures. The collection's purpose is to foster clearer understandings of ELT courses while serving to complement the several professional development resource genres outlined in chapter 2.

As your journey in language teaching continues to unfold, we trust that examination of the *Understanding* collection will support the ongoing emergence of your own *sense of plausibility* as a teacher, your own *robust reasonings,* and related insights into language instruction possibilities. As language teachers, all of us should continue to explore emerging possibilities in the courses we offer; extend their potentialities; examine professional development resources; and share and discuss with colleagues, supervisors, mentors, students, and friends our personal understandings and explanations of our efforts. As an overview of instructional themes to support such efforts and prior to introducing the individual course descriptions featured in chapters 6 through 23, the next two chapters describe and discuss each component of the organizational framework for writing that contributors adapted and applied in modified ways throughout the remaining sections of the *Understanding* collection.

Chapter 4

A Framework for Discussion—Part 1

John Murphy and Patricia Byrd

Labour well the Minute Particulars. . . .

. . . .

[Those] who would do good to another, must do it in Minute Particulars
General Good is the plea of the scoundrel hypocrite & flatterer:
For Art & Science cannot exist but in minutely organized Particulars
And not in generalizing Demonstrations of the Rational Power.

. . . .

General Forms have their vitality in Particulars: & every
Particular is a Man [or a Woman].

       —William Blake, *Jerusalem* (Paley 1991)

Chapters 1 through 3 outlined some of the background, rationale, and precursors to the collection. Chapter 2 also included discussion of 14 general principles of ELT. We now turn our attention to the *Understanding* chapter framework since it is the structure around which the collection's remaining chapters are organized. To make it more accessible, our discussion of the framework spans two chapters, the first half in chapter 4 and the second in chapter 5. Our purpose is to provide reference points for thinking about, describing, and analyzing the discussions of English language teaching (ELT) featured in chapters 6 through 23. That is, the chapter framework is designed for readers to use as a conceptual lens. Though a sequence might seem implied by the order in which its components are presented in table 4.1 and the subsequent discussion, we encourage anyone interested in working with the *Understanding* framework in reference to her or his own teaching to modify the sequence and connections between its components as necessary.

The remaining sections of this chapter and chapter 5 present the framework's 13 components in the sequence shown in table 4.1. Chapter 4 focuses on the first 7 components: setting, conceptual underpinnings, goals and objectives, syllabus design, activity types, learners' roles, and teacher's roles.

TABLE 4.1. Skeleton Outline of the *Understanding* Chapter Framework

Heading and Focus	Required/Optional
Setting	R
Conceptual underpinnings	R
Goals and objectives	R
Syllabus design	R
Activity types	R
Learners' roles	R
Teachers' roles	R
Instructional materials	R
Lesson particulars	R
Affective concerns	Opt
Culture	Opt
Assessment	Opt
Caveats/Final thoughts	Opt

Note: See corresponding questions in table 1.1.

The framework's second half is presented in chapter 5, which treats the components of affective concerns, culture, instructional materials, assessment, lesson particulars, and caveats/final thoughts. Set aside in a block within the body of each of the 13 sections, we also present a series of questions and topics to keep in mind while examining chapters 6 through 23. These items appear near the end of each section under the heading "Applying the *Understanding* Lens" and are intended as aids for those interested in comparing, contrasting, or in other ways analyzing some of the local approaches to ELT appearing in subsequent chapters. We encourage you to revisit them as points of reference while reading about the contributors' courses.

Setting

What is the setting for the course? All instances of English language teaching take place within particular settings and evolve under local sets of circumstances. The framework's initial section calls for as clear a description as possible of the instructional context in which the targeted course is offered.

Here you will find discussions of such topics as the part of the world in which the course is offered, the type of instructional program, the nature of the institution (e.g., public or private), and other contextual factors that may influence how the course is offered. Contributors discuss such learner characteristics as ages, ethnic backgrounds, levels of education, career goals, community status, and other relevant background information. Sections on setting provide clear signals on the general purposes of the targeted language course. For example, a course may focus on teaching English as a Foreign Language, general life skills, English for Academic Purposes, or other areas.

A special feature of setting discussions is that learners' English language proficiency levels are indicated in a consistent way. For purposes of uniformity throughout the collection, contributors use proficiency guidelines of the American Council on the Teaching of Foreign Languages (ACTFL) (1986) as their reference points when characterizing the language abilities of learners they typically meet in the course. Through several readily available sources (e.g., James 1985; Omaggio 1993; Stansfield 1992) the ACTFL proficiency guidelines target nine levels of proficiency each in listening, speaking, reading, writing, and cultural awareness. Now available "in the public domain," the full set of ACTFL descriptors may be found on the World Wide Web by linking into the Summer Institute of Linguistics's (SIL) Home Page: <http://www.sil.org/>. In addition, the same organization provides an even more direct link to the ACTFL descriptors through the following URL: <http://www.sil.org/lingualinks/ LANGUAGELEARNING/OtherResources/ACTFLPROFICIENCYGUIDE-LINES/>.

Minimally, each chapter's setting section includes proficiency level specifications for at least one language skill prioritized in the course. For example, learners' ACTFL listening levels may be cited if the course highlights attention to listening instruction. Alternatively, an ACTFL reading level may be more appropriate for courses highlighting the teaching of reading. Some contributors specify ACTFL levels for more than one facet of language (e.g., listening and speaking in a general oral communication course). ACTFL levels are introduced to illuminate what the chapter author considers to be an average proficiency level of the kinds of learners who typically enroll in the targeted course. Proficiency level specifications are used throughout the collection to illuminate course background, constraints, and instructional possibilities.

Attention to setting characteristics early in each chapter is intended as a significant step away from generic discussions and toward helping to establish a basis for examining and comparing contributors' local understandings and explanations of English language teaching. For example, Janet Graham and Susan Barone's chapter 22 targets the teaching of speaking to groups of international graduate students at a private university in the United States, a setting quite different from the ones described in Tim Murphey's chapter 11 and William Acton's chapter 12, which target the teaching of speaking to EFL undergraduate students in Japan.z

---

Applying the *Understanding* Lens: Setting

When comparing setting sections across courses, look for features that might make a difference in how a course is offered. Some points to consider: What are some of the distinguishing features of the institution or program housing the course? What is the course's administrative context? How might this context impact the teacher's way of offering the course? Are you already familiar with such contexts for teaching, or are they very different from your experiences? What types of instructional resources are available? What is the overall length of the course? How many hours of instruction are there per lesson and per week? Does the teacher discuss some of the physical characteristics of the classroom? Are learners' proficiency levels described? For just one skill area—or several? After reading this section, are you able to identify, or infer, what some of the learners' needs might be? Based upon this brief introduction to their circumstances, how would you characterize students' chances for success in learning English? Which of the general ELT principles listed in table 2.4 in chapter 2 might you anticipate as being especially relevant to this instructional setting? Is there anything left unmentioned concerning the setting you would really like to know more about?

Conceptual Underpinnings

What are the theory, principles, or related concepts serving to support the teacher's way of offering the course? In this section contributors present their own accounts of relevant theory-principles underlying their efforts as teachers. A few contributors discuss theory-principles widely acknowledged in contemporary discussions of language teaching. Even more of them articulate conceptual underpinnings (CU) considerably more individualistic in nature. In contrast to our purpose for introducing general ELT principles in chapter 2, the charge contributors accepted for the purpose of CU sections was to *voice whatever they believe to be* the theory-principles underpinning their efforts as the teacher of the course. We asked contributors to avoid impulses to rely too heavily on what might be considered the conventional wisdom of the field (e.g., principles of "communicative," "task-based," or "content-based" language teaching). As discussed in chapter 2, we believe it is important to be aware of general principles widely acknowledged as important conceptual supports for contemporary practices of English language teaching and learning. However, for the purposes of the course-specific discussions we asked contributors to avoid excessive references to theory-principles commonly associated with either global methods or generic approaches to language teaching and to focus instead on whatever theory-principles they find relevant to their local contexts of teaching.

The collection's CU sections are tied directly to the *theory* end of the *theory-practice* continuum hotly debated in contemporary discussions of ELT (Clarke 1994). To help ensure a range of different voices and perspectives, we encouraged contributors to develop their discussions of conceptual underpinnings in ways appropriate to their sensibilities as writers, course developers, and teachers. A chapter's CU section provides a window into the teacher-contributor's rationale for her or his way of planning and teaching the targeted course. The section addresses questions of why teachers structure and go about teaching their courses in particular ways. Partly in response to the long line of ELT specialists who argue that the field of language teaching has been remiss in this area, the *Understanding* framework's CU section celebrates language teachers' capacities as theorizers. Since a CU section focuses on whatever the teacher believes to be foundational theory-principles serving to support her or his ways of teaching in a specific course, it offers an opportunity to learn about some of the reasoning beneath surface features of teaching.

Applying the *Understanding* Lens: Conceptual Underpinnings

What learning principles are reflected in the course? May any of them be linked to (or contrasted with) one or more of the 14 general principles presented in table 2.4 of chapter 2? Based upon your reading of this section, would you be able to describe some of the reasoning behind the teacher's plans? Do you agree with any of the teacher's reasoning? With which aspects might you disagree? What are some of the teacher's understandings associated with the teaching of second language listening, speaking, reading, or writing? Are you able to trace any sources of the teacher's understandings? Does the contributor's discussion of theory-principles in this section seem consistent with the rest of the chapter? Is any aspect of second language acquisition theory, or more general learning theory, reflected in how the contributor organizes the course? Do you know of any other writer(s), discussion(s), or approach(es) to ELT that could serve to support some of the ways of teaching discussed in the chapter?

A major theme in the *Understanding* collection is that different settings may lead teachers to different aspects of theory and alternative modes of reasoning in their efforts to better understand students' learning and their own teaching. Thus, we caution against dismissing prematurely whatever theories or reasonings individual teacher-contributors discuss as being useful for their particular courses. CU sections should be read not to evaluate the "correctness" of the teacher's theories or reasonings but to better understand how conceptual supports individual teachers carry with them in classrooms unfold in the real world of ELT. Even if you disagree with an individual teacher's theories or reasonings, examining the collection's CU sections provides opportunities to read about classroom teachers' own understandings and ways of offering their courses to learners. A fair question to keep in mind while reading each of the local-perspectives chapters is whether or not the contributor has succeeded in discussing the course's conceptual underpinnings in ways internally consistent with the rest of her or his chapter.

Goals and Objectives

What will students be able to do by the end of the course? For the course goals and objectives section, we asked contributors to indicate as clearly as possible what learners should be able to do by the end of the course as a result of having participated in it successfully. Such specifications have been handled in a range of different ways throughout the history of ELT. When advising contributors, we followed Nunan's (1988) recommendations for presenting course goals and objectives to others, a format repeated with increasing detail, elaboration, and conviction by Brown (1994a), Graves (1996), Long and Crookes (1992), and Richards and Lockhart (1994). From these specialists we adopted the idea that explication of course objectives should focus directly on what *learners* will be expected to do and less on what the teacher will offer or what learning opportunities the course itself will provide. Even though teachers' actions in classrooms and the nature of learning opportunities within them certainly are germane, when it comes to specifications of course goals and objectives we find it useful to emphasize the actor word *learners* as well as the action phrase *to do* for purposes of clarifying "what *learners* will be expected to be able *to do*" by the end of the course.

In their discussion of task-based approaches to language teaching, Long and Crookes (1992) indicate that course objectives need to illuminate end points for instruction. Some of the many different terms for labeling course end points include learning objectives, criterion tasks, behavioral objectives, and learning outcomes. In our view, instructional end points should be tied to authentic purposes for using the target language. Such purposes focus on the *things learners will need to be able to do competently in settings outside the classroom.* For example, learners preparing to succeed in university settings will need to be able to take and coordinate study notes while both reading and listening for academic purposes. Learners studying for such purposes need to be able to coordinate these two types of study notes in order to prepare for the kinds of essay exams typically featured in university courses (Leki and Carson 1994, 1997; Murphy 1996a). Shih (1992) discusses alternative ways of designing EAP courses and course objectives to meet such purposes. In a very different instructional setting, L2 English speakers planning to be department store attendants may need to be able to understand, clarify, and negotiate customers' complaints when working at customer service counters. A third illustration, Eggly (1998) prepares nonnative English-speaking physicians and interns to be able to form and maintain healthy doctor-patient relationships with First Language (L1) English-speaking patients during medical interviews. Purposes implied by these three examples suggest very different sets of course-specific goals and objectives tied to learners' particular needs.

Applying the *Understanding* Lens: Goals and Objectives

Has the teacher been explicit in stating course goals and objectives? Where objectives appear, are they presented in language that is clear, sufficiently elaborated, and easy to understand? Has the teacher stated course objectives in terms of what learners will do in the course, what language content or topics will be covered, what the teacher will do, or through some other focus? In what settings beyond the classroom will learners be using English or in other ways applying what they have learned in the course? What does the teacher expect learners to be able to do upon completion of the course, in the real world outside the classroom, as a result of having been successful course participants? As listeners? As speakers? As readers? As writers? Or in other ways as members of an English-speaking community? If you do not find clear answers to such questions, do other chapter sections help to clarify? If you were the teacher of such a course, what course objectives would you want to include? Do you know of other ELT courses sharing the same, or any comparable, learner goals and objectives?

Syllabus Design

How is the course organized? What are its overall design and trajectory? Most English language teachers would agree that manners in which courses are organized affect ways in which they are perceived and experienced by learners. For many teachers the organization of a course becomes clearest only retrospectively, when looking back once the course is over. Though hindsight can be revealing, language teachers need to be as clear as possible with respect to their initial plans and decisions for organizing an ELT course. Since most of the *Understanding* contributors have offered their courses multiple times, they are well positioned to be aware of how their courses are organized, including initial stages and some of the modifications that commonly evolve once a particular iteration of a course is under way. In this section, contributors discuss the nature of the supports around which their courses are organized.

When examining these sections, it is useful to be aware of some of the broad options in course syllabus design rarely stated directly in the work of English language teachers. Since linguistic prepackaging is a characteristic feature of many approaches to ELT, one aspect to look for is whether or not the course presents learners with language samples in a series of prearranged pieces of syntax, lexis, morphology, or phonology. If it does, are such prearranged pieces presented to learners one at a time, in clusters, or within stretches of either written or spoken discourse, or are they left implicit within the structure of the course? Citing Wilkins 1976 as an antecedent to their work, Long and Crookes (1992) find course trajectories highlighting prearranged pieces of language (including language functions) to signal a category they call a "synthetic" syllabus (28). Synthetic course syllabi pivot on the assumption that learners will be able to resynthesize the pieces of language presented during instruction in order to be able to use them during subsequent instances of authentic communication. Alternative course structures may involve much less, little, or even no linguistic prepackaging of this kind. For example, course structures may be scaffolded around broader portions of language or more extended experiences in using the target language (Nunan 1991b). In ELT settings worldwide, relatively holistic language learning experiences have been gaining prominence in recent decades. Course trajectories of this second type contribute to what Long and Crookes (1992) call an "analytic" syllabus type (28). Ways of organizing ELT around analytic features pivot on the assumption that learners will be able to detect for themselves some of the systematic patterns of syntax, lexis, morphology, or phonology in the new language based upon "innate knowledge of linguistic universals . . . which can be reactivated by exposure to natural samples" of the target language (Long and Crookes 1992, 29).

Though the analytic versus synthetic distinction is useful to keep in mind, in actual practice most ELT courses reveal hybrid features since they are likely to incorporate aspects of both syllabus types. Planning instruction around hybrid features may be an effective option since several decades of research into language learning styles and strategies suggest that even within a single course learners differ with respect to their language learning preferences and strategic inclinations (Oxford 1992; Larsen-Freeman 1991). With these considerations in mind, it may be useful to envision synthetic versus analytic syllabus features as opposite ends of a continuum that encompasses a very wide range of possibilities (as depicted in table 4.2).

Contributors' ways of organizing instruction in reference to the analytic-synthetic continuum are just one of several features to keep in mind when examining plans for ELT instruction. A second feature pivots on ways language teachers envision the possible impacts of their initial plans. Many of the courses included in the collection reveal teachers struggling to find a balance between (*a*) what they know they would like the course to include ahead of time and (*b*) their interests in being responsive to learners' specific needs and suggestions for possible changes once a course is under way. As readers we might ask, Does the course's trajectory seem relatively preset in advance, or do some components only take shape once the course is under way? For example, do learners' experiences with processes of learning affect ways in which a course unfolds? Chapters 7 through 10 and chapter 22 are interesting examples of this struggle to find a balance between preplanned syllabus decisions and more interactive decisions negotiated with

TABLE 4.2. Continuum of One Set of Macrolevel Options in ELT Course Syllabus Design

Analytic	Hybrid	Synthetic
"Present the target language whole chunks at a time, without linguistic interference or control" (Long and Crookes 1992, 28).	A hybrid syllabus includes significant features of both analytic and synthetic course design.	Feature considerable degrees of linguistic intervention and control in the presentation of language forms
Presents holistic experiences in using "target language samples which . . . have not been controlled for structure or lexis [or phonology] in the traditional manner" (Long and Crookes 1992, 28)	Compatible with proposals for a focus on form in both communicative and task-based approaches to language teaching (e.g., Fotos and Ellis 1991; Williams 1995)	Explicit concern for the presentation of target language samples that have been predigested and controlled for structure, lexis, or phonology ahead of time by, for example, the teacher, a curriculum developer, or a textbook author
Supported by research into the nature of the L2 acquisition process (Larsen-Freeman 1991; Ellis 1994)	Supported by growing numbers of classroom textbooks and basic series (Nunan's Atlas series [1995]; Brown's Vistas series [1992])	Supported by centuries of tradition in many instructional settings worldwide and by marketplace expectations in ELT textbook design
With an analytic syllabus "we are inviting the learner, directly or indirectly, to recognize the linguistic components of the language behavior he [or she] is acquiring, we are in effect basing our approach on the learner's [hypothesized] analytic capabilities" (Wilkins 1976, 13).	Li's (1998) suggestions for applying CLT principles in EFL settings	"The synthetic syllabus relies on learners' assumed abilities to learn a language in parts (e.g., structures and functions) which are independent of one another, and also to integrate, or synthesize, the pieces when the time comes to use them for communicative purposes" (Long and Crookes 1992, 28).
Some well-known approaches to language teaching such as Counseling-Learning/Community Language Learning, the Direct Method, and task-based language teaching reflect many features of analytic course syllabi.	Compatible with discourse- and genre-level approaches to the teaching of grammar (e.g., Byrd and Reid 1998b; Byrd 1995)	Some well-known approaches to language teaching such as the Audio-Lingual and Grammar-Translation Methods, Total Physical Response, and Silent Way reflect many features of synthetic course syllabi.
Whole language instruction (Rigg 1991), language experience approaches (Gunderson 1991), extensive and silent sustained reading, content- and theme-based teaching (Stoller and Grabe 1987), process approaches to writing instruction (Zamel 1982)		Intensive analysis of sentence-level syntax (e.g., as prioritized in many traditional classroom settings throughout the world)
		The production processes of most, though not all, ELT publishing houses reflect synthetic syllabic expectations in course syllabus design.

Compatible with Morgan's (1997) and Greenberg's (1997) proposals for pronunciation instruction as tied to themes of social change, praxis, and emancipatory education

Activity-recipe teacher resources, such as Campbell and Kryszewska's (1992) *Learner-Based Teaching*, Day's (1993) *New Ways in Teaching Reading*, Hedge's (1988) *Writing: Resource Books for Teachers*, and Whiteson's (1996) *New Ways of Using Drama and Literature in Language Teaching* seem more compatible with analytic syllabus types.

Compatible with Morley's (1994) proposals for multi-dimensional curriculum design in speech-pronunciation instruction

Harmer's (1991) proposal for "Balanced Activities Approaches" to ELT (41–42); Tarvin and Al-Arishi's (1991) reconceptualization of communicative language teaching in EFL

Compatible with the phonetic-level, segmental end of Morley's (1994a) dual focus continuum; and with many contemporary ELT pronunciation texts as discussed by Levis (1999)

Activity-recipe teacher resources such as Gerngross and Puchta's (1992) *Creative Grammar Practice*, Rinvolucri's (1984) *Grammar Games: Cognitive, Affective, and Drama Activities for EFL Students*, Rinvolucri and Davis's *More Grammar Games: Cognitive, Affective, and Movement Activities for EFL Students* (1995), and Ur's (1990) *Grammar Practice Activities* seem more compatible with synthetic syllabus types.

learners. Though these five courses address the needs of very different student populations, in each case a teacher finds ways of adjusting designs for instruction to meet themes, topics, and competencies that only become apparent as the course is unfolding. The following are some additional questions to keep in mind when examining how ELT courses are organized.

Applying the *Understanding* Lens: Syllabus Design

How does the course begin? Where does it end? Is there a series of signposts along the way? Does the teacher make plans autonomously or through collaboration? If asked to, could you describe any of the course's recurring features? Is the course organized around message-oriented communications, that is, those highlighting expressions of meaning? Or, does the course seem to prioritize language-oriented communications highlighting language usage? Do features of grammar, lexis, morphology, or phonology receive prominent attention? Might course organization depend upon alternative domains such as survival or vocational abilities, functional uses of language, real world tasks, learning strategies, discourse genres? Is there an interplay between any of these, or some other, domains? Where might you place the course on the syllabus type continuum depicted in table 4.2? In the case of a hybrid course, what seems to be the teacher's starting point or primary point of reference? Are there topics or themes incorporated into the course that stretch across successive units of instruction? If so, how are they prioritized and sequenced? Are there opportunities for anything to be negotiated by learners once the course is under way? Has the teacher incorporated ways of eliciting students' preferences for what they would like to learn from, or contribute to, the course?

Activity Types

What types of classroom activities feature prominently in the course? This section focuses attention on labels and brief descriptions of the recurring types of learning activities commonly incorporated within the course. Phrases such as *learning tasks, pedagogic tasks, instructional techniques, learning opportunities,* and *classroom procedures* are just some of the many headings writers and teachers commonly use to signal what we refer to here as classroom activity types. Many different taxonomies have been proposed to group and categorize the kinds of activities represented in ELT classrooms. Some typical ones are reflected in Brown's (1994a) and Crookes and Chaudron's (1991) taxonomies of (1) *controlled,* (2) *semicontrolled,* and (3) *free* activity types. Other writers use slightly different labels such as *directed, guided,* and *communicative* language practice. Morley (1994a) prefers to call them *controlled, guided,* and *extemporaneous* classroom activities. Within their discussion of reflection-centered ELT, Tarvin and Al-Arishi (1991) discuss relationships between *task-, process-,* and *synthesis-oriented* activities. However we refer to them, a major distinction between types of ELT classroom activities depends upon the relative degrees of control, intervention, and initiative envisioned for teachers as compared with learners during segments of language lessons.

In this section, teachers discuss the kinds of recurring classroom activities and patterns of learner interactions highlighted as part of the course. We find the activity categories mentioned previously to be helpful when comparing activities different teachers tend to use and when relating them to our own preferences as language teachers. As added support for readers, *Understanding* contributors provide specific labels for individual activity types in each chapter. We asked contributors to (1) decide upon a list of recurring activity types consistently represented in the targeted course, (2) label each one with a concise and memorable name, and (3) compose a descriptive paragraph for each of the activities incorporated into the chapter.

Applying the *Understanding* Lens: Activity Types

What are the kinds of classroom activities and related learner behaviors typically incorporated within lessons? For example, does the course tend to favor closed-ended or open-ended activity types? Are memorization, comprehension, or application activities sometimes featured? Since language learners depend upon contextualized illustrations of language, how are contextual supports incorporated into the activity types featured in the course? Are some activities designed to foster critical thinking, values clarification, or other analytic abilities? For each of the activity types introduced, is it relatively more teacher controlled or teacher guided, or does it call for learners to make decisions and use language in more spontaneous ways? Which of the activities seem more clearly message oriented? Are there other activity types that might be focused more directly on language usage? Does the teacher sometimes give explicit attention to either processes or strategies of language learning? If asked to do so, would you be able to describe the kinds of student grouping arrangements favored in the course? Could you rank order the various activity types the teacher describes according to what seem to be their relative degrees of importance? If you were to compare this course to some other included in the *Understanding* collection (or to some other course with which you are familiar), what are the relative degrees of control and initiative taken by learners during frequently occurring classroom activities?

Learners' Roles

Of the many alternatives possible, *what roles do learners actually play in the course?* As is readily apparent to anyone interested in the field of either second or foreign language teaching, language learners are major players in the realization of classroom lessons, and of whole courses, as the accumulating impacts of their contributions continuously emerge over time (Allwright and Bailey 1991; Wright 1987). Of course, teacher and learner awareness of the pivotal nature of learners' contributions to classroom potentialities shifts in and out of focus within the perceptions of all those involved. Such awareness may fluctuate widely as individual lessons, and whole courses, unfold. Themes highlighted in this section reveal that (1) learners are implicit collaborators in the realization of language lessons and (2) learners' roles can have both facilitating and debilitating impacts on the quality of ELT lessons. As one language teacher puts it:

> A group of learners in a classroom with a teacher comprises a learning community. The human element—both verbal and non-verbal, visible and barely perceptible—shapes human interaction qualitatively and may perhaps furnish the key to what happens [within the classroom] (i.e., the processes) and what eventuates (i.e., the outcomes). . . . It has been said that one can't teach a language—the best one can do is to make the conditions right for others to learn. (Wajnyrb 1992, 28)

Prabhu (1992) also calls attention to some very human elements ever present in language classrooms. As illustrated in his discussion, language learners' roles unfold within a complex arena of social interaction. Such roles have tremendous impacts on language lesson possibilities. Prabhu (1992) discusses these issues as follows.

Behind the conventionalized roles and routines of a lesson are a group of individuals . . . with varied personalities, motives, self-images, fears, and aspirations, levels of tolerance, and degrees of maturity. . . . Learners . . . perceive the teacher as being friendly or unfriendly, helpful or hostile, tolerant or vindictive, and so on, both to themselves and to different fellow learners, and try to act in a way that protects or enhances their own varied self-images. Such a play of personalities takes place not just between the teacher on the one hand and learners on the other but, in a more fierce form, between learners themselves, in a highly complex and multilateral form. There are likes and dislikes, loyalties and rivalries, ambitions and desires to dominate, injured pride and harbored grudge, fellow feeling and jealousy, all creating a continual threat to security and self-image . . . Perhaps the most immediate and pervasive concern for teachers and learners alike in classrooms is to guard against a loss of face and, to the extent possible, to win approval, sympathy or loyalty from others as a safeguard against future hazards to "face." (229)

With the backdrop of such complexities, this section provides opportunities to examine some of the diverse roles learners play in ELT courses. By looking back on roles learners typically have played in the past, some contributors also describe what learners seem to be expecting of themselves and of their peers while participating in the targeted course. These chapter sections depict how roles played by learners are envisioned by the teacher-contributor along with how they are featured within the course.

Applying the *Understanding* Lens: Learners' Roles

What are the teacher's expectations of learners? What kinds of contributions are learners expected to make during lessons and during the course overall? Has the contributor been clear when describing circumstances in which learners are expected to interact with classmates? How and under what conditions do such interactions take place? In the course, are there opportunities for learners to assume any leadership responsibilities? To what extent do learners participate along with their teacher in a shared construction of lesson events? What might be some other roles learners play? A close examination of learners' roles is critical since the best of contemporary teaching and research suggests that learners themselves are primary agents when it comes to the essentially internal, though socially mediated, process of second language acquisition (Larsen-Freeman 1991). What are some of the course's characteristics that help to facilitate and enhance this process?

Teacher's Roles

What roles does the teacher play? Along with learners, the teacher is assumed to be a primary player in language courses. In most classrooms worldwide, teachers are the most visible players. The prominent role a language teacher tends to play is not necessarily something to be avoided. As Nelson (1998b, 1995b) points out, teachers from nations such as Australia, Canada, Great Britain, New Zealand, the United States, and other English-dominant parts of the world face special challenges when they work with English language students from educational backgrounds with alternative orientations to learning (as in parts of Africa, Asia, Eastern Europe, the Middle East, and South America). Some of the related challenges we might anticipate as ELT teachers include differences between a teacher's and learners' perceptions of power distances, gender roles and role relationships, anticipated classroom communication patterns, motivations for language study, tendencies toward either individualistic or collectivist styles of teaching-learning, degrees of tolerance for ambiguity in classrooms, and strategies of uncertainty avoidance (see Hofstede 1986).

Educators from one of the English-dominant nations mentioned previously who teach in nonwestern (i.e., non–Anglo/European) settings may find it necessary to learn to feel at ease with teacher roles somewhat more prominent than ones more familiar within their own educational backgrounds and training. Under appropriate circumstances, teacher prominence can instill confidence and feelings of security within learners. One reason is that it may match classroom communication patterns students not only anticipate but prefer. However, even in such settings excessively prominent roles played by a teacher sometimes begin to interfere with students' learning experiences. A complication ELT teachers sometimes face is the debilitating impact of *excessive* teacher prominence. If carried to an extreme, teacher prominence can defeat some of the central purposes for language instruction. Even in parts of the world where teachers are expected to play a prominent role in classrooms, a teacher who monopolizes available speaking time, for example, may be missing chances to provide even more efficient learning opportunities. Our reason for introducing this theme is not to suggest that teacher prominence be avoided in certain settings but to illustrate a dimension of a teacher's role that merits focused attention from all of us as language teachers. Such matters are not easily resolved. Lindsay Miller's chapter 14 illustrates the situation of a teacher facing the challenge of working to reconcile teacher roles on these dimensions. Of course, role relationships between teachers and learners in all classroom settings and in all parts of the world are incredibly complex, even when cultural and ethnic backgrounds are shared by the teacher and learners. Table 4.3 depicts some of the more familiar ways in which language learners and teachers tend to perceive the roles played by "the teacher" in ELT classrooms. As the format of a continuum is intended to imply, the roles teachers play in classrooms are not only complex but overlapping. Perhaps an even better way to envision table 4.3 would be as a Venn diagram with overlapping circles joined together by a shared shaded area at the center. Such a depiction might highlight even more clearly some of the complexities of teachers' shifting roles and role relationships with learners in classrooms.

However we envision them, the various facets of a teacher's roles blend together and interconnect in more and less obvious ways. One teacher may be a clear and decisive leader inside the classroom while simultaneously being perceived by learners as a good listener, encourager, and friend. A teacher of another style may be perceived as a good listener, encourager, and friend yet less decisive when it comes to exercising what would be appropriate degrees of managerial control over lesson events. On such dimensions, there are few immutable rules for teachers to live by. Ultimately, the roles a teacher plays in a language course acquire definition, relevance, and meaning through the shifting actions, responses, and perceptions of everyone involved since acts of teaching (and learning) are anchored in social, interpersonal, and intellectual domains as well as in external activity and responses. Not only are a teacher's roles incredibly complex, they are continuously being redefined through dynamic social interactions in classrooms. Patterns of communication in language classrooms call for teachers to be creative, resourceful, and flexible while moving in and out of a wide range of overlapping roles tied to the needs, expectations, values, and beliefs of all those participating (Johnson 1995). Richards and Lockhart (1994) discuss some of the complexities of a language teacher's role as follows.

> Teachers cannot be all things to all people, and the teacher's role may change during the lesson [and/or the course overall]. For example, in the opening phases of a lesson where the teacher is modeling new language patterns, the teacher may be particularly concerned with planning and quality control. At a later stage of the lesson where students are working independently, the teacher's role may be that of a facilitator. The way in which teachers interpret their roles leads to differences in the way they approach their teaching. (106)

In these sections you will find experienced teachers' discussions of the roles they believe themselves to be playing in the courses they describe. The

TABLE 4.3.   Continuum of Roles Language Teachers Play in Classrooms

Teacher as "The One in Charge" →				Teacher as "A Learner"
Leader	Director	Facilitator	Guide	Listener
Decision maker	Instructor	Resource	One who serves	Observer
Drill conductor	Manager	TL model	Encourager	peer
Planner/Organizer	Main speaker	Provider of comprehensible input	Collaborator	Archivist
Disciplinarian	Learner trainer	Cultural informant	Conflict resolver	Team member
Needs analyst	Technician	Negotiator	Motivator	Friend
Course developer	Knower	Elicitor	Counselor	One who follows students' leads
Materials developer	One who prompts	Mentor	Team member	
Provider	Quality controller	Researcher	Problem solver	
Linguist	One who intervenes	Advocate	Empowerer	
One who sets things up	Assessor	One who monitors	One who cues	
Evaluator		Feedback provider	Coach	
Tester				
Expert/Specialist				

Note: TL = target language

following are some questions to keep in mind while examining what they have to say.

Applying the *Understanding* Lens: Teacher's Roles

What are some of the roles the teacher typically plays during lessons? Can you describe what seem to be some of the teacher's recurring classroom actions and behaviors? Could you discuss what might be the teacher's perceptions of her or his roles? How about learners' perceptions? When comparing different chapters in the *Understanding* collection, do you notice ways in which teachers' roles and relationships with students may differ across courses? Across skill areas? Proficiency levels? Instructional settings? (Also, consider other courses with which you may be familiar.) Use table 4.3 as a reference point for identifying some of the roles the teacher plays within the course. Examine other chapter sections such as the setting, goals and objectives, learners' roles, or activity types sections to see if they illuminate additional facets of a teacher's role in the course. Can you infer connections between your understanding of the teacher's role in the course and any of the general principles listed in table 2.4 of chapter 2? How does the teacher within this particular course make opportunities available for either internal or socially mediated facets of second language acquisition to take place? Compare how you, your colleagues, or some other teachers make such opportunities available.

We have reached the end of chapter 4's discussion of the first half of the *Understanding* chapter framework, including the components of setting, conceptual underpinnings, course goals and objectives, syllabus design, activity types, learner roles, and roles of the teacher. Discussion of the framework's second half continues in chapter 5, which focuses on the remaining components of affective concerns, culture, instructional materials, assessment, lesson particulars, and the contributors' caveats/final thoughts tied to the courses they describe.

Chapter 5

A Framework for Discussion—Part 2

John Murphy and Patricia Byrd

> My signs are my rain-proof coat, good shoes, and a staff cut from the woods.
> —Walt Whitman, "Song of Myself"

In chapter 4 we introduced the first half of the *Understanding* chapter framework. We continue the discussion in chapter 5 by focusing on the framework's six remaining components. Near the end of the chapter, the section on lesson particulars extends our previous discussion of the rationale and intended purpose for the *Understanding* collection. Chapter 5 closes with guidelines and suggestions for examining the contributors' local-perspectives discussions of ELT as featured in chapters 6 through 23. The next component of the chapter framework focuses attention on affective concerns.

Affective Concerns

How are affective considerations addressed? English language teachers realize that emotions and feelings are essential features of life within language classrooms. Some teachers consider their ways of responding to affective considerations to be crucial for language learning to be successful (Bailey 1983; Mendelsohn 1999; Moskowitz 1979). Others go as far as to characterize learners' affective states as a causal factor in the acquisition of an L2 (Asher 1996; Krashen 1985). Along with attention to cognitive and linguistic concerns, more than a third of Brown's (1994a) widely cited synthesis of teaching principles is devoted to affective considerations. His several discussions of these themes (see also Brown 1994b) include principles of language ego, self-confidence, risk taking, and the language-culture connection. In addition, several of the implications for language teaching drawn by Kumaravadivelu (1993, 1994a), Larsen-Freeman (1991), and Pica (1994b) in their separate reviews of SLA literatures highlight closely related themes. Without requisite levels of affective support that can only be provided via the efforts and goodwill of a teacher and peers, the ELT classroom can become a "scary," an "alienating," and even an "intolerable" place for learners (Mendelsohn 1992, 72) .

We trace our interest in providing opportunities to examine affective considerations to two additional sources: Allwright and Bailey's (1991) discussion of L2 learner "receptivity" (157) and Smith's (1982) image of "sensitivity" to learning opportunities (174). Both sources conclude that a healthy affective environment, though not necessarily sufficient, certainly is a prerequisite for learners to succeed in language courses. Beyond threshold levels, teachers sometimes need to provide even higher levels of affective support if L2 students are to continue in their expectations to be successful language learners. Though explicit discussion of "affective considerations" is optional in the *Understanding* framework, it is useful to examine each of the collection's chapters with such concerns in mind. One thing is certain, even when taught by teachers with the best of intentions, language courses present learners with a plethora of anxiety-provoking experiences. When examining this feature of particular courses we try to recognize some of the precautions teachers take, or strategies they have developed, for cultivating and supporting the emotional well-being of learners as course participants.

Applying the *Understanding* Lens: Affective Concerns

In what ways does *the format* of the course serve to support the emotional well-being of learners? In what ways does *course content* or the *teacher's roles* or other facets of the course? Is the course structured in ways fostering and strengthening learners' anticipations of success? After examining the whole chapter, what is your impression? Do you think students participating in such a course will consider it worthwhile to try to do their best? Is there anything about the course that might spark (or dampen) learner motivation? Do course structures leave room for students to pursue some of their own interests and needs? Are opportunities provided for learners to become more self-sufficient and autonomous as language learners? In what ways do course features help to ensure that learners will remain open and receptive to (1) the teacher's way of teaching, (2) course content, (3) instructional materials, (4) the teacher as a person, (5) the kinds of activities featured in the course, (6) the idea of working with classmates, (7) opportunities for performing successfully in the course, (8) the idea of becoming an even more competent English language user (cf. Allwright and Bailey 1991)?

Culture

What roles do culture and/or cultural considerations play in the course? During the final quarter of the twentieth century, the discipline of ELT matured well beyond earlier eras when the role of culture in the teaching of second or foreign languages implied little more than exposing learners to the fine arts (e.g., dance, film, music, painting, sculpture) or literary canon of the target language culture. Recent decades have witnessed considerable expansion of what teachers consider to be culturally relevant topics in ELT courses. As Kumaravadivelu (1994a) reminds us, many English language classrooms are multicultural settings where a teacher and learners, sometimes from very different parts of the world, meet for language learning purposes. First language culture, target language culture, interlanguage culture, and features of intercultural communication are topics receiving considerable attention at the present time (Flowerdew and Miller 1995; Hinkel 1999; Pennycook 1996; Watkins and Biggs 1996). Their impacts on ELT are being recognized, discussed, and debated in substantive ways by contemporary language teachers (e.g., Atkinson 1999; Carson 1998; Nelson 1998a; Spack 1997).

Due in large part to differing cultural backgrounds and variations in learner expectations, difficulties arise when ELT approaches identified with English-dominant parts of the world are "exported" to alternative cultural settings (Ellis 1996; Li 1998; Ting 1987; and Valdes and Jhones 1991). Some of these difficulties include role expectations of teachers and learners, power distance relationships, learner-centered versus instructor-centered teaching, implied challenges (even when unintended) to traditional styles of teaching, and learners' perceptions of classroom communication patterns. A pervasive theme still expanding in the field is resistance of teachers and learners from non–Anglo/European parts of the world to ELT approaches developed in English-dominant nations. Like most dimensions of human activity, processes and procedures of ELT are inextricably linked with the cultural values, beliefs, and expectations of all parties involved.

Another reason for changes in how teachers perceive and understand the role of culture in ELT classrooms is awareness that in English-dominant regions of the world ESL courses teem with learner diversity. Such diversity in learners' cultural backgrounds has shifted teachers' attentions to the impacts on teaching and learning of students' differing predispositions, responses, and preferences as English language learners. In classrooms where cultural diversity is the norm learners meet peers with alternative ways of perceiving the world (Hinkel 1999; Kumaravadivelu 1994a; Nelson 1998a)—ways that carry special challenges for everyone involved. One challenge is that a teacher or learners may perceive topics tied to students' differing predispositions, responses, and learning preferences to be inappropriate for class discussion. When this happens, such topics may remain unspoken, unacknowledged, and neglected. Thus, potentially useful learning opportunities may be missed.

Fortunately, alternative ways of viewing the role of culture in language teaching are emerging. When handled well by teachers, student diversity can become a useful resource for purposes of both language and culture learning. English language teaching has always provided instructors with opportunities to serve as cultural guides, but continuing student diversity in ESL populations provides opportunities for learners to serve as each others' guides as well (Kumaravadivelu 1993). Some teachers explore ways of fostering learner awareness, tolerance, and understanding of what often are the many cultures represented in even a single course (Kumaravadivelu 1993). For teachers and learners interested in exploring such themes, the fostering of cultural tolerance and understanding is one of the more intriguing potentialities of ELT classrooms worldwide. Several contributors discuss ways of taking advantage of cultural diversity to live up to such challenges in their courses. Jo-Anne Wilson-Keenan, Jerri Willett, and Judith Solsken's chapter 7, Robert DeVillar and Binbin Jiang's chapter 9, and David Mendelsohn's chapter 17 are especially interesting on this dimension. Though optional in the *Understanding* collection, this section is an opportunity for contributors to highlight what they consider to be culture-related dimensions of their courses. Even when this aspect of a course is discussed only indirectly by contributors it is important to begin to recognize ways in which the roles of culture and cultural considerations impact ELT courses.

Applying the *Understanding* Lens: Culture

When considering the role of culture, we suggest using a chapter's setting section as a starting point to examine and reflect on the possible impacts of learners' cultural backgrounds, the local culture in which the course is offered, and ways in which related considerations are being incorporated in the course. For example, does the course exploit learners' cultural backgrounds as possible resources for learning? Has the teacher found ways of fostering learner awareness and understanding of either the target culture or some of the other cultures represented in the class?

Would you characterize the materials, topics, and activities woven into the course as culture sensitive, as culture neutral, or perhaps as biased in any ways? Do course materials, topics, or patterns of communication seem either problematic or especially helpful on such dimensions? If you were offering such a course, in what ways might you modify the teacher's plans in order to be true to your own understandings of the role of culture in language teaching? Chapters 11 through 14 are of special interest since they are examples of teaching English as a foreign language in non-English-dominant (non–Anglo/European) parts of the world. Brian Morgan's chapter 8 and Donna Brinton's chapter 16 merit close attention as well, since both contributors explore ways of incorporating students' cultural backgrounds as resource materials while exposing students to alternative ways of perceiving the world.

Instructional Materials

What types of instructional materials are included in the course? In many language classrooms a commercially published textbook functions as the primary anchor for the course. In some settings a textbook may serve as the only course syllabus. There are situations, of course, in which teachers or learners have good reasons to resist the use of commercially published materials. Nevertheless, published materials often provide language teachers with opportunities to work with high-quality resources potentially more useful than anything they would have time to develop on their own. Beyond a core textbook, such opportunities may be facilitated through an accompanying workbook, an instructor's manual, audio recordings, video recordings, computer software, and other instructional supports. The following are just a few of the reasons why published materials often serve as essential tools for purposes of ELT.

Learners may expect them.
There may be a set of appropriate materials available through one or
   more commercial publishers.
Teachers may have insufficient time to create their own materials.
Not all teachers are skillful as materials developers.
The institutional setting may call for consistency in instructional
   materials across different courses offered by different teachers.

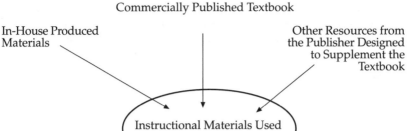

Fig. 5.1.   Instructional materials used in ELT courses

Figure 5.1 depicts a range of possibilities with respect to instructional supports used in ELT courses.

In some programs teachers focus their courses on a commercially published textbook that provides a reasonable match with their curricula. In other courses and programs, teachers combine a published textbook with additional supplementary materials either made available through a publisher or generated "in-house" by a local committee of teachers, by an individual teacher, or even in collaboration with learners. In some settings, in-house materials are designed not by the teacher of the course but by some other member(s) of the teaching staff. The reasons for these alternative structures and procedures are multiple and may include such considerations as the following: (1) there may be an effective match between a published text and program/course goals; (2) teachers who are interested in and skillful at materials development may decide to create materials focused on the particular needs of their program; (3) desire for content consistency across multiple sections of a single course may call for the selection of a published text to use throughout a program; (4) in some settings, the population of learners is so small, or their needs so specialized, that suitable published materials are not available—a situation that often leads to the development of sets of in-house materials; (5) since few if any textbooks are completely congruent with course goals, learners' interests, and learners' needs, textbooks are often supplemented with additional resources. In chapter 7, Wilson-Keenan, Willet, and Solsken illustrate the use of learners' families and family visits to the classroom as resources for generating instructional materials.

Whatever forms instructional materials may take, and however they might be developed, in this section contributors discuss the kinds of materials they depend upon for teaching purposes. Their comments are not limited to commercially published textbooks but extend well beyond them to include such alternatives as more loosely organized materials, library materials, newspapers, video recordings, audiocassette recorders, camcorders, computer software, Internet resources, community resources, in-house course packets, forms and questionnaires to be completed, charts, transparencies, pictures, wall posters, objects, and other forms of realia.

Applying the *Understanding* Lens: Instructional Materials

Do students buy anything? Are materials made available through the teacher, program, or institution? Is there a textbook or another set of materials serving as an anchor for the course? Are there any supplementary materials? If a course packet is used, what kinds of materials are included in it? What might be some criteria for their inclusion? Does the teacher discuss the role and importance of whatever instructional materials are found to be useful in the course? Based upon your reading of the chapter, are you able to identify the sources and purposes of the kinds of materials used? Do course materials seem compatible with students' needs? In your view, would anything about the materials mentioned seem especially intriguing (or possibly distracting or boring) from learners' perspectives? If you were to offer such a course, would you work with similar materials? Alternative materials? Contrastive ones? If published sets of materials are mentioned in the chapter, consider looking them up for purposes of your own review. In reference to figure 5.1, which of the six categories of materials are incorporated into the course? Which others potentially could be? What decisions might you make as a teacher of such a course with respect to instructional materials?

Assessment

How is learner assessment accomplished? A teacher's strategies for assessing learner progress in a language course can take many different forms. They

might include both informal and formal procedures, formative and summative assessment options, holistic and discrete-item formats, oral and
written modes, live feedback provided spontaneously in the midst of lessons, delayed feedback made possible via video recordings, and peer responses to learners' contributions, among a range of additional possibilities.
For language learners to continue to progress in their control of the target
language, formative feedback on how well they are doing is essential.
Mendelsohn (1992) reminds us that ELT classrooms can become frustrating
for learners without some combination of appropriate feedback from both
the classroom teacher and peers. In most ELT courses teachers coordinate
a combination of informal (usually more frequent) and formal assessment
options.

Applying the *Understanding* Lens: Assessment

What information is given—not only in the section titled "Assessment"
but in a contributor's chapter overall—about how assessment issues are
addressed in the course? What does the teacher assess? Bearing in mind
that most language learners depend upon feedback on how well they
are doing, how does the teacher monitor students' efforts? Are any
feedback procedures mentioned? If so, what purposes do they serve? Do
grades seem to receive significant attention? Are there less formal ways
of providing students with feedback on how they are doing? Are some
forms of assessment included as part of the regular routine of teaching?
Do assessment results impact what subsequently takes place in the
course? Do students ever receive peer feedback? What features of
learner progress would you be likely to assess if teaching such a course?
Do you come away from the chapter with an understanding of how
learner progress is tracked or how feedback is provided to learners during the course?

Lesson Particulars

> General Forms have their vitality in Particulars.
> —William Blake, *Jerusalem*

*What are some details of communication and interaction patterns that have actu-
ally taken place within the course?* Regardless of our background and expectations as teachers, the nature of our professional preparation, the theories
we may subscribe to or generate on our own, the charges we accept when

we agree to teach a course, or the number of times we might have taught it, everything culminates as a series of lessons in which a teacher and learners meet on a regular basis for purposes of language learning. Each classroom lesson is supported by a teacher's and learners' implicit as well as explicit contributions. A finite series of such lessons, each one with a beginning, a midpoint, and an end, aggregate to become a language course. Contributing to such aggregations, language lessons and whole courses are socially interactive events made up of people with personal strengths and weaknesses; explicit and implicit agendas; overt and covert moods, assumptions, and predispositions. As another way of calling attention to the situated nature of language teaching, we asked each of the contributors to include what we call a lesson particulars (LP) section. In most instances these sections describe at least a portion of an actual lesson. They are intended to illustrate the kinds of communications and events that typically occur within the targeted course.

Contributors explored a range of options for presenting LP sections. Not all the sections are in narrative form. Some precursors to this component of the *Understanding* framework are Day 1990 (54–57), Larsen-Freeman 1986 (90–95), and Morgan 1997 (440–43). A very early example appears as the "blackboard composition" section of Clarke's (1984, 578) classic journal article titled "On the Nature of Technique: What Do We Owe the Gurus?" Clarke's illustration of what we call lesson particulars begins as follows.

> After the business of the class (roll taken, graded papers returned, questions regarding the midterm exam answered) is taken care of, I announce that we are going to write a blackboard composition on "Love and Marriage in the United States." For several weeks we have been reading, talking, and writing about the mores and morals of Americans. The topic has generated a great deal of interest. . . . everybody has accumulated a wealth of information, insight, and opinion on the topic. I give the class precisely seven minutes to get organized. . . . Some seem to meditate, eyes half-closed, chins resting on palms, pencils tapping lightly; others scratch notes furiously, apparently driven by inspiration which they fear will escape them; . . . Most seem gratifyingly engaged in the activity, although one student appears to be sleeping, and another arrives late and does not really get down to work before the time is up. At the end of the seven minutes, I announce to the students that they are to compare notes and to discuss their musings in pairs and small groups. They know that the object of their discussion is to produce a list of main ideas around which we can build an essay. I do not indicate a time limit here but rather, circulate among the groups, eavesdropping on the discussions and commenting on the growing lists of main ideas. After about ten minutes, I call the class to order. A

student raises his hand. His group believes that the title of the composition should be changed to "Love and Courtship in the United States." Marriage, they contend . . . (578–82)

Allwright and Bailey (1991), Ernst (1994), Johnson (1995), and Murphy (1993) illustrate yet an additional way to introduce authentic lesson events by featuring verbatim transcripts of extended lesson segments accompanied by prose discussions. What all of these sources share is the care taken to present detailed illustrations of at least a portion of an actual lesson. As Freeman and Johnson (1998) propose, when it comes to classroom teaching "the general resides in the particular" (404). Thus, part of the contributors' charge was to provide LP illustrations that reflect the broader spirit of the course.

We trace the inspiration for our way of envisioning and labeling this section to the excerpt from William Blake's epic poem *Jerusalem,* presented at the heads of chapters 2 and 4. Over recent years Blake's images have provided ongoing inspiration for our own work as language teachers. We believe there are several useful connections between Blake's images and the spirit of the *Understanding* collection. Parallel to Blake's images of "Minute Particulars," by *"lesson* particulars" we mean the inclusion of descriptive details concerning teacher's and learners' actions and behaviors during an authentic language lesson. As illustrated earlier, many theory-to-practice discussions of ELT include something along the lines of LP descriptions. Such discussions remind us of the grounded nature of our efforts in classrooms and of the tangible sources of questions we tend to ask ourselves as teachers. We may extend Blake's observation that "Art & Science cannot exist but in minutely organized Particulars" to suggest that the specifics of our teaching behaviors not only matter a great deal to learners but reach to the very heart of our profession. Such connections further imply that an individual teacher's way of offering an ELT course is a particular and local, rather than a global, endeavor.

As captured in the spirit of the excerpt from Whitman's ([1891] 1992) *Leaves of Grass* given here and as the epigraph to the book, language teachers are in good company since most professional activities are grounded in local journeys of seeing and searching.[1]

---

1. We would like to acknowledge the contribution of John F. Fanselow (personal communication, October 24, 1990) in calling these lines from Whitman's "Song of Myself" to our attention.

I tramp a perpetual journey, (come listen all!)
My signs are a rain-proof coat, good shoes,
    and a staff cut from the woods,
No friend of mine takes his ease in my chair,
I have no chair, no church, no philosophy,
I lead no man to a dinner-table, library, exchange,
But each man and each woman of you I lead upon a knoll,
My left hand hooking you round the waist,
My right hand pointing to landscapes of continents
    and the public road.

Not I, not any one else can travel that road for you,
You must travel it for yourself.

It is not far, it is within reach,
Perhaps you have been on it since you were born
    and did not know,
Perhaps it is everywhere on water and on land.

—Walt Whitman, "Song of Myself"

While we "tramp" along our own pathways of learning to teach as best as we can, for good and ill our actions and behaviors in classrooms affect students' learning experiences and lives. Beyond the scope of LP sections, one of our intentions is that the *Understanding* collection's five initial chapters will serve as something like a "left hand hooking you round the waist." To continue with Whitman's images, we believe many of the course-specific themes contributors discuss in chapters 6 through 23 are pointing to some of the "landscapes of continents and the public road" being explored by contemporary English language teachers. Part of the challenge we face in classrooms is to find ways of ensuring that the potential impacts of our plans, decisions, and behaviors as teachers are appropriate for our local settings and as tailored as we can achieve to meet the needs of learners in our courses. At the same time, we should be mindful of ELT perspectives beyond the scope of our particular experiences. Ultimately, these are "perpetual journeys" tied to a sense of what is truthful in our local settings of English language teaching and learning that all of us must travel for ourselves. Fortunately, some of the language learners, colleagues, ELT courses, teacher development courses, conferences, workshops, books, and other professional resources we spend time with along the way help to ensure our journeys are in good company.

Examining Blake's references to the vitality of "Minute Particulars" also reminds us that in language courses, theories-principles can only enter the world of experience through acts of teaching and learning. Blake's image of limits to the "generalizing Demonstrations of the Rational Power" places in an interesting light the research literature of our field—what Freeman and Richards (1993) categorize as "science-research conceptions of teaching" (193). Contemporary research literatures are important sources of information and inspiration for teachers. Since they are a dimension of our continual search for clearer understandings and explanations, science-research conceptions play essential roles in our efforts to grow as professionals. Pica (1994b) and Kumaravadivelu (1993, 1994a) illustrate that science-research literatures often speak directly to the needs and interests of language teachers. But while they serve as important reference points, few of us place research discussions at the heart of the *local understandings and explanations* of our efforts as language teachers (Clarke 1994; Freeman and Johnson 1998; Gebhard and Oprandy 1999). Rather, language classrooms themselves and the complex nature of events taking place within them are even closer to the heart of the profession. LP sections illustrate this theme while celebrating the classroom as the place that matters most. Whether we envision acts of teaching as "a science, a technology, a craft, or an art" (Freeman and Richards 1993, 193); as an expression of values (Edge 1994); as an articulation of beliefs; as a demonstration of assumptions about teaching and learning (Johnson 1994); or as any combination of (or all of) these contributors to our local understandings and reasonings as teachers, the language classroom remains the centerpiece of teachers' efforts . . . and of the profession itself.

Partly in response to this theme, it seemed essential to include a section devoted to something along the lines of what we call lesson particulars within each of the collection's chapters. The following is an excerpt from the original prompt presented to contributors.

> Begin by imagining that an ethnographer who is a specialist in descriptive classroom observation techniques were to visit a representative lesson of your targeted course. Further imagine that you have asked the ethnographer to compose a careful prose description of a particularly interesting portion of the lesson observed. As a basis for your work in composing the lesson particulars section, what might a relatively polished and readable version of the ethnographer's field notes include?

Within each chapter, the LP section is an opportunity for readers to envision some of the details, atmosphere, and events of at least a segment of a lesson representative of the targeted course. As much as possible, contributors were asked to include details of classroom events and behaviors from an observer's perspective. Minimally, an LP section should be both authentic and representative of communications and events typically taking place within the contributor's course. It is a window opening onto at least a brief scene of teaching.

Applying the *Understanding* Lens: Lesson Particulars

When examining LP sections, some questions to keep in mind are, Is the account believable? Are the events depicted consistent with the chapter's other themes and sections? Who are the participants in the lesson segment? What happens? What kinds of events might have led up to the ones illustrated? What might have followed them? Does the LP section illustrate any of the teaching ideas mentioned in the chapter's activity types section or discussed elsewhere by the contributor? Is the section consistent with the contributor's discussion of conceptual underpinnings of the course? Is it consistent with any of the general ELT principles listed in table 2.4 of chapter 2? What elements do you believe were captured in the LP section? Keeping in mind that LP sections necessarily are limited in scope, what elements were missing? Do any of the elements depicted remind you of your own teaching or learning experiences? Does the contributor discuss how the LP section was generated? If you are currently teaching, what procedure(s) might you explore for producing such a snapshot of your own teaching? What are some elements of the spirit of your teaching you would hope to capture?

Caveats/Final Thoughts

Is there anything else you would like other teachers to know? In this final section of the *Understanding* framework, contributors have the option of including anything else they feel readers should know about the targeted course. Some discuss lessons they have learned about teaching, complications they encounter when offering the course, future directions for course development, and other issues they would like readers to keep in mind should they ever have an opportunity to observe or teach a similar course.

Conclusion

Attention now turns to ways in which 18 different teachers, or teams of teacher-collaborators, applied the *Understanding* chapter framework as a mechanism for describing local understandings and explanations of their work in language courses. Contributors treated the various sections of the framework in sometimes similar, and at other times dissimilar, ways. In keeping with our theme of context-specific approaches to language teaching, we expect to find variations in the ways contributors ended up working within the chapter framework. As writers, they are using prose discussions to share with others their understandings and explanations of a highly complex and socially interactive endeavor—their own teaching. Realizing that teacher-writers vary with respect to their reasonings about teaching as well as their preferences for self-expression, we asked contributors to view the framework as flexible and to find opportunities for the emergence of their own voices. Our reason for outlining and describing the framework in detail in chapters 4 and 5 may be summed up in the following adage: "it is unwise to introduce variations on a theme without first presenting the theme" (Clifford Hill, personal communication, October 7, 1978). Now that the "theme" of the *Understanding* chapter structure has been presented, we trust variations in ways contributors worked with it serve to strengthen the quality of their discussions. While working your way through remaining chapters, you might keep the following advice from Larsen-Freeman (1986) in mind. In the original source, the author was discussing readers' possible responses to the global methods of teaching she surveyed. Since our focus is quite distant from considerations of global methods, we have taken the liberty of substituting words and phrases used throughout the *Understanding* collection to refer to an individual teacher's *local approach to teaching* in places where words and phrases tied to global methods originally appeared.

Applying the *Understanding* Lens: Conclusion

Elbow (1973) says there are two basic games one can use when one is looking for truth and faced with conflicting assertions. One can play the "doubting game" or one can play the "believing game." If you play the doubting game, you try to objectively assess each [teacher-contributor's approach] while you are looking for weaknesses in it. If you play the believing game, you take each [approach] one at a time and try to believe in it in order to understand it. You try to imagine yourself the originator or practitioner of the [teacher's local approach] and to see things as they do. . . . if you do not allow yourself to first believe, if you do not allow yourself to enter into [someone else's approach to teaching] and understand it from the inside out, then you may be too quick to dismiss [it] or the principles or techniques which comprise it. Thus, as you [continue with your reading of the *Understanding* collection], we encourage you to review what you have experienced, to seriously entertain the principles and techniques of each [teacher's individual approach], and then to hold them up to the filter of your own beliefs, needs, and experiences.[2]

As Larsen-Freeman goes on to advise, ultimately you are the one who will be responsible for making relevant connections to your own teaching situations, just as you are the instructional specialist learners will be depending upon to make informed and appropriate plans, decisions, choices, responses, and reactions while teaching ELT courses. We believe each of the course descriptions provided in chapters 6 through 23 illuminates important aspects of teachers' plans, choices, and decision making. Examining and comparing descriptions of real courses currently being offered in the field of ELT is one way to learn more about facets of teacher thinking, understanding, and reasoning that are integral to the language instruction process—especially if we are willing to suspend disbelief, temporarily, while learning about each contributor's course. Clarke (1984) reminds us that when it comes to local considerations of ELT it is the individual teacher "who is in the position of authority" since she or he is the only one who "can decide what to take and what to leave, whom to listen to and whom to ignore" (591). The *Understanding* collection will have met one of its central purposes if it serves as a touchstone supporting, but not constraining, your own efforts and teaching decisions.

As illustrated throughout the rest of this book, language teaching is a complex decision-making process. Teachers vary with respect to the exciting, creative, inspirational, critical, commonplace, routine, and even troubling decisions they are called upon to make, day in and day out, in language classrooms worldwide. We believe the many dimensions of language teaching suggested in chapters 6 through 23 imply enticing worlds of pos-

---

2. Material adapted from *Techniques and Principles in Language Teaching* by Diane Larsen-Freeman. © 1986 Oxford University Press. Reproduced by permission of Oxford University Press.

sibilities. These chapters illustrate how other teachers have responded to the *Understanding* framework's potential as a means for thinking and writing about experiences in language teaching. We trust the conceptual lenses presented in chapters 4 and 5 will be helpful for at least one of the following purposes: (1) to foster clearer understanding of the contributors' courses from the "inside out"; (2) to make it easier to recognize similarities and contrasts between features of what might be very different courses and ways of teaching; and, through the process of learning to examine closely the work of other teachers; (3) to clarify some of your own values, beliefs, and understandings as a language teacher.

One way to proceed in reading this book is to examine the collection's table of contents and the additional chapter information depicted in table 1.2, identify two or more course descriptions that interest you, and use them as starting points for further reading in the collection. Since each chapter is introduced by a concise editors' preface that previews its scope and focus, another option is to read several of the prefaces in succession before settling on a single chapter to examine in depth. In fact, reading all of the editors' prefaces in one sitting provides a quick overview of the *Understanding* collection's local-perspectives chapters and is a strategy for becoming more familiar with the rest of the book that we highly recommend. At the same time, some readers may prefer to follow the sequencing of chapters as originally presented. In addition to the editors' prefaces, a section titled "Prompts for Discussion and Reflection" closes each chapter as additional support to readers. These sections are intended to prompt further engagement with the contributor's discussion and with possible connections to teaching in other settings. Also, the many "Applying the *Understanding* Lens" windows appearing throughout chapters 4 and 5 are intended for periodic review while reading chapters 6 through 23. You may be examining this book alone, or you may have opportunities to discuss some of its content with colleagues. In either case, the following is a listing of supports to refer back to during your reading.

Table 1.1: Framework for *Understanding* Chapters 6 through 23 (13 questions)

Table 2.4: Fourteen Principles to Support English Language Learning and Teaching (followed in the body of the chapter by a series of prose discussions tied to the principles)

"Applying the *Understanding* Lens" Windows (Interspersed through the bodies of chaps. 4 and 5, each window is tied to one of the

questions listed in table 1.1 and repeated as a topic heading in table 4.1. Over a dozen such windows are presented.)
Prompts for Discussion and Reflection (located at the ends of chaps. 6 through 23)

In addition to these supports, the *Understanding* collection's Internet site is introduced and described at the end of the book in chapter 24.

Part 2
General Purposes Instruction

Chapter 6

English in the Workplace at Goodwill Industries

Marjorie Terdal, Janice Ruhl, and Carolyn Armstrong

Carolyn Armstrong and Janice Ruhl are English language teachers at Goodwill Industries in the northwest United States. Carolyn teaches entry-level English in the workplace to the company's employees. Her classes are offered on-site, and students are given release time from work to attend. Taking advantage of this arrangement, Carolyn ties her curriculum decisions and teaching materials to students' current jobs. Two primary sources serve as input: (1) information on students' needs based upon individualized needs assessment procedures and (2) a list of foundation skills and competencies developed by a national government commission. As informed by these sources, Carolyn and Janice generated a list of 30 basic survival English competencies and 50 basic workplace competencies, all stated in terms of performance objectives. Thus, the course described in this chapter incorporates topics, communicative functions, and themes designed to help students reach carefully identified competencies.

In the classroom, activities feature tasks and materials designed to help students develop skills for success in their jobs at Goodwill and to enhance their lives outside of work. Students write stories about themselves, their jobs, and their families. The stories are used for reading comprehension, vocabulary lessons, and other forms of language practice. Their stories are also shared in published form with managers and other Goodwill employees as indications of what students and the language program have been able to accomplish. Because it is a workplace setting, Carolyn and Janice find they need to play a number of roles in addition to those more familiar to English language teachers.

Setting

In 1998, Goodwill Industries of the Columbia Willamette (GICW) was in its third year of an in-house program for employees whose native language is not English. The ESL program is one of several programs that fit with Goodwill's mission to provide vocational training, employment, and job placement for people with special needs. Goodwill is a nonprofit agency that receives donations of used goods, which are then processed and displayed in retail stores. The Columbia Willamette is a successful retail store operator and among all 187 Goodwill units in North America one of the biggest employers of people with special needs.

Many nonnative speakers of English face vocational disadvantages that impact the quality of their lives. For those nonnative English (NNE) speaking employees unwilling or unable to attend community college ESL classes, the GICW program is a welcome benefit. Two full-time year-round ESL instructors, Janice Ruhl and Carolyn Armstrong, assess the English language skills of all newly hired NNE speakers, negotiate with store managers for classes based on test results, and provide instruction in various Goodwill stores throughout northwestern Oregon and across the Columbia River in Vancouver, Washington. In its first phase, the GIWC ESL program consisted of two levels, one meeting for 30 weeks and the other for 20 weeks. The extra time in the 30-week course was used to address survival English and literacy needs. Concern for employees with limited literacy led to the addition, in 1998, of a basic literacy course (now called Level A), in anticipation of the more in-depth workplace ESL topics and competencies covered in the 30-week and 20-week courses (now called Levels B and C).

As with most workplace ESL programs (for representative examples, see Belfiore and Burnaby 1995), the Goodwill curriculum is customized and grows out of the students' needs in the employment situation. It is organized around hands-on communicative tasks that employees need to master in order to function successfully at work and in the community. Responding appropriately to a customer's solicit for assistance and demonstrating safety procedures at work are just two of the many tasks for which Carolyn and Janice have created materials specific to the Goodwill work setting.

Students are from Latin America, Southeast Asia, Africa, Eastern Europe, and the former Soviet Union, with a majority from Mexico. They have varied educational and employment backgrounds and range from 18 to 62 years old. About half of the members of the program have had nine years or less of schooling and are not completely literate in their native language. Others have attended high school, postsecondary technical schools, and even universities in their native countries. A few students have never attended school before. Before coming to the United States, some were professionals; others were farmworkers, small business owners, or general laborers. Many of the older women were homemakers. At Goodwill they work as production workers, donation attendants, cashiers, maintenance staff, and dockworkers.

These Goodwill employees attend ESL classes during their regular work shifts and are paid for this time. Classes meet in break, supply, locker, and conference rooms in various Goodwill stores. They are held two or three times a week for a total of three hours a week, at whatever time can be negotiated with the site manager(s). The class described in this chapter meets Tuesday and Wednesday mornings from 7:30 to 9:00 in a supply room. It is a 30-week, Level B class for workers who classify as Novice-High on the ACTFL speaking and listening proficiency guidelines. Students in Level B have basic literacy skills in their native language and can handle routine entry-level jobs that do not require much oral or written communication. They can ask and respond to simple questions in English; have some control of basic English grammar; and can read short, simple sentences related to their immediate needs.

Lesson Particulars

It is 7:30 A.M. and the second week of the 30-week course. The six women in this class are all from Mexico, have lived in the United States from 3 to 10 years; and, except for one of the younger women, who graduated from a Mexican high school, have all attended school in Mexico for 6 to 9 years. The women are seated around a rectangular table in an 8- by 12-foot corner of an L-shaped room. Boxes of supplies line two walls of the small, windowless room. Taped to the wall beside the table are a map of the world; enlarged copies of pictures from the textbook being used in the course, Huizenga and Weinstein-Shr's (1996) *Collaborations: English in Our Lives, Beginning I;* and a sheet of paper with the conjugation of the verb *to be* in present tense. Sticky-backed notes are fastened to various objects in the room with corresponding labels written in English: *door, light, ladder, pictures, radio, clock.* At one end of the table is a small whiteboard. Carolyn, the teacher, has carried in a large box of supplies and a cassette recorder, portable because there is no electrical outlet in this room. Each student has a copy of the textbook that was provided by Goodwill and a three-ring binder with blank lined paper and handouts Carolyn and Janice created.

As the class begins, Carolyn writes several letters, in capitals, on the whiteboard and then asks students to make up words from the letters. Students talk to each other, mostly in Spanish, and come up with the words *goodwill, dog, so, win.* Carolyn writes them on the board and then quickly goes over an exercise from the textbook that students had completed at home.

She then tells the students to close their eyes and listen to the story of Linh Dang, taken from their textbook. The women repeat the story chorally. It is six sentences long. Next, the students working in pairs have their first practice with dictation. One woman reads aloud a sentence from the story while her partner writes it. Carolyn tells them they can ask their partner to spell out some words, if needed. When one of the older women is having obvious difficulty, Carolyn allows her to look at the text and copy the sentences. After five minutes, they switch partners to give each person an opportunity to write. In two minutes one pair has finished, another is half through, and the third has yet to begin—evidence of the multilevels even in this class of six students. Carolyn then asks everyone to take turns sharing similar information about themselves. When Angelina, one of the youngest women, says, "I am 90," Carolyn smiles and then politely says, "You are 19," with the primary stress and vowel sound, /iy/, on the final syllable. A little later, Maria, whose English level is the lowest in the class, says, "I am for Mexico," which Carolyn tries to modify by asking, "Do you mean you are 'for' or 'from' Mexico?" Maria responds "from Mexico." Carolyn then gets the entire class to repeat the correct form after her. Both Carolyn and the students laugh with each other a lot, indicating they have already established comfortable rapport and a relaxed atmosphere in the class. To conclude this activity, Carolyn asks the students to write about themselves, following the pattern of the textbook story of Linh Dang. Most look in the book and copy the model. Carolyn walks around the table, praising their attempts and offering help. When Sofia asks about the spelling of *married*, Carolyn asks two other women to spell it, and then she writes the correct spelling on the board.

It is now 8:05, and Carolyn introduces a new activity. She passes out a handout with sketches depicting different jobs at Goodwill (see app. 6.1). She asks questions trying to elicit the names of jobs with which the students are familiar: *sorter, donation attendant, hanger, pricer, tagger, cashier, stocker*. Several students can explain what a person in a particular job does, such as "sorts," "donation," or "hang clothes," but most of them do not seem to know more precise words and descriptors for the positions. Carolyn writes the name of each job on the board. She then points to the chart on the wall with the conjugation of *be* and says, "We can use these words to talk about these jobs." Carolyn writes students' sentences on the board: "They work at Goodwill." "She is a cashier." "I am a coder." She makes sure everyone participates by calling them by name: "Angelina, what is your job?" "Imelda, who is your supervisor?"

Carolyn next holds up enlarged photographs of real Goodwill employees and says, "This is Tinh. He's in the Portland store. What's his job?" to which students reply, "He is a bedding pricer." Students relate easily to these authentic photographs of fellow employees. About this time, the store manager and another employee walk into the storeroom to get some supplies. Rather than being flustered by the interruption, Carolyn asks the students, "What's her job?" and chats briefly with the manager before resuming the activity.

The next activity involves another handout showing Goodwill jobs. Carolyn asks *wh-* questions as a way to help students talk about the sequence involved in different jobs they are familiar with. Students become quite animated when asked what happens to the money customers spend in the store. Some begin in Spanish, and then the more proficient students provide a possible word in English. They eventually generate a long list, including *pay employees, buy trucks, pay rent, office in Portland, people with disabilities,* and *bank.* One by one, Carolyn writes most of these on the board and then reviews how to say them and their meanings with the class.

In the last 10 minutes, Carolyn distributes an exercise to spell out names of jobs at Goodwill by filling in missing letters in an alphabet puzzle. She helps the class with the first two items, and then as the faster students catch on, she goes around the table to assist those who are working at a slower pace. The highest level student, who finishes quickly, then helps others who seem to need the support. At 9:00 the women leave the room to return to their jobs on the floor.

A few minutes after 9:00, Carolyn goes out to visit and interact one-on-one with students as they work. She walks around the store and production area, speaking for about five minutes with each of the six women in the class. Carolyn also has a few exchanges with other employees and students in her next class at this site. She asks questions practicing the structures just learned in the classroom: "What is your job?" "Tell me what you do." "What is Imelda's job?"

Conceptual Underpinnings

The class described in the preceding section illustrates several of the principles underlying many English in the Workplace (EWP) programs. *EWP* is the term used to describe English language programs tailored to meet

TABLE 6.1.   SCANS Workplace Competencies

Label	Example Competencies
Resource management	Organizing; planning; allocating time, money, materials, staff
Interpersonal skills	Working on teams, teaching others, serving customers, leading, negotiating, working effectively within culturally diverse settings
Information management	Acquiring and evaluating facts and data, organizing and maintaining information, interpreting and communicating information, using computers
Systems management	Understanding social organization and technological systems, monitoring and correcting performance, improving existing systems, designing new systems
Technology	Selecting equipment and tools, applying technology, maintaining and troubleshooting equipment

Source: Information from Secretary's Commission on Achieving Necessary Skills (1991).

the needs of a particular group of learners at a specific company. EWP programs are growing because of (*a*) the increasing number of limited English proficient workers in the North American workforce and (*b*) the perception that today's workers do not possess the skills required for a changing workforce. Johnston and Packer (1987) and the U.S. Department of Education (1992) agree that technological, demographic, and global economic forces are reshaping the workplace throughout North America and requiring higher level skills than ever before.

The Secretary's Commission on Achieving Necessary Skills (SCANS) (1991) has identified foundation skills and competencies necessary to succeed in today's workplace: (1) general foundation skills (e.g., basic reading, writing, arithmetic, listening, speaking, interpreting, as well as organizing new information and ideas), (2) thinking skills (e.g., creative thinking, decision making, problem solving, ability to reason), and (3) personal qualities (e.g., responsibility, self-esteem, sociability, integrity, honesty, self-management). As depicted in table 6.1, SCANS also lists five additional categories of essential workplace competencies.

In response to the increased awareness of a perceived skills gap (we use the word *perceived* deliberately because we believe employers often see this gap as larger than it actually may be), employers and educators often work together to develop programs for their workers. EWP programs include a variety of approaches, often referred to as "work centered" as opposed to "worker centered" (McGroarty and Scott 1993). The work-centered approach is usually competency based, with competencies defined within the workplace context, such as those presented in the SCANS framework. Critics argue that such competency-based programs ignore workers' wider range of full communication needs. An alternative is the "worker-centered" approach, also referred to as "participatory" or "learner centered" (see Gillepsie 1996), through which curricula are built around issues drawn from the learners' lives at work and in the community (Auerbach 1992a, 1992b). Proponents of the worker-centered approach argue that it is more holistic and encompasses the participants' fuller social identities, rather than focusing solely on their work identities (Sarmiento and Kay 1990; McGroarty and Scott 1993).

Employers seeking a quick solution to a perceived skills-based problem are more likely to choose a work-centered approach, whereas those who are responsive to their workers' communicative needs outside of the workplace may support a longer-term, more worker-centered approach. Closely related to the issues of work-centered versus worker-centered approaches is the distinction between *training* and *education*. Businesses are more familiar with the concept of training, which Grognet (1995) defines as relatively short term, nonsequential, and separate. In contrast, educators tend to prefer broader and more inclusive facets of education that are longer term, sequential, and more directly connected to general life experiences.

In line with Goodwill Industries' mission to provide vocational rehabilitation and social, educational, and employment services as well as other opportunities to people with vocational disadvantages, we designed the GICW ESL program to enhance the vocational potential, independence, community functioning, and quality of life for the participants. A large part of the program's curriculum focuses on language needed for successful oral and written communication in the workplace. However, NNE speaking employees are viewed by Goodwill management and their ESL teachers as whole people with language needs and interests, some of which may fall outside the realm of workplace ESL. Thus, the program includes general survival competencies and workplace competencies (see table 6.1) and combines elements of both work-based and worker-based approaches. By providing employees with release time from work to attend classes, GICW management has demonstrated serious commitment to its employees. Management further validated the program by hiring two professionally trained full-time ESL instructors and giving them adequate pay, benefits, time, and funding to continue developing the program.

Goals and Objectives

The procedures involved in developing and teaching a customized workplace ESL course are different from those used in adult ESL programs that focus on more general language needs. The process, which in this case is ongoing, involves interviews with management, workers, and supervisors to determine needs; presentations in management training to build support for the program; observation of workers on the job doing basic skills tasks; collection of work-related materials; and language assessment of prospective learners to determine their current level of language skills. Results of the needs assessment procedures provide a basis for curriculum development. Belfiore and Burnaby (1995) offer an in-depth discussion of procedures for conducting effective workplace needs assessment.

The primary goals of the Goodwill ESL curriculum are (1) to help working students acquire the vocabulary, language structures, cultural information, and practice they need to perform their jobs successfully; (2) communicate with supervisors, customers, and co-workers; and (3) understand Goodwill's rules, policies, and benefits. Some additional goals are to use the content matter of the workplace as a bridge for the discussion of issues outside Goodwill settings and enable students to apply what they learn to other areas of their lives.

The learning objectives identified for the course are stated as competencies rather than as mastery of linguistic structures. Each unit in the curriculum includes performance objectives or competencies that have been determined to be essential to real-life communicative competence on the Goodwill work site. The syllabus lists 30 basic survival English competencies, including these examples of skills that learners will be able to perform by the end of the course.

> Identify, state, and print the letters of the alphabet and numbers from 1 to 100
> Exchange simple, common greetings and good-byes
> Read prescription drug labels and doctor appointment cards

The syllabus also lists 50 basic workplace competencies that learners will be able to perform by the end of the course, including these examples.

> Respond appropriately to a customer's request for help to locate an item in the store
> Fill out a request form for a vacation and submit it to the manager

Read and explain simple warning labels on cleaners and warning
    signs
Report an injury to a supervisor

Listing objectives in the form of competencies facilitates the requirement
that workplace programs demonstrate results in terms of worker behavior
and workplace productivity. By including two types of objectives, some
specifically related to the workplace and others more basic for survival in
the world beyond the workplace, the curriculum supports the instructors'
and company's belief that instruction should concentrate both on what the
workers need to learn for success on the job and what they want to learn
for their daily lives.

Syllabus Design

The syllabus is framed around, but not limited to, workplace language needs
(see table 6.2). It has several characteristics of a task-based syllabus, as described by Long and Crookes (1992). The tasks are identified through needs
analysis and include performing workplace skills such as reading a work
schedule, asking for a tool, and filling out a leave request form. Instructors
then develop and sequence pedagogic tasks, which students work on in
the classroom. This process leads to a relatively structured syllabus, preplanned by the instructors, although learners participate in the selection of
tasks that they identify as necessary for successful communication in their
work areas. The version of the Level B 30-week course serving as the centerpiece of our discussion was organized around the sequence of topics,
communicative functions, and themes shown in table 6.2.

Activity Types

Activities used in a workplace ESL class are similar to those used in many
other nonacademic ESL classes. The focus is on learner-centered, task-based
instruction and development of requisite communicative skills needed to
function successfully at work and in the community. Grognet (1996) summarizes the following characteristics of a learner-centered class as it relates
not only to EWP but to adult ESL teaching in general. (1) Classroom activities are negotiated between learners and the teacher, with the workplace
context as the starting point for classroom interaction. (2) Problem-solving
activities are essential because they help learners become more confident
in their ability to work in teams and to negotiate language at work. (3) The

TABLE 6.2.   Syllabus Elements—Topics, Communicative Functions, and Themes

1. Personal information
2. Schedules and time cards
3. Learning to learn
4. Maintaining positive relations/making small talk
5. Talking about the job
6. Communicating with supervisors, managers, and co-workers
7. Health
   7.1. Body parts
   7.2. Health problems
   7.3. Health insurance
8. Safety
   8.1. Injuries and accidents
   8.2. Safety gear
   8.3. Safety problems
   8.4. Fire and earthquake
   8.5. Ladder safety
   8.6. Safe lifting
   8.7. Infectious diseases and blood-borne pathogens
   8.8. Hazard communication
   8.9. Dangerous donations
9. Money and paychecks
10. Customer service

classroom is collaborative, with opportunities for learners to interact with others and to monitor their own progress. Grognet continues with a list of useful instructional strategies including the following: (4) using language that is authentic to the workplace, (5) ensuring that activities are relevant to the lives of the learners, (6) progressing from visual to text-oriented material, (7) emphasizing pair and group work, (8) following a whole language approach (see Rigg 1991), (9) presenting grammar as a discovery process, and (10) integrating cultural skills with language skills.

Janice and Carolyn have incorporated many of these teaching characteristics and strategies into their classes at Goodwill. They use a variety of grouping strategies, particularly pair work, since students work in an environment where workers are organized into teams and where there is a great deal of social interaction on the job. In the personal identification lesson, Carolyn moves from controlled input in the form of a six-sentence paragraph in the textbook, to guided practice in which students substitute information about themselves, to more communicative practice when students generate original sentences about jobs at Goodwill. Controlled activities include listening to and repeating chorally a story from the textbook, dictating to one another, writing from dictation, and completing exercises on work sheets. Guided activities include asking each other questions about what they like and do not like about their work responsibilities, filling out time schedules and production forms, and interviewing co-workers outside of class. Each activity begins with an oral presentation and practice phase before moving to reading and writing practice. By the end of the 30-week class students have moved well beyond individual sentences to connected discourse as they write stories about their experiences both at home and at work for publication in a student book.

Because students in Level B are at a fairly low level of literacy in English, Carolyn frequently uses Language Experience Approach (LEA) techniques (see Gunderson 1991). Students tell the teacher what they want to say about their experiences at work or in the community while the teacher writes out their words. Later, students read their own words and copy them into their notebooks. In the lesson described earlier, Carolyn shows pictures of various employees at Goodwill and asks students to describe what their jobs entail. She then writes the responses exactly as dictated on the classroom whiteboard and assists the students in reading back what she has written. Although there is no explicit teaching of grammar rules, Carolyn does not ignore grammatical errors. Instead, she listens carefully while considering when and how to provide appropriate information to learners. Tailoring her responses to meet the needs of the class, Carolyn may draw attention to more significant errors—ones that in her perceptions seem to be interfering with intelligibility—if the moment, phase of the lesson, and learner readiness seem right.

Recently, midway through the 30-week course, Carolyn was conducting a lesson focused on schedules and daily routines. She asked students to interview each other about their daily activities and later to share what they learned. At one point Maria said, "Angelina pick up her daughter at 6:30." Carolyn first wrote the sentence as produced and then explained to the class, "When we say 'I,' 'you,' 'we,' 'they,' we say 'pick up.' When we talk about one other person, we put an '-s' on the end of it." She then called on one of the more proficient students to repeat the sentence correctly and then on Maria to practice the form, too. Subsequently, Carolyn modeled a modified version of the original sentence so that students would hear and see the accurate form. As a rule of thumb, she avoids using grammatical terminology such as *verb* or *third person singular* in her explanations to the class.

After each class the teacher does "floor work" with employees. Floor work is a concept borrowed from rehabilitation programs that strive to place people with disabilities in competitive work situations. In that setting, a job coach spends two to four weeks at the job site teaching the employee how to do the job and evaluating her or his ability to do it at a competent level. In the ESL program, Janice and Carolyn use floor work to interact one-on-one with students as they work. Floor work links language use in the classroom with real-life situations since it provides more personalized, communicative, extemporaneous practice. The teacher follows each class period with a walk around the work site, asking each student questions similar to those just practiced in the classroom and checking progress on the students' competency lists (see app. 6.2; also see Internet apps. 6.1 and 6.2).

Each lesson integrates material from previous lessons; uses authentic materials (such as safety signs and photographs of situations related to the students' jobs at Goodwill); and provides opportunities for students, teacher, and supervisors to evaluate progress. For example, a lesson on "calling in sick" is preceded by lessons on body parts, ailments, going to the doctor, and reading prescriptions. The "calling-in-sick" lesson includes cultural expectations in American workplaces, specific Goodwill procedures, role playing in the classroom, and practice calls to the teacher at the ESL office. The preparatory-stage lesson is followed by role-playing calls to a dentist, a pharmacist, a child's teacher, or anyone else the student wants to be able to talk to on the phone. After completing the calling-in-sick unit, students phone their supervisor (who has been alerted that the mock calls may be coming) from the classroom to report that they are sick and cannot go to work. Supervisors use a simple form to check whether the employee identified self, satisfactorily answered questions, and used appropriate clarification techniques.

Students' co-workers and supervisors often provide evidence of the ESL program's success as the following example illustrates. About midway through the 30-week term, Sofia was absent from class. The supervisor shared with Carolyn after class that Sofia had, for the first time ever, called to say she was sick, had the flu, and couldn't come to work. The supervisor had no trouble understanding her. Before making this call to the supervisor for herself Sofia would always go through a translator to make such a call. For the employee who had always had someone else make the call for her, and for the supervisor who had never spoken to the employee on the phone before, this was a momentous occasion.

Learner Roles

Because learners in this workplace ESL class are receiving release time from their jobs to attend the class, they are expected to attend regularly, be punctual, participate actively in the class, and complete outside assignments. In class, students are encouraged to speak and write, using whatever linguistic skills they possess, knowing they will not be criticized for trying. If a low-proficiency employee can call in sick and say, "Me Rosa. Sick today. No work," it is considered to be successful communication in this setting since it indicates Rosa is active in using her limited language skills. Learners whose skills are more advanced are encouraged to lend assistance to their classmates, thus promoting dependence on peers rather than on the teacher. Peer-to-peer collaborations support the development of teamwork skills needed for success in the workplace.

Adult learners use their considerable background knowledge, not only of the job they perform but also of the world around them. When they can not talk in detail about a situation, they are encouraged to use alternative communication strategies to express their meanings. For example, students in the GIWC class are allowed to use their first language to assist a peer when needed. Auerbach (1993) reports several benefits of using the first language in an ESL class, including reducing of affective barriers, facilitating development of thinking in English, and actually increasing English language use during lessons.

Teacher Roles

Belfiore and Burnaby (1995) discuss the many responsibilities of the workplace ESL educator, including negotiating a contract with the company, carrying out needs analysis, preparing the syllabus, creating and adapting materials specific to the workplace, and developing an evaluation plan, as well as building and maintaining constructive relationships within the company. Janice and Carolyn note that open lines of communication with store managers and supervisors are critical to the success of the program and go well beyond simply arranging schedules. Managers and administrative staff may have little understanding of language acquisition, literacy issues, and the link between language learning and culture. Teachers often find themselves in the position of educating co-workers as well as students. At the same time, EWP teachers have to learn and appreciate the perspective of business-oriented managers focused on retail operations, production, and the bottom line.

Within the classroom, a major role of the workplace ESL instructor is to provide learners with the language they need to perform work-related tasks. Carolyn makes sure input is comprehensible by using gestures and visual aids; explaining and demonstrating workplace vocabulary; repeating and reinforcing key terms; and using simple, clear speech. Her role is more than just providing learners with comprehensible input. In addition, she offers feedback so that students will know when their language is appropriate and understandable to others. She is also a facilitator of activities that allow maximum opportunity for practice. During group or pair activities, she monitors each group to make sure everyone understands directions and is participating and that the group is on task and is able to complete the task in the allotted time. As a supportive teacher, Carolyn offers help and encouragement when needed and also provides feedback on the final product of the learners' efforts.

Unexpected circumstances require the workplace instructor to be flexible. Janice describes walking into her Level B classroom one day and learning that one of the students had just suffered a major on-the-job injury. Though the class had not yet reached the unit on safety in the workplace, she scrapped her prepared lesson and launched into an impromptu safety unit. She focused on teaching students the language needed to identify the cause of an injury and how to report it to a supervisor. On another occasion, the break room where her class usually met was taken over for an employee meeting on open enrollment for insurance. The unexpected employee meeting provided an opportunity to stay and help the nonnative speakers understand the vocabulary and concepts in the various insurance policies offered in their benefits package.

Instructional Materials

Many of the materials in an EWP class are customized for the workplace setting. To generate them, Janice and Carolyn spend many hours observing workers on the floor at Goodwill, talking with supervisors and co-workers about communication breakdowns, and collecting samples of workplace realia. Materials used in the Level B class include line drawings of workers at Goodwill illustrating different jobs and merchandise that employees work with; activity sheets providing practice with vocabulary needed on the job; role-play dialogues that cover basic communication practice such as reporting a safety problem or asking for a schedule change; student-generated descriptions of their jobs; and work sheets on Goodwill policies, procedures, benefits, and paychecks.

In the third year of the Goodwill ESL program, Janice and Carolyn decided to supplement the customized materials with published textbooks. For the Level C class they selected *Working It Out* by Magy (1998), a recent workplace ESL text. Students in Level B use Huizenga and Weinstein-Shr's (1996) *Collaborations: English in Our Lives, Beginning I.* This book is organized around language functions and structures and teaches basic and higher-order skills within a personal narrative context. Although it is not designed specifically as a workplace text, these teachers use it as a springboard for discussion of workplace concepts and themes.

Each year Janice and Carolyn assemble students' stories in a collected volume entitled *Our Stories.* On each page is a photograph of the student author taken at the workplace and a story the student has selected for publication. In a recent edition, one older woman with developing literacy skills drew four pictures representing key events in her lifetime and wrote one sentence about each sketch. Another student wrote a few short sentences describing his job and family. Preparing their work for publication provides a reason for students to revise and edit their writing because they know their piece will be read by a wider audience, including their supervisors, native English speaking co-workers, family, and friends. The collection of stories also provides authentic reading material for subsequent groups of students, and the photographs are used for vocabulary lessons. The entire volume is shared with managers and supervisors and distributed more widely as an indication of the success of the program and as an in-house marketing tool to expand the ESL program by attracting the interest of managers at other Goodwill sites.

Assessment

Because of the need for accountability in any EWP program, students' progress and the effectiveness of the program are monitored continuously. At GIWC all nonnative employees are tested to determine the level of their English skills using the Basic English Skills Test (BEST) developed by the Center for Applied Linguistics (1989). The oral interview, which tests speaking and listening, takes 20 minutes and is individually administered. The literacy test, which tests reading and writing, takes one hour and can be administered to a manageable size group of students at the same time.

Scores on the BEST are interpreted as Student Performance Levels (SPL) and are described in behavioral terms in the BEST manual. Those with a literacy SPL of 0–2 (Novice-Low on ACTFL) are placed in the new basic literacy, Level A class regardless of oral proficiency. Most students in the Level B class may be characterized as Novice-High on ACTFL, but in many cases their speaking and listening levels are higher than their reading and writing abilities. Students in Level C are similar in oral proficiency but stronger in reading and writing than the students in Level B. When the BEST is administered again at the end of the course, learners have often advanced two SPLs. Student records are maintained on a database that includes personal information, pre- and posttest results, class information, and follow-up information (e.g., their work responsibilities at 6 and then 12 months after completing the course).

Learners' self-assessment of their own performance and progress is an important aspect of the overall evaluation process. Instructors keep track of each student's progress on a competency list. Students get a copy of the competency list, and managers get one for each employee in the program as a record of student progress (see Internet app. 6.1). The teachers also try to involve supervisors actively in creating opportunities for learners to use the language learned in class and in checking progress toward mastery of competencies. An evaluation survey for managers and supervisors asks for their responses to specific questions about improvement in such areas as following instructions, changes in self-confidence, and understanding of safety rules. Students fill out a different survey asking them to rate their improvement in specific uses of English at work and to answer open-ended questions about the class, the materials, and their plans to continue studying English. This input and the day-to-day contact with supervisory staff provide critical information for the ongoing process of reexamining and refining the curriculum.

Caveats/Final Thoughts

There are several unusual features of the GICW ESL program. Rather than focusing on short-term training for management-level employees, GICW funds an employee education program for the entry-level worker out of revenue earned from the retail operation that the employees are working in. GICW has made a commitment to long-term education that is both work centered and worker centered. Unlike many EWP programs that are taught by independent contractors, at GICW the ESL instructors are company employees. They have ready access to information, events, and people that an independent contractor would have to spend time and energy discovering. Janice and Carolyn continue to conduct ongoing needs assessment to refine the curriculum. Already they have piloted a class for maintenance workers and another class focusing on writing skills for workers who would like to move up to a supervisory position at Goodwill. They are working on ways to incorporate more problem-solving activities within lessons and to make the classes even more learner centered.

Prompts for Discussion and Reflection

1. How do the authors characterize the kinds of students who take the workplace English course at Goodwill? What might be students' reasons for taking the course? What are the company's reasons for offering the course?

2. With a partner, review the error correction techniques Carolyn uses in the section on lesson particulars. Who conducts the error correction? What kinds of errors are corrected? What techniques are used? Discuss ways in which some of the techniques used may be (in)compatible with your understanding of general ELT principles.

3. In the section titled "Conceptual Underpinnings" the authors make a distinction between *education* and *training*. How might you distinguish between these general orientations toward learning and teaching? Which aspects of the course seem closer to one orientation or the other?

4. The chapter's coauthors seem well aware of possible tensions between "*worker*-centered" versus "*work*-centered" ways of envisioning the course and its potentialities. When conflicts arise between an instructor's preferred orientation and that of a company such as Goodwill, how might such conflicts best be resolved? How might a workable balance be found in such settings so that effective language instruction may take place?

5. Many EWP classes meet in break rooms or storerooms, as does the class described here. However, the latest Goodwill stores are being designed and constructed with employee classrooms in mind. What kind of equipment and technical resources would be reasonable to recommend if a Goodwill industrial engineer asked you to make suggestions for a proposed facility? Discuss what features a classroom dedicated for purposes of ELT at such a location should have.

6. Contemporary approaches to ELT recognize that second/foreign language instruction needs to include a focus on form as well as a focus

on meaning. If you were teaching this class, would you try to integrate more teaching of grammar or pronunciation? If so, what techniques might be appropriate and useful with these students?

7. ELT instructors of adults often struggle with finding out-of-class opportunities for students to practice/apply knowledge gained in the classroom. In the Goodwill program, instructors use "floor work" to evaluate learners' abilities to apply knowledge. How could this concept be adapted to other ELT settings with which you are familiar?

8. The authors contend that teaching English in the workplace is different from other ELT settings. Do you agree? What makes EWP teaching different from other nonacademic adult ELT classes? (Compare with chap. 8 by Brian Morgan; chap. 9 by Robert DeVillar and Binbin Jiang; and chap. 10 by Anne Burns and Pam McPherson in this volume.)

9. One feature found in most EWP classes is the use of authentic materials from the workplace. This feature is consistent with other contemporary ELT approaches that support the use of authentic materials relevant to students' lives and needs. What would you consider advantages and problems in working with such materials? What would be some of the advantages and problems in working with published materials (such as generic ESL texts) not specifically designed for teaching EWP?

Miniprojects

10. Write a want ad for an instructor of an EWP class. Include a brief description of the job and qualifications needed for the job. Then, design a list of 10–12 questions you would ask of applicants for the EWP teaching position during initial job interviews. If time permits, role-play such an interview or a series of such interviews.

11. Select a company (preferably in your area), gather some in-house materials the company produces, and examine them. (Many companies post such materials on the Internet.) Try to determine ways in which some of the materials could be used for EWP instructional purposes. Then, create a lesson using these materials to help low proficiency level students reach one or more competencies this chapter's coauthors discuss.

12. Locate an EWP (or job-specific) course in your area and arrange to observe one class. Try to talk with the instructor before or after the observation. Then write up a brief report of what you have been able to learn about the course.

What Do You Do at Work?

He *cleans* the bathroom.   She *manages* the store.   She *takes* the money.
He *buys* the merchandise.

She *tags* clothes.   He *unloads* the truck.   He *takes* donations.

She *prices* items.   She *sorts* clothes.   She *hangs* clothes.

She *stocks* items.   They *shop* for clothes.

I Helped a Lot of Customers Yesterday.

What did you do at work yesterday? Check Yes or No.

	Yes	No
tagged clothes	❑	❑
helped customers	❑	❑
stocked shelves	❑	❑
priced items	❑	❑
sorted clothes	❑	❑
took donations	❑	❑
gave a reciept	❑	❑
cleaned my work area	❑	❑
hung clothes	❑	❑
took a break	❑	❑
used a hand truck	❑	❑

Verbs

Present Tense	Past Tense
sort	sortes
tag	tagged
help	helped
stock	stocked
clean	cleaned
price	priced
supervise	supervised
manage	managed
take	took
eat	ate
give	gave

Appendix 6.2. ESL Student Evaluation Level A

A—student absent X—practiced XX—mastered NA—not applicable

Competency

1.0 Basic Skills
- say, read, write, sequence alphabet
- match capital and small letters
- read personal information sight words
- read, write, recite numbers 1–100
- write numbers 1–10 in words
- write numbers from dictation
- read, recite, sequence days of week
- read, recite, sequence months of year
- read, write, say dates
- match abbreviated date form to full form
- use calendar to locate dates
- read, write, say time
- match analog to digital time
- identify coins, bills by name and value
- read, write, say prices
- produce requested amounts

2.0 Personal Information
- respond to yes/no personal information questions
- distinguish between/orally spell first/last name
- read sight personal information words
- fill out simple personal information form

3.0 Schedules and Time Cards
- state own work schedule
- fill in own schedule on schedule form
- read + interpret simplified Goodwill (GW) schedule
- request interpreter for schedule change
- identify holidays stores are closed
- request interpreter to report time card problem

4.0 Learning to Learn
- indicate comprehension lack/need for repetition request
- request an interpreter

5.0 Maintain Positive Relations/Small Talk
- introduce self
- greet/address co-workers throughout day
- use leave-taking expressions
- express gratitude
- express likes and dislikes

Competency

6.0 Talking about the Job
- read, write, state names of store, manager, supervisor
- state job performed
- name, read, write tools used in own job
- identify, read, write merchandise worked with
- ask for a tool or supply
- read workplace sight words

7.0 Communicating with Supervisors
- indicate lack of understanding/need for interpreter
- get someone's attention and ask for help
- report a problem/ask for an interpreter
- ask to have a task demonstrated
- understand relation between performance and review

8.0 Health

8.1 Body Parts
- name, locate, read limited number of body parts
- name, locate, read limited number of internal body parts

8.2 Health Problems
- name, read a limited number of common illnesses
- identify very basic points of GW sick policy
- find sick pay and sick bank on pay stub
- role-play simplified call-in sick to supervisor
- read a medical/dental appointment card
- role-play call to 911 to ask for ambulance
- read dosage information on simplified drug label

8.3 Health Insurance
- identify the name of health insurance plan
- identify health insurance deduction on pay stub
- fill out health insurance form

9.0 Safety

9.1 Injuries and Accidents
- identify a limited number of typical work injuries
- categorize injuries as big or small
- role-play reporting injury to supervisor
- get a co-worker's attention and ask for help

9.2 Safety Gear
- name safety gear required for own job
- ask supervisor for safety gear

Competency

9.3 Safety Problems
- identify safety problems at work from pictures
- report or show a safety problem to supervisor
- warn co-worker of impending danger

9.4 Fire and Earthquake
- lead instructor on fire evacuation route
- identify procedure for fire in trailer
- recognize/identify fire extinguisher location
- role-play calling 911 to report a fire
- demonstrate best inside places during earthquake

9.5 Ladder Safety
- identify which types of ladders used at work
- ask for a ladder or stepstool

9.6 Infectious Diseases/Blood-Borne Pathogens
- identify cold spread prevention techniques
- recognize danger of needles, sharps, blood, fecal matter
- role-play showing/reporting infectious material to supervisor

9.7 Hazard Communication
- identify location of material safety data sheet (MSDS) in store
- role-play asking manager for copy of MSDS sheet
- recognize warning pictures for hazardous material

9.8 Dangerous Donations
- name, identify variety of dangerous donations
- role-play reporting dangerous donation to supervisor

9.9 Money and Paychecks
- identify vacation pay, bank, taxes, overtime on pay stub
- multiply hours worked by hourly wage
- role-play reporting problem with check to supervisor
- explain key points of employee shopping policy
- explain holiday pay

10.0 Customer Service
- tell customer they will get someone to help them
- recognize and respond to store pages

11.0 The Future
- name other positions at GW
- name other kinds of jobs
- identify own skills
- identify preferences

Chapter 7

Families as Curriculum Partners in an Urban Elementary Inclusion Classroom

Jo-Anne Wilson-Keenan, Jerri Willett, and Judith Solsken

———

Jo-Anne Wilson-Keenan teaches young children in a public elementary school in the northeast region of the United States. She and her collaborators describe a community-oriented language arts program in her combined first and second grade classroom that focuses on *families as curriculum partners*. The chapter illustrates not only how ESL children can be assisted to integrate both socially and academically into target language communities but also how to help native English speakers (teachers and children) to recognize and value the knowledge ESL learners bring to school settings. Equally important, the chapter focuses on strengthening relationships with families so children's success with English does not alienate them from their homes and communities. A series of activities tied to what the authors call the "Family Visit" is the center of Wilson-Keenan's interdisciplinary language arts curriculum. Each child's family is invited to the classroom to share something about their lives. Although the actual visits are short, they generate a variety of reading and writing activities that serve as starting points from which the academic and social curriculum gradually develops. Wilson-Keenan connects the ideas that arise during Family Visits to the academic curriculum as the children write about their lives at home, dedicate stories to their families, correspond with family members about school experiences, and select books based on interests developed at home. Thus, through the visits, families become partners in the curriculum development process. These practices are grounded by mutual engagement of children and their companions in the literate practices of the school and by community support for learning. The chapter's lesson particulars section describes one Family Visit in detail to show how the family, teacher, and children work to create a supportive space for an ESL child and how other children connect to the family's experiences.

———

Setting

In this chapter we describe a community-oriented language arts program with a focus on families as curriculum partners. The program, implemented in Jo-Anne Wilson-Keenan's combined first and second grade classroom, was part of a collaborative curriculum development and action research project with Jerri Willett and Judith Solsken from the University of Massachusetts. Jo-Anne took primary responsibility for curricular decisions, while Jerri and Judy took primary responsibility for data collection and management. However, in our conversations during team meetings we regularly blurred the conventional status-laden boundaries between "teacher" and "researcher" as we reflected on the data and developed strategies for achieving the pedagogical goals of the project. Interpretations presented in this chapter were reached through dialogue and are fully shared.[1]

Jo-Anne's school serves a low-income and multicultural community. At the time we began our work together, the student body was approximately 53 percent Puerto Rican, 23 percent African American, and 24 percent European American. The children's families ranged from single-parent, two-parent, and grandparent households to extended, foster, and blended families. Some children spent time in more than one household, and some had a parent in prison. A high proportion of the children would commonly be described as socially and academically "at risk": 86 percent qualified for a free or reduced-cost lunch under federal guidelines, and 67 percent met qualification for Special Needs Services. Many of the children spent part of their day in other classrooms that served various needs (e.g., special education, ESL, bilingual).

Jo-Anne's heterogeneously grouped classroom included both native English and nonnative English speakers from Puerto Rico, Poland, and Cambodia. Using the ACTFL guidelines, the children's English language proficiency ranged from Novice-Low to Native proficiency in speaking and listening and from Novice-Low to Advanced Plus in reading and writing. However, since the ACTFL guidelines were not designed to describe the proficiency of children, our conception of what is termed an *educated person* in the ACTFL descriptors is a native English speaking child between the ages of five and eight who is performing at appropriate, satisfactory levels in school.

---

1. The work was partially supported by a grant from the National Council of Teachers of English.

Conceptual Underpinnings

An important issue facing a growing number of teachers is how to assist second language learners to integrate socially and academically into their target language communities (Coelho 1994; Deegan 1996; Hruska 1998). The elementary language arts program we describe in this chapter illustrates not only how ESL children can be assisted in this process but also how to help native English speakers (teachers and children) to recognize, appreciate, and validate the knowledge ESL learners bring with them. Equally important, our chapter focuses on developing and strengthening relationships with the children's families so their success with English does not alienate them from their homes and communities.

Cummins (1986) argues that efforts to improve the education of children from dominated societal groups have been largely unsuccessful because unproductive relationships between teachers and students and between schools and communities remain unchanged. He says that "the required changes involve personal redefinitions of the way classroom teachers interact with children they serve" (18). While teachers who work with second language learners may appreciate the difficulties faced by the children's families, their mandate to integrate children into the mainstream as quickly as possible sometimes intensifies unproductive relations between the children's homes and school. These unproductive relations can come back to haunt us in the long run when families find themselves powerless to support their children's education (Wong-Fillmore 1989). Redefining home/school relations requires that (1) the children's language and culture become incorporated into the school program; (2) community participation is encouraged as an integral component of the children's education; (3) pedagogy promotes intrinsic motivation on the part of the students to use language actively to generate their own knowledge; and (4) professionals involved in assessment become advocates for students rather than legitimizing the location of the problem in students (Cummins 1986; Flores, Cousin, and Diaz 1991; Moll 1988; Nieto 1996). By putting family participation at the center of the curriculum, we were better able to gradually redefine relations between families and school, while simultaneously witnessing shifting relations between ESL and mainstream children.

Inviting families to become curriculum partners, however, makes sense only in a classroom guided by a vision of education in which curriculum is created through collaborations between learners and their teachers (both schoolteachers and family teachers), rather than by specialists who have already made decisions for them (Long and Crookes 1992; Short, Harste, and Burke 1996). Such a vision is grounded in some commonly held key assumptions about language, literacy, and learning between first and second language teachers and researchers (e.g., Freeman and Freeman 1998; Hudelson 1994; Moll et al.1990; Short, Harste, and Burke 1996; Whitmore and Crowell 1994), as listed here.

Literacy and oral language acquisition are profoundly social phenomena, an insight that is often overlooked in cognitive studies of language and literacy acquisition that focus on individuals rather than the communities in which they are apprenticed (see Gebhard 1999; Heath 1986; Hudelson 1994; Pease-Alvarez and Vasquez 1994).

Children are eager to learn about their social worlds. If they are immersed in language rich environments where they use language for meaningful and varied purposes, they will work hard to learn to read, write, listen, and speak. When exploring problems that interest them, children continuously discover new insights about the structure of language. On the other hand, when language is broken down into bits and pieces with no recognizable purpose and without contextual support, learning and teaching are difficult and frustrating (Edelsky, Altwerger, and Flores 1991).

Mutual engagement of children and their companions in the literate practices of the school and community provides support for learning language and literacy needed to accomplish cultural and personal goals. Such an apprenticeship draws on children's experiences and strengths and includes collaboration, shared understanding, and the gradual transference of responsibility to help children adapt to new situations, solve problems, participate in a wider social life, and develop new tools of learning (Heath 1993).

Children are better able to support one another in the risk-taking adventure of learning when they assume ownership of, and responsibility for, building and contributing to the classroom community (see Peterson 1992). Moreover, when the language and knowledge that children bring with them to the classroom are respected and valued, bridges are created between home and school, the known and the unknown, and their first and second languages. These bridges lead to learning processes that are both easier and more rewarding.

Teachers and families working together can better facilitate this active construction of meaning and knowledge by helping one another recognize and appreciate their children's nascent explorations. Together, they can better demonstrate varied uses for reading and writing in two languages, and they can help children use reading and writing for multiple purposes. Children

who witness their parents and teachers working together are better prepared to envision a place for themselves in both their own communities
and the wider world.

Goals and Objectives

Our goals and objectives are intentionally broad to encompass the individual paths that children's learning takes, while fully expecting that all
children will become readers and writers who can explore the world in a
meaningful and socially responsible way. We aim to

construct a multicultural classroom community
foster home/school collaboration
create a language rich environment
strengthen academic learning
facilitate English language and literacies development
support children's bilingual language and literacies development
facilitate children's active and meaningful construction of knowledge
recognize the unique knowledge, strengths, talents, and interests of
  each child
challenge children to tackle complex and interesting problems

As will be illustrated in later sections, Jo-Anne's classroom truly is a
heterogeneous and inclusive classroom with children of different ages,
languages, cultures, and academic experiences, so it is difficult to specify
what all children will know by the end of the program. With respect to
general objectives, we expect all children to make substantial progress in
learning to

read and write
use reading and writing to learn about science, math, and social
  studies
develop languages and literacies other than English
tackle complex problems with curiosity and perseverance
respect others in the multicultural community
value their own community and family knowledge

The educator's role is to ensure that all children are given the opportunity to read, write, analyze, communicate, play, experiment, inquire,
create, and synthesize. But we do not expect all children to develop at the

same rates or in the same way. Children who come from bilingual house-holds will progress more rapidly in developing biliteracy than those who do not. Children whose families have read to them since birth will understand what reading is about sooner than those who have not had this experience. Also, children who have schoolteachers for parents are likely to know decontextualized phonics and math facts better than those who do not. Some learners may take longer than others in becoming competent readers and writers. Jo Anne takes deliberate steps to bolster the positions of all children in her class as successful learners in the process of becoming readers and writers.

Syllabus Design

As mentioned earlier, course curriculum is created through collaborations between learners, teachers, and families (for further discussion see descriptions of the "negotiated syllabus" in Long and Crookes 1992; "integrated curriculum" in Enright and McCloskey 1988; and "curriculum inquiry" in Short, Harste, and Burke 1996). Weaving reading and writing into thematic strands around ideas that arose initially during Family Visits, Jo-Anne negotiated an interdisciplinary curriculum that incorporated the interests and contributions of everyone involved.

The content of the syllabus in Jo-Anne's classroom emerged from several different sources: the mandated curriculum; bodies of knowledge and practices that the children's communities and families used to survive, to get ahead, or to thrive (called "funds of knowledge" in Moll 1992); the children's individual and collective interests; the social justice issues that underpinned our action research project; professional judgments about the children's language and literacy development; and Jo-Anne's knowledge of multicultural children's literature (for guidance in selecting multicultural literature, see Barrera, Thompson, and Dressman 1997; Harris 1992; Manna and Brodie 1992; Rudman 1993; and Samway and Whang 1995). The following example illustrates part of what the negotiated curriculum process was like in Jo-Anne's classroom.

> Hector's mother, together with his extended family, demonstrated how to sew a quilt (with more proficient bilingual children translating between Spanish and English when needed). The children decided to use the quilt in the class library as a "reading quilt," which they eventually "passed down" to next year's class. During the conversations that took place while Hector's mother demonstrated quilt making, the children talked about quilts passed down in their own families, and they told stories about brothers and sisters arguing over their

quilts. Some of these oral stories were written down by the children and became part of the class library. Jo-Anne added several books to the library that featured quilts. She read Hopkinson's (1993) *Sweet Clara and the Freedom Quilt* to the children, a story about a slave girl who had sewn together a quilt whose design was a map of the land that showed the way to the start of the Underground Railroad. Classroom conversations centered around the institution of slavery, the Underground Railroad in Springfield (Massachusetts), and the ongoing exploration of local history. Jo-Anne was able to incorporate many concepts from mandated social studies curriculum into the readings, conversations, and projects that developed from the quilt made by Hector's mother.

An important insight gained from our collaborative research was that a curriculum decision in Jo-Anne's class often emerged in the give-and-take of what may have appeared to be noninstructional conversations as the children made connections to the visitors, the teacher, school subjects, and each other through stories. In the quilt example, the special knowledge that Hector's mother had about quilt making gave rise to casual conversation among the children about their own experiences with quilts in their families. This talk provided a thematic anchoring point around which Jo-Anne could (1) gather a wealth of materials, (2) connect to the interests and needs of individual learners in the class, and (3) develop a variety of instructional themes and goals. As the children learned about one another's families through their quilt stories, they were constructing the kind of multicultural learning community Jo-Anne had envisioned.

Activity Types

The Family Visit was the center of the community-oriented language arts program featured in Jo-Anne's class. Visits were more than entertaining diversions from the work of learning to read and write. In addition, there were times when the children could use reading, writing, listening, and speaking in authentic ways to communicate across the two worlds that were most important to them—home and school. Here they could explore roles not available to them in either world. The visits served as nodes from which the academic and social curriculum would gradually develop and connect in ways that were understandable to the children, their families, and their teacher. Thus, through the visits, families became partners in the curriculum process rather than mere observers.

Each family guest was invited to share something about her or his life with the class. After introductions, the family member would make a presentation to the class. The visits ranged from elaborate and well-planned performances to informal talks around family photos. If appropriate, Jo-Anne would help some of the families get started, but as the class became more experienced with the visits, the children would often play this facilitative role. When the presentation began to wind down, the child of honor would call on her or his classmates to ask questions. Questions would quickly evolve into stories the children would use to connect to the themes introduced by the family member.

After the families shared their knowledge and experiences with the class, Jo-Anne would locate literature that echoed some of the same themes. Just as important to the children's academic learning, the visitors brought into the classroom the languages and cultures of the diverse communities served by the school. Children heard a myriad of languages and dialects, and they learned about the different ways that families live, eat, work, play, and celebrate.

Family Visits generated a variety of different authentic reading and writing activities. Some reading and writing occurred spontaneously during the visit, such as the time when Jo-Anne, the children, and the family made a list of safety rules to think about during summer vacation in response to the "danger stories" that the children swapped during the Family Visit. Sometimes the content of a visit would reverberate throughout the day as children engaged in more routine activities. A partial listing of some of the many language arts activities featured in Jo-Anne's class would include writing workshops (Calkins 1994); authors' circle, read alouds, and mini-lessons (Short, Harste, and Burke 1996); class meetings and other positive discipline strategies (Nelsen, Lott, and Glenn 1986); literature study and literature circles (Samway and Whang 1995); shared reading, and conference approaches to reading (Hornsby, Sukarna, and Parry 1986). The following narrative illustrates how themes and connections made during Family Visits became incorporated into the daily life of the classroom and became more richly elaborated and synthesized over the school year.

Rosa's family gave a hamster to the class, and it had babies shortly thereafter. The children wrote a class letter to the family both thanking them for the hamster and telling them about the happy event. The children designed a chart detailing who was responsible for feeding and cleaning the cage and another chart for documenting what the hamsters were doing at particular times of the day. They hoped this second chart would help them learn more about the behavior of hamsters in a systematic, hands-on way. To her great surprise and delight, one day Jo-Anne found a letter addressed to the hamsters taped to the cage facing inward so that the *hamsters could read it!*

Jo-Anne filled the class library with literature for the children to read. The children made productive use of the class library to help them care for the hamster and to stimulate ideas for writing their own stories. Children shared their stories in authors' circle, gave feedback to one another, and revised their stories until they were ready for publication. After the stories were entered into the computer, the children's own books were placed (and featured) in the class library. In a class meeting the children decided to sell the baby hamsters to other classrooms and donate the money to people in need. Sharee's father, who served as a minister in a local church, was in charge of finding a person who could benefit from the money. The children made posters and together created a chant, modeled on Silverstein's (1974) poem, "Sister for Sale," to advertise the hamsters. They traveled from classroom to classroom performing the chant and holding up the signs that they had made. After selling all of the baby hamsters, they counted the money, composed a letter, and created a large card on which everyone printed their names. Then, they sent the card to Sharee's father, who wrote a moving thank-you letter to the class telling them about the person who benefited from their gift.

Through such episodes, the children learned that as readers and writers they could organize their lives and act on the world in new ways. They also learned the conventions of letter writing, advertising, and documenting observations. Emergent readers and second language learners were apprenticed as they worked side by side with more fluent readers and writers to dictate the chant, compose the letter, write down observations of the hamsters, and sign up for jobs on the chart. New words and ideas were made comprehensible for the second language learners as they worked closely with more proficient peers on the posters they would carry from classroom to classroom. Peter, who had arrived recently from Poland, had such beautiful handwriting that the native speakers were eager to be his partners. With the children completely engaged in the task of getting ready for the sale, Jo-Anne was able to give minilessons to the second language learners to ensure they understood what they were writing. When a family's stories and knowledge connected the activities around which the children's days were organized, it was obvious to all that the children and their families had something important to contribute.

Role of the Families

Families were part of the everyday life of the classroom, whether the children were talking about family activities during sharing, writing about family stories, or making connections between books read in the classroom and events in the community. The influence of Family Visits and the family members' stories recounted in class reverberated across activities and time. Children could be heard invoking past visits, and some would continue to participate in the community engendered in Jo-Anne's class long after they had been promoted. For example, Hector and his mother, who had sewn the "reading quilt" for the class, had gone on to participate in sewing the community AIDS quilt the following year. They returned to Jo-Anne's classroom to share their experiences and were proud to find the reading quilt still hanging in the classroom.

Visits to the classroom also helped families to understand what was going on in school and to make connections between school and their everyday activities at home. These connections emerged from authentic interactions rather than merely from the school explaining to parents how to support their children's learning. For example, through participation in the classroom, Cynthia's parents had come to understand how language, reading, and writing were connected to everyday activities, despite their initial concerns about a classroom so different from their own school experiences. Together with her mother, Cynthia made a video showing the family preparing a typical Puerto Rican meal. By then, Cynthia's mother trusted that Jo-Anne would use the video to promote the children's reading, writing, and math. Seeing her contributions become the stimulus for a class cookbook, math lessons, and children's writing sent the message that the school believed in her ability to support her child's learning.

In the last analysis, it was not so much the content or style of the Family Visits that was important but the meaning of the visits for each child (e.g., *my family and community are respected by the teacher and the other children, and my family supports my taking risks in learning to read and write*). Knowing they were supported by strong and vibrant home/school relations, the children were able to take up more varied roles than they might have otherwise been able to assume. The children in Jo-Anne's class saw themselves, and were often explicitly labeled, as teachers, learners, connectors, authors, organizers, challengers, linguists, scientists, researchers, storytellers, peacemakers, translators, and advocates—in short, the varied roles that emerged out of their engagement in this very active and busy classroom. To play these roles, they had to make decisions, negotiate with others, and solve problems.

Role of the Learner

Many children prepared their families for the visit and negotiated a "good face" for them in the classroom. They introduced family members and handled turn taking. How active they were in the presentation depended on the family, although Jo-Anne worked hard to keep the focus on the child who was being honored with a family's visit by directing questions to the child. Even the less active children, however, helped their families negotiate visits in ways that were not immediately visible.

Upon close analysis of transcripts, for example, we were able to see that Omar was attempting to help his mother think up suitable topics of conversation and stay clear of topics that he felt were inappropriate (such as the trouble he got into at home). This role was a complex one for Omar since what counted as appropriate for class discussion differed among his classmates, teacher, and mother. He was clarifying details his mother talked about, making them more accessible to this particular audience, and pointing out things about the classroom that he knew would please Jo-Anne. The following excerpt records an episode when Omar quietly and respectfully coached his mother on appropriate language practices for the Family Visit without undermining her status as both his mother and the honored guest.

Mrs. Cardenas:	well, he likes baseball
	I mean, . . .
	basketball
	I mean, forget it (*uses hand gestures very dramatically throughout what follows*)
	he don't pay too much attention to school
	because all this sports you know (*Omar looks at her with his hand partially covering his face*)
	He really sometimes
	I gotta talk to him
	"O. J., I'm talking to you" (*said directly to Omar as if in a play*)
	. . .
Omar:	Ma
Mrs. Cardenas:	what?
Omar:	they don't know who O. J. is, Omar (*very quietly and respectfully to his mother*)
Mrs. Cardenas:	Omar
	I know
	but we call you O. J. at the house
	. . .
Omar:	We go to the pool (*Omar says softly to his mother rather than to the class*)

Through our (the teacher and her collaborators') cultural lenses, Mrs. Cardenas's focus on Omar's misdeeds seemed inappropriate for the occasion, although the topic resonated with the children and evoked some wonderful stories. We later came to understand that we had misinterpreted the way Mrs. Cardenas seemed to construct her son as a "mischievous boy." Rather, she was attempting to construct her family in a positive light by showing that they were guiding their naturally mischievous son down the right path, as any responsible Puerto Rican family would do.

It took us many hours of analysis to realize that Omar was attempting to negotiate positive faces for his family, teacher, and himself across very different cultures. Omar understood that Jo-Anne, his mother, and his classmates did not have the same meanings as he attempted to construct himself simultaneously as a respectful Puerto Rican son, a protective brother, an adventurous risk-taking boy, an active self-directed learner, and a proud member of Jo-Anne's class. It was a humbling experience for us as this realization brought about a deeper appreciation of the complexity of the children's roles in these visits (for a more detailed analysis of this visit, see Willett, Solsken, and Wilson-Keenan 1998).

Role of the Teacher

Jo-Anne's role in the classroom could be broadly characterized as supporting and facilitating the children's learning. Because families were central to the curriculum, Jo-Anne's support and facilitation often took the form of extending the children's engagement with the stories and themes that came out of Family Visits and connecting them to the academic and "social justice" curriculum. For example, Jo-Anne added some scarves to the dress-up trunk, which the girls used to create costumes for themselves. The scarves reminded the children of the clothes worn by a classmate named Aziza during her family's visit the previous year. Aziza had dressed in wide pants, a shirt, and a flowing pink headdress, called a "kemar," with a gold cord around her head to show her classmates what they wore for the feast at the end of Ramadan. During the visit one of the children had commented that Aziza looked like an African princess. Months later when the children were playing with the scarves, Aziza was inspired to write a story called "The African Princess." Jo-Anne, noticing their continued interest in the African princess theme, helped the girls extend Aziza's story into a play, which they eventually performed for the class and parents.

In Jo-Anne's classroom we found the same potential in the use of drama as Heath (1993). In ways very similar to the inner-city youth Heath observed, children in Jo-Anne's class also engaged in the accomplishment of a group goal; they used a "rich communication array—including spoken, gestural, spatial and written means"; they willingly practiced and mastered the skills needed to perform well; they responded "not for and to teachers but to their imagined audience"; they drew on their community's funds of knowledge; they set high standards for themselves in preparing for their performance. In her article Heath (1993) urges language teachers to think about "the power of drama and the fuller uses of role playing for bringing out performance that reflects the fullest possible range of linguistic competence of students" (185).

In Jo-Anne's class, the "African Princess" play generated even more reading and writing as the whole class read their parts as the "chorus" and prepared the invitations and the program. During the playwriting episodes, Jo-Anne showed the children where Africa was on the map; read Steptoe's (1987) *Mufaro's Beautiful Daughters: An African Tale* to them; guided their analysis of characters and story structures; helped them investigate facts about the African landscape to include in their play; and pointed out the conventions of writing a playscript, invitations, and programs. She also used the children's texts as a source for minilessons on word study, phonics, grammar, and punctuation.

The Family Visits also presented opportunities to extend the critical analysis of social issues in the classroom. The purpose of these critical analyses was not to tell the children how they should think but to open up critical dialogue about important social issues. For example, during their visits, families would contribute to an ongoing dialogue about gender stereotyping. By including the diverse views of the parents in these critical dialogues, the children could hear different points of view and begin understanding that they did not have to share the same views as their teacher and classmates (for further discussion, see Wilson-Keenan, Solsken, and Willett 1999).

Jo-Anne's most powerful role in the classroom was as an engaged and active learner who was curious about the world. She wondered with the children and investigated topics she didn't know about so that she could explore with them, learning from books, their parents, and her own experiments. She was a critical thinker who examined her own practices for biases. One of her personal concerns was the violence portrayed in movies and television—especially the Ninja Turtles and the martial arts. But with the help of a parent who practiced the martial arts, she came to a different understanding of the code underlying martial arts. She was also open to a critique by one of the children, who pointed out that *Three Billy Goats Gruff*

(Asbjorn and Moe 1957), a familiar children's classic from the dominant culture, was more violent than any cartoon she had seen on television. Jo-Anne was an author who shared her poems and writing with the class, and she was a family member with her own history and family stories. Finally, she was a learner who struggled with learning to read in Spanish (as a new language) in full view of the children. Her implicit message conveyed through such consistent teacher behaviors was "We're all learners in this classroom."

Instructional Materials

The children and their teacher organized their lives with one another through literacy: they learned about and acted upon the world, organized their materials and activities, and documented and celebrated their growing competency through reading and writing—and thus, their everyday lives in the classroom and at home served as the material through which they learned about language and its uses. In addition to organizing their school lives, children used literacy to connect to their families. Thus, their reading and writing in school were often motivated by their families. Children wrote about their lives at home, dedicated their stories to their families, corresponded with them about their experiences at school, and selected books based on interests they had developed at home.

The room was visually vibrant with print of all kinds and students' own products illustrating their authentic engagements with reading and writing. With the help of their teacher, peers, and families, they learned to communicate what was important to them. A quick survey of Room 8 only begins to suggest how the rich material of classroom encounters served as instructional materials for reading, writing, and speaking.

Hanging from the ceiling were charts with class-composed chants, rules for running class meetings, lists of interesting bilingual words, Venn diagrams analyzing characters and plots of their favorite stories, and "thank-you letters" for Family Visits. Large numbers of multicultural trade books with their colorful and intriguing covers beckoned the children to read them. Interspersed with children's literature were the children's self-authored books, thoughtfully illustrated and often dedicated to family members, and library books with information about the current thematic study. Visible and accessible for all children to use were equipment, writing and drawing materials, the children's work files, and portfolios. As the year progressed, the walls, ceiling, and other available surfaces became covered with artifacts and products of the children's thematic studies and projects.

In a prominent location, a large bulletin board emblazoned with the words *The Relatives Came*, borrowed from Rylant's (1985) book of the same title, provided a record of each child's Family Visit. The children with their families designed, labeled, and arranged the display. On the board were a time line drawn by Kelly's mother to show the stages of development that her brother went through as a baby; Aziza's mural of herself dressed in festive clothing; photos of Omar and his baby sister; Kate and her sister's costumes for competitive dance.

The activities and materials of this classroom sent a powerful message to the children that they were readers and writers, that reading and writing were part of their day-to-day life in the classroom and at home, and that everyone involved was convinced they would succeed.

Lesson Particulars

Carmen Pedron was a new student in Jo-Anne's classroom. In the process of transitioning, she spent part of the day in a Spanish-medium classroom and half the day in Room 8. Jo-Anne invited Mrs. Pedron to visit the classroom so that the children could learn more about Carmen and her family. She explained that most of the families had visited the classroom: some families had shared photographs, treasured objects, or family stories, while others merely talked about their interests and experiences. Cynthia's mom, for example, cut Jo-Anne's hair. Robert's grandmother described her experiences as a child at Riverside Park, a local amusement park. Aziza's father played his African drums. The following excerpts describe how Mrs. Pedron's visit unfolded.

> *Mrs. Pedron, the children, and Jo-Anne have been encouraging Carmen to talk. Eventually Carmen introduces the topic of pets. Mrs. Pedron helps her talk about two big dogs that she used to have (although the use of incorrect tenses made it difficult for the class to realize that she no longer had the dogs). Mrs. Pedron clarifies that she now has a small dog.*

Mrs. Pedron:	Yeah. She have a dog right now and the name is Colly. It's a dachshund. It's a hot dog=
Carmen:	=hot dog.
Mrs. Pedron:	a small ones
Girl:	You got one?
Mrs. Pedron:	Yeah. It's a small one. It's a girl. A hot dog.
Boy:	Hot dog. They're long .

| Mrs. Pedron: | It's a small one. Like this (*demonstrating the length with her hands*). |
| Boy: | Ever see a Cocker Spaniel? We had to get rid of ours because he was biting. |

. . . Children continue to talk about their dogs. Then, Mrs. Pedron points to Aretha, who broadens the topic.

Aretha:	I have a cat. I have a cat and one day when I was watching TV and his name is Snoopy. I was watching TV and he was eating upstairs. He was standing on the bed and he mashed the button and it made the TV came up and my mommy didn't know what happened. My mommy's saying, "What happened? What happened?" And, and, we said, "We don't know." And he got back on the TV again.
Mrs. Pedron:	(*smiles and says to Carmen*) Dile de la perra, de lo que hace la perra [tell them about the dog, about what the dog does]. Qué tú le dices siéntate y ella se sienta [that you tell her to sit and she sits].
Jo-Anne:	Put your hands down a minute. Let Carmen tell us as much as she can first.
Carmen:	(*after a moment of hiding behind her hands she begins speaking*) When my mother tells the dog to sit down, she sits down and when they tell her to roll, she rolls.
Jo-Anne:	Your little dog? Your dachshund?
Mrs. Pedron:	Yeah.
Jo-Anne:	Does the dog do what you say, Carmen, or just what your mother says?
Carmen:	What my mother says.
Mrs. Pedron:	Yeah.
Jo-Anne:	Just your mother? It doesn't obey you?
Aziza:	Cause she knows her. She'll . . . I betcha that . . .
Mrs. Pedron:	She knows everybody. Me, I give her the food, the water, take the bath, go outside to use the bathroom, everything.
Aziza:	Maybe she knows you'll get on her case, too.

As the excerpt illustrates, Mrs. Pedron, Jo-Anne, and the children work to create a supportive space for Carmen to talk about something she knows well. While the spotlight is on Carmen and her family, the children's comments help to make the occasion more informal. The children's clarifications help the visitors negotiate meaning in English (e.g., tense and number), but they also signal their interest in the topic. We learned an important lesson early on that the children's comments tended to put the families at ease and increased the flow of communication.

Jo-Anne resisted the "interview" style of interaction that teachers are prone to use when faced with embarrassing silence. She knows that her minimal prompts will get the conversation rolling without it becoming teacher dominated. Originally, Jo-Anne had attempted to cut short the children's stories so that the child being honored by the Family Visit stayed in the limelight, but she later discovered that the children's stories helped to raise their interest in the visitors and thus raised the social status of the child being honored. Indeed, in this visit Aretha's impromptu story opens up numerous stories from the class. This particular excerpt is followed by contributions from 11 different children (7 girls and 4 boys, out of which 4 children were Puerto Rican) about their dogs and cats. Five of the children tell extended stories about the unusual antics or trouble their pets get into. Each story builds on the details provided in previous stories. As has been the norm in other Family Visits, either Carmen, her mother, or Jo-Anne nominates speakers. Jo-Anne reminds the children who interrupt or who do not seem to be attending to the nominated speakers to be more courteous, but she does not prevent the children from making responses that serve as signals of involvement and interest.

Informal rules that emerged over the year required that children connect in some way to the topics being raised by the guests. The children's topics were connected in interesting and surprising ways to the family's topic even when they at first seemed off topic. Moreover, these connections were the primary way that children learned to empathize with one another and learned about one another's cultures. A child sometimes asked Jo-Anne if she or he could raise a new topic, which Jo-Anne sometimes allowed— especially if the child was struggling to communicate in English. Children typically attempted to create dramatic, unusual, or silly stories out of the details introduced previously into the general conversation and to get an appropriate response from their audience. Guests developed, extended, or expanded topics that emerged from the ongoing conversation or switched topics completely.

At this point in the visit under discussion, Carmen has begun to take more control of the visit and decides to change the topic to her upcoming trip to Puerto Rico, a topic that Jo-Anne has supported in previous Family Visits.

Carmen:	June 23rd we're going to Puerto Rico.
Jo-Anne:	Tell us more. (*Carmen talks to her mom in a whisper*) Who are you going with? Are you going to see someone there, Carmen? Tell us.
Carmen:	My grandmas.
Jo-Anne:	Your grandmother? And what kind of place does she live in, in Puerto Rico?
Mrs. Pedron:	She don't know. She's only . . . She have one and half. One year and a half when she come.
Jo-Anne:	When she came? Okay.
Mrs. Pedron:	And she xxx and umm (*pauses to think*)
Jo-Anne:	In Spanish.
Mrs. Pedron:	Out of the city. It's a (*speaks in Spanish to Carmen*)
Jo-Anne:	Out of the city?
Mrs. Pedron:	Yeah. Outside.
Jo-Anne:	Is it a farm?
Mrs. Pedron:	No. No. The other grandmother she have . . . is living in the, like in the, in the farm (*uses her fingers to count*) have the pigs, chickens, everything.
Jo-Anne:	We were just reading a book about that and I was trying to read it in Spanish and English and Carmen's been helping me.

Here, Mrs. Pedron is struggling to say what she wants to say in English, so Jo-Anne encourages her to use Spanish. She knows that the Puerto Rican children will help to translate for the rest of the class and that, as they do so, their bilingualism will be seen by the other children as an asset. But Mrs. Pedron declines and continues in English, which prompts Jo-Anne's attempt to position herself as a learner of Spanish and Carmen as a teacher.

In the interaction that follows the excerpt presented here, Carmen does not take up Jo-Anne's connection to reading bilingual stories about farms but continues to talk about her trip to Puerto Rico, telling about a trip to the beach her family was planning. Two other children tell stories about their trips to Puerto Rico, and Jo-Anne questions them to see if they are going to be anywhere near where Carmen is going. Then Carmen calls on Mitzi to tell about her trip to Puerto Rico. Jo-Anne adds drama to her story by telling the children that Mitzi and her cousins are going "by themselves," which suitably impresses the children. Mitzi also talks about a trip she's taking to Boston on the weekend, which opens up the conversation for non–Puerto Rican children to join in.

In the early days, Jo-Anne might have resisted the children's moving away from the topic introduced by the family, but analyses of classroom transcripts revealed that allowing the children to connect their own lives to those of the families was an essential part of building the classroom community. The children in this visit connect to Carmen's family as they talk about going to Riverside Park, Boston, and the beach. Eventually, Miriam returns the discussion to Puerto Rico for a moment but then tacks on her trips to Las Vegas and New Jersey.

The next child's contribution joins together the various topics introduced by different children into a short narrative about getting hit by a boxing glove when visiting relatives in New York and being thrown on top of a dog. The story connects tangentially to Puerto Rico because many of the Puerto Rican children visit relatives who live in New York, but it also connects to many of the previous topics about pets getting into trouble, trips to other places, and a dramatic escapade told about a cat being thrown against a wall by a dog. Nevertheless, Jo-Anne senses that the story will lead the children far away from the visitors' topics, and she shifts the conversation.

Jo-Anne worked hard to ensure that all of the children had a chance to talk during Family Visits (and thus connect to the family) while simultaneously keeping the conversations focused on the family's interests and experiences. Sometimes, when looking at transcripts of visits, missed opportunities and a premature closing down of the conversation became evident. After closely examining the transcripts to see how these visits developed, Jo-Anne gradually developed a better sense about when to shift the conversation, when to encourage further development, and when to remind the children to make space for their visitors.

In this particular visit Jo-Anne decides that she needs to return to her own agenda—that is, to position Carmen and her family as teachers, herself as a learner, and bilingualism as a worthy goal.

> *Carmen reads aloud in English a story from a book of bilingual stories, a story that Jo-Anne had struggled reading in Spanish earlier in the day. Then a child invites Carmen's mother to read the same story in Spanish.*

Child:	(*To Carmen's mother*) Can you read it in Spanish now?
Jo-Anne:	Now you're gonna hear . . . somebody who knows what they're doing [*i.e., reading Spanish*].
Carmen:	The title is "Cumpleaños" (*She reads the story in Spanish*) . . .

Girl:	That was quick too! (*She is referring to the way that fluent Spanish sounds*)
Jo-Anne:	A lot quicker than I can read it. Will you read us the one before the chickens? People, I was saying "gallina" (*pronounces double L as an English /l/ sound*)
Mrs. Pedron:	Gallina (*pronounces the Spanish sound correctly with a /y/ sound in the middle of the word*).
Jo-Anne:	Carmen, have your mom read the Spanish. She's going to read it so much better than I can.
Mrs. Pedron:	(*She reads the story in Spanish*)
Girl:	She didn't read . . . you didn't even read it for one minute.
Boy:	For one second
Jo-Anne:	Room 8 people, I'm going to give you a break. If you wanna talk some more with Carmen's mother, you can do that. (*Group breaks up. Some children stay to talk with Carmen's mother*)

While Jo-Anne is a monolingual speaker of English, she still supported the children's bilingualism. The children, seeing how Jo-Anne struggled with learning to read in Spanish, were less likely to judge negatively their parents' struggles with English, and they were more likely to see their own struggles with reading and writing as part of learning rather than as a sign of failure. Jo-Anne modeled her interest in and awareness of the structure of language, and she talked about her own strategies to make sense of text.

Caveats/Final Words

When JoAnne first began inviting families to her classroom, it was not clear whether these seemingly simple conversations were worth the amount of time it took to set up the visits or whether they took too much time away from the academic curriculum. We worried that we might unintentionally position the families in ways that were embarrassing or that made them feel inadequate rather than honored. Jo-Anne struggled with how much to guide the conversations and how much to control the children. She found that her classroom became more unpredictable, requiring her to become more spontaneous. Like most teachers, she felt the pull toward the formal knowledge and authority structures of the school, especially when a visitor was present. The children also struggled with the sometimes contradictory demands of their parents, peers, and teacher. Should they tell a story that would make their friends laugh but might risk adult reprimand? What should they do when their parent raised a topic that might not be understood or appreciated by the class? The families also struggled with concerns about which kinds of topics were appropriate for school. They wondered whether they should act like formal teachers and whether to scold their children in front of the class if they behaved inappropriately.

Over time, however, parents, the classroom teacher, children, and researchers came to appreciate the richness of these classroom conversations and their importance to the children's learning. The research team noticed how much the children looked forward to the visits. They beamed with pride when they introduced their family member(s), and their friends responded with great interest to what the guest(s) had to say. We noticed it became easier to arrange the visits because the children had already prepared their families for our telephone calls. During sharing time, the children began to talk more about their families than about the latest movie or television show, and they showed more interest in one another's lives. Jo-Anne was able to give homework that included families in appropriate ways. The parents started asking to meet some of the other parents, having heard so much about their visits from the children. Families found ways to be involved in the classroom even when they were unable to visit the classroom. They kept daybooks with the teacher and sent in videotaped home literacy practices. Families also participated in the class's assessment portfolios by collecting examples of their children's oral and written language use in the home.

Jo-Anne's familiarity with the families made it much easier to relate to each child and to help them connect in a personal way to the academic curriculum. Moreover, she began to learn more about the children's communities and to recognize the families' talents and strengths, where others tended only to see deficits. As the families began to feel comfortable in her classroom, they began to show their appreciation for the effort Jo-Anne put into her teaching and their willingness to support her. Classroom interaction shifted from a few dominant children monopolizing the floor to a more equitable distribution of talk among all children. The Puerto Rican children, in particular, began to find their voices in the classroom. The more closely we examined the transcripts of these visits, the more we understood that simple conversations have the power to transform many people's lives.

Prompts for Discussion and Reflection

1. In what ways did families associated with Wilson-Keenan's class become partners in the curriculum process?

2. Compare and contrast the roles of families, learners, and the teacher in connection with Family Visits. Discuss any insights you might have from your own experiences related to any of these issues.

3. Discuss the importance of changing more traditional relationships between home and school and how Family Visits address the challenge of changing these relationships.

4. The authors describe language and literacy learning as profoundly social. How do their assumptions lead to practices that differ from traditional practices such as those founded on cognitive-based approaches that typically focus on individual learners and skills?

5. What questions or insights has this chapter raised for you as a language teacher in thinking about your own relationships with families? And with connections to other dimensions of students' lives beyond the classroom?

6. Examine table 2.4 in chapter 2. Identify (and discuss with others) ways in which any of the 14 ELT principles listed are supported (or not supported) through course features Wilson-Keenan, Willet, and Solsken describe in this chapter. To start, give special attention to principles 13 (*language and culture are inextricably interconnected*) and 14 (*the process unfolds within social phenomena*).

7. Discuss ways of modifying or extending the activities described in this chapter to develop reciprocal relations with families. If you teach adults, what more could you do to support adult learners in developing reciprocal relations with their children's teachers?

8. Family Visits with adolescent learners might not be the most effective way to build reciprocal relations with families. How might Wilson-Keenan's approach to a community-oriented language arts program differ if she were working with adolescents in an ESL setting? Or adolescents in an EFL setting? Or children in an EFL setting?

9. A key principle in language learning is that learners need to "negotiate meaning." How might the roles of the child and family members in Family Visits provide opportunities for such negotiation? How might native English speaking students also participate in and benefit from negotiations of meaning during Family Visits in an ESL context (mixed class)?

10. Discuss how the practices described in this chapter reflect and extend other contemporary approaches to ELT (such as communicative, content-based, task-based, or other participatory approaches).

11. Reflect on your fears and concerns regarding families as curriculum partners and develop a plan for addressing those fears and concerns.

Miniprojects

12. Recall that students in this language arts course include both L1 and L2 speakers of English. Imagine you are the parent of one of the children in Jo-Anne's class. You have been invited to visit the class and asked to share something about your life in order to fulfill your role as a partner in the curriculum process. You know that the visit will last from 30 to 60 minutes. How would you prepare? What would you plan to talk about? What resources might you bring? Join with others and design either a short-term role play or longer-term simulation that would help illustrate this process.

13. One of the ways that teachers can confront their fears is for the teacher, family members, and the child to write a story together about a family experience. In the process the teacher and families discover how they can work together to help children learn. Find a family other than your own with which to write a story, drawing on the knowledge and experiences of the family, and reflect on the experience. Alternatively, compose a story with members of your own family. In addition to writing the story, document the process through notes in a journal. Discuss what you learn about the process with colleagues.

Chapter 8

Community-Based ESL:
Exploring "Critical Citizenship"

Brian Morgan

———

This chapter's central premise is that language teaching should take different shapes in different contexts. But as Brian Morgan demonstrates, eclecticism and experimentation, for their own sakes, are insufficient responses to the need for instructional flexibility and innovation. In describing a "community-based ESL pedagogy," Morgan argues that (1) teaching decisions should be responsive to locally situated social, political, and linguistic contexts in which language instruction takes place and (2) social needs and experiences play central roles when it comes to course syllabus design. Morgan conceptualizes community-based ESL instruction as a form of "critical practice," a conception reflecting his interest in participatory approaches to language pedagogy (see Auerbach 1992a, 1992b; Morgan 1998). The chapter features several themes tied to political dimensions of ESL students' lives. To illustrate, Morgan introduces a course unit on a sovereignty referendum within Canada, specifically in Quebec. Building from this unit, he discusses larger issues of how best to offer citizenship courses in ESL programs from a perspective of critical practice.

The setting for his chapter, a Chinese community center in Toronto, is significant in several ways. Many of the students, recent immigrants from Hong Kong, were evaluating the 1995 Quebec referendum on sovereignty in light of China's 1997 reacquisition of Hong Kong from Great Britain. Ongoing comparison of these two historic events became one of the course's integral components. In addition, L1 literacy skills and principles of word formation became significant classroom resources with which to examine controversies surrounding the specific wording of the Quebec referendum. Morgan's chapter illustrates that social concerns are often as important as linguistic ones in attracting ESL students to community language programs and that language teachers can address such concerns while organizing courses and lessons in ways relevant to students' needs, interests, and life situations.

———

Setting

In Toronto, with the highest immigration rate in Canada, a great deal of ESL instruction takes place in traditional academic settings. At the same time, many ESL programs for adult refugees/immigrants flourish in less formal learning environments such as community agencies, religious centers, work sites, and shopping malls. This chapter describes an ELT course that takes place at a community agency for Chinese immigrants located within one of the city's long-established Asian neighborhoods. Known by Torontonians simply as Chinatown, the area is a dense mix of residential and commercial property combining street vendors, restaurants, and a wide array of small businesses advertised prominently in Chinese, Vietnamese, and English. Our agency occupies the entire third floor of an older office building, notably nonacademic in appearance, and one that houses several Chinese and Vietnamese businesses, including a bookstore, a stereo shop, and a grocery in the basement.

Characteristic of these types of ESL programs, language instruction is only one of many important services that occur at the site. Many newcomers visit our agency to receive advice (in Cantonese, Mandarin, or English) on housing, health care, employment, and other immigration concerns. A women's support group, seniors' program, and Chinese language school for children are also very popular. Many have learned about our ESL classes through attendance at monthly seminars on topics such as "the citizenship process," "menopause and osteoporosis," and "the Employment Standards Act," to name a few. In fact, the popularity of services provided has been as much of an incentive in maintaining mandatory attendance figures—required for continued ESL funding from government sources—as meeting specific linguistic needs.

As a result of the many events and programs the center offers, the physical space apportioned for ESL instruction is somewhat constrained. In all, there are seven classrooms available to be shared by the 33 ESL classes that take place during regular evening and daytime schedules. Conveniently, all but two of the ESL courses are part time, anywhere from 3 to 12 hours per week, which eases some of the scheduling difficulties involved. The two full-time courses run 5 hours a day, 25 hours per week. There are approximately 450 students and usually around 10 to 15 students in one classroom at any given time. Some classrooms are windowless, and others have just enough space for a person to walk between compact rows of desks. For the 19 teachers on instructional staff, there is a small teachers' room equipped with a photocopy machine, several tape recorders/players, a number of ESL reference books, and class materials for their use.

Considerable program flexibility has evolved around the need for attracting and retaining an optimum number of students at the center. For example, continuous intake and mixed streaming are mainstays of the ESL program. Some students have been in the course I describe in this chapter for several years and others for only a few weeks. From the first week of September, when the course begins, to its completion at the end of July, students drop in and out of classes at will. Many students, for example, go on vacation for months at a time, often returning without having practiced or spoken English for the duration. Officially, an absence of two weeks requires permission to reenter from the teacher as well as possible loss of place in the program, but again, funding and attendance requirements lead to a programmatic culture that tends to accommodate all students interested in either entering or returning with relatively few, if any, conditions.

Funding and attendance demands are also influential in the organization of the various classes into basic, intermediate, and advanced levels. For instance, I teach the only course in our program designated as "advanced." Its designation and composition, however, are as much a consequence of scheduling and the relative distribution of students at the agency as they are a reflection of any standards of language performance or competencies (see ACTFL 1986). Although there are three classes called "intermediate," the students in the advanced course tend to come from the one intermediate class scheduled at roughly the same time in the morning. Thus for the morning sessions, the placement of a new student in either the "advanced" or "intermediate" level is often determined by the relative numerical strength of these classes at the specific time of entry assessment. The ambiguity around class levels is further compounded by the fact that close friendships with other students and teachers, personal schedules, and familial responsibilities often take precedence over consideration of language proficiency levels in student placements. The cumulative effect in my own class has been a student body with language abilities ranging from ACTFL Intermediate-Low (especially in terms of speaking and listening) with occasional ACTFL Advanced level students passing through on their way to university study or professional employment. Fortunately, teachers are relatively free to choose skill areas, topics, and methods of teaching with which they are most comfortable and that satisfy the expectations and abilities of the specific student group they have at any given time. The overall result, in short, is that both L2 proficiencies and pedagogical choices can vary considerably across similarly defined levels within the program.

In the class I will be focusing on, most students do not see the wide discrepancy in their L2 abilities as a complication or deterrent. Though the time slot for class is relatively short (from 9:30 A.M. to 12:30 P.M. every

Tuesday through Friday morning), several regulars spend over two hours a day in transit even though other ESL programs might be closer to where they live. Some attend almost every day of the year, which is remarkable considering the fact that Toronto is a city in which most service and business transactions can be done in Cantonese. Such commitment of time and travel indicates that valued common interests outweigh L2 proficiency and other differences in motivating students to attend our ESL program. Specifically, shared sociocultural experiences, a common first language, and a community agency that supports and promotes these values draw students to the program and enhance the lasting friendships and program loyalties that have developed over time. For the course and particular lesson described in this chapter, 15 students were in attendance, all of whom claim Chinese ethnicity. With the exception of 1 student from Malaysia and 1 from Taiwan, all of the students come from Hong Kong. Half are over the age of 50, and 11 are women. Most are retired and financially secure; outside of homemaking duties only 2 students have paid employment. As this profile indicates, many common points of reference characterize students in the class and their expectations about learning and using language. For further discussion of the ESL population in this program and in courses I teach, see Morgan 1997 and 1998.

In the Advanced level course, my aim is to introduce and develop general communication skills for life in the city of Toronto. To achieve this end, one must always consider whom and what purpose the general language skills are to serve. Prolonged focus on an externally defined set of core functions, tasks, or even "survival" ESL skills would be inappropriate and might actually threaten the long-term survival of the program by discouraging students from attending. The key point is that ESL classes such as this exist and are shaped by unique social conditions based on strong social bonds. For teachers, such determining factors often need to be foregrounded and sometimes critically examined when organizing relevant language lessons.

Conceptual Underpinnings

I have taught in the setting described previously for almost six years and have also been involved in curriculum development, preservice training, and in-service training for similar programs. From early on, I felt that a lot of ESL theory and methodology seemed too general and overly focused on cognitive and descriptive dimensions of language and language learning. For example, classroom textbooks designed for teaching the types of ESL learners who are attracted to community centers do not adequately address their particular life conditions and experiences. As a result, I began to conceptualize my work around what I call a "community-based ESL pedagogy." In this approach, I conceive of social needs as equal to and often prior to linguistic concerns. Cultural, political, and linguistic practices that enrich community life or threaten its cohesion are key elements I look for when selecting, adapting, and designing instructional strategies. To help me think about and organize my practice in such terms, I have explored a wide range of critical and postmodern theories concerned with notions of social identity, discourse, and power. In my teaching I have tried to identify the social possibilities these perspectives might generate within traditional ESL areas such as assessment, grammar, pronunciation, and L2 literacy (see Morgan 1995–96, 1998). While applying critical theory to ESL teaching, I have also come to recognize that the knowledge base of ESL and the direct experiences of its practitioners have much to offer and to learn from critical pedagogies (i.e., poststructuralism, cultural studies, feminist pedagogies) in ways that further the emancipatory goals to which they aspire. Consequently, I view my work in terms of a constructive dialogue, where radically different assumptions about the nature of language and the world around us and possibilities for knowledge are compared and evaluated with the hope of discovering compatibilities that enrich ESL pedagogies.

In the fall of 1995, the class became interested in the Quebec referendum on sovereignty, which was being hotly debated across Canada. While examining the referendum in preparation for class, it seemed to me that one of the key issues was confusion over the actual meaning of the referendum question and the word *sovereignty*. Subsequently, I was inspired by a *poststructural* understanding of language, in particular by the concept of *différance* as formulated by the French theorist Jacques Derrida. "Différance" (see Weedon 1987), with the graphic substitution of an *a* in its spelling, intentionally conflates the two distinct meanings of the French verb *différer* (Derrida 1982). These two distinct meanings roughly translate into English as "differ" and "defer." The co-occurrence and interplay between these two signs serve visually to undermine the certainty with which we attach words and meanings to things and ideas in the world around us. It seemed to me that Derrida's twin notion of "différance," the dispersal and deferral of meanings throughout a language and over time, would be a useful way to go about conceptualizing L2 vocabulary in the context of the Quebec referendum. Instead of seeking stable, denotative meanings in class, we might try to identify how the signs *sovereignty* and *independence* differed provisionally in relation to each other and other signs in language.

For example, we could analyze how certain politicians avoided providing concrete policy details when asked to substantiate the terms that voters were being asked to pass judgment on. Instead, a politician might simply provide other words or phrases—equally abstract and ambiguous—as substitutes. When asked to define these new terms, she or he might provide others, and so on. Hence, the dispersal of meaning throughout language— an endless "passing of the buck" through linguistic means. Similarly, we could analyze this process over time, observing how the ultimate meanings and final ramifications of "sovereignty" were never clearly outlined because they were constantly being revised (their deferral), based on whether a federalist or separatist leader was being consulted and on the results of their most recent polls (see Cherryholmes 1988).

Interestingly, one of the resources that made this approach possible was my students' "traditional" literacy strategy of "bottom-up" or lexis-centered reading (see Parry 1996; Bell 1995) and their reliance on bilingual dictionaries in this process. Through close analyses of key referendum vocabulary, many students realized that feelings of confusion and uncertainty are not necessarily the products of their L2 limitations. Rather, such ambiguities can reflect political strategies that, intentionally or not, position newcomers in ways that discourage them from participating in public life. When such critical language awareness encourages students to explore unfamiliar issues and to speak and write about them, or guides their actions as citizens, the movement from reflective to transformative pedagogy is realized.

Lesson Particulars

In the fall of 1995 the Quebec referendum had been on everybody's mind in class, not just for the instability it posed for Canada but also in relation to unfolding events in Hong Kong leading up to China's reacquisition in 1997. As my students, most of whom come from Hong Kong, examined the implications from one set of events, they reappraised the other.

The day after the Quebec legislature introduced the referendum question, I brought in an article from a local newspaper (*Toronto Star,* September 8, 1995) that examined its controversial aspects. The question: "Do you agree that Quebec should become sovereign, after having made a formal offer to Canada for a new economic and political partnership, within the scope of the bill respecting the future of Quebec and of the agreement signed on June 12, 1995?" (Stewart 1995, A12). Not surprisingly, most students had trouble with the 43-word question's complex clausal and phrasal structure. Like most Canadians, the students were unsure what the word *sovereign* meant or what Quebecers were specifically being asked to vote on. I resisted providing a definitive answer for either and told the class that the article I brought from the newspaper (Stewart 1995) might help clarify some of the questions and difficulties they had. I then distributed a copy to each student (see app. 8.1).

We initiated our discussion of the newspaper article as a whole class activity (see the activity types section, which follows). After we completed this stage, I placed students in small groups for a speaking activity. On the blackboard I wrote a number of vocabulary items (i.e., words and phrases) and various comprehension questions related to the article, which I wanted the students to discuss.

A. Vocabulary: What do these words and phrases mean in the article?

> *intentionally vague, a strong attachment to Canada, an argument over semantics, referendum, decentralization of powers, a mandate, a blank cheque*

B. Discuss in your group.
1. What do the federalists/separatists think about the referendum question?
2. What's your opinion?
3. Name three federalist and sovereignist leaders.
4. Has there ever been a similar problem in your native country?

The vocabulary discussion in the postreading activity helped many students to rethink and clarify the types of difficulties they experienced when examining the referendum question. In the article, *intentionally vague* was a referendum descriptor used by a provincial premier in the context of claiming that Quebecers "would not be fooled" (Stewart 1995). This leader echoed the concern of many federalist politicians, who argued that the fuzziness of the question was a subtle intent to deceive voters. Similarly, the federal referendum minister noted in the article that there was no reference to the word *country* after *sovereign* or any mention of *independence* or *separation* (Stewart 1995). In contrast, one of the leaders of the sovereignist Bloc Quebecois was quoted as saying that "the question was clear" and that federalist complaints were just "an argument over *semantics*" (Stewart 1995).

Focusing on this dispute through the examination of key vocabulary (a "bottom-up"strategy) was important in that it indicated to students that the source of indeterminacy could be external to their own L2 competencies/ interlanguage development. Discussion over *intentionally vague* and *an argument over semantics* emphasized that the authoritative meanings were not just "out there" waiting to be gleaned from the best dictionary or transmitted through a "banking" mode of pedagogy in which an all-knowing teacher deposits timeless "truths" into the "empty" minds of students (see Freire 1997). Rather, these word meanings were being covertly "deferred" and "dispersed," in Derrida's sense. The dispute, in this perspective, was not so much on which meaning was most correct but about whose frame of reference would gain ascendency: literal or figurative, denotative or connotative, textual or intertextual, our history or yours? When opportunities occurred, I reiterated this perspective to the students.

One of my students explained that the confusion reminded her of the Basic Law negotiated between England and China for the postcolonial administration in Hong Kong. Another student referred to Hong Kong as an analogy to explain Quebecers' mixed sentiments. In reference to "a strong attachment to Canada," she said, "Hong Kong people love China but have a strong attachment to England." This observation was particularly important in that it evoked experiential meanings/texts that were a powerful illustration of why and how a choice between the terms *sovereignty* and *independence* might be of pragmatic consequence. Expanding on her comment, I then asked the students which word would be easier to vote "yes" for if you had mixed feelings? They all selected *sovereignty.*

The metaphor of a "blank cheque," used by another prominent federalist politician to describe a possible outcome of a "yes" vote, was very popular and also served as an excellent illustration of deferred meaning. We went over the literal and figurative movement between both signing a cheque and marking a ballot without having either numbers or names on the form. The meaning of *mandate* was compared to *blank cheque.* I pointed out that they both had the same referential identity but that the former term was relatively neutral while the latter was explicitly intended to have negative connotations. The term *decentralization of powers* was an opportunity to talk briefly about the various levels of government and *respective* jurisdictions in Canada. We also talked about the implications of decentralization, particularly around national standards for health care and immigration policies.

One discussion around question 4 in part B (i.e., *Has there ever been a similar problem in your native country?*) prompted several thought-provoking exchanges among students. Several students said that something like the Quebec referendum could never happen in China because the leaders would be arrested and shot. One student stated that a country cannot function with these types of internal disputes constantly going on. He then suggested that the Canadian army "should be sent in" to prevent this and future referenda from occurring. An older student replied that "I wouldn't want my grandson to have to go to Quebec to fight in a war." For myself, I was reminded how much we take for granted in Canada. Such exchanges—especially when expressed from survivors of warfare and revolution—reminded me of the underlying fragility of civil conduct and of the surprising ease with which relations of mutual respect can deteriorate into violence. As a language teacher, I also reflected on the many complex ways that language can be used to incite or prevent conflict among social groups. These thoughts would later inform other lessons pertinent to community issues and citizenship initiatives.

Goals/Objectives

Several factors complicated my efforts to assess learners' needs and set learning objectives in earlier iterations of the advanced course. First, the length of the course, continuous intake, and the long-term attendance of many students (in some cases for several years) worked against any predetermined notion of fixed needs and outcomes. Indeed, many learners in the class would be uncomfortable with the idea that the advanced course could be "completed" since it would go against their demonstrated belief that learning, at any age, is a lifelong endeavor over which one cannot achieve complete mastery. Second, in the past, I worked with needs assessment forms at the beginning of the year only to be frustrated by most students checking off everything as a priority or stating that whatever I teach is fine. For some, their experiences of formal, teacher-centered learning leave them uncomfortable with the idea of providing input on course direction. In my experience, a new student is more likely to invent a face-saving excuse (for the teacher's benefit) and drop out of the course rather than propose substantive changes more suitable to her or his needs.

In my current teaching, needs assessment in the course is more of an informal, ongoing, formative process based on firsthand observations during lessons or occurring when a student suggests a topic or skill area she or he would like to try in class. Often at the beginning of class, casual discussions will alert me to an issue that has been recently examined in the local Chinese media. As in the case of the Quebec referendum, students ask me for more information. Taking up these ideas—in groups or whole class discussions—the specific social and linguistic dimensions of a problem become more recognizable. Thus, new needs emerge as a consequence of classroom interactions rather than prior to them.

A final goal I aim for in the course is the following. Partly as a result of their participation in the course, I expect students to be better informed as Canadian citizens and better able to infer meanings and read between the lines of media accounts of important social issues.

Syllabus Design

Recently, I participated in the drafting of an adult ESL curriculum defined as task-based, communicative, and organized around theme-based units. The intent of the document was to augment existing practices and/or assist new teachers rather than impose rigid standards across the many diverse adult ESL programs in the city. For the advanced course, a theme- or topic-based syllabus is in keeping with the type of priorities I highlight in community-based ESL pedagogy. An important provision is that topic selections favor the life situations, local issues, and power relations that characterize a community program. Most often, a topic will be generated informally through classroom discussions or proposed by a student, after which I might survey the entire class to assess their general interest (see the discussion in Long and Crookes 1992 of "Type B syllabuses" in which students' preferences have significant impacts on instructional plans). Current events, as reported in the English and Chinese media, tend to be favored. And often such topics will generate secondary or related topics of interest.

Once a topic is selected, the adult ESL curriculum recommends its exploration through a task-based approach, focusing on the completion of "real world" tasks—those most likely to be encountered outside of the school environment—as the unit of instruction (see Nunan 1988). One of the major challenges a focus on such real world tasks poses for the advanced course is that in Toronto almost the entire gamut of typical ESL target tasks can be done in students' L1, Cantonese. Thus, the intrinsic motivational factor in simulating "real world" situations is somewhat undermined.

Another related problem is that a focus on task alone as the unit of instruction (cf. the discussion of strong forms of task-based instruction in Skehan 1996) is not a particularly credible teaching approach when working with students whose predominant experiences of language education have been through rote learning, grammar and translation, dictation, drills, and teacher-centered pedagogies. In spite of the formidable research suggesting the benefits of primary attention to meaning in the acquisition of form, most students in the advanced course would be skeptical of instruction that did not integrate a substantial degree of "direct" focus—

"consciousness-raising" if you like—and review of structural items, vocabulary, and pronunciation during the progression of a lesson.

In the advanced class, such needs and expectations fall in line with Skehan's (1996) description of a weak form of task-based instruction, in which primary task activities are complemented by pretasks and posttasks [*editors' note:* both examples of "pedagogic" tasks] that allow for focused instruction on the formal properties and items of language necessary for task performance (see Long and Crookes 1992). For example, the referendum activity described earlier was organized around the primary task of reading an authentic, unformatted text (i.e., a newspaper article) for information on the referendum. This activity involved analysis and evaluation of a complex range of cohesive and rhetorical elements used to position readers around a particular social issue. A necessary pretask, one spontaneously determined by initial student inquiry, required comparison and contrast of the key vocabulary terms *sovereignty* and *independence.* Through group discussions, in which L1 translation and bilingual dictionary use were incorporated, students foregrounded several areas of dispute that were central to the debate over the ambiguities and social consequences of the referendum question discussed in the article. Later, during group discussions of the article, I noticed that several students were having problems expressing their intentions, predictions, and feelings about the future. As a posttask, I organized a lesson that reviewed several forms of lexico-grammar used to express varying degrees of likelihood. Students wrote sentences about what they thought Hong Kong would be like after 1997 and what Canada would be like after either a "yes" or "no" vote in the Quebec referendum.

In a course with continuous intake and mixed streaming such as ours, pre- and posttasks conveniently allow the teacher to reintroduce formal properties of language covered earlier as well as to recontextualize them in new form-function relationships that promote long-term acquisition.

Activity Types

Reading newspaper articles is one of the activities students say they enjoy most in the advanced course. The types of instructional techniques we use can vary, but the approach followed for the referendum article has evolved into a kind of standard most favored by students and reflective of their own L1 literacy experiences. As mentioned earlier, some form of pretask related to the content of the article (usually spoken group activities) will precede in-class reading work. Most often this will involve a combination of relatively closed- and open-ended questions designed to encourage various descriptive, interpretive, experiential, and critical meanings around texts (see Cummins 1996). A descriptive phase of the lesson focuses on information explicitly provided in the text. To prepare learners for the Quebec referendum article, for example, I might ask, "Who is the premier of Quebec?" "What does the referendum question ask?" "When will it happen?" "Why are federal and provincial politicians arguing about the referendum question?" In contrast, personal interpretive and experiential phases try to link textual meanings to learners' experiences. For this assignment, I would try to pose questions that indirectly relate the referendum to Hong Kong's situation (since most of the students tend to frame it that way) by asking questions such as, "If you lived in Quebec, how would you prepare for the referendum?" "What would a yes/no vote mean for your family?" Or, I might try to initiate an understanding of what motivates many Quebecois: "If you felt that your language and culture were in danger of disappearing, what would you want your political leaders to do?" A critical meanings phase deals more abstractly and through critical analysis with the issues in the text. Here I would ask a question such as, "In which ways does the referendum on sovereignty strengthen or weaken the future of Canada?" Finally, Cummins (1996) also discusses a creative action phase in which a teacher tries to encourage concrete action as a consequence of course readings and related discussion. As preparation for the newspaper article we were about to read, I might ask, "What can Canadians outside of Quebec do to participate in the referendum?" knowing that many Canadians traveled to Montreal in 1995 to rally support for the federalist side at a series of huge public rallies. (Others sent letters of support or phoned friends and relatives in Quebec to talk about the issue.)

After various problems and insights from group work are collectively discussed, each student is given a copy of the 625-word article. First, I have an individual student read a passage (several paragraphs) out loud, after which I repeat it with emphasis on pronunciation difficulties. This technique draws support from research indicating that exposure to the correct phonological shape of words contributes to depth of word knowledge in the mental lexicon (Ellis 1994a; Corson 1995). From a social perspective, as well, the provision of oral input partially compensates for the gendered division of labor within the home and community, where immigrant women, who make up the large majority of my class, find their access to spoken English restricted (see Goldstein 1997; Norton 2000).

Next, I ask if there are any comprehension problems or unfamiliar ideas stemming from the passage. Usually students' requests pertain to specific words. This response reflects a belief shared by many students whose L1 is Chinese that "vocabulary learning is at the heart of mastering a foreign language" (Rubin and Thompson 1994, 79). The prodigious burden and strategies involved in learning the complex, ideographic writing system of Chinese seem to underlie Chinese learners' preference for bottom-up or lexis-centered approaches in L2 reading (see Bell 1995; Parry 1996). In this approach, the denotative meanings of lexical items are first established, followed by the application of existing knowledge of L2 grammar to figure out their interrelationships. Next, more generalized descriptions are made. And finally, as Parry (1996) experienced, "only as [students] advanced towards a translation of the text did they feel able to relate it in any meaningful way to their experience" (680).

Based on my experiences at the ESL center, I follow two alternating strategies in response to Parry's observation. When the meaning of a word is requested, I try to defer providing a gloss or definition and instead point out, modify, or extrapolate from contextual cues and various cohesive textual elements for inferencing. This teaching strategy can be frustrating for two reasons: (a) some students follow a bottom-up strategy exclusively and are reluctant to guess; (b) others who are more willing to experiment with alternative strategies may have insufficient depth and breadth of vocabulary knowledge (especially in a specialized subject area such as politics and Canadian history) to enable successful inferencing to occur (see Qian 1998; Wesche and Paribakht 1996). The other approach, utilizing what some are already doing, is to have several students check their bilingual dictionaries, compare in their L1, and then translate the denotative meaning to me orally so that we might collectively judge its contextual and intertextual appropriateness for the specific passage in the text. This oral cross-referencing and negotiation in L1 help illuminate multidimensional qualities of vocabulary that would otherwise not be gleaned through isolated dictionary use. Thus in a direct and experiential way, our normal classroom routines provide evidence of the limitations of exclusive and isolated dictionary use. At the same time, it is important to reiterate that close bilingual and morphological analyses of key words such as *sovereignty* actually enabled my students to comprehend the controversial aspects of the referendum question in ways that might elude many native English speakers. For instance, when students said they would find it easier to vote "yes" to *sovereignty* their conclusion was based on an earlier activity in which the associated lexical variant, *sovereign,* was identified as inferring the coexistence of a nominally higher power, suggesting a more agreeable compromise for Quebecers, who have spent generations with the British monarchy as the symbolic rulers of Canada.

After reading the article, students are placed in small groups to review and answer the types of questions and lexical items described previously in the section on lesson particulars. Often, words and questions are selected based on queries during the initial reading.

Instructional Materials

Every Wednesday, 15 copies of the *Toronto Star* newspaper are delivered to the community center for our use and become a kind of focal point of instruction for the week. Stories of interest, especially about Canadian society, may lead to supplementary or background material selected from the numerous books on Canada in the staff room collection. Or, pronunciation problems during a reading might lead to a review of various segmental and supersegmental aspects of oral communication such as linking and word or sentence stress. A class set of Gilbert's (1993) *Clear Speech: Pronunciation and Listening Comprehension in North American English* ESL speech-pronunciation textbook has been very popular for such purposes. Similarly, difficult grammatical material from a newspaper article may direct our attention to an area of review or introduction. A number of good reference books are available. Lately I have been using the high-intermediate and advanced texts from the Focus on Grammar series made available through Longman (Fuchs and Bonner 1995; Maurer 1995). Other classroom materials include articles self-selected and brought in by students; the occasional composition from one of the avid writers in the class; or a lesson from my personal collection of looseleaf materials gathered, saved, and collated over the years.

Learners' Roles

From the selection and sequencing of content to the allocation of time on task and choice of methods, almost every aspect of the advanced course reflects students' ongoing contributions. In the lesson described earlier, for instance, the pretask was initiated by someone who went up to the board and wrote out Chinese translations for both *sovereignty* and *independence*, which set the direction for an impromptu class debate on vocabulary. The techniques for the reading task, similarly, were based on valued L1 literacy practices—also by request. In addition, the following day a student brought in an article from the local Chinese press that took up the same issue. I made copies for group work and had students compare the content of the Chinese version with the one from the *Toronto Star*. Since I cannot speak

Cantonese and only know a few phrases of Mandarin, I had each group outline their findings to me in English.

In this last activity, the student who brought in the supplementary article was acting as both learner and researcher—a typical occurrence in the advanced course. The fact that he chose a Chinese publication was significant as well. First, it reinforced the importance of the topic for this community. Second, his research data was specifically generated for my benefit. As a non-Chinese individual, I would be alerted to the various meanings and associations (i.e., Hong Kong's postcoloniality) that the Quebec referendum held for Chinese Canadians, new immigrants, or investors from Hong Kong. Equally important, because of my past teaching experiences in China and my expressed interests in Chinese history and culture, students know that such contributions will be appreciated and may allow us to shape the direction our lessons might follow. In this way, students in the advanced course are encouraged to see themselves as critical coinvestigators, a role synonymous with Freire's (1997) notions of dialogue and problem posing. In class, many learners offer opinions, ideas, and experiences that can, at times, fundamentally challenge my own commonsense values and subsequently provoke new ways of thinking about language and public life. Conversely, such collaborative activities help ESL students view Canadian citizenship as more of an active and continuous process, one potentially strengthened by their international experiences and critical insights.

Teacher's Role

In order to make relevant social needs and experiences central to syllabus design, one must also be immersed, to some degree, in the general concerns of the community agency and the broader constituency it represents. Otherwise, one risks framing local issues in excessively narrow and patronizing ways. This backdrop to one's teaching does not mean that a teacher needs to master the local language, history, and culture but that she or he demonstrates a sincere interest and openness toward the values embodied therein.

In the classroom, I often participate in and instigate casual discussions around developments in China, Taiwan, Hong Kong, or Toronto that might be of particular interest to Chinese Canadians. Sometimes I inquire about a particular Chinese recipe or borrow a CD or tape of traditional Chinese music. Often, I try to use a Chinese analogy or anecdote—either historical, geographic, or linguistic—to help explain a difficult idea. And after our class is over, I often join the students for a casual Cantonese-style *dim sum* lunch at one of the local restaurants, where the relaxed atmosphere can be more conducive to frank discussion. Over time, the close friendships that have developed between me and especially the students who have attended for several years have made it much more possible to engage in dialogue, in Freire's sense. Together we are able to examine controversial topics such as the Gulf War (see Morgan 1992–93), community policing, gender, and family roles in thoughtful and potentially transformative ways. Perhaps most important, my students' experiences and values continuously challenge my own assumptions about Canadian life and inspire my curiosity as a language teacher (Morgan 1998).

Conclusion/Caveats

Citizenship is inherently difficult to teach. As Sears and Hughes (1996) note, misunderstandings about the meanings of citizenship education frequently occur because "the same language means different things to different people" (126). Fashionable concepts such as "the educated citizen" and "active" or "responsible" citizenship often operate in the public sphere as educational slogans, whose consensual appearance can serve to disguise particular social and political interests. The important point to reflect upon is the degree to which a "one size fits all" or global approach to ESL teaching and learning discourages students from identifying and promoting their own interests in the public sphere. In arguing for a community-based ESL pedagogy, I believe we can at times conceptualize social outcomes as equal to, or of greater importance than, linguistic ones. By exploring critical social issues through the particular experiences and skills of our students, we may in fact broaden the parameters of our profession in many exciting and beneficial ways.

Prompts for Discussion and Reflection

1. What are some differences between community-based ESL programs and the kinds of programs that take place in K–12 schools, colleges, and universities? According to Morgan, how do these differences influence syllabus design in community programs?

2. How did the local setting of this chapter and the cultural, political, and linguistic experiences of the students involved influence the organization and classroom treatment of the unit on the Quebec referendum?

3. What rationale does the author give for his conceptualization of a community-based ESL pedagogy? What other issues besides language learning seem central to this conceptualization? Discuss any connections you can infer between your understanding of Morgan's way of teaching and any of the 14 general principles listed in table 2.4 of chapter 2.

4. In the conceptual underpinnings section, the author seems to imply that particular theories of language and of language teaching influence how we might define and teach the notion of citizenship in ESL classrooms. What "language" theory and/or language teaching theory does the author view as most suitable for developing critical citizenship? Why?

5. The author conceptualizes community ESL as a form of critical practice. What is your understanding of this term? In what other contexts have you encountered it? To what degree is critical practice (in)applicable to teaching contexts you are familiar with?

6. Examine table 2.4 in chapter 2. Identify (and discuss with others) ways in which any of the 14 ELT principles listed are either supported or disconfirmed through course features Morgan describes in this chapter. To start, give special attention to principles 1 (*learners rely on knowledge and experience they bring to the process*) and 8 (*learners require access to contextualized illustrations of language*).

7. In relation to the larger goal of exploring "critical citizenship," in what ways was this unit on the 1995 Quebec referendum successful and/or unsuccessful? If you ever have an opportunity to teach such a unit, what would you do differently?

8. In this ESL setting, where continuous intake and mixed streaming are common features, the author organizes his syllabus around topics/themes and a "weak" form of task-based syllabus design. What other options for syllabus design are possible in continuous intake programs such as the one described in this chapter?

9. The author describes how relatively closed- and open-ended questions can encourage a variety of *descriptive, interpretive, experiential,* and *critical* meanings around a newspaper article or classroom text. Select a story or an article that you could use in your own teaching and try to formulate a question for each of the literacy phases as described in the activity types section of this chapter.

10. As exemplified by Brian Morgan and throughout the *Understanding* collection, the ELT profession appears to have rejected a "one-size-fits-all" approach to language pedagogy. If no single method or theory

is viewed as universally applicable, on what basis should teachers make informed decisions? What other theories and disciplines should teachers investigate in order to provide language instruction that is relevant to particular classrooms and community settings?

Miniprojects

11. The author believes that in community-based ESL programs social needs are in some cases even more important than linguistic concerns. But this doesn't necessarily mean that we have to exclude one when we choose the other. Select a typical ESL competency or skill area (pronunciation, grammar, reading, speaking, etc.) and explore how teaching in this area might be contextualized in ways that account for issues of identity (e.g., race, gender, ethnicity, sexual orientation, social class).

12. Following the types of critical-reflexive perspectives discussed in this chapter, reconsider a language curriculum or syllabus you know about by way of the following questions: How did the syllabus get organized this way? What are the historical and ideological values that have shaped it? Are issues of language, power, and identity made central, marginal, or invisible in the document? Given the administrative contexts of an ESL program you are familiar with, what possibilities are there for modifying the syllabus to account for the types of critical, social concerns addressed in this chapter?

13. Taking Morgan's unit on Quebec sovereignty as an illustration of instructional possibilities, identify and discuss possible plans for teaching a comparably newsworthy issue in a setting closer to your own experience. What issue(s) could be highlighted in your own setting(s)?

14. Along with other contributions to the field, Brian Morgan has published three journal articles and a book that reflect his interest in "critical theory" and "participatory" forms of ESL instruction (see the bibliography). His 1992–93 classroom-focused article in *TESOL Journal* is entitled "Teaching the Gulf War in an ESL Classroom," and "Promoting and Assessing Critical Language Awareness" is the title of a second article in the same journal (Morgan 1995–96). Locate and examine one of these additional discussions or one of Morgan's other contributions to the field and compare it to the chapter just completed. Afterward, discuss with others any insights you have gained into the philosophy of Morgan's work as a language teacher. In what ways does Morgan's philosophy seem compatible with, or perhaps different from, your own?

Appendix 8.1

Parizeau "Lacks Courage" Federalist Leaders Insist: Won't Ask "Clearly" What Quebec Wants

Edison Stewart, Ottawa Bureau

The Quebec referendum question shows a lack of political courage because it omits any explicit reference to making the province a country, the federal referendum minister says. "The (proposed) question is: 'Do you accept that Quebec becomes sovereign?'" Labor Minister Lucienne Robillard said yesterday. There is no mention of making Quebec a sovereign "country," Robillard said. And that's because Premier Jacques Parizeau "lacks courage, political courage, to ask Quebecers clearly what they want," she said. Parizeau "realizes that Quebecers are very proud to be Quebecers but at the same time they have a strong attachment to their country called Canada," Robillard said in a telephone interview from her pre-referendum tour in Quebec.

"The real question is: Do we want a new country called Quebec only, and not Canada?" she said, standing in for Prime Minister Jean Chretien, who declined any comment. Bloc Quebecois Leader Lucien Bouchard called it an argument over "semantics" and insisted that the question is clear. Robillard, Chretien's lead minister for the vote, said the question is also confusing because it commits the Quebec government, after a referendum victory, to proposing an economic and political partnership to the government of Canada. Bouchard said yesterday the rest of Canada "will have no choice" but to negotiate with Quebec as an equal. Robillard said some Quebecers might take the proposed partnership as a promise that there will be no independence without an association with Canada.

But only the rest of Canada could approve such an association and "we all know it is not acceptable for anybody in the rest of Canada," she said. The question is also confusing because it refers voters to the proposed bill on sovereignty and a June agreement between Parizeau, Bouchard and Action Democratique du Quebec Leader Mario Dumont, neither of which most Quebecers have read, she said. Robillard also told Quebecers a federalist victory would open the door to decentralization of federal power to the

Stewart, E. 1995. Parizeau "lacks courage" federalist leaders insist. *Toronto Star,* September 8, p. A12.

provinces. Reform Leader Preston Manning said the wording of the question doesn't really matter. " The question that Quebecers are voting on, and how their vote will be interpreted by (other) Canadians, is just that simple: Does Quebec want to separate from Canada?" he said.

Federal Progressive Conservative Leader Jean Charest said a Yes vote would give a "blank cheque to Jacques Parizeau to go out and do whatever he wants, whenever he wants." And for Parizeau to propose a new marriage with Canada within a year of a vote to divorce doesn't make sense, he said. "Name me one single government or person elsewhere in the country who has a mandate to break up their own country. No one. We're into the black hole if ever that were to happen." But, a number of premiers, including Ontario's Mike Harris, said yesterday that the question means only one thing for Quebecers: a Yes vote is a vote for separation, pure and simple. "There's no realistic basis for any premier in Quebec to suggest (an economic and political partnership) is a remote possibility," Newfoundland Premier Clyde Wells said.

Premier Frank McKenna of New Brunswick was equally blunt. "I don't think it's a winning question, I think it's a confusing question and I think Quebecers will see through the duplicity," said McKenna, who was on the election trail in his province. "They're saying do you want to be a sovereign country within Canada and you cannot have it both ways." Alberta Premier Ralph Klein said Quebecers will not be fooled, even though the question appears to be intentionally vague.

"If I were a voter, I would go into the polling booth thinking I'm voting for some kind of sovereignty association where in fact, the preamble makes it quite clear that Quebec wants to become a sovereign country."

Chapter 9

Building a Community of Adult ESL Learners

Robert A. DeVillar and Binbin Jiang

———

The coauthors of this chapter discuss how Binbin Jiang and 30 adult students enrolled in an ESL course she teaches built a classroom community through pedagogy consistent with Jiang's understanding of second language acquisition (SLA) theory. The course lasted for one year and targeted learners at a low level of language proficiency. As the instructor, Jiang took what she perceived as some of the social, psychological, and linguistic factors affecting student learning in her class and applied her understandings of SLA to classroom practice. In the chapter she and her coauthor describe ways in which specific classroom activities and teaching strategies may be planned to increase student motivation, promote cross-cultural understanding, and foster cooperative learning.

DeVillar and Jiang suggest that six salient features contributed to the effectiveness of the course: (1) a nurturing classroom environment promoted a community of adult ESL learners with positive attitudes toward learning English; (2) meaningful activities that students perceived as meeting their needs increased motivation and participation in learning; (3) integrated instruction in listening, speaking, reading, and writing that drew on material from students' lives promoted learning of English; (4) realia, pictures, and other instructional techniques the teacher used to contextualize linguistic input helped to ensure that language forms were more accessible to learners; (5) students were more likely to expand their active use of L2 structures when they were guided and supported by their teacher as they collaborated in group projects and other interactive activities; (6) their teacher may have contributed toward minimizing learners' perceptions of social and psychological distances from English language speakers in general because she was conscientious in encouraging and assisting students during daily learning activities. Jiang's experiences illustrate that an understanding of and appreciation for SLA theory can have a healthy impact on a teacher's instructional practices and the quality of students' learning opportunities.

———

Setting

The Valley Adult School (VAS) is located in an exceptionally high revenue–producing agribusiness sector in central California. Defining characteristics of the city are its cultural and linguistic diversity and majority-minority population status. Based on 1996 census data of U.S. county/metropolitan areas, the county's population is 751,000, 44 percent of whom are classified as white (non-Hispanic), 41.2 percent as Hispanic, 9.5 percent as Asian or Pacific Islander, 4.5 percent as African American, and 0.7 percent as Indian or Eskimo (Frey 1998).

The school itself serves nearly 17,000 adults, of whom as many as 80 percent are Asian American, African American, Hispanic American, or Native American. Students attend VAS to become proficient in the English language—in the general sense, as well as for vocational purposes—and to attain formal educational levels that will increase their marketability within the employment sector. They tend to have low incomes and receive welfare stipends as well as assistance in job searches while they are continuing successfully with their studies. To meet the diverse needs of adult learners in the wider community, VAS offers a variety of programs, including citizenship preparation, vocational education, GED preparation, high school diplomas and independent study, basic and parent education, and competency-based ESL. For the adult ESL component, there are seven levels of classes ranging from Novice-Low to Advanced-Low in relation to ACTFL proficiency standards.

The class discussed in this chapter was at the second lowest level with students entering the course at the Novice-Mid ACTFL speaking proficiency standard. Thirty students regularly attended the 40-week course during the 1995–96 academic year. In addition to ESL-focused instruction of three hours per day (five days a week), the students also received three hours of vocational ESL (VESL) training (five days a week). The students in the class were involuntary immigrants from very low income backgrounds, tended to have little to no formal education, were widely distributed in their age ranges and family size, and represented five ethnic groups (Hmong, Hispanic, Laotian, Mien, and Ethiopian). Most students were Hmong, Laotian, and Mien women (many had lived, or had even been born, in refugee camps due to dislocations resulting from the Vietnam War more than two decades ago), who accounted for 67 percent of the class population. Hispanics represented 27 percent of the class population and Ethiopians 6 percent. All students except one were married and had between 3 and 15 children in their families. Among the 30 students, 27 (90 percent) received Greater

Assistance for Independence (GAIN), a form of government support program that helps refugees enroll in language and job training classes, monitors their attendance, and assists them in identifying subsequent employment opportunities. These heterogeneous student characteristics provided significant challenges to the instructor, not the least of which was to develop a harmonious learning environment characterized by social cohesion. Students' ages ranged from 20 to 60. Seventy-three percent of the students were between 20 and 40 years old. The age span, nevertheless, was even greater, as 17 percent of the students were at least 51 years old. The formal education level of 80 percent of the students was exceptionally low by U.S. standards, ranging from no formal schooling at all to some form of elementary schooling, and, by this same standard, generally low for all the students in the class. The following discussion shows how the instructor (one of the coauthors), Ms. Binbin Jiang, assessed, adapted, and integrated the instructional context with her knowledge and skills, as well as with the students' qualities and needs, to form a cohesive community of learners conducive to the learning of English.

Conceptual Underpinnings

The learning of a second language (L2) by immigrant nonnative speakers of English is an important step in becoming integrated into and enjoying comfortable status in the host culture. *Acculturation* is the process of language and cultural adaptation and integration and the influence of that process on immigrants (e.g., DeVillar 1994, 1998). Schumann (1978a, 1978b) developed an early model of acculturation relating the effect of social and psychological distance between the learner and native speakers of English to the learner's ultimate level of attainment in English language proficiency. He proposed eight social factors influencing the extent of social distance: (1) social dominance, (2) integration pattern, (3) degree of enclosure, (4) cohesiveness, (5) size, (6) congruency, (7) attitude, and (8) intended length of residency. Schumann further hypothesized that this set of social factors and the affective factors of (9) language shock, (10) culture shock, (11) motivation, and (12) ego-permeability were the main causal variables determining second language acquisition in naturalistic (outside-of-the-classroom) settings. Thus, according to Schumann (1978a), a learner's ultimate level of attainment in second language oral proficiency depends upon the extent to which the learner's perceptions of social and psychological distances between her- or himself and the host culture are promoted or inhibited. The greater a learner's perception of social and psychological distances, the less probability of full acculturation or, more specifically, nativelike acquisition of spoken language (Acton 1979, as cited and discussed in Brown 1994b).

In the ESL class discussed here, social and psychological factors reflected a strong probability of a negative second language learning situation for the learners. *Social dominance,* for example, was a complicating factor since 90 percent of the students were GAIN recipients (i.e., nonnative residents of very low income status); as such, their "standard of living, level of education, degree of technical development, and political power" almost certainly assured a social distance from the majority of U.S. Americans, the target language group (Schumann 1978b, 77). Relative to *enclosure* and *cohesiveness,* students generally were isolated from mainstream society. The students lived in their own densely populated and generally low-income ethnic communities. Their marginality tended to translate into high enclosure within their own cultures, which fostered high internal cohesiveness but cultural and linguistic segregation from the wider community. This latter phenomenon especially did not bode well for successful L2 acquisition.

Another factor that could negatively influence this particular L2 learning context was the degree of *incongruency*—that is, the relative distance of the students' cultures from the dominant U.S. culture along many dimensions, including language, religion, and customs. The *attitude* of the students toward native speakers in the United States varied, but attitudes tended to be more negative among older members of the class. The students' intended length of residence in the United States, on the other hand, was mostly long term. Finally, relative to *affective* factors, although most of the students in the class had been in this country for some time, at the beginning of the school year, they demonstrated high levels of stress, confusion, and lack of motivation in learning English.

Schumann's research and the interpretations he and many others draw from it provide insights into some of the possible conditions that lead to the success or failure of second language learners within naturalistic (i.e., noninstructional) and, by extension, formal instructional settings. Larsen-Freeman and Long (1991) discuss additional factors by considering the importance of the role of linguistic and cognitive variables in second language instruction and acquisition. Second language teaching can be facilitated by principles that focus on the innate human ability to learn language (e.g., Chomsky's proposed construct of Universal Grammar consisting of "a set of innate, abstract, linguistic principles, which govern what is possible in human languages" [Larsen-Freeman and Long 1991, 230; see also D'Agostino 1986]). Pedagogically, such assumptions may be translated into instructional practice in the following form: in order to facilitate learning, instructors need to demonstrate their belief in the ability of all students to acquire an L2 and provide a learning context in which students' motivations to learn the L2 will be nurtured and maximized. According to Enright and McCloskey (1985), effective language teaching includes provision of generous amounts of comprehensible input and takes into account the learner's previous linguistic experience, as well as her or his prior cognitive, social, and cultural experiences. ESL instructors, therefore, should design curricula to meet students' needs and design lessons meaningful to students in a comprehensible manner. To surmount the social and psychological barriers that many adult learners encounter, Schumann (1978b) suggests "finding language instructors who have a deep understanding and acceptance of the learner's inadequacies, anxieties, and insecurities . . . [to] enable the learner to overcome the trauma of language shock and culture shock" (106).

Cummins's (1981) model of language proficiency builds upon effective L2 input through the notion of context-embedded instruction in L2 teaching and learning. He characterizes context-embedded instruction as "interpersonal involvement in a shared reality that reduces the need for explicit linguistic elaboration of the message" (Cummins 1981, 11). Because of their limited English, context-embedded instruction is essential to students in beginning level ESL classes. The instructor can use pictures, realia, activities modeled by the teacher and the language aide, and books and prints that have rich illustrations to provide meaningful instruction. In the adult L2 situation described here, Binbin Jiang facilitated communication through (1) the use of appropriate reading materials with pictures, (2) slower and shorter utterances in instruction, and (3) the assistance of a multilingual aide.

According to Swain (1985), the role of input presented to learners by a teacher or other target language sources must be complemented by comprehensible *output*, that is, production of second language utterances—whether through speech or writing—by L2 students themselves. Swain (1985) argues persuasively that comprehensible output serves "to provide opportunities for contextualized, meaningful use [of language] to test out hypotheses about the target language, and to move the learner from a purely semantic analysis of it" (252). In other words, comprehensible output includes contextualized interaction, precise language use, hypothesis testing, and form-focused production. Swain concurs with Long and Porter (1985), Long and Sato (1983), and others who suggest that input made available through interactive negotiations of meaning is essential for L2 acquisition. She contends that "the role of interactional exchange in L2 acquisition may have as much to do with Comprehensible Output [as produced by learners] as it has to do with Comprehensible Input [as directed to learners by others]" (Swain 1985, 236).

In summary, the theories briefly introduced here share the principle that efficient L2 learners actively construct and reconstruct meanings through collaborative interactions with others (e.g., classmates, teachers, other target language speakers). Further, through negotiations of meaning with others, learners extend their abilities beyond considerations of L2 development in that such interactions also help students make sense of their new contexts of experience. Working from these conceptual underpinnings, Binbin Jiang took as a fundamental guideline for the course the provision of a positive learning environment. She was conscientious and deliberate in working to build trust, understanding, and support in her interactions with students, and she designed class activities to decrease their psychological and social distance in learning English.

Goals and Objectives

According to Freeman and Freeman (1994), language teaching is more effective when instruction in four modes—speaking, listening, reading, and writing—is offered in an integrated manner. Given the proficiency level of this group of students and their immediate needs, developing their conversational English skills was of primary importance (i.e., these are called Basic Interpersonal Communication Skills in Cummins 1981). In developing such oral language abilities, the main focus is on the students' everyday needs so that they are able to go shopping, for example, and to use community services available to them. Along with speaking and listening skills, the development of reading and writing was given some attention, since one of the goals of the GAIN program is to help students find employment. In fact, instruction in listening, speaking, reading, and writing was integrated in order to help students to become more independent English language users. Students in the course needed to be able to read instructions, fill out applications and other forms, ask questions, obtain information, and cope with everyday life.

The course highlighted both institutional and instructional course objectives. All ESL courses at VAS are part of a predetermined curriculum including textbooks and workbooks as well as assessment procedures and instruments. The formal goals of the course were for students to reach Novice-High ACTFL proficiency levels in speaking, listening, reading, and writing through hands-on activities, role plays, and opportunities for cooperative learning. As carrier topics for language learning, the content areas incorporated within the course included the following.

Topics

1. Consumer economics (shopping, food and consumer goods, clothing)
2. Community resources (transportation, maps and directions, housing and home safety, calendar, places in the community)
3. Health and family care (family, body, illness symptoms, appointments, emergency situations, medicine labels, simple first aid, dental health)
4. Government, law, and culture (traffic tickets; holidays; federal, state, and local officials; citizenship).

Complementing these four content areas, students also received explicit instruction in syntax and grammar focusing on sentence types (e.g., simple statements—affirmative and negative; *yes/no, or,* and *wh-* questions and answers; compound sentences) and appropriate use of language functions (e.g., expressing information, agreeing, disagreeing, giving commands, introducing and taking leave of someone, making requests). In short, upon completing the course students were expected to be able to function at ACTFL Novice-High levels as speakers, listeners, readers, and writers within the four content areas listed here. To these aims, their teacher was conscientious in her efforts to

Teacher's objectives

build a mutually respectful community of culturally diverse learners

provide scaffolding to help learners with conceptual understanding through the use of collaborative group work

meet students' needs through integrating the four modes of listening, speaking, reading, and writing

use activities that build upon students' own life stories and experiences

increase students' confidence through encouragement, first language support, and instruction embedded in clear contexts

introduce aspects of the target language culture through celebration of U.S. holidays, as well as use songs and games to help students understand the new culture and lower their anxiety levels

make appropriate use of multilingual aides in the classroom to help facilitate the teaching/learning process

Syllabus Design

The syllabus of the course evolved from textbook based to three alternate forms of L2 instruction: learner based, content based, and theme based, each taking place in accordance with students' specific needs. In the beginning of the school year, the course syllabus was based closely on the textbook, *Crossroads 1 Students' Book* (Frankel, Meyers, and Stevick 1991). This novice level book is designed for adult learners and contains 10 instructional units, all corresponding to the required competency content areas of the course.

The textbook, to reiterate, was the main syllabus at the beginning of instruction. Ms. Jiang adhered closely to the textbook's contents at this stage, complementing and supplementing it with additional activities to help students understand the content and its contexts and to improve their performances. As students became more comfortable with the teacher and each other, and more confident in expressing their own needs and concerns in English, they shared their impressions as to the kinds of activities they enjoyed, how long they would like them to last, and how they might be modified. When certain activities did not work, Ms. Jiang and her students conferred, discussed the problem(s), and explored new ways of teaching and learning together. Over time, the syllabus became more and more flexible, negotiable, and diverse in activity design and implementation. The students' participation in the refinement of the syllabus became an essential component in the overall learning process. Long and Crookes (1992) refer to this latter type of instructor-student negotiated syllabus as a Type B Process Syllabus.

The general structure of individual lessons had the following recurring pattern: warm-up activities, journal reading and writing, textbook-based study, general writing, and group project work. *Warm-up activities* included greetings, mingling, socializing, sharing news, asking and answering questions, and from the teacher a brief introduction of the day's learning goals and planned activities. This introductory period varied from 15 to 30 minutes and was even longer at times when special situations occurred. For example, on one occasion the class learned that a student had just had a car accident and was sent to the hospital. On another, the members of the class were specially concerned about the departure of the multilingual aide. At such times, the warm-up period might be extended in order to give students opportunities to express and discuss their concerns. More often, Ms. Jiang would use the warm-up period to gain a sense of students' readiness for planned activities and to solicit students' feedback on recent activities as well as other suggestions for how the course might be modified to better fit their interests and needs.

Journal reading and writing started in the middle of the year. Journal sessions lasted about 30 to 45 minutes, depending upon the nature of students' topics and the class's relative interest in addressing them. After finishing with this activity, Ms. Jiang turned the class to their *textbooks.* Another 45 minutes would be spent on a particular section of the textbook, which was sufficient for the students to become familiar with the language structure(s) and vocabulary featured in a unit. The final section of the class involved the students in *group project work*. During this time, the students worked together on projects related to the specific theme upon which the class was focused.

Activity Types

Six recurring activity types were featured in the course: group work, sharing time, simulations, card rotation, journal writing, and general writing. Ms. Jiang incorporated these activities into phases of lessons based on pedagogical values described in earlier sections, particularly with respect to her goals and objectives for learners in the course.

Group Work

At the beginning of the semester, many students felt shy about speaking in class. As some students did not speak very much English, they felt more comfortable working with partners or in small groups of four. The number of students in a group was based on the types of activities: for conversational activities, students worked in dyads most of the time; for writing projects or some simulation activities, they worked in groups matched along different ethnicities and various degrees of English proficiency. Thus, members generally communicated in English, although L1 support was available from either the multilingual aide or peers. Peers with greater proficiency often helped less proficient peers in English understand content-related meanings through the native language, which, once understood, served to free the less proficient peer to practice expressing content in English. For this Novice-Mid level class, some students could not communicate with either the teacher or other class members in their group projects without the assistance of more capable peers or the multilingual aide. L1 support from peers who are relatively more capable, as well as from the multilingual aide, was an important feature of this Novice-Mid level course.

Sharing Time

Many different cultures were represented in the class. Therefore, it was important to help students appreciate each other's cultures and to create a cohesive atmosphere in order to help them overcome some of the social and psychological distances they were experiencing at the start of the course. Culture sharing, cooperative group learning situations, and activities designed to build self-esteem and improve student motivation contributed to the development of a positive environment in which students were able to learn successfully. The sharing time was held once a week when students brought in crafts, musical instruments, stories, family pictures, and food from their own cultures to share with the class. This activity helped to increase students' self-esteem and enhanced their self-confidence in learning and performing in English. The sharing time also helped them to get to know one another better, which, in turn, helped students feel they were all part of a large family. As a result, they were willing to help each other in their collaborative group work and, ultimately, to become integrated into the wider society.

Simulations

In order to make learning more meaningful and authentic to the students, the instructor was deliberate in relating the students' learning to their daily lives. Early on, students explained that learning to use the telephone was important for both emergency use and everyday living. In a unit dealing with emergency procedures, the students practiced conversations in the classroom with real telephones and engaged in role-playing situations. For example, the students practiced how to make emergency calls to the hospital and doctor, just in case the Laotian woman in the class who was pregnant went into labor. Students learned to listen to directions and to report emergencies over the phone. They also learned how to report concerns, such as informing school personnel of a child's absence due to illness. When students studied the unit on shopping, they engaged, singly and through group projects, in making up menus, comparing prices for various foods from ads in the local newspaper, and composing related shopping lists. Each group then presented to the rest of the class, explaining what they wanted to prepare, what they needed to buy, where they had decided to purchase the items, and how much they thought they would have to spend. Later, when the class had potluck lunches, students decided to explain how to prepare the food they contributed. The group particularly enjoyed learning the names of less familiar foods as well as cultural and family traditions associated with them.

Card Rotation

In this activity, students chose two cards with questions on them. The questions were composed by the teacher and covered all the units students had been studying, thus serving as a meaningful review of course material and vocabulary. Students paired up and took turns reading the questions and answering them. Then they formed different pairs. When necessary, students were able to seek help from each other or ask for assistance from the teacher, the class aide, or other peers. Over time, and given the popularity of the card rotation activity, it evolved into one of the warm-up activities featured at the beginning of most lessons.

Journal Writing

In order to help develop English reading and writing proficiency, students were responsible for two activities designed to enhance these skills: (1) reading illustrated children's books based on self-selected themes and (2) writing in a common classroom journal on a daily basis. This latter activity was one of the favorite activities—for both Ms. Jiang and the students—because it engaged the whole class in a writing project to produce a collective journal that evolved through different students' contributions over time.

The idea of writing a class journal may be traced back to the VESL instructor (another teacher) in the students' afternoon class. On a regular basis, the VESL teacher wrote a class journal on a portion of the blackboard that included weather conditions of the day and some current news events for students. Students copied what the VESL instructor wrote on the board in their own notebooks as a controlled writing task. However, the students explained in Ms. Jiang's ESL class that they needed much more time and practice to better understand and learn the words and sentences their VESL teacher introduced. Several months into the course, some of the students expressed frustration that they could not understand many of the words used in their afternoon VESL course and were not able to pronounce them very well. Ms. Jiang soon realized that students were describing a component of the VESL instructional format that from students' perspectives lacked comprehensibility. In order to help the students understand and learn better, and with the VESL instructor's collaboration, encouragement, and support, Ms. Jiang made arrangements to read the previous day's VESL journal aloud. Her strategy in modeling the material aloud was to make the language it contained more accessible and easier for students to work with from their own copies. Students explained that they enjoyed Ms. Jiang's effort when working with the VESL journal material because it gave them a chance to review the words and phrases they were responsible for learning, to understand them better, and to practice reading aloud themselves. Some students were especially interested in asking for help with the accurate pronunciation of specific words.

As a result of this first phase of journal activities, students suggested that the ESL class take responsibility for composing a daily journal all its own. Ms. Jiang agreed with their suggestions. Collaboratively they developed procedures for the whole class to participate in composing a daily ESL journal focused on the events that took place in the ESL class and on the learners' families. The students decided on the specific people and activities they wanted to include in the journal, as well as their comments. As a result, the journal from Ms. Jiang's class was centered on student-generated material that seemed particularly meaningful to the group. Through the journal, students became the writers of their own lives while participating in a mutually respectful learning community. They became more enthusiastic about reading their own journal entries aloud not only in the classroom but also to their families and friends outside of class.

Over the span of several weeks, the journal writing activity evolved into the following procedure. Before writing, the students first shared their experiences as a class through discussion. Afterward, the class collectively discussed and negotiated the vocabulary, form, and content of the entry to be included in the classroom journal. During this process, the students received assistance from the instructor, who provided scaffolding related to the vocabulary and grammatical structures needed. After completing the entry, the students practiced reading their journal aloud and received help from the instructor in their pronunciation and in clarifying the meanings of new words.

General Writing

A meaningful way in which to introduce and develop students' own writing is through immersion in literature of all kinds (Weaver 1994). Students in Ms. Jiang's class seemed very interested in reading biographies, and many of them explained that they read biographies in their L1s and were beginning to try to do so in English. As this topic was repeatedly mentioned, the instructor realized that every student had her or his own story to tell. Thus, Ms. Jiang initiated a unit on writing (auto)biographies by talking about and writing about her own life story. Following her model and starting with time lines, students began to write about their own lives. The class was also introduced to other forms of written expression, including poetry and informative reporting. By the end of the semester, each student chose one or two of her or his best writings, and the whole class compiled selected writings into a yearbook. Entries included pen pal letters, a story about a car accident, changes around the home once an infant is born, biographies of presidents from the different countries students were from, and writings—accompanied by drawings—about the students' homelands.

Role of the Instructor

An important role of any ESL teacher of adults is one of mediation (Freeman and Freeman 1994). She or he is in an excellent position to provide scaffolding, modeling, and direct instruction in support of language learning (Cazden 1992). In her role as mediator in the students' learning process, Ms. Jiang regularly provided encouragement, first language support, context-embedded instruction, and opportunities for students to work together. One important way she found to provide students with encouragement was by demonstrating faith in them as learners during daily teaching routines. First language support was given to most students through the use of bilingual materials and with the help of a multilingual aide. An important asset to the course, the multilingual aide was able to speak a number of the languages represented in class including Hmong, Lao, Mien, and English. The aide also provided demonstrations and gave short summaries of stories and activities in some of the students' primary languages. The instructor and the aide worked together to provide context-embedded instruction intended to make learning more comprehensible, and therefore easier, for learners. Their efforts in working together harmoniously carried the added benefit of serving to model collaborative teamwork for the class.

In talking about the class, Ms. Jiang explained that when learning seems "easier" to students they tend to display more self-confidence and are willing to take more risks. This insight into her own teaching illustrates Smith's (1983) description of a teacher's role: "Clearly, teachers play an important role in demonstrations and in creating classroom communities where students feel free to risk and engage in learning" (as quoted in Freeman and Freeman 1994, 51). At the beginning of the semester, the students had said such things as "Teacher, I don't know how to read and write." The instructor would always make replies such as "Yes, you are learning how to read and write," in order to affirm that they were in fact learning and making progress and to break the psychological barrier and lower their anxieties. In fact, from the very first day, the instructor told the class that they all could learn and that she would do her best to help everyone learn. She also spent considerable time outside of class with individual students who needed extra help.

Planning lessons to suit students' levels of understanding and maintaining instructional flexibility when necessary are essential to a successful lesson. For instance, when Ms. Jiang saw some frustrated expressions on the faces of students who were reading passages of children's literature, she arranged a class meeting and discovered that the texts were beyond the students' reading levels. She then asked the students what types of books they would prefer. A couple of days later, she brought in a variety of books within the students' expressed areas of interest from which they selected what they wanted to read.

As this sequence of events illustrates, it is very important for teachers to be flexible and make the most of teachable moments, especially those that are unplanned. For instance, the morning everyone learned that a classmate had just had a car accident and had been sent to the hospital, everyone was concerned about him. The instructor thought it would be an opportune moment to learn to write a sympathy card and asked the students if they liked the idea. That day, the class ended up making cards with beautiful drawings instead of following through with their teacher's planned lesson. The student who received the cards was moved by them emotionally and wrote a heartfelt letter of appreciation addressed to the whole class.

Role of Learners

A basic premise of the course is that effective, long-term learning takes place when students engage in meaningful activities, work in dyads or small groups, take an active role in the learning process, collaborate with one another, and exercise choice during classroom activities. As their classroom teacher, Ms. Jiang guided students in working collaboratively and provided meaningful learning contexts in which they could participate actively during lessons; help each other; and collaborate during dyad, small group, and whole class activities (for elaboration of these principles, see DeVillar and Faltis 1991, 1994; DeVillar, Faltis, and Cummins 1994). Collaboration extended beyond student-student relationships and became integrated into the instructor-learner relationships as well. As her students developed heightened self-esteem and motivation in learning English, they became more active in class activities, helped one another in their group projects, and took even more active roles in deciding what they wanted to learn and how they were going to learn. They negotiated with each other and their teacher the types and ways that learning activities were being planned and presented.

Students' roles in the learning process in this Novice-Mid level class were also developed through engagement in group writing projects. In one particular activity, students were placed into several groups by the instructor in order to write paragraphs of several types (e.g., descriptive, narrative) based upon photographs Ms. Jiang had taken of them during sharing time and other classroom activities. Each student contributed what she or he could to the writing within the particular group. For example, one person would take the role of scribe and editor; others helped with the vocabulary—providing extemporaneous definitions of English words, seeking definitions in the dictionary, or assisting with the spelling of a word; and others would assist with tenses and structures of the sentences. Still others helped with the layout, for example, by determining how to combine the photographs with the writing. Then, each group shared its text-and-image work with the class before placing the individual project on the bulletin board. The level of pride exhibited by students with respect to their projects was very high. Meaningful, participatory group activities of this kind helped students to reduce inhibitions, to increase their motivation, and to develop confidence and self-esteem, all of which contributed to their ability and willingness to work together, engage in communicative negotiation, and exercise choice as they developed proficiency in English.

Lesson Particulars

The following is a description of one component of a larger instructional unit. Incorporated within the unit was a shopping project that occurred about 20 weeks into the course. This description characterizes three related activities during a three-hour class period.

Activity 1. When the instructor enters the class, she greets students with brief phrases in their native languages. She then puts dozens of index-size cards with English phrases, sentences, and questions relating to the shopping unit on the table, as well as cards from previous units. She says, "Please come to the front, choose two cards from the table, and find a partner to talk to." The students select the cards, and each begins reading the questions on the cards to her or his respective partner. The partner answers one question and then asks a different question from her or his cards. For example, one student asks, "How much is this bottle of aspirin?" and the partner answers, "Three dollars and fifty-nine cents." Although the questions are written out on the cards, students respond extemporaneously. While the students are talking, the aide and instructor walk around to help students with particular questions, including requests for assistance in pronouncing certain words, such as *drugstore, together,* and *toothpaste.* Students continue to alternate questioning each other from the multiple questions on each of their cards for about 10 minutes, at which time the instructor says to the class, "Once you have finished talking to your partner, please move on to find another person to talk to. If you want to change your cards, you can come to the table and exchange them." In a few cases, Ms.

Jiang suggests partners to students who seem uncertain about who to talk to next.

Activity 2. The next activity is journal reading. The content of the students' classroom journal entries centers on the shopping unit with which they are already involved. Once the activity is under way, half of the students read their journal entries from the day before to the person sitting next to them. Then the instructor asks volunteers to read their entries to the whole class. Later, she asks some questions about the contents of particular journals to check the students' reading and listening comprehension. During the activity, Ms. Jiang is also able to check learners' speaking abilities since they are responding to her questions.

The following journal entry is written by a woman in the class named Lily. "Today is Monday, November 27th. It is a sunny day. I had a good weekend. On Friday, I went shopping with my husband. We bought rice, eggs, chicken, beer, tomatoes, and lettuce. My husband likes fried rice and Blue Ribbon Beer. I like tomatoes and onions. I cooked fried rice and vegetables for dinner. He drank beer, too. We also visited friends this weekend." Having noticed the quality of what Lily has written and since she is one of the top students, the teacher asks Lily to read her journal entry to the class as a model. After the student finishes reading, the teacher then asks the rest of the class questions such as, "What did Lily buy last weekend?" "What did she cook for dinner?" "What does Lily's husband like to drink?" In addition, Ms. Jiang asks the students to recognize the tenses (present and past) used in the journal entries. This grammar aspect of the activity is voluntary, so whoever wishes to answer does so.

Activity 3. The final activity is the shopping skit—a culmination of the shopping unit. Students have been engaged in this unit for approximately one hour a day for the previous three weeks, and they have been working on the shopping skit for several days in class to prepare for today's activity. They enter the class with plenty of realia—such as empty soda bottles, cereal boxes, and cans—to decorate the class with the decor of a supermarket, including different aisles for the various items. They place prices on each of the items being set up for display. The instructor brings out a cash register and artificial money as props. Students are formed into groups of four, in which each student will have a particular role. One person is designated to be the cashier; one, the employee; and the other two, shoppers. As students alternate between roles, all students first learn how to use the cash register and basic sentences relating to both employee and consumer, such as "May I help you?" "Where is the milk?" and "Here's your change." The students seem to be enjoying doing the shopping, comparing prices, and making up lists. Here is an excerpt of one group's shopping skit.

> Tom, a shopper, enters the Supermarket (the classroom) and is greeted by Mary, the employee of the store. Mary says, *"Good morning. May I help you?"* Tom replies, *"Good morning. I want to buy some cereal and Mountain Dew."* After quickly glancing at the aisle numbers, Mary replies, *"Cereal, aisle two; Mountain Dew, aisle five. No, aisle four."* Tom says, *"Thank you"* and goes into the aisles. Mary starts to greet Nancy, the next customer, who is asking for a different set of products, which requires giving different information. After five minutes, Tom comes to the Cashier Stand with his cereal and Mountain Dew. Harry, the cashier, hams it up, acting very happy to see him while saying, *"Good morning. How are you?"* He takes the cereal box and slides it through the simulated bar code machine, reads the price aloud to Tom, and uses (redundantly) the keys to punch in the $4.99 price on the box. Then, Harry takes two bottles of Mountain Dew from Tom, repeats the same routine, and informs his "customer" that *"The total is six dollars and forty-nine cents."* Tom pays Harry while saying, *"Here is a twenty dollar bill."* Harry gets the change from his mock register drawer and replies, *"Here is your change, thirteen dollars and fifty-one cents."* Tom takes the change and is going to leave when someone from the audience shouts out, *"Count the change!"* Everyone laughs. Harry counts the money for Tom and says, *"Thank you"* and *"Have a good day."* Mary takes out a plastic bag, puts the goods into the bag, hands it to Tom, and says, *"Good-bye."* Everyone applauds their good performance. Then it is time for the next group to go on.

Conclusion

Overall, the yearlong teacher-student negotiations and community-building processes indicate the following: (1) a supportive, nurturing environment promotes the formation of a community of adult ESL learners with positive attitudes toward learning English; (2) designing meaningful and authentic class activities to more directly meet students' needs increases their levels of motivation and participation in learning; (3) integrating speaking, listening, reading, and writing activities in ways drawing upon students' lives and own experiences positively promotes the learning of English; (4) using realia, pictures, a multilingual aide, and theory-informed instructional techniques leads to more comprehensible and context-embedded classroom input, thus making it easier for students to learn; (5) collaborating in group projects and interacting with other students for meaningful purposes build upon existing L2 structures and increase opportunities for both comprehensible input and intelligible output to occur so that everyone in the class benefits; and (6) encouraging and assisting students in their daily learning activities result in <u>lower anxiety</u> levels and help to minimize <u>students' individually perceived</u> social and psychological dis-<u>tances from English speakers.</u>

Prompts for Discussion and Reflection

1. Work with two or three of your classmates and review the chapter's first section. What are some of the learners' characteristics relative to ethnicity, educational background, age, and social-economic status? Building from this initial review, discuss your expectations of what would be appropriate goals and objectives for the class. Then compare what your group settles upon with those actually provided in the chapter. See how (dis)similar they might be. As your discussion continues, try to elaborate on the areas of agreement and disagreement between Jiang's goals and objectives and ones you might view as even more appropriate.

2. Review the section titled "Conceptual Underpinnings" and identify any specific principles Jiang based her classroom practices upon. Discuss your own understanding of the principles cited, as well as any reasons you may be able to infer to support Jiang's choice of principles and evidence of how she seems to have applied them in her teaching.

3. Are there any descriptions of teaching activities included in the chapter that you might be interested in adapting to more closely fit your own style of teaching? What about them resonates with your own understanding of ELT? How would you adapt them in your own teaching?

4. In the section on syllabus design, the authors explain that course organization evolved from textbook based, to learner based, and eventually to content- and theme-based instruction. What events or experiences do you think caused this evolution in course design and related teaching decisions? Would your plans for the course have evolved in similar ways if you were the instructor?

5. After reviewing the chapter's section on instructional materials, compare the materials the instructor mentioned with the kinds of materials you use in your own teaching. Do they have anything in common? What do you think might have been some of the reasoning behind the teacher's choice of instructional materials? Is there any kind of material mentioned in the chapter that you have not used before but would like to try? If you were teaching the class described here, what activities or materials would *you* have chosen that are different from those the co-authors described?

6. Do you find that there are opportunities in the course Jiang offered for students to have some impact on how the course actually unfolds? If yes, can you find a specific example you could explain to others? Why might it be beneficial for learners to have such opportunities? What are some of the ways in which you provide such opportunities in your own teaching? (Alternatively, compare the teaching of some other teacher whose work you are acquainted with.)

7. What are some of the course contexts in which learners are provided opportunities to use language as a means for either exploring or negotiating meanings with one another? Discuss any reasons you either know of, or can infer, why it is important for language learners to have opportunities to negotiate meanings with others.

Miniprojects

8. Take another look at the final paragraph in the chapter's conclusion. Try to relate each of the six themes the coauthors reviewed to one or more of the general ELT principles introduced in table 2.4 of chapter 2. Alternatively, do the same with any other set of second language learning or teaching principles with which you are familiar.

9. In the section on instructional materials, the authors mentioned that the course featured *Crossroads 1 Students' Book* (Frankel, Meyers, and Stevick 1991) as the main textbook, especially in the beginning of the school year. Talk to other teachers (or review publishers' catalogs) and ask them about other possible textbooks that might be used in such a course. Make arrangements to gain access to one of them. If you are enrolled in a teacher education course, prepare to introduce one such textbook to others (e.g., through class discussion, poster presentation, e-mail discussion, lecture).

10. There seem to be instances when students in the course are depending upon clear and carefully worded directions from their teacher. In preparation for in-class discussion, make arrangements to observe someone else teach and take written notes on the classroom teacher's ways of giving directions. What does the teacher say? How much time does it take the teacher to provide clear directions? Does the teacher modify her or his speech in particular ways? How? Does it seem that the teacher's directions are understood by most of the members of the class? Describe a situation in which you learned the importance of providing clear directions.

11. Compare these authors' discussion of "sharing time" as it appears

in the chapter's activities types section with Wilson-Keenan, Willett, and Solsken's discussion of Family Visits in chapter 7. How are they similar or different? What are their respective purposes? What theories of language learning would you be able to propose to support their respective purposes?

Chapter 10

An Australian Adult ESL Settlement Classroom

Anne Burns and Pam McPherson

———

In Australia, the Adult Migrant English Program (AMEP) has developed over the past 50 years into the major educational component of the national government's immigration policies by providing language instruction to assist new immigrants in their early settlement needs. In their chapter, Anne Burns and Pam McPherson situate the course specifics of an Australian adult ESL classroom within the broader goals and curriculum of this national program. While Burns provides a "macroperspective" on the AMEP as it operates nationally, McPherson illuminates how national themes are realized within the context of a single course. Their chapter illustrates that what happens within a single English language course reflects broader educational, organizational, and political factors. Some of the elements highlighted within Burns's macroperspective are AMEP commitments to (1) adopt a learner-centered approach, (2) analyze affective and psychological factors associated with recent immigration, (3) work within the curriculum framework and documents of the national program, (4) develop syllabus specifics in collaboration with the learners, and (5) integrate assessment processes and tasks that meet national requirements. For the course featured in this chapter, McPherson's way of meeting these broader AMEP goals includes minimizing her students' classroom anxiety and neutralizing the need for learners to reveal personal information. As the classroom teacher, McPherson uses a "whole text" approach to developing written and spoken language skills, recycles text types for consolidation and practice of language skills, and implements a scaffolded teaching-learning approach that includes explicit instruction on language function and form. The chapter concludes with reflections on key principles supporting classroom teachers' efforts in the AMEP: diversity, flexibility, learning choice, and teacher-learner collaboration.

———

Written from the collaborative perspective of two colleagues with long-term associations within the Australian Adult Migrant English Program (AMEP),

———

this chapter focuses on the teaching of adult immigrants in a beginner settlement classroom. Anne Burns began as a part-time teacher in community and migrant[1] resource centers, teaching newly arrived immigrants for seven years before moving into program administration, teacher education, and research. Pam McPherson has taught adult ESL learners for 13 years, specializing in beginner, refugee, and special needs classrooms. We combine our personal association, joint experiences of changing curriculum, policies and practices, and integrated perspectives on the theoretical and practical constructs influencing the teaching of immigrants in an Australian classroom. We attempt to show how the lesson particulars (the microlevel) of practice in a recent "on arrival" class are mediated by the policy and curriculum structures of the AMEP (the macrolevel).

Setting

Pam's Classroom Teacher Perspective

It is Monday morning, 9:00 A.M., in the Stage 1 course I teach in a Sydney teaching center, one of several such AMEP centers spread across the metropolitan area. The 25 students in the class range across Novice-Low, Novice-Mid, and Novice-High levels with respect to the language proficiency guidelines provided by the American Council on the Teaching of Foreign Languages (ACTFL). Today, these adult students are arriving to class one at a time. They come from very diverse backgrounds, including South America (Chile and El Salvador), Asia (Vietnam and the People's Republic of China), the former Yugoslavia (Bosnia and Croatia), Eastern and Northern Europe (Poland, Romania, Bulgaria, and the former USSR), and the Middle East (Turkey, Iran, and Afghanistan). For four hours daily, five days a week, over a 20-week course, we meet in a well-equipped, modern, and pleasant classroom in an adult immigrant teaching center. The class demographics reflect the current source countries of immigrants to Australia and to the AMEP center where I work. Students whose needs are being met through the refugee and humanitarian program predominate. The psy-

---

1. As used in this chapter, the term *migrant* refers to immigrants who have been accepted as permanent residents. It does not carry pejorative connotations sometimes associated with the same word in other contexts.

chological, affective, and emotional factors normally associated with im-migration—such as separation from friends and family, culture shock, and change in societal status—are heightened by students' recent experiences as refugees. While some students' immediate practical needs are being met through established family and ethnic community support networks, one of my objectives is to be alert to other emerging psychological and linguis-tic factors. Developing English to cope with immediate settlement needs is a critical concern. This aspect of their lives involves constant renegotiation of course content to identify (*a*) organizations and people with whom stu-dents need to communicate and (*b*) goods and services they need to obtain.

Anne's Macroperspective

These students form part of the approximately 40,000 learners taught an-nually across Australia in AMEP classes. Established in 1948 as part of the Commonwealth government's postwar immigration policy, the AMEP con-stitutes a major response to a need for English instruction in early settle-ment, offering students an overall learning entitlement of 510 hours within their first three years of arrival in Australia. Students in the program re-flect immigration categories of humanitarian/refugee, family reunion, and skilled/business migration. Program entry structures allow for learning at beginner, postbeginner, and intermediate stages through three Certificates in Spoken and Written English (CSWE) designed to enable the achievement of "functional" English (ACTFL Intermediate-High level). The programs offered through the AMEP have goals related to students' settlement needs. These include organizing accommodation, finding employment, accessing health and medical services, arranging schooling for children, and so on. Specializations are offered through vocational, further-study, and community-focused course pathways. Skills modules such as reading-writing, pronunciation, and orientation to learning are additional options also available to students.

Approximately 29 AMEP service providers offer classes at the present time. Many of them are administered at multiple locations varying in number from 1, to 15, to as many as 20 through a single organization. There is also a thriving distance learning program—in operation for nearly four decades—for which enrollments are increasing due to greater demands for flexible learning arrangements. In sum, the nationwide AMEP is a settle-ment English language program considered to be an essential component of support for recent arrivals to Australia.

Lesson Particulars

Pam's Classroom Teacher Perspective

Greetings abound as the members of my class arrive: "Good morning, Teacher," "Good morning, Pam," "Hello, Miriam, how are you today?" These are good signs. In this third week, friendships and alliances are forming, providing positive foundations for the style of collaborative learning I favor. Some students sit at the octagonal tables that seat four to five and chat quietly until class begins. Others sit alone at the single tables. In the last lesson, the students talked about problem incidents. Anna's experience with a sick daughter the day after she arrived led to an animated discussion about visiting the doctor and the difficulties she encountered. Following that discussion, students decided that "visiting the doctor" was a priority area for language learning. In this introductory lesson I hope to establish an understanding of the sequence of events and vocabulary associated with a visit to the doctor. We begin with "making appointments." I show a short video about a man visiting a doctor's office. The scene is mimed by professional actors using props that provide contextual clues as the man enters the office, seeks an appointment with the receptionist, and consults the doctor. I listen to the students' comments as they watch. Students are saying such things as "he sick," "go to doctor," "what your name," "sign here," "come in." The students' collective knowledge of the text structures and language forms will be activated later when we work through a guided dialogue.

I stop the recording and ask for everyone's attention. For now, we discuss the steps the man uses to get an appointment and compare the video illustration with students' own experiences. I ask questions to scaffold the vocabulary development needed for this context: "Who is this?" "What is she doing?" "What is he writing?" and record the learners' responses on the board. I replay the scene, and together we reconstruct the action sequences. In the third replay I ask students to focus on the number and context for questions the man asks and to suggest what information he might need. As they brainstorm, I write key words and concepts on the board: "appointment," "free today," "time." Then we work together to construct the appropriate forms for these questions, and I write them on the board. To consolidate and extend textual knowledge, I give each group of students the actual questions used by the actors written on separate strips of paper and play an audiotape version of the exchange we have seen on video. As they listen to the dialogue they place the question strips in sequence. We compare their sequences with their earlier brainstorm suggestions, and they are pleased to find their predictions of typical questions are quite accurate.

Soon we will move on to a speaking activity in which students will practice asking these and similar questions of each other. The students will also use a daily schedule sheet showing time slots taken by various appointments. On the schedule sheets, their task is to make an appointment with each class member, negotiating times, places, and events. The first student completing the entries "wins."

To prepare for the speaking phase of the lesson, first we practice question forms: "Can you come at . . . ?" "What time are you free?" "Which day are you busy?" Then, the students race through the activity, and Hasan eagerly claims the lead. I check his schedule sheet against others: "Linda, do you have an appointment with Hasan at 4:30 P.M. on Thursday?" "When is your appointment, Suresh?" Discrepancies emerge, and we realize that there have been some misunderstandings over appointment times and venues. As Linda and Hasan compare their schedule entries with others, they identify a problem with the exercise. "She say 'five' and I write 'nine,'" says Hasan. "He say 'Thursday' and she write 'Tuesday,' " notes another. I wonder aloud what we can do to avert this problem, and Iman suggests, "We check what we say." I replay the audiotape, asking the class to listen for ways the speakers in the recording might have illustrated how to negotiate understandings: "How does he check the time?" "What does she say?" They quickly identify comprehension checks and clarification requests (tied to solicits for repetitions of time and place) as effective strategies, along with some samples of the actual language used. For example, after one person says, "I'll see you at the coffee shop at 4 P.M.," another person asks, "Did you say 4 P.M. at the coffee shop?" The students begin to practice these with each other, extending them by trying out different times and venues until someone notes that it is time for our class to pause for the coffee break. The students gather their belongings and start moving toward the door. As I turn to prepare the video for the next lesson, Sharmila calls to me from the doorway, "Teacher, we'll see you in this classroom at 11:30 A.M.?" "Yes, Sharmila, 11:30 A.M. in this room," I reply.

Conceptual Underpinnings

Anne's Macroperspective

Over the past 10 years, ESL teaching in Australia has been influenced by the contributions of genre theorists who draw on systemic functional linguistics (Halliday 1994). The Certificates in Spoken and Written English I (CSWE I) curricula and teaching practices have been shaped by the following key tenets from systemic functional linguistics.

Language is functional and draws on interrelated systems of discourse, grammar, and vocabulary to make meaning in particular ways for specific purposes.

Language can only be understood in relation to its cultural and social contexts of use. It both shapes and is shaped by such contexts.

Language is a resource used to create whole and meaningful texts that are purposeful within their social context. Texts may be as short as a single word (*Exit, Caution*) or as long as a novel or the video recording just described.

The functional model incorporates three planes of meaning creation.

Discourse text level. What is happening in the context? What is the topic of the text? Who is taking part, and what are their interpersonal relations?

Lexico-grammatical level. Syntactic and lexical patterns that make up textual phrases, groups, and clauses.

Expression level. Phonology (sound) of spoken language or the graphology (symbol system) of written language.

The related concepts of genre-based teaching refer to the notion of different text types, or genres, which are ways of achieving social goals or purposes through language that have evolved culturally. Examples of genres are service encounters, recounts of recent events, narratives, personal histories, anecdotes, and book reviews. Genres are characterized by recognizable schematic structures; that is, they have distinctive beginnings, middles, and ends through which their social function is achieved.

Within the AMEP curriculum framework, systemic functional and genre theory are complemented by broader discourse-based concepts (McCarthy and Carter 1994) such as language variation, including analysis of the linguistic similarities and differences between spoken and written language; pragmatic analysis of conversational and discourse strategies; and critical discourse analysis focusing on the relationships between language and the cultural values and practices of social groups and organizations. In sum, the linguistic base of the curriculum draws on a functional, textual, and socially oriented view of language.

Pedagogical interactions in genre-based teaching are motivated by concepts of "explicit" teaching. To frame teaching decisions within this approach, a "teaching-learning cycle" is used as a reference point involving related episodes of knowledge and content building, discourse/text mod-

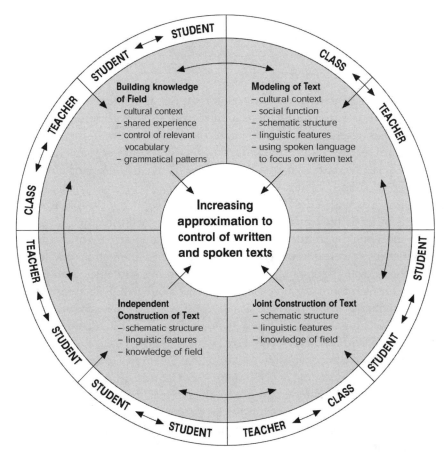

Fig. 10.1.   The Teaching-Learning Cycle (From Burns and Joyce, in Burns 1991. Diagram reproduced from *English for social purposes* by Hammond et al. p. 17, based on a concept by Callaghan and Rothery with permission from the National Centre for English Language Teaching and Research [NCELTR], Australia. © Macquarie University.)

eling, joint discourse/text construction, and independent construction (for a detailed description, see Hammond et al. 1992).

The teaching-learning cycle derives from Bernstein's notion of "visible pedagogy" (1990, 73), where teacher-led interaction is given equal value with learner-centered interaction and what is to be taught and assessed is made explicit. The cycle also draws on the notions of "apprenticeship" (the gradual, but deliberate, induction of the learner into the skills and knowledge required) and "scaffolding" (the support of "novice" learners through collaboration with more "expert" others) deriving from the work of Vygotsky ([1934] 1978) and Bruner (1986).

Pam's Classroom Teacher Perspective

Teaching AMEP settlement programs requires understanding the functional and text-based foundations of the CSWE, as well as the genre-based approaches described earlier. However, other dimensions of my work as a classroom teacher reflect my understanding of recent language learning theories. I draw particularly on two areas that have had growing currency in the AMEP since the mid-1980s: adult learning theory and collaborative teaching/learning. Adult learning theory (e.g., Knowles 1990) holds that adults prefer active learning roles and modes aligned directly to their social, vocational, or cultural goals. Since adults gain varied world and life experiences as well as knowledge through previous interactions and learning, they develop personal repertoires of learning strategies that are reapplied in classroom learning. Adults are best motivated by learning necessary to enhance immediate life situations or when there is real interest to satisfy. Learning is also facilitated by application to familiar contexts relevant to needs previously clarified by learners themselves.

Cooperative or collaborative learning has emerged as a significant concept in language learning (e.g., Nunan 1992). Genuine, purposeful learning interactions between and among learners and teacher are fundamental to cooperative processes. Opportunities for practicing and negotiating meaning and exchanging information are increased, and shared decision making means that teachers encourage students to work together rather than individually or competitively. Applications of these concepts affect the nature of classroom relationships: students begin to assume some of the responsibility for course content and to work together to achieve common learning goals. Research indicates positive impacts of cooperative approaches to teaching such as face-to-face interaction, greater opportunities for practice, enhanced group dynamics and affective interactions, increased opportunities for negotiations of meaning, and heightened motivation (Long and Porter 1985; Larsen-Freeman and Long 1991).

Goals/Objectives

Pam's Classroom Teacher Perspective

My major goal is to help students develop language skills and discourse strategies necessary for initial settlement interactions. Some of the students' more pressing needs are to understand Australian cultural and social systems such as the following: how the transportation system works; what happens when their children go to school; where to obtain information about employment, social security, public facilities, and services such as medical services (as depicted in the section on lesson particulars). The concept of "community access," of enabling learners to begin communicating independently and effectively with the organizations, groups, and individuals they encounter, is a key principle of the curriculum. The spoken and written language competencies of the CSWE I focus on such areas. By the end of the 20-week course, students should be able to (1) demonstrate understanding of a spoken information text, (2) request information/goods using spoken language, (3) provide personally relevant information using spoken language, (4) read public signs (e.g., traffic signs, public notices and advertisements, public transportation symbols, shopping center postings), and (5) complete a simple formatted text such as an employment application.

Anne's Macroperspective

Central to AMEP curriculum goals is a learner-centered approach focused on settlement needs, affective/psychological factors, spoken and written communication skills, cultural diversity, multicultural sensitivity, and strategies for independent learning. Increasingly from the early 1990s, government demands for greater evidence of learner progress and program accountability have led to an emphasis on assessment and outcomes reporting through the competency-based CSWE. To gain a certificate, students must achieve 12 to 14 criterion-referenced competencies. Since the conceptual underpinnings of the curriculum come from text-based linguistics, learning competencies are expressed in terms of students' abilities to use various spoken and written genres encountered in everyday life. Examples of spoken genres at the beginner level are the following: give personal information; retell events in order to entertain or inform; and request information, goods, and services.

Syllabus Design

Pam's Classroom Teacher Perspective

In terms of practical development, the syllabus for our unit of study is derived by mapping the genres outlined as CSWE I competencies onto areas selected as course content. I express these areas as "themes," or topics related to the situational contexts typically encountered by new arrivals to

TABLE 10.1.   Syllabus Topic Areas

Topic/Theme	Unit of Work	Spoken Genres/ Text Types	Written Genres/ Text Types	Cultural Knowledge
Accommodation	Finding accommodation	Making inquiries in person Making appointments Asking for specific requirements	Newspaper advertisements Window advertisements	Finding accommodation through real estate agents, local newspapers, city newspapers
Education	Talking to the teacher	Making appointments Teacher-parent progress interviews	Absence letters Attendance notes Event permission notes Excursion notes	Education system in Australia Expected modes of communication with school
Health	Getting sick	Making appointments Talking to the doctor	Appointment cards Medicine packages	Health care system in Australia
Transport	Getting around on public transport	Buying tickets Asking for timetables Asking about routes	Transport timetables Transport routes Electronic destination boards Tickets	Public transport system in Sydney/Australia

Australia. Some examples include obtaining accommodation, seeking employment, accessing retail services, and dealing with government agencies. As I am not initially aware of each student's migration status and personal circumstances, ongoing needs analysis and formative language assessment are central to my decision making in the beginner settlement course. To inform this process, early in the course I lead students through a sequence of activities in which they create an identity for a hypothetical recent migrant to Australia and select the kinds of experiences and situations that person might be likely to encounter during her or his initial settlement phase. Through the development of the "migrant" narrative, I try to integrate themes relevant to learners' current concerns.

The 20 students in this class selected the four topics listed in the left-hand column of table 10.1. From these topics, subunits of work identifying typical spoken and written texts as well as likely dimensions of cross-cultural knowledge were developed.

After determining the main topics with the students and creating a plan for distributing the subtopics throughout the course, learner-centered explication of the syllabus topic areas can begin. Students work in groups on a topic (e.g., "health" in the visit to the doctor lessons). I guide them through typical generic stages of the texts (e.g., openings, negotiations, transitions, closings), language features, and structures associated with these stages. Following a number of guided practice tasks, students work together to develop mastery of the linguistic elements and generic stages. As the course progresses, individuals begin to ask for practice in specific text types that usually arise from personal experience. Generally, students' personal requests spark the interest of the whole class; they provide opportunities for discussing real problems and practicing discourse strategies (asking for clarification, seeking feedback, attracting attention) that lead to more effective communication.

Anne's Macroperspective

The CSWE are a broad curriculum framework individual teachers use as a basis for deciding upon syllabus specifications for particular groups of learners. Deriving from the learner-centered, needs-based, process-oriented, and communicative approaches to language teaching adopted from the early 1980s (Nunan 1989b; Tudor 1996; Yalden 1983), the open-ended nature of syllabus design is intended to promote flexible teaching-learning processes responsive to learners' heterogeneous needs and their genuine roles in everyday life.

Activity Types

Pam's Classroom Teacher Perspective

Activity types are intended to form a linked sequence, based on the topics and associated spoken and written texts I negotiate with learners. To reduce the pressure refugee learners may feel if asked to disclose personal experiences (especially early on in the course), I use a "hypothetical." This strategy involves developing along with learners a "migrant family profile" centering on experiences of migration, typical social encounters, and tasks confronted by new immigrants. Whatever tasks the students develop are collected in a portfolio and discussed in reporting sessions where each group recounts the activities of their character(s) and displays the texts they have developed. These texts are compared among groups, and the story line events become topics of considerable discussion.

Specific activity choices are also motivated by factors of course intensity, lesson objectives, students' needs to engage with various text or language features, and my interpretations of adult learning processes. Due to the linguistic and cognitive demands placed on beginning learners in a 20-hour-per-week course, I try to strike a balance between activities that are (*a*) linguistically more complex and cognitively demanding and those of (*b*) high interest level and lower cognitive demand. My practice is to pace learning activities across the five days of class each week by taking students' energy and concentration levels into account (e.g., Monday morning enthusiasm vs. Friday afternoon fatigue). Learning objectives that target new discourse features also help to define activity choices: introducing stretches of whole texts that are unfamiliar, linguistically complex, or longer than those previously encountered. More challenging texts usually require even closer attention to learners' responses to ensure that members of the class are maintaining pace and interest.

To introduce a new text, for example the doctor-patient exchanges illustrated earlier, I adopt a whole class approach where I retain control of the interaction, eliciting and introducing new discourse structures and drawing attention to features typical of this text type. Through teacher-controlled activity, I monitor individual reactions and productions while keeping the whole class focused on the same activity. With this beginner group, I continue this kind of activity for approximately 30 minutes, encouraging questions and eliciting contributions but maintaining attention on the whole text. For the events depicted in the lesson particulars section, I worked with the doctor's office video recording for such purposes.

What follows the teacher-controlled lesson phase is a series of five activities that provide opportunities for integrated instruction in terms of topic and content. Later activities build upon initial lesson phases and give students a chance to control their own pace and level of engagement with the language features being introduced. Students may practice some of the textual features, for example, by providing personal identification information through the following kinds of activities.

Sequencing. In preparation, a dialogue is cut into sections representing the introduction, body, and closure of the exchange. Learners listen to the dialogue on tape and place the sections in sequence.

Sentence strips. Learners follow the preceding sequencing procedure; this time the dialogue has been cut into shorter sections approximately one line in length.

Surveys. Students are given a list of information to gather from their classmates, and they practice some of the question forms introduced by collecting the targeted information.

Information gap. In a small group format, each student is given one piece of information. By collaborating and sharing information with others, the group creates a complete text.

Vocabulary puzzles/games. I use a range of individual, team, and group games that help students to memorize meanings of vocabulary.

A key principle for follow-up tasks is learner choice. Whenever possible, learners may decide for themselves whether to work in groups, in pairs, or alone. This principle accords with my interpretations of adult learning— classroom tasks should relate to authentic, everyday, real world needs. I select activities that allow for rehearsal of linguistic features embedded in everyday discourses, which enable learners to work toward achieving CSWE competencies.

Anne's Macroperspective

The text-based nature of the curriculum includes the notion of "building the context" of particular fields or topics and shifting activity types across a continuum of related spoken and written texts. Thus, the teacher may keep the topic constant while introducing activities and texts that explore the specific social and cultural context. Classroom activity types might include brainstorming; vocabulary work; viewing visuals such as posters, videos, television programs; using written realia; undertaking role plays; listening activities; reading stories or recounts; making cross-cultural comparisons; going on visits or field trips; listening to instructions and carrying out practical procedures in the classroom. Through such activities students are assisted in moving from more concrete to more abstract language and from more context-embedded to more decontextualized uses of language and hypothetical situations as their proficiency in English grows.

Learners' Roles

Anne's Macroperspective

While it is widely recognized that AMEP learners may enter the program with extremely diverse culturally and experientially based learning expectations, a major goal for the 20-week course is that they will develop strategies to continue learning beyond their formal entitlement to language instruction. This goal implies introducing students to some of the learner roles that most of them are encountering for the first time: negotiating course content, analyzing personal learning styles and strategies, experimenting with new modes of learning, becoming active rather than passive learners, developing interpersonal skills as learners, sharing responsibility for learning with the teacher, self-assessing and self-monitoring, and having input into course evaluation.

Pam's Classroom Teacher Perspective

Learners in the AMEP come from a wide range of cultural backgrounds and educational experiences. They have widely divergent expectations about the way language learning should be undertaken in the classroom. Learner diversity and differing expectations of the very nature of the language classroom create major tensions in needs-based syllabus design. My preference is to encourage learners to provide input into the syllabus as much as possible and to recognize their own role in learning. Such a preference sometimes means I am challenging students' implicit cultural assumptions about (1) the teacher as transmitter of knowledge and (2) the learner as passive receiver. For example, Anna's experience with her sick daughter had prompted intense interest among the members of the class on the previous day to the lesson illustrated earlier. Consequently, I decided to work with topics related to medical issues and procedures during the following class. Thus, Anna's discussion of her experiences with her daughter served as input for the subsequent class. The following is a list of some learner characteristics I try to take into consideration while teaching.

Learners may be unfamiliar with the generally informal nature of adult teacher-learner roles and relationships in Australia.

Learners may be inexperienced or uncomfortable negotiating learning needs with teachers they tend to regard as authority figures.

Learners may believe that decisions about learning rest solely with the teacher.

Learners may consider it impolite to promote personal needs/ideas above those of classmates.

Learners may be unfamiliar with the range of social transactions required to meet settlement needs and therefore experience some difficulty when asked to assist in identifying or prioritizing such needs.

My approach is to have early discussions about their previous experiences of language learning in both formal or informal settings and to raise awareness of effective learning strategies. As well as fulfilling formal participation requirements such as regular attendance and punctuality, the curriculum requires learners to participate in (1) goal clarification processes, (2) a range of different kinds of activity types, (3) assessment tasks, and (4) monitoring their own learning progress with the support of teacher feedback. I frequently introduce the notion of learner choice, encouraging students to consider shorter-term learning goals and longer-term life goals, as well as how they will participate actively in specific classroom activities.

The hypotheticals that frame initial classroom activities encourage learners to recognize variation in out-of-class needs and their own roles in mediating the demands of different communicative situations. They also expose learners to ways of adopting new classroom roles. Through gradual movement from early teacher-centered (controlled) and structured (guided) activities that identify different contexts for migrant characters, learners begin to work together in a project-based format, choosing more specific communicative pathways and practicing the language that reflects their own needs and aspirations. This process also allows me to identify individual interests or goals.

Teacher's Roles

Pam's Classroom Teacher Perspective

Depending on situational considerations, I adopt one of three types of personal teaching roles, evolved over my years of teaching the AMEP beginner course: professional, guide, and facilitator. In my professional teacher role, I see myself as someone who has knowledge of the language and of the Australian cultural context in which it is used. I also have specialist knowledge *about* the language: how it is used semantically and syntactically to convey meaning in different social contexts. I am also a specialist interested in exploring ways to convey that knowledge to others. In my role as guide, I see myself as a collaborative leader, monitoring learners' progress and helping them make informed decisions about situations and contexts relevant to their lives and the discourses to be studied. Finally, I am a facilitator, providing tasks and resources to enable learners to achieve learning. These roles are interwoven on three levels: during the course as a whole, during individual lessons, and during individual lesson segments, with different roles being foregrounded at different times. Initially, I emphasize the professional teacher role, to place the focus and pressure on me rather than the learners. As the learners become more familiar with the nature of classroom relationships and course demands, I become increasingly a guide and facilitator. Role shifting also occurs throughout each lesson as I introduce new tasks. Over time, I expect learners to gain awareness of their own roles in making decisions about class content, learning tasks, knowledge gaps, and individual or group learning modalities, thus enabling me, at times, to fulfill a less prominent role in the classroom.

Anne's Macroperspective

The move toward genre-based approaches in the AMEP has generated criticism of extreme versions of learner centeredness that assume nonintervention on the part of the teacher. The concepts of apprenticeship and scaffolding underpinning Australian genre approaches, which are embedded in the processes of the teaching-learning cycle, imply a shifting role for the teacher between teacher-centered and learner-centered interaction. These shifts depend on how much input and guidance are required during either form-focused or more communicative tasks. Dealing with new knowledge or language structures is likely to require more explicit instruction and teacher intervention. Learner-centered instruction is seen increasingly as teacher sensitivity to learners' progress in terms of when direct input and explicit instruction can be gradually withdrawn once appropriate scaffolding is in place.

Instructional Materials

Pam's Classroom Teacher Perspective

Instructional materials in the beginner course reflect three main categories from which I select according to lesson objectives: (1) authentic materials (or "realia"), (2) teacher-made materials, and (3) publications focused on Australian content. Authentic materials, including a wide range of informational material, are used to increase learners' knowledge of the Australian community and systems. These materials may include application forms for housing, employment, and education programs. They also include dual language brochures in students' L1s and English from federal and local government authorities such as community health service programs and child care services. Libraries provide both information about services and opportunities to develop language skills. We use off-air recordings from television such as community announcements, commercial advertisements, popular television "soap operas," and news excerpts to compare discourse styles, speaking strategies, and paralinguistic features of native English styles of speech. Additional forms of authentic materials I use in the classroom include advertisements and articles from newspapers and magazines, radio news updates, and recorded public transport announcements.

The teacher-made materials I use may be divided into scripted, semiscripted, and pedagogical materials. Scripted and semiscripted materials arise from short recorded samples of natural speech or simplified written texts based on authentic data. These materials are presented to students in the form of short dialogues and may illustrate greetings, requests for information or service, and leave-taking. I use these to highlight particular textual features, lexis, or grammatical patterns. Pedagogical materials focus attention on specific features or may facilitate practice of isolated linguistic items. For example, such materials include tapes focusing on a particular phonological feature such as final consonants, work sheets for topic or vocabulary development, or exercises practicing subject-verb agreement, all of which may serve to scaffold the production of more extended texts. Finally, recent publications that feature Australian content provide other sources of classroom input. Publications such as Cornish's (1996) *Making Contact: Your Child's School* or Brown and Cornish's (1996) *Beach Street 1* are text based and include video- or audiotaped listening material offering local voices and characters that familiarize learners with Australian phonology, syntax, and discourse as well as cultural and social relationships. *Beach Street 1* features a story line that follows the lives of the residents of a block of apartments in a beachside suburb in Australia. *Making Contact: Your Child's School* is a video package designed to help parents gain the English language and literacy skills they need to communicate with personnel at their child(ren)'s school.

Anne's Macroperspective

The adoption of learner-centered and, more recently, text-based approaches has meant a substantial process of curriculum renewal in instructional materials. Major changes have seen a shift from the predominantly British and structurally based course books of the early 1980s to material drawing on local contexts, situations, and content (e.g., Clemens and Crawford 1986; New South Wales Adult Migrant English Service [NSW AMES] 1997) as well as adopting an integrated text-based orientation. The newer materials draw together related spoken and written tasks and aim toward modeling authentic interactions as closely as possible (e.g., Brown and Cornish 1996; Delaruelle 1997; Cornish and Hood 1994). Many resources have been developed collaboratively at the national or state level to complement the conceptual underpinnings of the CSWE (Burns and Joyce 1998). Some have emerged from research and curriculum development coordinated by the National Centre for English Language Teaching and Research (NCELTR), the federal government's AMEP research center (e.g., Willing 1989; Joyce 1998a, 1998b).

Most AMEP teachers adopt an eclectic approach toward instructional resources, seeing the use of authentic texts as the ultimate goal of instruction but drawing on more pedagogically oriented materials to scaffold the learning process. Few courses are driven by a single textbook. Rather, they tend to include a mixture of published resources, authentic texts, teacher-produced or learner-derived materials, visuals including video recordings and posters, and, increasingly, computer and multimedia resources. A full range of such materials and resources is utilized flexibly and at the teachers' discretion, according to perceived learning purposes.

Assessment

Anne's Macroperspective

The CSWE contains statements of outcomes couched as competencies. Each competency is assessed against specific criteria as in the following example (table 10.2) from Certificate 1 (ACTFL Novice Level). Ideally, these statements are shared with learners who can then track their own progress. Responsibility for integrating assessment into the course rests with teachers, and assessment tasks are intended to give learners maximum opportunities to demonstrate achievement in each competency.

Pam's Classroom Teacher Perspective

Students are unlikely to be familiar with the criterion-based nature of AMEP assessment, and so providing information about language skills to be assessed, texts on which assessments are based, and the structures and conditions for assessments is a continuous part of classroom discussion. I treat assessment integrally throughout the course so that individuals are assessed as they master the required texts. In practical terms, I try to facilitate this process by setting a date for whole class assessment after a period of informal formative assessment of classwork. If my observations indicate that most students can approximate benchmark levels or higher, we spend time reviewing the criteria and rehearsing assessment tasks and conditions on similar tasks. At this point, I usually provide further instruction for students having difficulty meeting the targeted performance criteria. Some students

TABLE 10.2.   Competency 5—Can Request Information/Goods Using Spoken Language

Elements	Performance Criteria	Range Statements	Evidence Guide
Can ask one-clause questions Can use appropriate vocabulary Can seek repetition or clarification	Asks one-clause questions including polar [yes/no] and wh- questions Uses appropriate vocabulary Seeks repetition or clarification as required	6 questions grammatically correct May reformulate each question yes/no and wh- questions Pronunciation errors should not interfere with meaning or dominate text. Face to face Questions and answers may be memorized. Interlocutor has experience with NESB (non-English speaking background) speakers.	Sample tasks Learner interview with teacher or counselor, e.g., questions about photographs Role play of buying a car or renting an apartment

Source: Information from New South Wales Adult Migrant English Service (NSW AMES) 1997.

may feel insecure and not ready for assessment. When such insecurities are expressed, assessment is deferred until the students have gained further confidence and language skills. On the other hand, some students request a "fast track" to the next certificate level by attempting a greater number of tasks and using more frequent assessment opportunities. Flexibility reduces pressure on students by allowing them to make individual decisions about their readiness for assessment.

Pam's Caveats/Conclusion

The nature of the immigration program and the English language services offered through the AMEP means that, in the courses I offer, groups of students demonstrate very diverse learning needs and goals. While the curriculum specifies the text types to be taught and assessed, it is flexible enough to accommodate learners' diverse needs and to allow for student choice of situations and contexts of language use. The principle of providing student choice in learning has become an essential one for me. It seems to enhance motivation and interest, as the students participate in decisions about what they will be learning in the course. Providing students with opportunities to make choices helps to develop collaborative learning practices in the classroom as learners discover shared interests, develop common goals, and enrich the teaching program with their ideas.

I have learned, however, that the firsthand life histories and experiences of students I meet in the course are not necessarily effective as resources to be incorporated as part of the teaching program. By introducing hypothetical migrant characters that can be scripted into various roles and situations, we are better able to explore possible sources of communication difficulties without embarrassment to individual students in the class. While students are often reluctant to expose their own experiences of communication breakdown, they are very willing (even anxious) to suggest typical areas of difficulty for a hypothetical character, often with much humor. The hilarious routines in which students have role-played unhelpful bureaucrats; abrasive office workers; or vague, forgetful teachers (like me) have been useful indicators of the kinds of linguistic and discursive skills that need to be prioritized in such courses. I also particularly enjoy the sense that we develop into a learning community that can collaborate on many aspects of curriculum design. To better serve this community, I try to focus on making my professional teaching skills and knowledge available as resources so that students and I can develop our program of learning collaboratively.

Prompts for Discussion and Reflection

1. Describe the language learning goals of the course Anne Burns and Pam McPherson discuss. What is the course preparing students to be able to do? How would you characterize the particular group of learners described in this account?

2. In what ways does the government policy framework influence the teaching and learning goals of the AMEP program overall and of Pam McPherson's course in particular?

3. A major theme underlying the discussion in this chapter is that classroom teachers do not operate in a vacuum. There is always a wider set of circumstances that needs to be taken into consideration. What are some of the programmatic, institutional, regional, and even national influences that impact Pam's teaching decisions and behaviors? Compare some of these with ones that impact your own teaching (or the teachers

in an ELT program familiar to you). Compare influences impacting Pam's teaching decisions and behaviors with those impacting other contributors featured in this book (e.g., Jo-Anne Wilson-Keenan, Jerri Willett, and Judith Solsken [chap. 7]), Brian Morgan [chap. 8], Lindsay Miller [chap. 14], Donna Brinton [chap. 16], Janet Graham and Susan Barone [chap. 22]).

4. How are notions of genre-based teaching applied in Pam's teaching program? To begin your discussion, what do the authors mean by the terms *genre based* and *genre-based teaching?* For example, identify which teaching activities seem to reflect such an orientation to ELT.

5. Discuss the notion of scaffolding in a language teaching program. What does the term *scaffolding* mean in this context? During which part of the teaching/learning cycle might it occur? Identify some teaching activities in the lesson that illustrate this concept.

6. The chapter describes some features of the course syllabus as resulting from collaborations between the teacher and students. Is this a good idea? Why or why not? What are some of the general ELT principles discussed in chapter 2 (see table 2.4) to which such efforts might be related? To what extent would you be interested in incorporating similar elements of collaboration between teacher and students in your teaching?

7. One of the teaching activities Pam McPherson discusses involves the use of a video to contextualize spoken interactions between a doctor and a patient. Discuss some of the ways you might use video resources in your own teaching or ways you have noticed that other teachers use them.

8. Anne Burns describes the goals of the AMEP program as focused on the settlement needs of recently arrived adult immigrants to Australia. On the basis of your own experiences, what might some of these settlement needs be? Alternatively, what are some of the more pressing learner needs in an ELT program with which you are familiar?

9. The roles of teachers and adult learners described in this chapter reflect Australian norms for relationships among adults in both social and educational contexts. From what you have seen in the chapter, how would you characterize the norms reflected in Pam McPherson's course? What assumptions are held about the teacher's role by your own teaching institution? By your colleagues? By your students? By yourself?

10. Burns and McPherson refer to the use of technology in their account of this lesson. Innovations in the use of technology for teaching and learning are now increasing rapidly, and teachers and researchers are engaged in a lively debate as to their place in ELT. Discuss ways that

other kinds of educational technology could be used in the kinds of lessons Pam offers and explain how they would support learning for these or similar learner groups.

11. In the chapter Anne Burns describes the genre theory and systemic-functional linguistics bases for the Certificates in Spoken and Written English curriculum. What other theoretical approaches to English language teaching do you see reflected in the learning activities? Can any of them be tied to the general ELT principles listed in table 2.4 of chapter 2?

Miniprojects

12. Discussion item 3 in this section raised the issue of teachers having to operate within a wider world of impacts on their teaching. Find evidence from other chapters in the *Understanding* collection to illustrate that teachers do not operate alone but need to be responsive to external considerations. Try to identify as much as you can concerning what some of these outside influences might be. Keep track of connections to your current or future teaching decisions and behaviors. Collaborate with others to generate an even more comprehensive listing of such influences. Later, arrange to interview several teachers about whatever might be influencing their teaching. Prepare a poster session, a panel discussion, a course paper, or an oral report that summarizes what you find. Include discussion of implications for your future as a language teacher.

13. In the section on instructional materials, Pam mentions three categories of teaching resources: authentic realia, teacher-made resources, and publications based on Australian content suitable for adult learners. Identify the kinds of teaching resources that are used for a course you (might one day) teach. Provide samples and describe to your classmates or colleagues rationale for their selection and how they are used.

14. Arrange with a colleague to observe each other's classes for a short time. (For preservice teachers, arrange to observe another teacher's class.) While observing, note the patterns of interaction between teachers and learners throughout the teaching session. Note incidences of scaffolding in formal instructional phases with the whole class and in interactions between the teacher and individual students. Later, discuss with your colleagues the ways that scaffolding can be adjusted to meet different learner needs throughout a language lesson. Prepare a lesson plan for a single class and note the points where you will need to provide more or less scaffolding for learners.

Part 3
English as a Foreign Language

Chapter 11

Videoing Conversations for Self-Evaluation in Japan

Tim Murphey

———

This chapter and the next address very similar student populations, though there are striking contrasts between the authors' respective courses. Tim Murphey teaches a university-level EFL course in Japan focused on enhancing learners' speaking abilities. Along with colleagues who work within the same department, he uses a classroom configuration of two video cameras and four VHS machines to record students' five-minute conversations on a regular basis. After presenting a student's, and then a teacher's, narrative of classroom events, Murphey discusses some of the technical needs and background research to support an approach to ELT he calls "videoing conversations for self-evaluation" (VCSE).

Murphey arranges weekly VCSE classroom activities into a three-part sequence of prevideoing, video day "performance," and postvideoing phases. During other phases of the course, students also experiment with self-talk and learn discourse conversation strategies, such as the use of shadowing (Murphey 2000a), clarification requests, and summarizing. While working with copies of their videos as homework, learners are sometimes asked to transcribe all or portions of a conversation, answer focus questions, or view a videotaped conversation with others (more often with peers, occasionally with their teacher). Toward the end of the semester when students have 10 or more video clips of their own speaking performances, they write a paper comparing the quality of their work as speakers during early performances in the course with more recent ones. The focus of their paper is to document their own progress as English speakers.

The VCSE procedures Murphey describes increase student awareness and encourage students to adjust speaking performance based on external feedback

———

An introductory training video (Murphy and Kenny 1996) (Murphey 2000a) about the VCSE process is available from the National Foreign Language Resource Center at the University of Hawaii at <http://www.lll.hawaii.edu/nflrc/Videos.html>.

———

that video recordings make possible. Since VCSE permits learners to view themselves as others see them, students in Murphey's course have access to a tangible record of their conversational strategies and evidence of their development as speakers of English during the course.

————

Lesson Particulars

To demonstrate what this chapter is about, I invite readers first to see and hear what happens from both a student perspective and a teacher's view in the procedures known as videoing conversations for self-evaluation (VCSE). My understanding of how students feel (their apprehensions, fears, and joys) comes from reading over 40 action logs over the past four years, each log written by a student going through the VCSE procedure and reporting her or his impressions. These student reflections impact my teaching decisions, strategies, and behaviors. By reading the lesson particulars section first, you will have a background for the more abstract conceptualizations in the rest of the paper and an image of the ways in which the teacher and students use video technology inside and outside of the classroom in support of course goals.

A Student's View

Imagine that you are a student in a language class that meets three times a week and emphasizes student talk. On the first day your teacher says you will be videotaped weekly conversing in your second language (L2). For the third class you are to bring a new VHS cassette with your name written on it to use in producing these videos. The idea of videotaping sounds interesting and a bit scary to you. The teacher gives you some material to practice, but you are not really sure how to practice or what to prepare.

On the first video day you are very relieved to discover that while the four people selected to sit before two video camcorders are being recorded, everybody else is having conversations, too. And everyone is changing partners at about five-minute intervals. This arrangement allows you to rehearse your conversation several times before you are the one called up to record. Immediately after your turn being recorded with a classmate, you are given back your cassette. Then you have a few more conversations while other members of the class are being recorded.

By the end of class you have spoken with six partners and learned a few new things from what your partners said. You used some of your first language (L1), but most of what you said today was in English (your L2), and, more important, you made some new friends. Your homework is to transcribe all of your video conversation as well as you can. With curiosity and a bit of dread you go home, or make your way over to the Audiovisual Center, to watch the recording.

Watching that first video is somewhat embarrassing. You look and sound funny to yourself, but you said a few things that you like. And you notice several things you would like to improve. Transcribing the conversation is hard, but it allows opportunities to notice a few errors you know you can correct in the future. In the next class, you pair up with the same person who participated in the video recording with you, and you read each other's transcripts. You notice some differences between the two versions. You or your partner had more words in some places, modified different things, and heard things somewhat differently. Your partner notices several other differences between the two versions you had not noticed. This collaboration is interesting. You notice you can learn from each other, and you want to do better next time. Working together, you both adjust your transcripts. Then you compare your work with yet another student's and see how others completed these tasks. It is fun to read someone else's conversation, and again you have the feeling of success, because the work in the course so far has been challenging yet easy to understand.

After a few weeks, you learn that the more you prepare for the videotaping, the better your conversations become, the more fun you have, and the more you learn. On one video day, four weeks into the course, your teacher gives your partner Mari's video back to you (and yours to Mari). Your task is to view all four of Mari's conversations recorded thus far in the course and to write a letter to Mari mentioning improvements and offering further suggestions. You have fun looking at Mari's three conversations with different classmates, as well as her last conversation with you. You notice she is more relaxed and talkative in later conversations. In the next class, you return each others' cassettes and exchange letters. You were a bit worried, but Mari's letter to you makes you very happy. Among other things, she has written that "you are improving." Now you feel like speaking even more.

As the semester continues, you notice that some topics the teacher chooses are easy to talk about, while others seem to be more difficult. You learn a few strategies that help you speak more fluently—phrases for gaining time to think, for expressing yourself even when you do not have the perfect words, for asking your partners when you do not understand something, and so on. You also continue to notice how your partners say things that you could try out for yourself. Video day becomes your favorite day in the course each week because you get to talk with several different classmates, and you notice you are speaking in the target language most of the time.

At the end of the term, you review all 10 of your recorded conversations and write a report comparing them, and you also explain how you would like to improve as a speaker and conversationalist even more. You are amazed at the differences between the first and last conversations: you are more comfortable speaking; your phrases are longer; you continue talking with partners with far fewer awkward pauses; and, best of all, you can see that you are even enjoying yourself in English—that, now, you *want to talk*. (For further discussion, see Murphey and Woo 1998.)

A Teacher's View of the Same Events

Now let's look at a teacher's view of video day. On video day, before class, you set up the video equipment and ensure everything is working properly. You put a card by the microphone in front of each of the two cameras with the day's date and topic. Each student brings a VHS videocassette wound to the end of the last conversation (to prevent previous conversations from being erased). Her or his name is clearly marked on the spine of the videotape with the list of past partners written on the top label. After removing the cassette boxes, students place their videotapes on the front desk. You choose cassettes at random in order to group partners for the recordings. Once everyone has participated in a warm-up conversation, you call up the first four students and insert their VHS cassette tapes into the four recorders. You start the Hi8 tapes in the cameras, the ones you keep for research or backup, and let the tapes continue to run without pause to the end of class. Once students are in place and all the machines are turning, you give everyone the signal to begin. You double-check that all machines are functioning properly, microphones are on, and the four designated students are visible within the viewfinder. You jot down the names of the partners on the Hi8 cassette covers to make it easy to locate conversations later on.

After five minutes, you signal that it is time for everyone to bring their conversations to an end by gently ringing a soft bell or by turning one of the class light switches off and on. The four students at the front of the room also finish their conversations ("Oh, I gotta go [looking at their watches].

Nice talking to you!"). These same four students retrieve their videotapes from you and return to the conversation area of the room to find new partners; at the same time, you call on a set of four new students to be video recorded.

All of this will be repeated five or six times in a class. After you and the students become more familiar with the process, there are actually a few minutes during each conversation for you to listen in or walk around the class and stimulate more interaction.

Setting

At Nanzan University, Nagoya (Japan), first- and second-year students in the British and American Studies Department meet three times a week (for 45 minutes each lesson) with a native speaker of English in an oral communication course (for a description of the whole curriculum, see Murphey 1997). In this chapter, I describe our three-times-a-week class meetings but give special attention to the course's once-a-week video-intensive segment. Most of the students have had six years of grammar-translation English language study in junior and senior high school before coming to Nanzan. Approximately 50 percent are Novice-Low (on the ACTFL Speaking Proficiency scale), and the others spread out above that level with one or two students being Intermediate-High or Advanced. Most students in their first 90-day semester jump from Novice-Low to Novice-Intermediate or Novice-High levels due in part to the VCSE procedures described in this chapter.

The goal of the course is to activate and further develop the students' latent listening and speaking abilities that have been neglected in their previous six years of grammar study. This semester I am teaching two sections of the course. There are 22 students in the section that serves as this chapter's centerpiece. My approach in the course is to optimize the amount of speaking interaction that is possible and to design procedures that allow students to both "go for fluency" and "focus on form" while recycling communicative language they consider useful. I find the set of video procedures developed by colleagues and myself over the past several years to enhance and intensify these possibilities.[1]

---

1. Thanks to Larry Davies, Clarita Filipinas, Tom Kenny, Duane Kindt, and Linda Woo for their support and inspiration throughout the process of developing VCSE procedures.

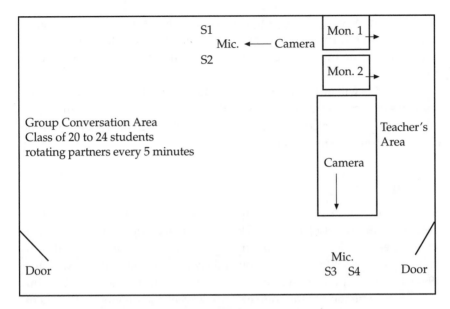

Fig. 11.1. VCSE equipment set up in a classroom

Instructional Materials

The equipment on video day consists of two video cameras that my colleagues and I use in specific ways. These cameras are lightweight Sony Hi8 Handycams that are attached to lightweight and portable tripods. Each camera is connected to two separate VHS players. Each pair of VHS players and a monitor are on a trolley so they can be moved to the appropriate classrooms on video day (see fig. 11.1). The equipment allows four students to be videotaped simultaneously in a 5-minute period; videotaping 22 students thus requires about 35 minutes. With changeover time included and a warm-up conversation at the beginning of class, 45 minutes is just about right. Currently, my colleagues and I are also experimenting with the option of storing the minimal necessary equipment (four VHS recorders, two Hi8 cameras with foldout monitors, and two microphones) in a large teacher's desk in one classroom. With this arrangement, setup time can be reduced from 15 to 3 minutes, and classes can rotate into the specially equipped room on prescheduled video days. Students buy their own VHS tapes, and teachers are able to reuse the same Hi8 tapes each time the course is offered or stockpile copies for research.

Conceptual Underpinnings

The background support for this local approach to teaching oral communication in Japan comes from a variety of areas: psychology, video use in therapy, the role of interaction in SLA, and classroom-based research on the importance of teaching for *fluency first*.

In psychology, Bandura's (1977) popular *Social Learning Theory* posits that most of our learning occurs as we observe "models." More recently it has been stressed that peers, compared with parents or teachers, are even more powerful models for learners (Harris 1995). I have discussed this concept as *"near peer" role-modeling* (Murphey 1998a): the modeling of peers who are close to the learner in age, ethnic origin, living situation, and proximity. Dowrick and Biggs (1983) suggest that choosing positive models to video and present to students has great promise for accelerating learning. Success has also been reported with *self-modeling* (Dowrick 1983), that is, recording subjects while they are engaged in desired behaviors and having them view these recordings repeatedly to reinforce constructive self-models. A VCSE approach incorporates both the viewing of peers and of self, which are usually positive and within the learner's capacity for replication and identification. While the use of video has already gained wide popularity among ELT enthusiasts as a medium for presenting language in context (i.e., listening comprehension or cultural learning) and as a starting point for different communicative activities, recordings of students using language for purposes of genuine communication have been less fully explored.

VCSE procedures are in line with four primary areas of contemporary SLA research. They encourage (1) a focus on form (Williams 1995), (2) input flooding (Trahey and White 1993), and (3) output flooding (Goto and Murphey 1997; Murphey 1998b) and more generally promote (4) collaborative dialogue (Swain 2000). These four areas suggest that repeated form-focused communicative interaction more efficiently enables the acquisition of targeted forms than would otherwise happen without such opportunities for interaction. In addition, as students are working together they are able to coconstruct meaningful interactions. Schmidt and Frota's (1986) seminal article on *noticing* and research in developing learners' metacognition—in other words, their ability to think about how they learn (Flavell 1979)—call for more involvement of the conscious mind in support of second language acquisition. When noticing and metacognition are encouraged during collaborative activities, there is even greater potential for learners to "push" one another's development as they interact within, and expand, one another's zone of proximal development (ZPD) (Murphey 2000b; Vygotsky [1934] 1962). With respect to language learning, the ZPD is that area in which language ability is constructed through negotiation with others. Learners operating within the same or proximate zones are more likely to be able to work together effectively as "near peer" role models (Murphey 1998a) as they display, try on, and borrow one another's attitudes, beliefs, and learning strategies. The degree of control that learners are able to exercise over the direction of their discourse opportunities is also important. Cathcart (1986) found that student-controlled discourse is characterized by a wide variety of communicative acts and syntactic structures, whereas teacher-controlled situations produced stilted language, single-word utterances, short phrases, and formulaic chunks.

VCSE procedures also find support in at least five of Kumaravadivelu's (1993) macrostrategies for L2 instruction. They allow teachers to (1) create a variety of learning opportunities in class, (2) utilize student learning opportunities and get students to create more of them, (3) facilitate interaction, (4) activate student metacognition, and (5) contextualize all input into short conversations repeated meaningfully with different partners many times.

Finally, MacGowan-Gilhooly (1991) describes a "fluency first" program of extensive interaction in which students

> become fluent in writing and reading before having to produce grammatically correct pieces or to comprehend academic material. . . . the quantitative and qualitative results of the several years of using the approach affirm its superiority over former traditional approaches. (1)

Similarly, a VCSE approach focuses on fluency first aspects of speaking and listening, involving great amounts of conversation with peers. By going for fluency first, much may be learned by default. For example, students can become more aware of particular points of grammar, vocabulary, and conversation strategies. Partially acquired forms develop cognitive depth through the many practice opportunities VCSE procedures make possible. Once students are conversing, it is easier to make adjustments (teachers do not have to guess as much), and learners are more motivated to fine-tune their production because they are able to relate their efforts to concrete experiences. To a great extent, second language learners gain confidence as conversationalists by participating in authentic conversations.

Objectives

The course engages students in intensive opportunities to interact with others via oral communication. Through VCSE procedures, all class members negotiate interaction (1) in extended discourse (usually in five-minute segments), (2) many times with different partners, and (3) within the same class period, and they (4) learn to feel in control and responsible for the quality of their efforts. As J. Murphy (1992, 1993) also points out, working with multiple partners over time helps to ensure that the recycling of topics and conversation strategies remains meaningful. Course structures serve to ensure that all students have a record of the work they have completed in class with their own VHS cassette copies to examine closely, evaluate, and learn from outside of class. The video recordings are generated on a weekly basis, so students are able to review and examine up to 10 conversations by the end of the semester in order to notice how much they have improved. Such procedures activate latent or untapped language and language abilities before, during, and after the students' video performances, thereby expanding their repertoire of linguistic capabilities. By the end of the course, successful students have acquired the skills and courage to initiate and continue conversations in English as well as to have an impact on another student's speech through shadowing and questioning techniques. In addition, they are less concerned with errors and more excited about interacting with other target language speakers.

Syllabus Design

My departmental colleagues and I have been applying and refining VCSE procedures over a six-year period. We are continually experimenting with different linguistic input, topics, and pedagogical procedures. The process of our exploration is shared openly with students, inspires what teachers and learners try to accomplish together in class, and, as much as possible, is negotiated between teacher and students. Teachers have access to student feedback through weekly action logs in which students provide formative evaluation of classroom activities. In the first two meetings of my own class each week, about half the time is spent presenting and practicing new target language material (e.g., specific conversation strategies, vocabulary, certain grammatical structures, etc.) within certain topic areas (sports, culture, music, language learning, etc.) to be used in the third meeting on video day. The rest of the time is filled with other teaching materials that carry less direct connections to students' video performances. Table 11.1 schematizes the VCSE process into three time periods along with the follow-up homework sessions, describes the respective activities in column 2, and lists theoretical correlates in column 3.

TABLE 11.1.   The Three Periods of the VCSE Process

Period	What's Taking Place	Theoretical Concepts
I. Prevideoing: class one	Teacher presents input/models. Students compare video transcriptions with previous partner. Students select items for use.	Socialization, negotiation/construction
II. Prevideoing: class two	Students practice noticing, awareness, and goal setting.	Learner training, facilitative anxiety
III. Video day: class three	Teacher records multiple performance events. Students talk to many partners and are videotaped with just one. Students notice and note items to learn from their partners.	Pushed output, collaborative learning, noticing, awareness, goal realization, recycling
IV. Postvideoing	As homework, students do multiple viewing and transcriptions of conversations. Do focused observations and feedback with forms or logs. Take partner's video home. Write self-progress report, review partner's progress, set goals for next time, compile a "noticing" list.	Learner autonomy, action research loop, expanding the ZPD, goal evaluation/setting, noticing, awareness, reflection

Activity Types

Given the cyclical nature of the procedures, each activity tends to feed into the next. For example, at the end of viewing and transcribing one video recording, the students make a list of things they notice and wish to change for the next video; these are practiced with new teacher input during the classroom conversations and targeted in their next recording. For discussion purposes we divide activities into three phases: *before videotaping, on video day,* and *after videotaping.*

Before Videotaping

In the two classes before videotaping, students are asked to target things they hope to do differently on the next video day and to use new target material or modeled input the teacher proposes. For example, one student's personal wish may be to smile and respond more quickly (things she perhaps *noticed* she was not doing in her most recent video and that her partner was doing). The new input may be *asking questions to get more details,* first modeled by the teacher and then presented in handouts. The student may practice these question types in several short conversations with different partners on the topic, for example, "What I did last weekend" in the first two days of the week's classes and again as telephone homework.

Students are also taught how to use self-talk to plan, practice, and rehearse conversations in their heads at any time (Manning and Payne 1996). During this phase, the students may be asked to list things they want to say. They might examine their list several times and begin practicing the items in order to get away from an overdependence on written notes.

On Video Day

On video day, students carry through with the culminating stage of their week's preparations by "performing" their conversation several times while learning to adjust what they have to say to different partners. They participate in conversations related to what they prepared and gain considerable practice in serving as good listeners. For example, as listeners they are taught to selectively and appropriately shadow (Murphey 2000b), that is, respond to, ask for details, and summarize the gist of what their partners have had to say. Previously, each of these strategies for active listening would have been a focus of direct instruction in the course. On video day students are asked to circulate with their notebooks and to write down the names of their conversation partners. Students also include in their notes any input from their partners that they would like to remember and/or might be interested in using themselves. Such input might include new vocabulary, less familiar language forms, interesting phrases, conversational strategies, and so on. At some point during the class, each person is called up along with a partner, and the two are video recorded having their five-minute conversation. Individual students may have practiced with others a few times before being videoed, and they may continue practicing a few more times after the recording is complete. Students learn and practice even when not being video recorded, but it is the video version of their conversation that will be analyzed at home. The video is a tangible record of their work and serves as a basis for forming future communication goals.

After Videotaping

In order to focus students on noticing even more, we have explored several ways for students to work with their video materials.

Evaluation forms. Students respond to a set of questions concerning their conversations: What did you notice that you said/did well? What mistakes did you make, and how would you correct them? What did your partner say that you might like to use? How about your partner's mistakes? What are your goals for next week's videotaping? [*editors' note:* cf. Janet Graham and Susan Barone, chap. 22 in this volume].

Transcriptions. Once students have generated an initial written transcription of what they said during a recorded conversation, they go back, relisten, and correct in the margin of their written versions as many of the mistakes they made while speaking as they are able to find.

Watching a partner's video. After a few weeks have passed (when students have recorded several conversations on their tapes), students exchange tapes with that day's partner and watch all of each other's recorded conversations (including the last one they just completed together). They are asked to notice things they might want to try using for themselves (e.g., strategies and language items) and to write short letters encouraging and giving advice to their partners. In this way, students have opportunities to see some conversations in which they are not involved and to analyze a peer's progress—both of which lead to increased self-awareness, autonomy, and metacognition.

End-of-term progress paper. At the end of a term, students are asked to watch all of their conversations once again and to write a paper comparing their first few and last few recordings. They are asked to comment on how they have progressed and in what ways they may need to progress even more.

Some of the advantages of the course's various viewing activities are the following: (1) students get to see some of their successful conversations repeatedly; (2) they develop strong images of successful experiences speaking English; (3) multiple viewings engender increased intrinsic motivation and excitement about participating in English conversations; and (4) positive images begin to supplant previous images of failures, or fears of failure, that may have dominated prior speaking experiences and even some of their initial VCSE experiences.

Learners' Roles

VCSE procedures encourage learners to switch from the role of "recipient of learning" to "creator" and "manager" of their own learning. The procedures involve a pattern of preparation, practice, performance, postviewing activities, planning, and goal setting. Thus, students are involved in VCSE procedures in a cyclical progression.

Teacher's Roles

With VCSE, teachers shift between more traditional roles of planner, syllabus organizer, and presenter of new information and the less traditional roles of observer, researcher, and coach. Planning and presenting weekly foci and organizing activities are stock functions of ELT classroom instruction. While a long-range top-down plan offers the advantage of a clear course focus, too detailed a syllabus can prevent adjusting to students' still emerging needs, interests, and ideas. On video day, however, the teacher's initial role is that of a technician. In the beginning, much of one's attention is given to the machines and making sure they are running well. As familiarity with the procedure is gained, increasing degrees of attention can be given to students.

Because teachers keep original copies of the video recordings (Hi8 tapes from the Handycams), they are able to view them and coach students individually with written comments. Teachers may also schedule counseling sessions and watch a taped conversation together with one or more student(s). If appropriate arrangements have been made for securing students' informed consent, a stockpile of VCSE recordings may serve as a basis for research. When teachers view VCSE recordings, they have a concrete record of students' performances in the course that may be used to examine the nature and quality of course instruction and learner progress over time. Thus, VCSE procedures provide a way for teachers to adjust their teaching to better address students' needs since a partial record of the course is available through the recordings. Students themselves can also become involved in participatory action research projects (see Gebhard and Oprandy 1999) if given appropriate support and opportunities to examine and reflect on their own experiences within the VCSE process.

Affective Concerns

For the first few weeks of the course, many students are uncomfortable and notice especially the silences and the robotic gestures and body postures, as well as their own and their classmates' lack of questions on the videos. After a few weeks, most students begin to find the videotaping fun and even rewarding. In their end-of-semester reports, students often comment on their gradually increasing abilities to fill silences, continue conversations, and notice pronunciation and grammatical problems. Numerous students have reported over the past six years that they are pleased with what they consider to be obvious improvements in their fluency. Many notice they have begun to use gestures, time, and pacing more effectively. They can express their feelings and are able to manage conversations more easily. Another recurring comment in their weekly action logs is that they feel better equipped to provide their conversation partners with appropriate support and assistance when needed.

Initially, one of their great fears is that the eyes of everyone in the class might be focused on them while they are speaking. Once VCSE is initiated, the relative privacy of the procedures goes a long way toward relaxing them, yet most students seem to retain enough positive tension (i.e., facilitative but not debilitative anxiety) to help them prepare for the videotaping event. The experience of seeing their progress convinces them they are improving and motivates them to want to improve more. Such experiences also validate the procedure: as one student recently noted, "Now, I have no hesitation to speak English in front of other people. This is the greatest thing for me through the videoing!"

When they witness through their video that indeed their goals are being attained, the "nothing succeeds like success" impact initiates an even greater push toward improved competence. Students wish overwhelmingly to continue with the procedure after a single semester, showing, contrary to Krashen 1998, that when comprehensible output is promoted in supportive ways it can become one of students' favored activities (see Dunn and Lantolf 1998; Murphey and Kenny 1998).

Perhaps it needs stressing that the technology and procedures work only as an extension and intensifier of good social relationships. It is important that feelings of trust are established during the first few weeks of the semester and maintained through continual rapport building between classmates and the teacher. Without a respectful, safe environment, the format of video recording may end up being too intimidating to be effective (Mendelsohn 1992). VCSE procedures, like other innovations and technologies (group work, project work, e-mail, etc.), depend primarily on healthy relationships in the course among everyone involved in the process. The method of assessment outlined subsequently goes a long way in helping to create constructive working relationships. It also promotes intrinsic motivation within learners.

Assessment

Students are continually being assessed throughout the semester through watching their videos, reading student-generated transcripts, and examining their action logs (for further discussion of student evaluations of class activities through action log procedures, see Murphey 1993). I give final grades based on students' self-evaluations of their own work, which are negotiated at a final interview with me. Assigning a final grade is a minor point; getting students to learn to assess themselves is the major goal. In this way, I am negotiating my role as teacher and allowing students to be involved in the assessment process. I believe consultations with students as part of the process of determining course grades increase intrinsic motivation. Regardless of how accurate their language is, I am convinced that the more they participate in well-structured conversations, the more they will learn. Thus, final grades in the course are dependent on the amount of effort learners put into the course, its structures and its procedures. Criteria for success are made clear during one of our earliest days of class since at that time I provide students with the form for summative evaluation. Some learners catch on right away and develop intrinsically rewarding behaviors. Others take more coaching. Rarely do students decline the invitation to play a part in the process of determining grades. Instructors have the freedom to create their own criteria for grading at the university where I teach (and probably at most universities in Japan). So far, students in VCSE course sections I offer have been making slightly more progress (although not significantly greater) on standardized tests than comparative groups of students being graded in more conventional ways.

Note, however, that *self-evaluation* in VCSE refers not to self-assigned grades but rather to the conscious act of examining one's performance as compared to (1) previous performances, (2) the performances of conversation partners, and (3) goals that are both predetermined and nascent. Thus, the procedure allows students to learn how to self-assess by using very specific, tangible data—their own recorded conversations—thus encouraging their autonomy and enhanced metacognition.

Assessment is normally in reference to student performance. However I provide students with opportunities to assess the procedures and technologies we are working with as well. For the most part, students have been extremely positive about learning through VCSE procedures. Since the course structures I am describing leave room to accommodate a variety of teaching styles and course foci, the procedures are popular with other teachers at our institution, as well. Qualitative data (student impressions of the benefits of the procedures and their increased fluency, comfort, and noticing) and quantitative data (words-per-minute rate increases, increases in strategy use, etc.) suggest that students benefit from VCSE through (1) repeated negotiated practice, (2) multiple opportunities for the "noticing" of learnable material (linguistic items, communication strategies, beliefs, attitudes, etc.) in their own and their classmates' output, and (3) control over the construction of extended discourse. Another benefit is (4) the increased desire to practice (Murphey and Kenny 1998).

Caveats/Final Thoughts

While teachers in other parts of the world may expect rather conservative educational styles in some Asian settings, many Asian institutions are open to innovation. By introducing innovations cautiously, in consultation with others, and with appropriate cultural sensitivity, much can be accomplished. Initially, VCSE procedures are costly. They assume that an administration is able to support the purchase, storage, and security of the equipment. Having a point person who is invested in the process and willing to work hard to ensure requisite levels of administrative support is essential.

Students also may show reluctance at first, some believing the common myths that they can only learn from their teacher, not their peers, and that it is wrong to make mistakes. In anticipation of such legitimate concerns, I provide readings (Murphey 1998b) in the course that contest some of these beliefs. Throughout the entire course, but especially early on, we talk openly about their reservations. Most objections are overcome within a few weeks as a new classroom culture forms with a new community of practice. During my years of teaching in Japan, I have noticed that having a foreign teacher in charge often leads Japanese students to accept and even anticipate less familiar styles of teaching. Even from the beginning of the course, they seem to expect something less conventional, and thus they may be more willing to try different things. I feel that because of this, non-Asian teachers in Japan may actually have more freedom to innovate than they might enjoy in their home countries.

Obviously, it is important to choose topics for conversation that are interesting (with student input and feedback) and to give students strategies that allow them to take control of the process and push themselves autonomously (e.g., to change the topic if it has become boring or explore new ways of presenting it). Opportunities for students to take control of their own learning are probably the most exciting spin-offs of a VCSE approach.[2]

Prompts for Discussion and Reflection

1. Discuss the time periods that VCSE activities are divided into. How many are there? How are they sequenced? For what purposes?

2. What do you think this teacher's students will be able to do by the end of the course as a result of having participated in it successfully? In what areas do you think they will still need additional work?

3. What are some of the concepts Murphey discusses that support the intensive student-student interactions described in his chapter? Compare Murphey's discussion, especially in the conceptual underpinnings section, with some of the general ELT principles shown in table 2.4 of chapter 2. Can you infer any connections between Murphey's ideas and the general principles listed in table 2.4 that might support Murphey's way of teaching oral communication in Japan?

4. How are the adages "participation precedes learning" and "we learn to speak by speaking" exemplified in the course and procedures Murphey describes?

5. What minimal technological hardware would one need to implement the procedures described in this chapter in a small class? In a larger class? Alternatively, how might Murphey structure such a course while targeting similar goals and purposes if video cameras and VHS machines were not available?

6. How might VCSE procedures be adapted for use in any of the following settings: a more advanced EFL course? International teaching assistant (ITA) training in the United States or Canada? A practicum course for preservice EFL teachers? Community-based ESL for residents of the United States, Canada, or Australia?

7. What additional forms of technology could be used to enhance VCSE procedures?

8. Discuss any aspects of VCSE procedures that encourage and inspire students to be more autonomous and metacognitive. Also discuss any aspects that might discourage them.

---

2. Thanks to Bill Acton, Pat Byrd, Brian Morgan, and John Murphy for feedback on previous drafts; and to Nanzan University for generous Pache I-A grants for several years to support this research.

Miniprojects

9. If you are studying in a TESL degree program, arrange for a student from another course to collaborate with you. Tell your partner that you will be asking her or him to work with you as part of your preparation for an upcoming class or exam. Decide upon two different topics from your respective courses you both consider to be important. Both of you need to prepare to explain your respective topics ahead of time. Secure your collaborator's permission to audio record your study session. Your partner needs to know that (*a*) you will be recording, (*b*) you will be playing the recording back after the explanation phase of your study session has ended, and (*c*) you will both have opportunities to talk about the experience. On the day you meet, record what happens and then listen to it together. Ask each other questions such as the following: How did knowing you were going to be recorded affect your preparation? How did listening to your presentation affect your self-image as a speaker? What was positive and what was negative about the experience? If we were to do it again, what aspects could we change to make the experience more beneficial? In private once you have completed this process, consider your own and your partner's experiences in light of Murphey's discussion of VCSE procedures. (Making arrangements to video record instead of audio record is an alternative way of working on this miniproject task.)

10. Develop a short presentation in a class you are teaching or taking. Plan to video record it and to try to make some sort of deliberate change that you think will help you get your message across to your audience (e.g., speak more slowly, gesture or smile appropriately, use the board or an overhead transparency in a certain way). Knowing that you will be videoed, notice how you might prepare differently. Keep a personal log of your feelings and impressions throughout the process. After the actual performance, view the video for certain things that you might learn from it. How did knowing that you would be videoed intensify your preparation and your performance? How did seeing it afterward affect you? Did it impact your idea of how you want to present next time?

Chapter 12

FocalSpeak: Integrating Rhythm and Stress in Speech-Pronunciation

William Acton

———

In addition to being a language teacher, Bill Acton is an accomplished dancer and dance instructor. As you will see in his discussion, he explores ways of linking his knowledge of the kinds of physical motions and sensory experiences implicit when one is dancing with the teaching of spoken English. Acton teaches university students in Japan. His semester-long course has two somewhat unorthodox features. First, he gives extensive attention to phrasal-, sentence-, and discourse-level stress placements, especially as such placements relate to students developing more native-like English rhythmic patterns in their speech. Second, Acton advocates the use of body movement (what he calls "speech synchronized gestures") to assist learners in developing firmer control over stress and rhythm features of spoken English. Early in the chapter, he posits a working definition of the concept of focal stress and builds a case for the systematic use of certain kinds of physical gestures to accompany focal stress locations. Acton suggests that English language learners should be assisted in consciously attending to appropriate stress placements whenever they are working with a fixed text (e.g., a new word, a phrase, a gambit, a sample of formulaic speech, a dialogue, a script, or an oral reading) as preparation for more extemporaneous speaking. He encourages teachers to explore ways of helping learners to figure out which word in a phrase or sentence would have the strongest stress (i.e., the greatest expenditure of acoustic energy) when produced by an English speaker. As Acton points out, listeners depend upon appropriate stress placements as key navigational guides while trying to understand other speakers of English. Whenever English language students are examining, analyzing, or practicing phrasal and sentence stress locations, Acton believes such activities should be accompanied by some kind of physical gesture to make both the stressed word and the most prominent syllable(s) within it kinesthetically more memorable to the learner. He concludes that systematic attention to focal stress coupled with speech synchronized gestures has real potential for the teaching of English speaking abilities.

———

Setting

Nagoya University of Commerce is a private business university of approximately 4,000 students. Its graduates often go to work for internationally oriented Japanese companies, where they are required to use English on a regular basis. For all students, spoken English competence is an indispensable asset in finding a job. Prior to coming to the university, students in the language program have studied English for up to seven years, beginning in middle school. Nevertheless, they seldom have attained an ACTFL speaking level beyond that of Novice-High. Typically, their speaking and listening skills lag considerably behind their English language abilities in reading, vocabulary, and grammar.

The overall curriculum is typical of Japanese higher education. For example, class sizes range between 30 and 50 students. The first- and second-year curricula consist of two semesters of general English study, with classes meeting a total of three hours per week and the possibility of up to six additional contact hours of electives each semester. This chapter describes a semester-long course titled Integrating English Skills (IES), which meets for 15 classes, each 90 minutes long. IES is one of about 24 courses required of students whose secondary concentration of study is English. In this course, third-year students work to develop an effective, functional command of the rhythm and process of English conversation. The key pedagogical tools of the course are as follows.

1. *Focal stress* (sometimes called *nuclear stress*). This tool involves extensive work with stress, rhythm, and intonation as signals that native English speakers use to direct and guide their listeners' attention (Levis 1999, 39).
2. *Directed physical motion.* A tool involving physical movements of the body (e.g., arms, shoulders, hands, torso) leading to speech synchronized gestures.

The emphasis of both these tools is on performing effectively in conversation, with acceptable discourse-level speech-pronunciation (rhythm, stress, and intonation).

Conceptual Underpinnings

The design of IES centers around two basic principles. The first is systematic attention to focal stress at clausal-phrasal, sentence, intersentential, and even broader levels of oral discourse. For the purposes of the course,

Focal stress practice // has made me sound // almost like a native speaker.

Fig. 12.1. Underlining to signal focal stress locations

attention to focal stress is essential to efficient development of spontaneous speaking abilities. The second principle is the use of kinesthetic (body motion) instructional procedures to teach Japanese learners to better integrate focal stress–based rhythms into their spoken English.

The term used here, *focal stress,* is one of several used by theorists and methodologists to describe the process by which native speakers of English emphasize and group words together in speaking, creating what are known alternatively as rhythm groups, thought groups, breath groups, or production groups (Gilbert 1994; Wong 1987). I will use the term *production group* for the remainder of the chapter. In the *FocalSpeak* system, the emphasis is on attending to the most strongly stressed (focal) word in a production group. For example, in the sentence shown in figure 12.1 the three underlined words (one in each production group) could be emphasized by the native speaker of English.

The double underlined word, speaker, signals the "sentence stress," or the most salient stressed word in the sentence overall. The other two single underlined words are most strongly stressed in each of their respective production groups. The concept of focal stress includes both types of stress assignment.

Course features that center on focal stress bring the learners' attention to the single word in the production group with the highest relevance. In so doing, the instructional plan is to move learners away from the word-by-word- or syllable-by-syllable-based speaking style typical of many Japanese learners of English. Concentrating on focal stressed words also brings together (1) the higher level, discourse functions of foregrounding and backgrounding (i.e., new or "given" information tends to be foregrounded, while old or "previously established" information tends to be backgrounded in spoken English) with (2) phrasal- and sentence-level stress and rhythm (i.e., suprasegmental features). The IES course calls to learners' attention the more manageable task of consciously emphasizing only the important, and more salient, focal stressed words first through controlled, then through guided, and ultimately through more spontaneous conversation practice opportunities.

At this time in the development of second language pedagogy, we do not have unequivocal empirical support for the general effectiveness of kinesthetic (motion-centered) approaches in pronunciation instruction. Support for movement-based approaches is still somewhat indirect and inferential. Along with other specialists, Bolinger (1983, 1986) and Lessac (1967) indicate the importance and efficacy of kinesthetic learning and intelligence. However, teaching materials, teacher resource materials, and contemporary practices in the teaching of pronunciation give significant attention to the role of kinesthetic, motion-driven stress and rhythm training for purposes of enhancing the intelligibility of learner speech (Celce-Murcia, Brinton, and Goodwin 1996; Gilbert 1994, 1995; Murphy 1996b; Wong 1987).

In pronunciation teaching, evidence is growing that physical involvement on the part of the learner and body motions (e.g., hand gestures, rhythmic clapping, simple dance steps) coordinated with rhythmic speech patterns facilitate learning (e.g., Acton 1997, 1984; Asher 1996; Celce-Murcia, Brinton, and Goodwin 1996; Chela-Flores 1998). Virtually every methods book and instructor's manual for teaching speech-pronunciation contain suggestions and directions for illustrating rhythmic patterning by coordinating body motion and movements of objects in the classroom. Few, however, go very far in treating ways of coordinating such procedures systematically (cf. Asher 1996; Celce-Murcia, Brinton, and Goodwin 1996). Acton (1984) describes a relatively controlled practice activity of this kind. The activity engages learners in simultaneously analyzing written transcripts and practicing speech-pronunciation tied to audio recordings of native English speech samples. As learners listen to the recordings, they also read along with the transcriptions. At later stages, once they know the material, learners begin to audiotape their own versions of the transcribed speech samples, using speech synchronized gestures as they speak. Among a set of other procedures, I suggest one way of incorporating kinesthetic teaching procedures when working with such material.

> In preparing [a] text to be read on tape, it is parsed into rhythm groups at constituent boundaries. The major constituents are then tied into, or associated with, the upper-body rhythms and facial expressions that are appropriate for the texts (that is, learners must "move" their bodies in accordance with the rhythm groups). The specific non-verbal movements focused on include, but are not limited to, those discussed by Bolinger (1983), who examines [body motion] gestures that may accompany certain intonation contours (e.g., head motions, body and hand movements). [In the speech-pronunciation class] students learn

to move their upper bodies in a gentle, unobtrusive rocking motion, coordinating that movement with sentence stress and contrastive stress. One intriguing feature of this technique is that it then makes perfect sense to ask a student to repeat an utterance or phrase silently so the instructor can [visually] check on the rhythm and stress. As the course progresses, the rocking motion becomes virtually imperceptible to the naive observer. (Acton 1984, 79)

The FocalSpeak process described in this chapter reflects an attempt to create a bridge between treatment of speech rhythm in isolation, the usual practice in pronunciation instruction, and spontaneous, more natural uses of rhythm during conversational interactions. In FocalSpeak instruction, conscious attention to rhythm and stress placement in English is tied to extensive, consistent involvement of the body and coordinated motions for purposes of identifying and producing appropriate rhythm.

Objectives

The general goals of the IES course are as follows: (1) to teach students how to speak with more native-like English rhythm in conversation, (2) to fill in some of the gaps in students' inventories of everyday conversational strategies and vocabulary, (3) to provide students with contemporary topics and vocabulary for conversation, and (4) to teach students how to be relaxed and confident in conversation.

The Japanese language manifests a more syllable-based (mora-based) rhythmic phonological structure than English. The Japanese speakers of English in my classes almost invariably impose syllable-based rhythms when speaking in English. English spoken in this Japanese-influenced way tends to result in a staccato-like, syllable-by-syllable delivery. The same speech features tend to be carried over to higher levels of proficiency as well. For Japanese learners to become more intelligible English speakers calls for learners' increased involvement with stress timing and English-like parsing of rhythm groups in spontaneous speech (Acton 1997). For example, when the sentence featured in figure 12.1 is produced by a Japanese speaker of English with little or no understanding of focal stress, it may sound something like the following (somewhat exaggerated here), where the speaker is stressing each word or underlined part of a word (syllable) equally.

Fo-ca-lu su-to-re-ssu pu-ra-ku-ti-su ha-zu may-do me so-un-do . . .

The perception of the native English speaker/listener would probably be that all elements of the sentence have nearly equal salience. In part due to the L2 learner's syllable-timed delivery, too many full vowels are appearing, and too few reduced vowels are used. In contrast to what are probably the learner's intentions, the speaker is actually overenunciating the vowel system of English. Such speech features can seriously interfere with speech intelligibility. The speaker's overuse of full vowels, for example, actually distracts the native English listener from being able to make sense of the speaker's intended message. Of course, such phenomena are not limited to Japanese learners of English. Chela-Flores (1998) discusses parallel phenomena in her work with first language speakers of Spanish learning English. Similar intelligibility issues arise in the styles of English spoken by learners from other syllable-timed languages as well (e.g., French, Italian, and many African languages).

To summarize, work on focal stress brings a learner's attention to word(s) in a production group that should be most salient to a listener's ear, as opposed to a word-by-word- or syllable-by-syllable-based speaking style typical of beginning level Japanese learners of English. Concentrating on focal stressed words also brings together the higher level discourse functions of foregrounding and backgrounding with phrasal- and sentence-level stress and rhythm, so that in spontaneous speech the learner has a more manageable task of consciously emphasizing only the relatively more important focal stressed words of conversation.

The basic design of the approach I use in IES centers around weekly lessons involving three components: (1) presentation of relevant lexical sets and model conversations, (2) development of focal stress skills, and (3) pair and group practice integrating (1) and (2). By the end of the course, successful students are prepared to participate in everyday business-oriented conversations using reasonably appropriate focal stress (and rhythm) conversational strategies and vocabulary.

Syllabus Design

The class consists of one 90-minute session per week for the 15-week semester with two of these sessions used for the required midsemester and final examinations. Thus, allowing for the introductory class, there are actually 12 working lessons of 90 minutes each. Generally, each of the 12 lessons is structured as follows.

1. Beginning and ending management functions, roll-taking, returning or setting up homework assignments, socializing, and so on (10 minutes)
2. Preparation for work of the day, often modeling focal stress tasks to be practiced; some brief work on problematic sounds (about 20 minutes)

3. Group-based conversation work, based on exercises and problem solving from the textbook (about 50 minutes)—key conversational strategies, phrases, and expressions. In this last segment, the focal stress work is integrated with general conversation activities.

Two basic components of every lesson are (1) kinesthetic anchoring and (2) speech synchronized gesture (hereafter SSG) practice. In kinesthetic anchoring, students practice using a motion of some kind as a memory aid to help later recall of a lexical item, phrase, short sentence, or process. In SSG work, students practice using gesture as simple accompaniment to connected speech rhythms that extend to broader stretches of discourse. Along with the assignment of focal stress, by midsemester, students will have learned to apply some type of kinesthetic anchoring to each focal stress location.

While kinesthetic anchoring can be done in many ways, perhaps the simplest technique (although not the most effective in that it generally fails to engage the torso) is to have students tap their fingers on their desks as they speak focal stressed words. Child learners of English as a first language do this kind of thing all the time. Think of the kinesthetic involvements of our hands and our whole bodies when partners play games based on stress timing and rhythm such as "patty-cake, patty-cake" while alternately clapping our palms, thighs, and so forth, within a repeated cycle, all while reciting the familiar rhyme. Another example is the engagement of our whole bodies while skipping rope and simultaneously reciting rhythms that echo the patterned motions of our legs, torso, arms, and feet. Similarly in kinesthetic anchoring, the key idea is to engage the body (and especially the torso) in marking and remembering words, rhythms, and locations of stress. By the end of the course, when students are attempting to use focal stress in spontaneous speech, the motion-anchored practice should at least be evident in upper torso motion.

The crucial kinesthetic features of the course are incorporated into the syllabus as part of a gradual process of training learners in focal stress placement and SSG. The gradual process can be characterized in five somewhat overlapping, and not mutually exclusive, stages arranged from more controlled, to guided, to extemporaneous practice.

1. Satisfactorily identifying focal stress locations in dictations and transcribed natural conversations while listening to native-style speech being produced either live by their teacher or via recordings of others' voices [*editors' note:* controlled practice]
2. Selecting appropriate focal stress locations in prepared texts without

hearing a spoken rendition [*editors' note:* guided practice; some elements of discourse analysis]

3. Actively using focal stress techniques in giving prepared oral readings and rehearsed practice of textbook dialogues, for example, and using accompanying SSG on each focal stress (see the preceding quoted material from Acton 1984)

4. Demonstrating acceptable focal stress patterning while reading (unprepared) an everyday language dialogue, [*editors' note:* guided, though a step closer to extemporaneous practice]

5. Using focal stress in simple, relatively spontaneous speech conversations with classmates (extemporaneous practice)

Another component of the syllabus consists of creating and maintaining an effective group process. Especially in the relatively large classes I teach, cooperative-style learning in small groups allows students to assist each other in working on integration of conversation with attention to the rhythmic patterning of English. The sequence of activities based on textbook materials, songs, and general class discussions gradually draws learners into more and more complex "rhythmic" conversations.

Activity Types

About 60 percent of class time is spent in active speaking practice. Several activities are incorporated within any given lesson. One of the first activities we do in the first five weeks of the course is called the "Syllablettes chorus line." Students are introduced to fundamentals of rhythm, stress, and intonation using Syllablettes procedures (Acton 1998), which later are used for developing better control of the expressive qualities of selected phrases or sentences. A feature of this activity is that individual students are assigned responsibilities for acting out the volume, length, and pitch (and possibly vowel clarity) for each of the individual syllables in a multisyllabic word or phrase. For example, five students are needed to illustrate through Syllablette procedures the rhythmic structure of a five-syllable word. Though I will attempt a prose description and discussion of Syllablette procedures here, the process is easier to introduce experientially (and kinesthetically) live in a classroom, in a teacher-training workshop, or from a video recording.

First, a small group of students gathers together at the front of the room or in some other conspicuous location. If a five-syllable word or phrase is targeted, then the group is comprised of five members of the class. While consulting with each other as a group, they quickly do the following.

Analyze the targeted word (phrase or sentence)

Decide upon its appropriate focal stress location

Divide up their roles in the group by assigning individual syllables
  to each member of the group

Identify any secondary stress or reduced vowel locations

Figure out specific sound components of their own individual
  syllables

Determine and agree upon an appropriate volume level for each
  syllable

Arrange themselves in the appropriate and agreed upon syllable
  sequence (i.e., they form a line in sequence with members of the
  group positioned side by side)

Following their rapid group consultations, they are now ready to proceed with their illustration of how an accurate enunciation of the word (phrase or sentence) would look. From a neutral starting position, and as part of the team representing the multisyllable word (phrase or sentence), each student acts the role of a single syllable by simultaneously

1. raising or lowering her or his body vertically to the appropriate pitch level (e.g., by standing straight up, stooping just slightly, squatting half-way or even closer to the floor),
2. moving either closer to or farther away from the adjacent Syllablettes in order to illustrate vowel length (i.e., corresponding distances between syllables), and
3. saying her or his syllable at the right moment at the agreed upon volume and in the appropriate sequence.

The effect simulates a snapshot of a chorus line of dancers captured in midair, but in this case the members of the group have choreographed a visual depiction of the rhythmic structure of an English word (phrase or sentence). In figure 12.2, from Acton 1998, you see the starting position (3) and the two higher and two lower positions (representing higher and lower pitch) in which a "syllable" may be produced in English.

For example, to produce a five-syllable sentence such as "How are you today?" where the word *you* is the focal word, students first all assume Syllablette position three. As they say their syllables, one at a time, they move to their own relatively higher or lower vertical positions. The Syllablettes effect is along the lines of how spectators form a "wave" at sporting events in North America. Other intonation and stress patterns are, of

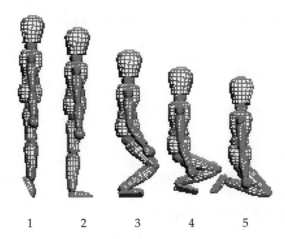

Fig. 12.2.   The five Syllablette positions/postures

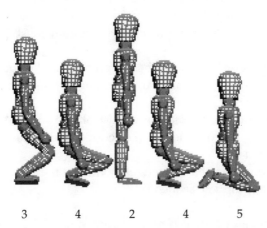

Fig. 12.3.   Five Syllablette positions/postures for the sentence
How are you today?

course, possible, but the one presented in figure 12.3 is probably the "expected" contour.

Note that there is more physical space between *you* and *today* because *you* is stressed and, consequently, the vowel is of considerably longer temporal duration. The students performing the roles of the third and fourth syllables (i.e., the *you* and the *to-* of *today*) leave more space between them to represent the lengthened, and more clearly enunciated, stressed vowel of *you*. With a little imagination it is equally straightforward for Syllablettes to represent other phonological processes such as linking, vowel reduction, and assimilation. To illustrate linking patterns, learners could, if culturally appropriate, link elbows. In Japan, where such public touching by "strangers" is not generally acceptable, I use two-foot loops of rope that learners link up when necessary. Syllablettes with reduced vowels can position themselves in vertical positions very low to the floor. Later on while working in groups, students are also asked to illustrate through written formats the volume, length, and pitch of phrases prior to carrying out almost any speaking or conversation exercise. Similar written tasks are incorporated into weekly quiz materials as well as into midsemester and final examinations.

Through such procedures, from the beginning of the course students' attention is drawn to the importance of information backgrounding and foregrounding based on stress, rhythm, and intonation. Celce-Murcia, Brinton, and Goodwin (1996) illustrate ways in which these essential features of spoken English are handled by native speakers at levels of interactive discourse. These authors state that

> the discourse context generally influences which stressed word in a given utterance receives prominence—that is, which word the speaker wishes to highlight. . . . the speaker places prominence [or, what I am referring to as focal stress in this chapter] on new information. . . . Allen (1971, p. 77) provides an excellent example of how prominence marks new versus old information; she uses capital letters to signal new information (strong stress and high pitch):
>
> X: I've lost an um*BREL*la.
> Y: A *LA*dy's umbrella?
> X: Yes. A lady's umbrella with *STARS* on it. *GREEN* stars.
>
> In this example, *umbrella* functions as new information in X's first utterance. However, in Y's reply, *lady's* receives prominence because it is the new information. In X's second utterance, both *umbrella* and *lady's* are old information, whereas *stars* and *green* are new information, thus receiving prominence. (176–77)

Similarly, Levis (1999) provides a four-line dialogue, a compilation of several dialogues created by ESL learners in his class (J. Levis, personal communication May 19, 2000), to show that "old" versus "new" focal stress locations can be made less ambiguous and are more clearly perceptible to learners through discourse-level illustrations that capture intersentential ties. Notice, especially, the dialogue's final line.

A: May I help you?

B: Yeah . . . I'd like a *LARGE* pepperoni, an order of bread sticks, and three large cokes.

A: OK, that's a *LARGE* pepperoni, an order of bread sticks, and three large cokes. Will there be anything else?

B: No, thanks. Wait a minute, you'd better make that a *MEDium* pepperoni pizza. (55)

Levis suggests that when learners are asked to create such dialogues, it is valuable to them since they have to construct the dialogue by applying "old" versus "new" concepts and it is valuable to their teacher, who may make the mistake of assuming that the whole system is rather transparent. In the IES course, focal stress becomes the central conceptual device for classroom practice and for working on integration of stress and rhythm into spontaneous speech. After students have become accustomed to doing "focal stress dictations," where they circle focal stress locations as they listen to spoken texts of various types, they begin to practice assigning focal stress (e.g., circling such words) in printed texts. Wong (1987) recommends using dialogue excerpts from well-known plays as effective resources for working on rhythm, stress, and intonation in context.

> Rehearsing and performing excerpts from carefully selected dramatic works is another way to review rhythm and intonation and to develop the students' sense of how these features are exploited to communicate meaning. . . . Find scenes that involve two characters that the students would not be embarrassed to play. The dialogue for each character should be balanced, so that one character is not doing all the talking. (75)

As far as finding excerpts from interesting dramatic works, I find edited collections featuring brief scenes for student actors, as are commonly used in university-level acting classes such as Handman (1978) and Schulman and Mekler (1984), especially helpful. Murphy (1996b) illustrates ways of working with excerpts from Neil Simon's *The Odd Couple* for purposes of teaching focal stress features similar to ones I highlight in the IES course. To give students some guidance on deciding where focal stress might be most appropriate, I suggest following guidelines and principles.

1. Usually there can be only a maximum of five or six words between focal stresses. This characteristic of spoken English limits the number of words spoken in one rhythmic "bunch" to something most beginners can handle in oral production. Of course, it is certainly possible that every word in

a short sentence be emphasized, as well. Wong (1987) gives the example of an astronaut exclaiming excitedly through his microphone about a satellite he had just repaired, *"There that bad boy goes!"* (22).

2. Usually there is a pause after each focal stress, although focal stresses generally come at or very near phrase or sentence boundaries, . . .

Ask <u>not</u> what your country can do for <u>you</u>, ask what <u>you</u> can do for your <u>country.</u>
   (A)   (B)   (C)   (D)
                                         —J. F. Kennedy

. . . occasionally there may be three or four words following a focal stress (compare locations (A) and (B) with locations (C) and (D) above).
3. Usually there will be a focal stress before ALL punctuation.
4. In linguistically unmarked utterances, focal stress tends to fall on content words, but in conversation it may sometimes fall on structure words. Levis (1999) uses the fifth line of the following five-line dialogue to illustrate an instance of focal stress on a structure word.

A: Hey, did you know that George is moving to Toronto?
B: No way! He just bought a house here.
A: He told me this morning that he was going next month.
B: Is this an April Fool's joke or something? He isn't moving next month.
A: Why don't you believe me? George *IS* moving to Toronto next month. (54)

5. Usually, the more focal stress, the more emotional the speaking style.

For L2 learners of English who have yet to develop adequate control of focal stress features, longer stretches of their speech can become difficult for L1 listeners to follow, especially if spoken rapidly.

Along with focal stress assignment, by midsemester, many classroom tasks feature extensive links to speech synchronized gesture. In other words, for every focal stress assigned, there will also be an SSG (e.g., a hand movement, head nodding, or toe tapping) at that same location in the sentence or phrase. We always use such gestures when practicing or rehearsing a written dialogue or conversation. SSGs are useful for getting a feel for a set of new phrases or expressions that will be used more actively in a later task, such as a role play or dramatization. During the 50-minute (approximate) segment of each class devoted to other types of oral communication opportunities, a range of more typical conversation teaching activities is employed. Most of these activities are based on the material in the textbook: pair work, information gap exercises, jazz chants, songs, role plays, interviews, oral readings, games of various kinds. Because students aspire to work in business settings, they are required to produce a final course project that involves writing, rehearsing, and recording an extended simulated interview with a prospective employer from an internationally oriented company. In the performance and scripting of the project, focal stress identification, analysis, and rehearsal figure prominently.

Learner Roles

It is critical for their success in the course that students assume at least three roles: (1) group members, (2) risk takers, and (3) guessers. Almost everything in the IES course, including most testing procedures, is done in groups. Exercises are carried out in pairs, if not in larger groups. Much of the group work is framed in cooperative group practice. Students are assigned a group and responsibilities within the group.

Using group work activities for English language teaching in Japan creates both advantages and challenges. University-level Japanese students do many things very well in groups. Once a learning task is decided and defined, they are unbeatable, but arriving at a clear plan and delegating responsibilities can be a long and tedious process. During the initial weeks of the course it is very important to take the time necessary to introduce students to both procedures and rationale for group work. Initial training in group work constitutes an essential phase of my teaching in Japan. In IES it takes careful planning, modeling, patience, and clear explanations.

For students to develop good conversational skills, they must learn how to behave appropriately in what I deliberately set up as a Western-style, student-centered classroom. Gradually as the course unfolds, tasks are assigned that provide incrementally more risk-taking opportunities. For example, learners gain practice in asking questions and providing their own opinions in ways sometimes antithetical to many of the schooling and socialization experiences in Japan. Especially at the start of the course, the Japanese learners I work with often find it difficult to act independently of the group.

Several aspects of the course require students to make guesses or independent judgments. For instance, the process of assigning focal stress to a prepared text is fraught with potential disagreements between partners, where sometimes more than one assignment of focal stress is perfectly acceptable. Eventually, students learn to trust their own intuitions and realize that their own focal stress "sculpting" of a sentence or broader stretch of discourse is probably just as good as any alternative being proposed by another student. With experience, learners understand that focal stress locations are flexible, subtle, and contingent upon the meanings a speaker is trying to convey.

Teacher Roles

My three key roles are probably authority, manager, and resource. The first role comes with the cultural territory. The experience of being an instructor in Japan (in my case for about 10 years) is, for many non-Asian teachers, a constant process of seeking balance between function and structure. The apparent luxury of having students who will do almost anything asked of them is mediated by the realization that, unless trained otherwise, they generally will do only what is specifically requested. Leading Japanese students into domains of autonomy and self-directed learning, where self-reliance is the objective, takes careful planning and tact. In a collectivist culture such as Japan, developing independent thinking and initiative in the classroom presents special challenges for the teacher and the students.

While in the class, I also see myself as a facilitator who is managing and providing learning opportunities. From the beginning to the end of lessons, I am moving around the classroom, sometimes taking the role of student, sometimes helping or clarifying, sometimes cajoling, and at other times consoling. My aim is to provide an environment where learners have almost no choice but to succumb, learn, and enjoy themselves. I try to accomplish this by attending to lighting, seating, background music, pacing, task transparency, agenda presentation, personal demeanor, and small group composition.

Inherent in the role of "roving manager" is the notion that I am also a ready resource for language input, linguistic rules, and, especially, considerations of focal stress assignment and SSG use. I never lecture. In addition to the text or materials, I usually carry a pen-size laser pointer and a wireless microphone. With the large class sizes, correspondingly large rooms, and the general cacophony of ongoing group work, being able at any time and from any location to talk to the class or point to the overhead projector screen is very effective (see further discussion in the instructional materials section).

I am required by the university to have two 70-minute examinations each semester. For each of the tests students are evaluated based on the following: (1) listening for focal stress, (2) assigning focal stress to written texts, and (3) functional conversational material from the textbook (using various modes). The two exams account for 50 percent of a student's grade. The remaining 50 percent is based on several additional tasks such as short speeches or conversations, final project, homework reports, Syllablettes exercises, daily quizzes, attendance/effort, and student self-evaluation.

Instructional Materials

The weekly lessons can use almost any good lower intermediate level student conversation text as the point of departure. A word of caution is in order, however. My review of sets of audio recordings provided by ELT publishers has shown that many are lacking appropriate focal stress features. Unless recorded dialogues, simulated interviews, scripted materials, and other speech samples are produced appropriately, they are not helpful for purposes of illustrating focal stress patterns. In many cases it is obvious that the actors/voices on the recording were given little guidance as to focal stress locations, resulting in unnatural emphasis patterns. I always take the time to preview such materials to see how focal stress is realized prior to making a decision to use a particular book, or book segment, in the IES course. Since the students will probably pursue careers in business, my choice of books is geared in that content direction. Some particularly interesting ESL speech-pronunciation textbooks from which I draw ideas and inspiration include Dauer (1993), Grant (1993), Hahn and Dickerson (1999), Hewings and Goldstein (1998), Gilbert (1994), and Miller (2000).

Although certainly not essential to a FocalSpeak approach, the classrooms in which I prefer to teach are equipped with a ceiling to floor projection display screen. For example, when considering alternative, acceptable focal stress assignments, it is most helpful to be able to quickly change on the screen the underlining, circling, boxes, or text positioning features I use to indicate focal stress. Use of laser pointers, along with wireless microphones, allows me to be heard and direct attention to the screen from any location in the room. Wireless microphones are always helpful in large classes, where the noise of group work can be difficult to talk over, and when clarity of the instructor's voice model is especially important. When students must both listen for focal stress (in the voice of the model) and watch for focal stress (in the speech synchronized gesture of the model or instructor), the ability to amplify the voice to appropriate levels is quite beneficial.

Lesson Particulars

In the following lesson segment, students are preparing for a party. Their first task is to discuss what they will need to buy. The basic open-ended exercise begins with the following lines, which they are later expected to expand into a full conversation.

"I have to go to Circle K // and the flower shop // before the game begins."
"Yeah! // It's three //-thirty // already!"
"Let's see. // We need . . . "

First the students decide where focal stress would be, based on the guidelines described earlier. Since there are 15 words in that first sentence, they know that they have to break it up into at least three groups with a focal stress in each. In the second sentence, the speaker appears excited, so there are perhaps four focal stress words. Note that, although I have marked each rhythmic break with "//," when students are ready I begin to withdraw such scaffolding.

Next, they decide upon SSGs, such as a head nod, upper torso nod, hand movement, arm movement, or pencil movement to accompany each focal stress. Again, any speech synchronized physical gesture is OK as long as it engages the torso, although by the end of the course students' gestures should become more and more subtle, well timed, and less and less overt. Once this phase of the task is completed, they practice the opening frame and then work through the party planning, while integrating motion and focal stress with each succeeding response or question. The assignment is for everyone to do the exercise twice, the second time with a different partner.

While walking around the groups during the exercise, I always look for a speaker's emotional investment in a line being delivered. That investment is evident in both the tone of voice and the character of the physical movement involved. I may ask that the line or phrase be done again for me, perhaps changing to a different SSG or changing the speed or size or direction of the gesture the student had originally chosen. The emotional content of a phrase, for example, in the second sentence in the preceding dialogue, "Yeah! // It's three //-thirty // already!" can be easily amplified or substituted by concentrating on the SSG/focal stress as the carrier or focus of the energy being expended. It is worth mentioning that focal stress mistakes or inconsistencies are less problematic than speech with little or no instances of focal stress in the first place. The aim is not to teach students the proper SSG or focal stress of every sentence or context in English. Equipped with the background of controlled, guided, and extemporaneous practice opportunities I provide in the IES course, learners are well positioned to continue developing an internal sense of what English focal stress and rhythm feel like. It is the essence of English kinesthetic stress timing.

Caveats

I recognize that I teach in somewhat unconventional ways, especially given the particular setting of my work (a Japanese university). There are several features of the course and its content that seem to contribute to its being well received by students.

1. *The curriculum.* There has been one instructor who teaches a beginning course, one generally taken before the FocalSpeak course I offer, who is also enthusiastic about suprasegmentals (rhythm, stress, and intonation). When students who have completed her class begin IES units on Focal-Speak, they have an advantage because the concepts I introduce are already somewhat familiar to them.
2. *The classroom management system.* Having taught IES many times, I have developed a good system for facilitating group work and task completion. Time is rarely wasted, and students are accountable for what they accomplish. The system easily incorporates and controls group work in connection with controlled, guided, and extemporaneous speech practice; the Syllablettes chorus line; focal stress exercises; and the other classroom procedures described previously.
3. *Singing.* When possible, singing is introduced into classroom lessons using focal stress preparation techniques similar to the ones described earlier. To complement or even replace one of the exercises from our course text, I may substitute a song, usually a blues or popular folk song.

The course is a very comfortable, and yet challenging, one for me to teach. When planning lessons, I need only think about the choice of course parameter, concept, sample of discourse, or learning activity. Near the beginning of lessons, and often during other lesson segments as opportunities arise, I may choose to shift or experiment with one of those choices, but my approach to the course has been relatively stable over the past several years. Finally, the process of describing the particulars of IES has revitalized my personal investment not only in FocalSpeak instruction but in teaching in other settings as well.

Prompts for Discussion and Reflection

1. Why might focal stress work be especially important in helping Japanese learners with English rhythm? Are there other groups of learners who might benefit from work in English rhythm? What are some of the characteristic features of spoken English that attending to focal stress addresses?

2. Discuss ways in which you can envision introducing focal stress rules or common patterns to English language learners. If you are aware of any such rules or patterns, what concepts might learners have to be aware of before you would be able to introduce them in a classroom setting? Where would you begin?

3. What are some of the ways in which Acton's efforts attempt to bridge the gap between direct and indirect approaches to teaching discourse-level stress?

4. Why would a group-based methodology probably be more effective within the instructional context Acton describes? Alternatively, what complications might you anticipate and why?

5. Beyond the format for depicting focal stress locations that Acton discusses in the section on conceptual underpinnings, what other visual marking system(s) for signaling focal stress placements might you find more appropriate in your own teaching? Why?

6. Working comfortably with physical movement and "speech synchronized gestures" in language teaching probably requires a moderately "unbuttoned" personality on the part of the teacher. What are some of the physical gestures Acton mentions? What other gesture types could you envision a teacher introducing? How would attention to "speech synchronized gestures" fit within your own teaching persona?

7. What technologies do you think would have to be in place in order to incorporate focal stress work in language teaching? What forms of technology are available in programs where you teach (or in programs with which you are familiar)? How might these forms of support be used to further enhance focal stress work either within or beyond classroom settings?

8. One of the potential drawbacks to Acton's ideas is that it may take a good deal of time to introduce the underlying concepts, model them, and begin to engage learners in focal stress work before any real payoff becomes evident. Discuss how much time it might take to introduce

Acton's suggested procedures and whether or not you would be able to justify the amount of learner training necessary in your situation.

9. Discuss ways in which Acton's work as described in this chapter may compare with other specialists' ways of teaching speech-pronunciation in ELT.

10. How, if at all, does this framework for focal stress work relate to any other approaches to teaching with which you are familiar (e.g., Total Physical Response, the Rassias Method) or to other approaches you may know about?

11. How might the FocalSpeak framework be of benefit to students in learning how to be more effective speakers and conversationalists in English? What is missing? How might you compensate for features you view as missing?

Miniprojects

12. In the section on activity types, review Acton's description of Syllablette procedures. Get a group of four or five other people to join you and explain to them Acton's idea for Syllablette procedures. Then, take a multisyllabic word such as *communicative* or *communication* and see if your group can figure out how to model the word through a "Syllablette chorus line." Once everyone has agreed upon and has a role as an individual "syllable" for one of these words worked out, start from a neutral position and at your signal get everyone to shift simultaneously to their respective positions. When you feel ready to do so, try some other words such as *enthusiastic, pedagogical,* or *innovative.* In addition to modeling multisyllabic words, do the same with brief phrases and sentences such as "Look at the time," "How are you feeling?" or "This is incredible!" Alternatively, if you have as many as a dozen collaborators try whole sentences such as "Working with focal stress can be exciting!" "Language teachers sometimes really are amusing!" or "Teaching a second language can be fun." Work with well-known lines from movies such as Clint Eastwood's "Make my day"; Humphry Bogart's "Here's looking at you, kid"; Robert De Niro's "Are *you* talking to *me*"; or Judy Garland's "There's no place like home." Go on to generate your own listing of multisyllabic words, phrases, and sentences that your group can illustrate through Syllablette procedures.

13. Take a conversation, script, or longer stretch of discourse from an ELT student textbook. Using the FocalSpeak conventions, identify what you perceive to be some of the more obvious locations of focal stress. After working your way through at least eight or nine lines, what

problems do you encounter? As your efforts continue, are some of these problems resolved? Do other complications arise? How would you prepare ESL or EFL learners for such experiences? Using the same (or similar) lines, work with them together with at least one English language learner. What do you need to explain? Have the learner read the conversation with you after you have identified some of the focal stress locations. How does the conversation sound? Natural? Awkward? Rhythmic?

14. The following URL links to a website titled "AI Screenplay Links: All over the Web!" that makes available complete screenplays for thousands of movies: <http://www.iscriptdb.com/>. Visit the site, then find and print out at least one scene from a movie of interest to you. Analyze the dialogue from the scene in ways Acton describes. What features of stress and rhythm could be used to illustrate in the classroom? Try working with it in collaboration with at least one English language learner.

Chapter 13

"Extensive Reading" for Japanese English Majors

Thomas N. Robb

———

A question Tom Robb explores is of great interest to English language teachers: Can EFL courses be structured in ways that encourage learners to become avid readers in English? Robb describes what he calls an "extensive reading" course. It is one of a series of seven courses for freshman English majors in the Faculty of Foreign Languages of Kyoto Sangyo University (KSU) in Japan. While Robb reports that many KSU courses require little preparation outside of class, he characterizes extensive reading (ER) as one of the most demanding courses English majors take during their university years. It requires up to five hours a week of preparation outside of class time. ER uses two distinct types of reading materials: (1) reading laboratory kits as produced by Science Research Associates (1999) for in-class work and (2) an outside reading library that provides access to a wide range of English language, primarily North American "youth literature." Some of the more popular titles in the reading library include old standbys, such as the Hardy Boys and Nancy Drew series, as well as more contemporary favorites by authors such as Judy Blume, Eve Bunting, and Beverly Cleary.

In addition to the broad goal of increasing the students' reading abilities (their levels of comprehension, speed, increased reading vocabulary, and reinforcement of basic grammatical structure through reading), an even more specific course objective is to foster more efficient reading habits, particularly to decrease students' reliance on dictionaries and to develop increased levels of tolerance for ambiguity. An incidental benefit of extensive reading is the considerable practice in summary writing required of students as proof of their having completed required reading tasks. Interspersed throughout his chapter, Robb references many Internet sites tied to the core themes he discusses.[1]

———

---

1. Since URLs for Internet sites sometimes change, please refer to the link corresponding to this chapter from the *Understanding* collection's Internet site for updated information.

Setting

Extensive Reading (ER) is one of a series of seven courses for freshman English majors at the Kyoto Sangyo University (KSU) Faculty of Foreign Languages. Other courses include an intensive English (translation) course; a grammar course; and classes in speaking, writing, and listening/pronunciation. The freshman English major program accommodates over 240 students per year. Students are divided into eight course sections of approximately 30 students each. As with most university level courses in Japan, classes meet 90 minutes each, once a week, for 30 weeks per year. Freshmen enrolled in our program normally also take up to eight other (non-English) courses each week, bringing their total workload per week to 15 class periods, each 90 minutes in length.

University freshmen in Japan have come through what is widely acknowledged to be an entrance-exam-oriented system. Most students enter university studies without ever having read more than two or three pages of English prose at a time and without ever having written sentences of their own creation in English. In terms of the ACTFL guidelines, English majors enter our program somewhere within the range of Intermediate-Low to Intermediate-Mid reading proficiency levels. Most of them are able to read in English and understand simple connected texts dealing with a variety of basic and social topics.

Overview of English Education System

Japanese students start studying English at the beginning of junior high school when students are between 12 and 13 years of age. Most students continue on to high school, where English is also a highly valued subject. Virtually all universities in Japan test English proficiency on their entrance examinations, a practice that assures the status of English as a major subject at all preuniversity levels. Because of the nature of university entrance examinations in Japan, most English language courses are very exam oriented. In the United States and Canada, it is much easier than in Japan for high school graduates to be accepted for admission into a college or university. However, it is somewhat more difficult for college and university students in the United States and Canada to actually finish their degrees. In contrast to the North American system, Japanese students tend to assume that once they have been admitted to postsecondary studies, their graduation four years hence is more or less assured. In many Japanese universities, in fact, instructors are reluctant to fail students who attend classes regularly even if they perform poorly in the course.

In Japan, a student's major is determined before she or he enters the university with applicants declaring their desired major as part of the admissions process. English study at the university level is, thus, of two distinct types. By far the most common variety is general education English, whereby students study English as a liberal arts subject in order to gain credits toward their graduation. However, about 20 percent of KSU's English majors also attain a certificate for teaching English at junior or senior high school levels. In addition, many universities offer opportunities to major in English literature or the English language. These students study English much more intensively, and they represent the population for whom ER is designed. Because ER is required for English majors, my colleagues and I who offer it are able to demand a good deal of work from students in the course, as long as students perceive the workload as justified and reasonable.

Conceptual Underpinnings

The three decades I have been teaching in Japan have taught me that there are three primary approaches to the teaching of reading in this part of the world. The first two are the most common: (1) *intensive reading* (i.e., grammar-translation or at least something very close to it; as practiced in Japan, intensive reading involves very detailed syntactic analysis, word analysis, and dual-direction translation of individual sentences), and (2) *skills building* (as featured in many commercially published reading textbooks targeted to the teaching of English as a foreign language). A more recent approach, (3) *extensive reading*, is the focus of this chapter.

Japanese instructors invariably favor the intensive reading approach. In contrast, most non-Japanese native English speaking instructors who have come to Japan from other parts of the world more commonly adopt a skills-building approach. The former choose texts from a wide variety of locally published materials. Intensive reading materials have been adopted widely in Japan and feature excerpts of authentic texts with numerous English-Japanese annotations/glosses in the margins of the pages. Examples include annotated anthologies of well-known literary works by major writers such as Joseph Conrad, F. Scott Fitzgerald, Ernest Hemingway, and Mark Twain. Other anthologies feature topical essays or shortened, annotated versions of standard nonfiction works such as Rachel Carson's *Silent Spring*. For teachers who adopt a skills-building approach, there are many ELT reading textbooks from major international publishers such as Cambridge, McGraw-Hill, Pearson Education, and the University of Michigan Press to select from.

"Intensive reading" refers to extremely close analysis of written materials, where students (and teacher) seem preoccupied with gaining as complete an understanding of each sentence's grammatical structure and lexis as possible. At the other extreme, "extensive reading" takes as its starting point a concern for increasing the volume of material to be read and neither assumes nor encourages complete understanding of the subject matter covered. Both intensive reading and skills-building approaches are widely criticized in Japan. Hino (1988) uses the term *yakudoku* (literally "translation-reading") to label some of intensive reading's disadvantages as follows.

> The yakudoku habit clearly is a severe handicap for the Japanese student. It limits the speed at which the student reads, induces fatigue, and reduces the efficiency with which s/he is able to comprehend. The meaning of the text is obtained via Japanese translation and is only an approximation of the original. (47)

Skills-building exercises suffer from a number of problems, too. One problem often cited is the lack of evidence that the discrete skills they focus upon are in line with contemporary L2 reading instruction theory and practice (Susser and Robb 1990). Other objections to the skill-building approach include those of Zamel (1992), who doubts the efficacy of the kinds of comprehension questions featured in "skills-building" collections. Zamel observes that questions featured in such collections "which immediately follow the assigned passage and which . . . call for a predetermined answer rather than the interpretation of the student reader . . . may, in fact, keep students from understanding the text" (464). Another problem stems from the fact that the readings in skills-based textbooks rarely feature full-length articles but, rather, present excised passages from longer works. Shih (1992, 295) argues that brief excerpts of this kind "deprive readers of important contextual clues." To move beyond such limitations, Shih goes on to advocate the use of whole, independent texts and textbook chapters in reading classrooms. Yet another drawback to both intensive reading and skills-building approaches is their reliance on "class readers." In each of the two approaches, all students in the class must be reading the same material, at a comparable pace, and usually at the same time, since the "class reader" serves as a structural basis for practically all course activities.

In contrast to both "intensive" and "skills-building" orientations, I use an *extensive reading* approach—what Gunderson (1991) terms *Sustained Silent Reading*—as a way to overcome many of the disadvantages of the other two approaches. For Japanese university students, who have already been exposed to six years of English in secondary school with a strong emphasis on grammar study and vocabulary acquisition, extensive reading provides an effective way to consolidate what they have learned and to advance their linguistic abilities. While teacher-selected assigned readings may not be especially pleasurable for some students, opportunities for reading in English to be intrinsically appealing increase when students are provided guidance and support for self-selecting their own reading materials. Of the three approaches discussed previously, only extensive reading permits a strong element of student choice since the other two approaches require adoption and use of teacher-prescribed class readers. (For further information on the ER topic in ELT, visit the "Extensive Reading Home Page" on the Internet: <http://www.kyoto-su.ac.jp/information/er/er.html>.)

Beyond the intuitive appeal of ER approaches, reading research indicates that one learns to read through reading. Grabe (1991) observes that "longer concentrated periods of silent [sustained] reading build vocabulary and structural awareness, develop automaticity, enhance background knowledge, improve comprehension skills and promote confidence and motivation" (396). Through a controlled experiment contrasting two groups of students using different approaches, Mason and Krashen (1997) demonstrate the efficacy of extensive reading compared to traditional intensive reading practices in the Japanese context. Their research illustrates that students not only improved in ability but also in their attitudes toward reading and the study of English.

Instructional Materials

As will be discussed in the section on syllabus design, ER makes use of two very different sets of instructional materials. These are (1) Science Research Associates (SRA) (1999) Reading Laboratory kits and (2) a course library that features a wide range of different kinds of books students use for outside-of-class reading. SRA Reading Laboratory kits have been popular and used extensively with elementary and junior high school students in English-dominant parts of the world for over 40 years. Since KSU students respond well to them, we have adapted these kits to our EFL situation and use them for ER's in-class component. SRA materials are arranged into reading difficulty levels according to a carefully structured color-coded system. While working with SRA materials, students advance slowly from one reading difficulty level to the next higher level by (1) passing a series of reading comprehension exercises at a comprehension level of 80 percent or higher and (2) finishing timed "Rate Builder" readings in four minutes or less. The color-coded series of reading selections, comprehension exercises, and rate building materials is attractively packaged and conceptually well structured by SRA. For a more complete description of SRA materials and their implementation at KSU, on the Internet see <://www.kyoto-su.ac.jp/~trobb/sraprogram.html>. See also the SRA's home page at http://www.sra4kids.com/teacher/reading/supplemental/phread.html>.

Along with the SRA materials mentioned previously, the course's other core set of instructional materials is an ER lending library. Due to limited open-stack space in the university's library, our department keeps its own collection of books for the ER course. We make them available on rollable library carts that are brought into the classroom at the start of each class. Students have ready access to the carts outside the instructor's office outside of class. The same carts also carry multiple sets of SRA material as well as a computer we use for record-keeping purposes. For class records, the computer system includes a database for tracking book popularity and tracking the pace of student progress.

Before being put into circulation, new books to be added to the reading library are numbered, assigned a "difficulty factor" (as will be described subsequently), and entered into the computer database. All of the outside readers have been obtained from two U.S. suppliers of books for "young readers," PermaBound (<http://www.perma-bound.com>) and Perfection Learning (<http://www.plconline.com>). The titles held include familiar materials such as the Hardy Boys and Nancy Drew series and more modern series such as the Baby-sitters Club and the Great Brain series, as well as works by authors especially popular with KSU students such as Judy Blume, Eve Bunting, Beverly Cleary, and Gordon Korman. Other items in the ER library inventory have been selected from the annual ALA (American Library Association) Notable Books for Children, concentrating on those titles suitable for English as a first language grade levels four through seven. Titles that prove popular with students over a couple of years are ordered in greater quantity with subsequent purchases. As will be discussed later, major works of great literature (e.g., F. Scott Fitzgerald's *The Great Gatsby;* Ernest Hemingway's *The Old Man and the Sea*) are excluded from the inventory since they are too easily available in translation. Students can and do, of course, read such material in their later years of study in the English language program.

Syllabus Design

As outlined previously, the ER course consists of two separate components: (1) the in-class component tied to SRA sets of reading materials and (2) the outside reading component where students are required to read an extensive amount of material in English over the 30-week span of the course. The materials they are required to read in the second component are whole books students select for themselves from the class library collection (see Internet app. 13.1, "Orientation to the Extensive Reading Course").

In-Class Component

As a reading teacher who works with EFL learners, I modify in significant ways the standard procedures suggested by the designers of SRA materials for working with their materials (see Internet app. 13.1). All students start out at the easiest color level (aqua). They need to read and demonstrate accurate comprehension of four numbered sets at this initial level before they are ready to graduate to the next. The four criteria for successful completion of an SRA set of materials at one's current level are the following.

1. Completion of the main "Power Builder" booklet and having passed the "How Well Did You Read?" quiz section with at least 80 percent accuracy.
2. Passing the "Learn about Words" (first section only) with 80 percent+ accuracy.
3. Reading the "Rate Builder" card and passing the quiz with 80 percent+ accuracy.
4. Reading the Rate Builder and completing its corresponding quiz within four minutes or less (just four minutes to complete both the reading and the quiz)

Each of these four components is described in detail in the instructional materials included in the SRA package from the publisher.

Homework Component

The students read texts they choose from the department's library collection for the course. The basic goal is to read 1,100 pages for a passing grade of 60 or up to 2,000 pages for the maximum grade of 100 for this component of their course grade. The two-semester course, which extends over an entire academic year, is divided into four reading periods, each of which has its own specific page requirements, as shown in table 13.1.

Intermediate values are extrapolated from these specifications.

TABLE 13.1. Page Requirements

	No. of Pages Required for 60 Points	No. of Pages Required for 100 Points
Period 1 (April–June)	200	400
Period 2 (June–Oct.)	250	450
Period 3 (Oct.–Nov.)	300	550
Period 4 (Nov.–Jan.)	350	600

Activity Types

SRA Classwork

After the first few weeks, each ER class session is similar in structure. Students work at their own pace with material from the SRA sets while the instructor checks each student's progress in the outside reading component of the course. Students first select a new reading at their current color level from the SRA kit left open at the front of the classroom. They read the prose selection and then complete two sets of comprehension checks ("How Well Did You Read?" and "Learn about Words") in their record booklet. Next, they check their answers against separate answer sheets and move on to a corresponding "Power Builder" timed reading. Proceeding in this fashion, most students are able to read and complete two or three sets of SRA materials in one 90-minute period.

Outside Reading

General ER course guidelines advise students to read on a weekly basis and to summarize the content in their personal ER notebooks, which are dedicated solely to this purpose. All of the books in the lending library are evaluated and labeled in relation to a "difficulty" factor (a simple measure of text density—the average number of words per page). Credit for the amount of reading completed is given on the number of "adjusted pages" in each volume (the number of pages actually read times the difficulty factor). Without such a compensation factor, students might be tempted to select a book according to the size of the typeface on the page rather than its content focus or their interest in the material. As a baseline, a book with 200 words per page is assigned an arbitrary difficulty factor of 1.0. A book with 400 words per page carries a difficulty factor of 2.0. The factor for any given book is extrapolated from these two benchmarks.

For their required summaries, students are expected to write approximately one page for every 40 "weighted pages" they have read. We refer to this weighting of pages read in class as the "40:1" ratio. For work submitted, adjustments in the requirements are made for variances in the size of the student's handwriting. The following guidelines are provided for summary writing tasks.

1. Your summary should contain only the most important sections in the story—who, what, when, where, how, and why.
2. Write the summary chapter by chapter.
3. Use the third person. (I, you → → he, she).
4. Do not use direct speech.
5. Do not copy exact sentences from the book.
6. Use every line on the page.

When writing their summaries, students are asked to specify the chapter title/number and the page range at the beginning of each summary section, as well as the date written. Having the students compose their summaries in chapter sections simplifies my task as instructor when I need to compare a summary with the original section of the book. It also makes it easier for me to see if the summary makes sense from chapter to chapter. Students realize that their summaries are supposed to flow smoothly and cohesively since they are summarizing the gist of each chapter in sequence. As might be expected, some students attempt to read and summarize just the first few pages of each chapter in an effort to lessen their workload in the course. Based on my subsequent feedback and comments, such students soon realize that such a strategy is counterproductive and that they will lose credit if they persist in doing so.

Training in Summary Writing

Prior to university study, most Japanese freshmen have had little or no opportunity to write English language sentences of their own creation. Most of them have never had guided experiences in summary writing, not even in Japanese. For this reason the course starts with a series of warm-up activities.

1. A short chapter from a book is presented to the students along with three brief summaries. Based on criteria presented to them, they are asked to decide which is the best summary.
2. The students read and summarize two short graded readers during the second and third weeks. The department has purchased a sufficient number of readers so half of the students are able to be using one while the others work with a different graded reader. Students then switch books for the second week. We have selected graded readers for the introductory phase of the course because (1) as the course begins, we want to ensure that the level of the reading matter is within the reach of all students while introducing the task of summary writing and (2) the reading selections are short and thus can be easily read in a single week. Available from a number of ELT publishers, graded readers are simplified versions of existing works of literature especially written for students at a specific level of syntactic and lexical mastery. Such series normally have a number of titles available at each of several levels such as "beginner," "elementary," "preintermediate," and so on. I examine students' summaries of the graded reader materials using a model summary as a guide with all key points underlined. Under my guidance, students compare my model to their own summary, counting how many of the essential points have been incorporated in their own versions. Casazza (1993) provides further discussion of "direct instruction to teach summary writing" generally applicable to ELT.
3. After three preparatory weeks, the students select their first book from the class library and begin to read on their own outside of class time. I continue to check the summaries throughout the course and provide further counseling on summary writing as needed.

Why Summaries?

Students' summaries of what they read outside of class are the primary means they have to demonstrate for course credit that they have actually read a self-selected book. Teachers in other environments have found other methods for student reporting, such as reading report forms or oral reports, to be effective. In our setting, I find written summaries to be a very efficient way to track whether students have read the book they have expressed interest in. In addition to checking assignment completion, summaries are also a good way to assess students' general levels of comprehension (Day and Bamford 1998). For the first few weeks, many students find that their summarizing efforts take even more time than it took them to read the original material. The fact that they spend so much time summarizing during the initial weeks of the course is probably due to their inexperience at writing in English and summarizing in general. Helgesen (1997) acknowledges that the writing of competent summaries in one's second language may be even more difficult than the act of reading needed to make summarizing possible. However, a bonus to summary writing is the marked improvement in the students' ability to write competent summaries over time. Regular review of the initial and final sections of students' notebooks at the end of the course convinces me that we are on an appropriate path.

Why Authentic Texts?

Many otherwise similar extensive reading courses (e.g., Helgesen 1997) use the vast collection of "graded readers" available, especially through British publishers. Our decision to avoid graded readers except for the first three weeks of the course is based on the following rationale.

1. Many graded readers are reduced versions of existing works of "good literature," and virtually all such material is readily available in Japan in translation. We try to avoid books for which translations are so easily available in order to remove any temptation students may have to read the text in Japanese with minimal reference to the English version.
2. Graded readers sometimes are even more difficult to comprehend than their source materials. Even if they are intended to be simplified versions, they may be particularly difficult for EFL readers due to a reduced level of information redundancy and stylistic awkwardness caused by the limitation in possible syntactic constructions (Susser and Robb 1990).
3. The authentic books we use are ones actually read and enjoyed by native speakers of English, which may translate as an intrinsically motivating factor for EFL learners.
4. KSU students who enter our program are already reading at a higher ACTFL level than students in many comparable programs in Japan. Therefore, we feel that KSU students are ready to begin reading authentic materials.

Record-Keeping Procedures

ER students are provided with a record booklet at the beginning of the course. The booklet contains a chart for recording their weekly outside reading (see Internet app. 13.2), a conversion chart for "real pages" to "adjusted pages" (see Internet app. 13.3), space for answers to 60 SRA sets of reading material (Internet app. 13.4), and additional orientation materials on various aspects of the course with the main points outlined in Japanese to ensure learner understanding (see Internet app. 13.5). (Continuing updates of these and other ER orientation materials are available on the Internet at <http://www.kyoto-su.ac.jp/~trobb/rules.html>.)

When the students return a book after finishing (or giving up on) it, they use their booklet as a paper record for entering the number of pages they have completed into the course computer. Periodically, class records are printed out and circulated to the members of the class so students can check their own sections for accuracy. This strategy allows students to gauge their progress compared to that of other members of the class. There usually are a number of outstanding performers in each class whose examples of accomplishment have a motivating effect on their classmates.

Tracking Book Popularity

Students evaluate each book they have read on the following scale: 0 (Terrible!), 1 (OK), 2 (Good), 3 (Great!). The students also enter this data into the computer database along with their personal record of pages read. On the basis of learner responses to the quality and interest level of particular books, additional copies of more popular titles are ordered each year. Books that consistently score poorly are removed from circulation. A copy of the book evaluations is also made available to the students as an aid to book selection. The most recent list of evaluation scores for books currently in use is posted on the World Wide Web at <http://www.kyoto-su.ac.jp/~trobb/evals.html>.

Teacher's Roles

There is limited up-front teaching in the ER course, except for the first few weeks when the teacher provides direct instruction in summary writing. The teacher acts mainly as a counselor, checking on each student's progress individually during the class session. I prefer to rotate through the classroom, sitting down next to each student to examine her or his notebook. I read through students' summaries weekly, glancing through what the students have written. While I may not have read some of the books students are reading, I find that competent summaries exhibit a smooth flow of ideas from chapter to chapter. If not, I might ask the student to produce the book, quickly read through a chapter, and provide further counseling, pointing out important details that have been missed or trivial points that should have been omitted, as appropriate.

Learners' Roles

As with most types of learning, the effectiveness of the ER course depends heavily on learners' attitudes and contributions. Students are responsible for their own learning to the extent that they must choose materials at an appropriate level and must learn to be conscientious in regularly completing assigned reading tasks. The guidelines of the course suggest to students that they read approximately 100 pages per week.

Lesson Particulars

In this section I present four illustrations of typical exchanges between a student and teacher during the weekly summary checking sessions. Although the illustrations are composites of actual events, they are reliable depictions of the type of interactive exchanges that typically occur during our weekly teacher-to-student discussions of students' summary writing efforts.

(Student 1: Sakiko is a good student who has been reading regularly each week. She is busy reading an SRA booklet as the teacher approaches. Teacher sits down next to student.)

T: Hi, Sakiko. Can you show me your notebook, please?
S: Here, have a look.
T: Hmm . . . Let's see . . . Your outside reading record says that you read 115 pages this week. That's very good. Let's see . . . at 40 pages per notebook page, you should have written about 3 new pages. . . . *(Teacher glances through the new pages, not reading everything but reading enough to see that the material appears to be a good summary in the student's own words.)*
T: Well, this looks OK. Do you like the book?
S: Yes, it's very interesting.
T: Good! Well there are still two more weeks before the end of the reading period. If you can continue at this rate, you will get 100 percent for this reading period! Keep reading!
S: Thank you.

(Student 2: Hiroko presents the instructor with summaries of three chapters from a book, a total of 50 pages read—a good amount for a single week.)

T: Well, this looks pretty good, Hiroko. Now, give me a minute to read some of what you wrote. . . . *(A few moments pass.)*

T: You know, in chapter 3, here, you say that Joe wanted to ask Anne to go to the prom with her, but in chapter 4, Joe is at the prom with Susie. I think you missed an important part of the story here. What happened? Why didn't Joe go with Anne?

S: He was too shy.

T: I see. Well, for a more effective summary, I really think you need to include a detail like that.

S: OK, let me try it again.

(Student 3: Yutaka previously has established himself as a slacker in the course. He hasn't done much reading, and today is the final day of the second reading period. Surprisingly, he comes in with the requisite number of pages read—at least according to the figures in his reading record.)

T: Well, this is a pleasant surprise. I see you managed to read enough pages.

S: *(Grins silently.)*

T: Now, let's take a look at the summaries. Let's see, you read 251 pages. So you should have about 6 pages in your notebook. Hmm . . . What you have is a little short, only 5 pages, but now let me take a look at what you wrote. *(The teacher looks over the pages for a few minutes.)* Hmm . . . I'm afraid that I can't follow the story from this. There seem to be big gaps in what is happening. Can you show me the book, please?

S: I returned it.

T: Well, go ahead and retrieve it from the book cart. I am sure a copy is there. We can take a look at it together. *(A few moments later Yutaka brings the book.)* Hmm . . . Everything that you say in chapter 3 happens on the first two pages. Now, let's see chapter 4. . . . Hmm . . . It seems to be the same. I'm sorry, Yutaka, but I can't give you credit for these pages. *(Teacher places an "X" at the top of each page.)* If you can write a good summary for the book, though, you can get credit for these pages in the next reading period, OK?

S: Yes.

TABLE 13.2.   Value of Student Activities

Activity	Value (%)
Performance on outside reading over the 30 weeks of the course (each of the four 6-week reading periods is valued at 15%)	60
Number of SRA sets completed/read	20
Highest color of SRA materials attained (more challenging sets yield higher grades)	20
Total possible score	100

Assessment

In addition to the procedures previously discussed to track student progress, students' grades are based on their performance on the outside reading and in combination with the in-class SRA activities according to the proportions shown in table 13.2. All of the students' notebooks and record booklets are collected at the end of the year and reviewed a final time by the instructor. The number of pages read is reduced for any shortcomings found at that point in the summaries, although this readjustment measure is usually necessary for fewer than 20 students of the 280 enrolled across course sections.

Caveats and Final Thoughts

The teacher serves a prominent supervision role in the ER course, guiding students, advising and in other ways supporting them, checking to see if the students are on task, and encouraging them to work harder. While a supervising role can be uncomfortable for some teachers, it is probably necessary in the context of KSU, where studying is not a high priority for many university students and where many learners expect their English instructors to take active roles as positive motivators whenever necessary. Students will normally complete 70 to 80 percent of what an instructor expects of them, so the instructor's expressed goals and the degree to which they are enforced are strong predictors of students' academic performances. Of course, there are some self-motivated students in our courses, and such students perform extremely well within the guided structure of the ER course. At the same time, we have tried to plan the course's format, procedures, and materials as a workable structure within which even poorly motivated, or weaker, students are able to succeed.

Over the past 30 years, I have learned that students in the course tend to procrastinate and postpone required reading until the last moment. When the extensive reading course was first implemented, the minimum requirement to pass was 1,000 pages for the entire year (approximately 27 class meetings of 90 minutes each). We soon discovered that many of the students were postponing the reading expected of them until the very end of the term. For the subsequent year, my colleagues and I agreed to revise course requirements by segmenting the academic year into four sections, with each succeeding term requiring incrementally more out-of-class reading. This strategy may not ensure our goal that students read on a weekly basis, but at least they now have to read, consult privately with their instructor, and be assessed in four installments. We have found the four-part structure a marked improvement over earlier ways of organizing the course.

We are still uncertain about the effect of summary writing on students' willingness to read, on their motivation for learning English, and on their personal investments in the idea of acquiring more English through reading. Students might read even more if they knew that they did not have to spend time writing a summary afterward. Part of our challenge is to continue to devise even more efficient ways to monitor student progress and to motivate them to read extensively in their target language. For such purposes, some programs use short reports. Another possibility is to prepare brief quizzes for each book available or to use the commercially produced "Accelerated Reader" program (<http://www.renlearn.com/>) widely adopted by secondary, junior high, and elementary schools across North America. In our setting, we find guided and supervised involvement with SRA reading materials in combination with "youth literature" an effective way to encourage extensive reading for Japanese EFL learners.

Prompts for Discussion and Reflection

1. In EFL settings, why would a teacher want to encourage learners to become extensive readers? What might some of the benefits be? What are possible benefits for ESL learners?

2. Have you ever worked with sets of programmed reading materials such as the SRA materials Robb describes? Describe what they are like. (In English-dominant parts of the world, many people may have used such materials during their middle school and/or secondary school years; compare also "accelerated reading" materials.) Why do you think Robb adopts SRA materials for in-class use?

3. In addition to the several book series Robb mentions, what would

be some other English language works of "youth literature" you think might work well in such an EFL course and program? Discuss rationale for those you would recommend to Robb.

4. The author describes most reading courses in Japan as falling into one of three categories: intensive reading, skills focused, and extensive reading. Where would you place the reading practices you have offered (will offer) students in your own teaching? Why were these types of reading practices selected for your curriculum? Discuss connections you are able to develop between any of these three categories of EFL reading instruction and two or more of the general ELT principles presented in table 2.4 of chapter 2.

5. In your (future) teaching situation, would there be any benefit in making a library of reading materials available? Could a library of reading materials be established? Where would the funding come from? Where could the books be kept? How might they be used to encourage extensive reading?

6. Current theory emphasizes a need for learner autonomy and for students to feel accountable for their own learning. The program described in this chapter, however, seems to require the instructor to supervise very closely the amount and quality of the reading done by students. How does Robb justify this position? Do you think that this degree of supervision is appropriate for the teaching situation described? Would you handle this aspect of the program differently?

7. Several other chapters in the *Understanding* collection focus on the teaching of reading in ELT. Compare and contrast Robb's way of organizing instruction with that of at least one of these other contributors: Brian Morgan (chap. 8), Janet M. Goodwin (chap. 15), Donna M. Brinton (chap. 16), David J. Mendelsohn (chap. 17), or Joy Janzen (chap. 20) or with the ways featured in some other course you may know about.

8. For students at the level you (intend to) teach, what would be some (in)appropriate types of materials to make available to them for purposes of extensive reading practice?

9. What was the rationale for excluding books for which a Japanese-English translation might be readily available? (Also consider books that are English translations from the students' native language.) In your (intended) teaching situation, do you feel these would be important considerations? What are some of the issues involved?

10. Extensive reading seems to have much in common with the "whole language" approaches to learning and teaching. Review the tenets of whole language at the following Internet site and compare them to

Robb's ideas for teaching extensive reading. Look especially for elements they share in common. See <http://www.ncte.org/wlu/08894f6.htm> for a summary of "whole language." Discuss possible connections between the tenets or themes you consider and any of the general ELT principles presented in table 2.4 of chapter 2.

Miniprojects

11. On the Internet, take a look at the "Extensive Reading Pages" at <http://www.kyoto-su.ac.jp/information/er/index.html>. Which aspect of extensive reading seems most useful to you? If you are working as a group, divide up the site according to the half dozen sections listed on the main page and report back to the class about any "gems" each of you may have found in your assigned section.

12. A recent (U.S.) National Reading Panel (NRP) report on reading concludes that it is not clear that children can become better readers by reading silently to themselves ("Reading Panel Urges Phonics for All in K–6," *Education Week*, April 19, 2000). Take a look at the original report at <http://www.nichd.nih.gov/publications/nrp/findings.htm> and Stephen Krashen's rebuttal at <http://www.kyoto-su.ac.jp/information /er/rdgpanel.html>. Considering both sides of the argument, what is your own position on this issue? Are there alternative issues to consider? How do these controversies relate to EFL teaching in secondary school or university settings? To ESL settings? Discuss any related themes in connection to a setting in which you work or may be working in the future.

Chapter 14

English for Engineers in Hong Kong

Lindsay Miller

―――――

Lindsay Miller describes a course developed within an English for Specific Purposes/ English for Science and Technology paradigm. He explains that the course titled "English for Engineers Part 1" reflects both a task-based and strategy-based approach and an attempt to encourage independent learning. Miller focuses on the learning demands made on students from Hong Kong upon entering an English-medium university. The learners he describes come from traditional Chinese-medium secondary schools where the focus of English language instruction is learning to pass tests. When these learners enter a university, they need to develop some of their listening-to-learn and reading-to-learn abilities, but equally important, they are also faced with having to interact in English for the first time with foreign professors in a range of settings. For example, learners need to acquire sociocultural insights and skills in order to interact with their instructors as university professors and not as high school teachers. These changes are important and fundamental to the learners successfully completing their three-year university program. In this chapter we see how Miller slowly leads learners to taking on more responsibility for their own learning and to understanding how they must acquire new roles.

The chapter concludes with a brief account of a follow-up second-semester English for Engineers course. Here, Miller extends the concepts of learner independence developed in the first-semester course to allow students greater say in their language learning. Miller's discussion suggests that by the end of the two-semester English for Engineers course sequence students will be in a better position to cope with linguistic demands and will be on the road to taking increased responsibility for their future language development.

―――――

Setting

The language course described in this chapter takes place at the City University of Hong Kong, an English-medium university with three large faculties: Business, Humanities and Social Sciences, and Sciences and Engineering. Within the three faculties, there are 17 separate departments.

Approximately 17,000 full- and part-time students study at City University (City U.). Most of them are Hong Kong Chinese who use Cantonese as their first language (L1). English for Engineers is a one-year, two-course program offered through the English department in consultation with the Department of Manufacturing Engineering. The course requires cross-faculty cooperation since the Faculty of Humanities and Social Sciences houses the English department while the Faculty of Sciences and Engineering houses the Department of Manufacturing Engineering. In this chapter, I will describe and discuss the first-semester course English for Engineers Part 1 (EEP1). I will use the title English for Engineers Part 2 (EEP2) to signal the second semester of this two-semester, yearlong course sequence. In EEP1, students attend one two-hour class each week for 14 weeks. In addition to in-class hours they are expected to spend an additional one to two hours in private study. The private study is usually done at home, although all students in the university have access to a fully equipped and well-stocked library. They also use our program's Self-Access Center, which is a dedicated language learning facility (see Gardner and Miller 1999). As offered through the English department, the EEP1/EEP2 sequence is compulsory for all first-year undergraduates majoring in manufacturing-engineering. Each year around 140 students enter the program for which the two-course sequence is designed. Students are randomly placed into class sections, and each class size is about 20 students.

Students enter City U. either directly from high school or after completing a diploma course in a technical institute. The former often have better use of English since they have completed form 7 in secondary school (the last level of high school, with students graduating at around age 19). The latter group leave secondary school at form 5 (the first level at which students can leave high school, corresponding with the slightly younger age of 16 or 17) to attend the technical institutes. Thus, students' ages when entering the manufacturing-engineering program range between 19 and 21. Nearly all students are male. Most of the engineering students have relatively low public-exam English scores. According to the ACTFL descriptors the majority of students fall into an Intermediate-Low to Intermediate-Mid range for listening and an Intermediate-Mid to Intermediate-High range for reading. Their scores are considered low by the teaching staff because the students are entering an English-medium university.

Conceptual Underpinnings

The IEP (Intensive English Program) course has been developed around three conceptual foci: a task-based approach, a strategy-based approach, and an attempt to encourage learner independence. I will discuss each of these in turn.

A Task-Based Approach

On entering the university, engineering students need to be able to function in English for the following specific purposes: (1) to listen to engineering lectures from native and nonnative English speakers (British, American, Australian, Indian, Singaporean, Chinese); (2) to read authentic engineering texts written in English; and (3) to interact in one-on-one tutorials in English (ask and answer questions, take part in discussions). In order to help the students meet these needs, I have developed a series of target tasks and pedagogic tasks (see Long and Crookes 1992) for the first-semester EEP1 language course. The target tasks include reading an authentic engineering text and listening to a segment of authentic spoken discourse on an engineering topic. The pedagogic tasks are specially prepared exercises and activities to enable the learners to complete the target tasks. The pedagogic tasks I design are based on my own interpretation of communicative language teaching principles and include such features as information gaps, choice of language function used to complete tasks, and listening to be able to make efficient use of feedback.

The preset pedagogic tasks come from an analysis of both written and spoken texts (i.e., written discourse samples such as reading selections and spoken samples culled from recorded listening materials) as presented by the material writers (myself and other staff members working on the course). In preparing pedagogic tasks we give first consideration to reading and listening skills that can be developed through the reading and listening materials we have selected. For example, some selections are suitable for scanning for numbers, whereas others are better suited for developing opinions. Attention is also paid to what can realistically be expected of learners who enter the course with intermediate level (ACTFL descriptor) reading abilities. Realistic appraisal of students' proficiency levels in reading and listening leads us to design tasks targeted to learners' abilities. The tasks are structured around a simple format of pre-, while-, and postlistening and pre-, while-, and postreading activities to facilitate overall language learning.

A Strategy-Based Approach

A second focus of the EEP1 course is to enhance learner awareness of strategies they already tend to use while completing targeted tasks and how they might extend their repertoire of language learning strategies. The following is the definition we will be using when discussing a learning strategy: "a specific mental procedure for gathering, processing, associating, categorizing, rehearsing and retrieving information or patterned skills" (Willing 1988, 7). The composite learning strategies a student uses signal the learner's preferred styles of learning: the ways that she or he likes or dislikes to approach learning tasks. The works of Stern (1975), Oxford (1990), and Wenden (1986), among others, are important influences in the features of course design described in this section. When introducing a new target task designed to enhance reading abilities, for example, learners may be asked to look at accompanying photographs, titles, and headings and encouraged to try to predict what kind of information they believe will be (or they would like to see) presented later in the text. They will also be asked *how* they are going to make predictions and seek confirming evidence from the text (a planning strategy) [*editors' note:* cf. Joy Janzen, chap. 20 in this volume].

When listening to a talk about manufacturing processes, learners may first be made aware that the speaker will speak fast and with an American accent that initially may not be clear to them and that may present unfamiliar challenges. They are encouraged to listen to the presentation for specific information and not to worry if they do not understand everything the speaker says (i.e., an empathetic strategy). Following each stage of completing a pedagogic task, learners are encouraged to reflect on how well they have been able to perform while completing the task (i.e., a self-monitoring strategy). By exposing learners to a range of language learning strategies, the intention is to provide opportunities for learners to discover for themselves what works best for them. Language learning skills and awarenesses introduced and practiced in EEP1 can then be transferred to the learners' content subjects.

Learner Independence

In conjunction with the two orientations to learning discussed previously, I have a commitment to lead learners toward language learning independence. Learner independence is a stage in the process of becoming an autonomous learner (Gardner and Miller 1996). By specifying learner independence as a goal in the EEP1 course, I try to ensure that lessons are as student centered as I can get them to be. This premise means that students are constantly asked to activate their prior knowledge about a topic and to contribute as much as they can toward the lesson. They are asked to monitor their learning and discuss how well they are doing. In addition, the tasks they attempt to complete are evaluated by way of feedback at the end of lessons (through teacher monitoring) and by students via written feedback forms (at the end of many classes, students are encouraged to write brief comments about what they liked and did not like).

Some of the skills learners need to develop in order to complete their degree program and that learner independence is targeted to help them achieve are (1) taking responsibility for their own learning; (2) interacting with professors in and out of class when they need help; (3) cooperating with classmates; (4) motivating themselves to improve their language (especially as many of the science students previously will have had negative language learning experiences); (5) coping with the unknown (in terms of complicated vocabulary and terms, professors with unusual teaching styles, etc.); and (6) developing sufficient degrees of self-confidence to be able to present their ideas in a second language. The structure, format, and underlying philosophy of the learners' secondary school educational experiences seldom prepare them adequately for City U.'s academic demands. Therefore, in the first-semester EEP1 course I incorporate learner independence as an integral facet of course philosophy.

Affective Concerns

Affective concerns are a major consideration in EEP1 because it is at City U. that many students participate for the first time in a course taught not only exclusively in English but also by a foreigner. In addition, in their previous schooling many students have focused on science subjects and consider themselves "not very good" at learning English. Very quickly I have to demonstrate that they can learn from a foreign teacher who only speaks to them in English. One way to give students confidence in their own abilities, and in their new teacher, is to use easy but engaging activities in the first few lessons. Short (10 to 15 minutes) icebreakers are useful for this purpose. Many of the ideas for such icebreakers I adapt in modified ways from "activity-recipe" teacher resource collections such as Bailey and Savage (1994), Nation (1994), and Nunan and Miller (1995). Using icebreaker activities at the beginning of lessons helps to ensure that all students are taking active roles in the course. These activities also help to build up students' confidence in working with a foreign teacher. In these first few lessons I make it a point to try to learn all the students' names and to use their names frequently. This strategy gives students a feeling of well-being and demonstrates that their teacher cares for them individually, an important feature of Chinese orientations to education. Although language classroom icebreakers and games do not form an official part of the course syllabus, they set the course off in the right direction and are essential to creating a mutually supportive environment in which to learn.

Course Objectives

EEP1 is the first half of a yearlong program. By the end of EEP1 students will (1) be able to read and learn from semitechnical articles from popular manufacturing journals and newspapers; (2) be able to listen to and learn from transactional (i.e., primarily one-way, information-transmission) types of academic lectures and other styles of spoken discourse on engineering topics; (3) have a heightened awareness of learning strategies that strengthen their abilities to complete reading and listening tasks; and (4) have developed strategies for autonomy as learners so they can continue their language learning after the EEP1 course has ended (and especially in EEP2).

Instructional Materials

The primary course text used in EEP1 is *Reading Skills: Authentic Readings for Manufacturing Engineering* (Costa et al. 1992). I depend upon this core text in combination with video work sheets that are used to develop students' listening abilities and focus on manufacturing-engineering topics. These have been specially prepared for the course and are distributed in class in a loose sheet format with three-hole punches for students to collate in three-ring binders. All of the students are provided with copies of the materials since many of the listening exercises require them to write on the pages (fill in a table, complete notes, show the stress on a list of words, etc.).

I decided when preparing the materials for the EEP1 course that formulas, equations, and the teaching of specific technical vocabulary used in content-focused manufacturing-engineering courses should be avoided. At our institution, we decided that the teaching of such specialized topics is more appropriate as the responsibility of engineering instructors and not of language teachers from the English department. Instead, I structure the course around material from popular engineering journals, most of which have semitechnical vocabulary and general interest content. For example, materials I have selected over recent years include topics such as new ways of processing food, facts about diamonds and the refinement process they go through, and engineering projects in high schools. By using more accessible topics and materials, I maintain my own and the students' confidence in my ability as their language teacher to handle the material well. Colleagues and former students agree that the reading and listening

TABLE 14.1.   Contents of the Reading Course (an excerpt)

Unit	Title	No. of Words	Synopsis
2	Electronic Assembly Systems	810	A journal article about choosing the right electronic assembly system using surface-mounted technology
5	Machine Retrofitting Work at School Attracts Industrialists	623	A newspaper article that discusses how a course in a technical college is attracting manufacturers' attention due to its inclusion of computer-aided design (CAD) and computer-aided manufacturing (CAM)
6	The Facts about Diamonds	1,038	A journal article about the many advantages to using diamond tools in the manufacturing industry

Note: For complete version, see Internet table 14.1.

materials included in the course are of interest to students and relevant to their field of study.

The *Reading Skills* text contains 10 units of work. In each unit there is an authentic text that originally appeared in one of several popular engineering magazines such as *Assembly, Manufacturing Engineering,* or *Cutting Tool Engineering.* In addition to these articles, I adapt others from the Hong Kong press that deal with issues of local interest to engineers. Table 14.1 gives the titles and brief synopses of the readings included in 3 out of the total of 10 units featured in the course. (For the complete version of table 14.1, please see Internet table 14.1.)

The video work sheets are based on *Manufacturing Technology* (Laleman and Priess 1994), an information video focused on the development of manufacturing technology in industry. This video, designed as an introduction to the science and technology of manufacturing-engineering, was produced in the United States and is aimed at secondary school students. I present it to EEP1 students in seven brief segments. Table 14.2 gives the titles and corresponding synopses for two out of the total of seven video segments featured in the course. (For the complete version of table 14.2, please see Internet table 14.2.)

Syllabus Design

White (1988) and Long and Crookes (1992) propose a distinction between two styles of ELT course syllabus design: Type A and Type B syllabuses. In

TABLE 14.2.   Listening Components Included in the EEP1 Course (an excerpt)

Segment	Title	Length (minutes)	Synopsis
1	Introduction to Manufacturing Technology	8	The first segment introduces the concept of what manufacturing technology is; why it is important to society; and common types of technology we use in our everyday lives.
2	The Manufacturing System (1)	7	This segment talks about input in terms of resources, processes resources must go through to be usable, and the outputs we obtain and use by manufacturing such resources.

Note: For complete version, see Internet table 14.2.

a Type A syllabus, course content is preselected by the materials writer, curriculum developer, or classroom teacher; the teacher makes decisions regarding what content is to be taught and how. In this syllabus style, content tends to be external to the learner, and the learner is assessed on mastery of whatever the prescribed content might be. In a Type B syllabus learners' needs are paramount, learners and teachers jointly negotiate what is to be learned, the process of course development is more interactive, there is an emphasis on the process of learning, and achievement is informed in part by learners' internal criteria. Though there are some features of Type B syllabus design in my teaching of EEP1, the syllabus comes closer to a Type A syllabus description.

The syllabus for the course is organized around specially prepared materials. In EEP1, I usually cover at least 6 of the 10 units from *Reading Skills: Authentic Readings for Manufacturing Engineering* (Costa et al. 1992). The units in the book allow students to practice a variety of reading skills and develop appropriate reading strategies such as predicting what the article is about, brainstorming vocabulary related to the topic, reading for the main idea, reading for specific information, developing a piece of writing from the text, and interacting orally in a group using the text as input.

I also try to cover at least five or six units from the *Manufacturing Technology* video materials. Here, the students focus on listening to authentic North American speakers using English to describe machines, define contemporary states of technology, and discuss issues related to using robots in industry, among other topics. This information-transmission type of spoken monologue prepares learners to listen to longer stretches of language on engineering topics and is similar to the type of spoken discourse they will be expected not only to understand *but to learn from* when attending engineering course lectures (i.e., not only listening-to-comprehend but *listening-to-learn* content material). The work sheets featured in the course help students focus on what they listen to, predict what they might hear next, take general and specific notes, and discuss the topic based on information from the video—all skills they will need to use when listening to lectures and attending tutorials.

Activity Types

During the course, lessons are organized around a simple format of pre-, while-, and postreading activities as well as pre-, while-, and postlistening activities. A typical sequence for a reading lesson begins with a warm-up activity designed to activate students' schemata for the topic (Gunderson 1991). This phase is then followed by reading the passage and completing tasks designed to activate further reading strategies. After completing three or four reading activities based on the text, the students use their knowledge gained from the reading to perform a postreading task (see example tasks in fig. 14.1).

The structure of listening lessons is somewhat similar. The class begins with some general discussion about the topic, or students are asked to recall what they viewed on video in the previous lesson. Then students participate in a note-taking activity based on a partial, incomplete outline with many gaps needing to be filled in. This format helps to focus their efforts and challenges listeners to extract the main points from the video segment. Afterward, the information from their then-completed notes is used as a basis for discussing the topic presented or a related topic. Alternatively, their notes may also be used for writing a summary. Figure 14.2 presents an example of such listening tasks. The activities in the course stress reading and listening tasks that encourage students to use specific learning strategies. Table 14.3 illustrates many of the types of strategies practiced during the EEP1 course. The table is based on Stern's (1975) conceptualizations and Grenfell's (1994) labels of learning strategies. The same table also exemplifies how such strategies are used in the course. During a pedagogic task more than one strategy may be used. For example, in a general discussion about an article, *communicative, experimental,* and *empathetic* strategies may all be used, whereas in a listening task, while students take notes from a talk, *active, practice,* and *monitoring* strategies may all be activated. In keep-

---

Unit 5: "Machine Retrofitting Work at School Attracts Industrialists"

Prereading: Prediction

Look at the title of the article and discuss the following questions with a partner.

1. What kind of school do you think the article will be about? Do you have any personal experience with this type of school?

2. Why do you think industrialists are interested in the retrofitting work done at the school?

While Reading: Flowchart

Complete the chart below describing the Computer Numerical Controls chain created by Mr. Lee's department.

CNC Chain Conventional Milling Machines are fitted with

_____ (fill in here)

which are connected to

_____ (fill in here)

and then are linked to

_____ (fill in here)

which reads

_____ (fill in here)

Postreading: Discussion

What do you think is meant by the last sentence in the article? How do you think the writer feels about technology in Hong Kong? Discuss the questions in a small group and then share your opinions with the class.

What language skills are most important when having a discussion? Are you good at discussing things? What would you like to improve so as to become better at discussions?

Fig. 14.1.   Examples of task types in the reading course

ing with Oxford's (1990) suggestions, I try to encourage students to develop, practice, and expand whatever might be their repertoire of preferred strategic options, but ultimately it is up to them to decide which strategies they choose to use to complete targeted tasks.

Unit 2: The Manufacturing System (1)   (a 7-minute video segment)

Previewing Tasks

1. *In your own words:* Look over your notes from the previous video segment. Turn your notes over and do not look at them again. Give a verbal summary of the video's first segment to a partner.

2. *Note-taking:* Listen to the segment from the video and complete the partial notes below.

The manufacturing system

A system =

_____

_____

e.g., _____

MS is made up of parts:

inputs   = _____

processes = _____

outputs   = _____

feedback = _____

MS is used by a company in-factory to make products.

Input
Natural resources   _____ e.g., _____
                          people/workers

_____

capital resources   _____

                          Helps manage people and money/sell products

_____

2 major technologies

1. Material technology   = _____

2. Management technology = _____

Fig. 14.2.   Examples of task types in the listening course

These must be used efficiently to get a good product.

Some examples of products = (a) _____ (b) _____

(c) _____

(a) goods purchased at store, e.g., _____

(b) changed raw materials for other manufacturers to use

(c) e.g., _____ made only for military

The purpose and goal of manufacturing are more than just making things.

1. _____

_____

2. _____

_____

3. *Summary:* Use your notes to write a short summary of approximately 100 words on Manufacturing Systems.

Ask a partner to check over your summary and give you feedback on (*a*) content and (*b*) sentence structure. You do the same for your partner.

Learners' Roles

Learners' perceptions of their roles in the EEP1 course have to be flexible in order to fullfill the learning objectives of the course. Learners enter the course carrying with them recent experiences within a traditional Hong Kong secondary school system where rote learning is encouraged, class sizes are large (+ 40), and classes tend to be very teacher centered. Confucian philosophy predominates in such settings (see Flowerdew and Miller 1995), which leads to "passive learning" and dependence on the teacher. An example is students' reluctance to volunteer answers in response to a teacher's whole class question solicits. Tradition-minded teachers in Hong Kong invariably use, and tend to overuse, "display" questions. These are questions to which (1) the teacher already knows the answer and (2) everyone else in the room realizes that the teacher already knows the answer. For example, a teacher who tends to use a lot of display questions might

TABLE 14.3.   Types of Strategies

Label (after Greenfell 1994)	Description of Strategy (after Stern 1975)	Examples of Ways Strategies Are Used in the Course
1. Communicative strategy	Using any language to convey meaning and ideas	Have a general discussion about a topic
2. Planning strategy	Doing something in preparation for reading/listening (activating schemata)	Brainstorm a topic and come up with a list of vocabulary that may be featured in the reading or listening tasks
3. Practice strategy	Using the language extensively in a controlled or semicontrolled way	Complete a language exercise focusing on specific items of grammar/vocabulary/usage, etc.
4. Semantic strategy	Focusing on understanding meaning as much as possible	Complete an intensive reading/listening exercise
5. Monitoring strategy	Monitoring own use of language either internally or from external feedback	Self- or peer assessment
6. Experimental strategy	Trying out the language to see how it can be used	Participating in postreading or postlistening discussion
7. Active strategy	Taking responsibility for learning	Self-monitoring of achievement/out-of-class preparation for lesson
8. Empathetic strategy	Relaxing when using the language, trying to enjoy the language experience, tolerating errors and ambiguity	Play language games/encourage classmates and be encouraged by classmates to participate in lessons

say, "In the opening paragraph there are three suggestions of how to protect the environment. What are the three suggestions, Siu Ming?" A challenge I am keenly aware of through my consultations with Manufacturing-Engineering faculty is that styles of teaching in their department depend upon considerably higher degrees of independent thinking, self-directed decision making, and autonomy. To lessen more traditional patterns of communication in the EEP1 course, a challenge I set for myself is to help learners develop more independence. Experience has taught me that developing such independence is difficult given students' many years of reliance on teachers.

When dealing with learners coming from a traditional secondary school background, the first few weeks of EEP1 serve as a transition and introduction to alternative patterns of classroom communication. Over the years I have found it useful to maintain styles of teaching that are already familiar and comfortable to students for several weeks. This initial phase is necessary before starting the process of beginning to introduce innovations from what their classrooms have been like in the past. Apart from the icebreaker activities mentioned in the section on affective concerns, a sense of the familiar and "normality" is achieved by continuing with some traditional learner roles. It would be fair to characterize this period as featuring teacher-centered lessons. In the past, attempts at early innovations and relaxing the rules of learning too quickly have not been well received. I find that at our institution students tend to flounder under such circumstances. They seem unsure of how to handle new roles if the roles are introduced too quickly. In the past, such uncertainties often resulted in misbehavior, frequent student complaints, and a frustrated teacher . . . sometimes for the duration of the course.

As the course continues, I introduce more and more instructional strategies that are less and less teacher centered. By the end of the course, students are expected to have developed clearer appreciations for the importance of learning to coordinate such options as working autonomously, collaborating with others, and making their own decisions on how to approach and complete course tasks. Over time, students come to realize that some of the previously unfamiliar learning strategies introduced in the course may, in fact, be useful.

Teacher's Roles

Anyone teaching EEP1 has many roles to perform, including the following: the traditional language teacher, the university "professor," the materials developer, the organizer, and the assessor.

Traditional role. As mentioned earlier, at the beginning of the first-semester course, the teacher has to adopt some of the traditional secondary schoolteachers' roles: (1) requiring everyone to be on time for class; (2) calling on students by name to answer questions; (3) checking that homework has been done; (4) maintaining class discipline; and (5) reminding students to use English instead of Cantonese, especially in pair/group work. As the course progresses, these schoolteacher-like behaviors become less obvious and less necessary. Students are encouraged to interact with each other and their teacher in a more personal way; students do not need to be reminded to be on time for class; they generally volunteer to answer questions; it is assumed that homework will have been done in preparation for the class; discipline is much less of an issue; and students become accustomed to using English with each other.

The "professor's" role. An explicit goal shared by our department faculty and also evident in most of the university's courses is to challenge students to become independent thinkers. Part of my job as an instructor of an entry-level university course is to find innovative ways to engage students in activities that will promote more independence in learning, more interactions with their professors, and more participation in class.

Materials developer role. Most of the materials used in the course have been locally designed by the staff at City University. I take on the role of materials monitor and update our course materials as necessary. Whenever possible, materials development is accomplished as a group effort. In our program such efforts are valued as part of a staff member's professional development responsibilities (see Miller 1995).

Organizer role. The learners are given more and more responsibility for their learning as the course progresses. As their teacher, I have to know when and how to organize the students into pair/group activities according to their strengths, weaknesses, preferences, and individual and group needs.

Assessor role. Although there is an ongoing emphasis on both peer and self-assessment during the course, I also serve a traditional role of being the overall assessor of students' performances. This role is in keeping with the university's requirements and supports administrative procedures for the courses we offer to be formally assessed and accredited.

Assessment

Students have an extended reading assessment halfway through the course, then another at the very end of the course. Reading sections for these assessments are taken from the textbook. Recently, I have been using unit 7's newspaper article "Asia's Position in the Manufacturing Industry" for the midterm test and unit 8's journal article "Kettles and Airfix and Design in Manufacturing" for the end-of-term exam. The exams provide opportunities for students to demonstrate their ability to deal with authentic and more extended reading experiences. The types of tasks students are required to complete on the exams resemble those practiced in class, such as reading to complete a diagram, composing summaries, providing their own interpretations and opinions centered on the article, and so on.

The listening test features note-taking and summary writing based on the final section of the video we use in the course that treats the topic "primary and secondary processes of changing raw materials into finished products" (see Internet table 14.2). Once more, students are given a task they have practiced many times before in class. Furthermore, the nature of the listening on the exam simulates a real-life criterion task/activity. In regular manufacturing-engineering courses, students attend lectures at which the instructor builds on previous lecture and reading materials. For assessment purposes in EEP1, the final section of the video allows students to activate and apply their prior knowledge from previous video segments and course readings. Because the culminating listening exam builds upon what they already have been studying, the task is more manageable and lifelike. All reading and listening tests are completed in class time, handed in, and graded by the instructor.

Lesson Particulars

Throughout the semester students are required to discuss what they are doing in the English lessons, why they think we are doing the kinds of things we do, and what outcomes of their learning in the course might be in terms of language development and its relationship to content-based learning. One such reflective session comes midway through the first-semester course. In this session, students are asked to discuss their experiences of attending lectures in English. The questions asked during the session deal with their perceptions of the course lecture as an event, problems they have when listening to lectures in English, and strategies they use to overcome any problems. The following is an excerpt from one audiotaped focus group session, a format planned in part to prepare them for tutorial meetings with course instructors. Those participating consisted of four ACTFL Intermediate-Mid level students and myself (*T* = teacher, *S* = student).

T: How do you feel about attending lectures?
S1: It's sometime useful but I sometimes not attend because it's useless.
T: Why do you say that?
S1: Because some teachers are good but some difficult to understand because they speak too fast.
T: Do you all agree?
S2: I think this is engineer course so must be in English but maybe too fast the speed.

S3: Yes, must be English.

T: Why?

S2: All notes and reference books in English so must be the lectures in English.

T: Do you think that, too, Derek?

S4: It depends who the lecturer is. Some of them only read to [from their] notes and that is difficult for us to understand, but some give good examples for us to follow.

T: What's the purpose of the lecture?

S3: To get main idea and then understand better details in tutorial.

S4: To give a chance for the lecturer to tell us the theory.

T: Is there anything we have been doing in the English class which helps you in your lectures?

S2: Yes.

S1: Yeah.

(*Long pause . . . everyone laughs.*)

T: And . . . ?

S2: We not get scared to listen to the foreigner.

T: Can you tell me more about this?

S2: When I first come and listen to foreigner speaking English I not understand anything (*at this point, in Cantonese, his classmates teasingly say to him, "You still don't understand"*) but now I listen very carefully and I not afraid to listen.

S1: In the [English] class we learn how to solve some problem when we listen.

T: Such as?

S1: I sometime ask my friend.

T: What helps you understand the lecture from the language point of view?

S3: Learn not to understand all the words. You tell, I mean you *show* us, not to understand [not to worry about having to understand] all the words is OK I can still understand. . . .

As we can see from this short excerpt, these typical EEP1 students are aware of some of the common problems Hong Kong students face at English-medium universities when they are expected to listen to learn from lectures in their new language. They realize that some of the sources of their problems, and some of the special challenges they face, may be traced to the lecturer's speed of delivery and choice of vocabulary and their own lack of familiarity with a topic under discussion. They also seem to be aware of some possible solutions. One compensatory strategy they mentioned is to ask a friend for help. Another is to learn to ignore and not become distracted by some of the nonessential vocabulary the lecturer might be using. In an effort to build upon and further extend such learner awareness, the first semester of the English for Engineers course offers opportunities for learners to enhance their reading and listening abilities. By the end of the course, students will overcome some of their reading and listening problems and become aware of a variety of academic learning strategies that they subsequently will apply in their manufacturing-engineering courses.

Conclusion

In the second semester of their first year of study, students continue developing their skills in a follow-up second language development and engineering-preparatory-focused course titled English for Engineers Part 2 (EEP2). As a complement to EEP1's attention to listening and reading, the second-semester course focuses on writing and speaking by way of a project structured to extend for the entire 14-week semester. As a team effort, students are required to conduct research on a manufactured product, compose a written report, and present their findings orally in class. Combined with the first-semester course, support for all four language skills is given significant and sustained attention during the students' first year at the university.

Whereas the first-semester course comes closest to a "Type A" syllabus design (see the syllabus section presented earlier), the second-semester course is structured around a significant number of "Type B" features. The students have a greater say in the direction of their learning in the second course and in how class meetings are structured and assessed, and they choose which areas of language to focus on. This is possible in the second-semester course because EEP1 has served as a transition phase in their learning that prepared them for such responsibilities. While working in teams on their projects, learners decide for themselves whether to focus the culminating presentation of the products they investigate on process descriptions, factual descriptions, or comparisons, among other options. This shifting in course structures from EEP1 to EEP2 is deliberate. Students enter the first semester of the two-course sequence directly from local secondary schools. But by the end of EEP2, they must be ready to function competently and to succeed in mainstream, English-medium manufacturing-engineering courses. Course one lays a requisite groundwork and gets them started along the right path for success, while course two comes even closer to simulating criterion tasks approximating the expectations of those who will be their manufacturing-engineering professors.

Prompts for Discussion and Reflection

1. Describe the setting for "English for Engineers 1." Compare Miller's setting to some other ELT setting with which you are familiar. How similar/different are they?

2. Discuss the conceptual underpinnings for the course described in this chapter. Are you familiar with these approaches in language education? What do they involve? Identify ideas you may draw from any of them for purposes of your own teaching. Do you think any of the approaches discussed by Miller might not work with your students? Why?

3. The instructional materials for English for Engineers have been especially prepared for the course. What are some of the advantages and disadvantages of preparing your own materials? What complications might you envision?

4. Look at the types of strategies listed in table 14.3. Consider a course that you are familiar with. With a partner, talk about how the tasks you ask students to complete may correspond with Greenfell's labels or Stern's descriptions.

5. Look at the examples of ways strategies are used in the course in table 14.3. Discuss other ways these strategies might be realized through classroom tasks.

6. In the course described in this chapter the teacher attempts slowly to change the learners' roles from more to less dependence on the teacher. Think of a course you are familiar with. Do students in that course progress through similar changes? How easy or difficult is it for ELT students to adopt new roles? Discuss any experiences you might have in this area as either a learner or a teacher.

7. At the beginning of the EEP1 course, the teacher's role may be described as rather authoritarian. Is it acceptable for a university teacher to perform such a role? How do you respond to Miller's rationale for this course feature? Compare Miller's understanding of the role of teacher in this regard with Tom Robb's discussion of the role of the teacher as a supervisor of EFL students' efforts in chapter 13.

8. There seems to be a contradiction in trying to promote learner autonomy and formally assessing the students' reading and listening skills.

Do you think that there is such a contradiction in this course? If so, how might an EEP1 teacher come even closer than Miller in trying to resolve it? What principle(s) presented in table 2.4 of chapter 2 might you use to support your position?

9. The transcription in the Lesson Particulars section is taken from a focus group with the teacher and a small number of students. Can you infer any rationale to support the use of focus groups in ELT? Think of the advantages and disadvantages of using focus groups as part of a course you teach. What constructive purposes might they serve?

Miniprojects

10. Find a short (400-word) newspaper article. Building from Miller's discussion, design three tasks around the article: one prereading, one while reading, and one postreading. Review the activity type examples before you begin.

11. In his conclusion, Miller described briefly (but had limited space to discuss in detail) the second-semester EEP2 course. Extending his discussion, how do you think the EEP2 course should be structured? What components would it include? Use the *Understanding* chapter framework as presented in table 1.1 (in chap. 1) to describe what you think its features should be.

Part 4
University Courses
(Credit Bearing)

Chapter 15

EAP Support for Matriculated University Students

Janet M. Goodwin

Janet Goodwin presents an English for Academic Purposes (EAP) support course for matriculated ESL university students. Each unit of instruction centers on a video recording of a single lecture, and accompanying authentic readings, featured in an undergraduate general education course. Students receive input in manageable chunks and focus not on academic lecture or reading content per se but on the process of learning to deal with such content. Goodwin emphasizes that EAP teachers must focus on students' academic needs—how learners can best acquire skills and strategies necessary to succeed in non-ESL university courses.

In addition to the content of a university lecture and readings, Goodwin's starting points for course design are academic tasks originally assigned in the general education lecturer's course. By blending both content- and task-based features, Goodwin's course benefits ESL learners in at least two ways: (1) since students are already matriculated into the university, tasks featured in the course are ones they grapple with each day; (2) the content featured in the course sets parameters and serves as a natural vehicle through which EAP pedagogical tasks may be realized.

In the section titled "Activity Types," Goodwin describes and discusses a series of 14 tasks that come in two stages: (1) processing content input and (2) using content knowledge to perform academic tasks. Each of the two stages has both skills-focus and language-focus components. In the first stage, activities focus on skills such as understanding a lecture, taking effective notes, and extracting important points from a reading. The language component highlights the actual language used in the lecture and readings, such as noting what discourse markers the lecturer uses to signal topic development and transitions. In the second stage, instruction in using content knowledge to perform academic tasks targets such skills as summarizing source material and analyzing essay questions. The language component highlights learning to use vocabulary and structures appropriate for academic discourse. Students also learn to edit language errors in their writing. Because the content (recordings of academic lectures and related readings) and tasks of a university course are brought into the ESL classroom, students in the course develop strategies for comprehension of content and completion of relevant academic tasks and assignments. Through engagement with videotaped lectures and authentic reading assignments, learners receive input in manageable but not simplified chunks. Goodwin explores ways of structuring the course so that students focus *not* on the content of academic lectures and readings but on the process of learning to deal with content effectively.

————

Setting

This course targets undergraduate ESL students who are matriculated at the University of California, Los Angeles (UCLA), a large public research university. All of the students taking the course are also enrolled in one or more mainstream (i.e., non-ESL) undergraduate courses, usually large introductory level lecture-based courses. Although some departments may require a minimum TOEFL score, most entering nonnative English speaking students are required to take the UCLA ESL placement examination (ESLPE), consisting of three sections: reading comprehension, listening comprehension, and an academic essay. This exam is designed to exempt students from an ESL requirement or to place them appropriately into one of four credit-bearing ESL courses: levels one, two, and three are multiskills; the fourth level course focuses on writing.

The proficiency of learners described here (level two of multiskills) corresponds with the ACTFL proficiency guidelines level of Intermediate-High in the areas of reading and writing. Students' listening levels vary from ACTFL Intermediate-High to Advanced, usually depending on the individual's length of residence in the United States. The population consists of both permanent residents and international (nonresident) students, predominantly from the Pacific Rim. Some are incoming freshmen, but a majority have transferred as juniors from community colleges in California. Most have chosen to major in mathematics, science, engineering, or business/economics; a consistent few specialize in the arts, usually dance, music, or design. Very few major in the humanities or social sciences, yet all UCLA undergraduates must complete a certain number of general education credits in order to complete a bachelor's degree.

The class meets five hours a week for 10 weeks with enrollment limited to 20. Students are seated in groups of three to four at square tables.

Since each table is placed at an angle, appearing to the teacher as a diamond rather than a square, no one has her or his back entirely to the front of the room. A blackboard and projector screen are located at the front of the room with whiteboards at the rear and on one side. The room is equipped with a videocassette player, two TV monitors, an overhead projector, a cassette player, and a set of ESL learner dictionaries (one dictionary per table). Elsewhere on campus, students have access to a video laboratory, several PC and Macintosh computer labs, and a state-of-the-art library system that includes an undergraduate library, an extensive graduate research library, and numerous discipline-specific libraries.

Conceptual Underpinnings

ESP/EAP

Language support courses for students in a formal academic setting fall into the realm of English for Academic Purposes (EAP), a subcategory of the broader field of English for Specific Purposes (ESP). ESP proponents believe that "language teaching must be designed for the specific learning and language use purposes of identified groups of students" (Johns 1991, 67). As a result, ESL research has often focused on examining the discourse of the target language situation. However, Hutchinson and Waters (1987) move beyond the context focus of earlier needs analysis studies in ESP and maintain that the primary focus of ESP instruction should be on language *learning*, not on language *use*. For example, instruction needs to take into account the learner's previous knowledge, cognitive processes, interest, and involvement. Just knowing and providing an authentic *context* for EAP students is not enough. If it were, then simply attending or auditing content courses would be sufficient for university ESL students to learn. What the EAP teacher adds to the equation is a focus on the learner's *academic needs*— how learners can best acquire the strategies and skills necessary to succeed in non-ESL content courses.

EAP Needs Analysis Research

Numerous needs analyses have examined the academic demands placed on university students (e.g., Kroll 1979; Johns 1981; Ostler 1980; Bridgeman and Carlson 1984; Horowitz 1986; Ferris and Tagg 1996a, 1996b). Among the pedagogical recommendations made in such studies, Horowitz (1986) advocates writing tasks that teach students to select relevant data, reorganize the selected data, and then encode this reorganized data into academic English. Based on a review of academic listening research, Chaudron (1995) notes the importance of background knowledge for lecture comprehension and of making learners aware of discourse markers, pauses, and nonverbal features. In terms of note-taking skills, Chaudron emphasizes training in recognizing main and subordinate points, using abbreviations, and maintaining an organizational structure in one's notes for later reference. Ferris (1998) points out that many ESL students already function well in small groups. She suggests that EAP instruction should focus instead on whole class discussions. Ferris also stresses the importance of teaching students how to ask questions of clarification and repetition in a lecture so they may become more participatory as learners in academic settings.

Authenticity as a Basis for Syllabus Design

The studies mentioned previously reflect the need for *authenticity*, that is, using real language contexts and tasks when designing an EAP syllabus. Ferris and Tagg (1996b) report that content-area professors are consistent in commenting about ESL students along the following lines.

> ESL students need to move out of their comfort zone in preparing for college coursework: They need to hear subject-matter professors giving actual lectures, to communicate with native speakers, to grapple with technical texts and vocabulary, and to practice authentic writing tasks. (313)

The authentic nature of both the content and the tasks of the EAP course described here makes it a "content-based" course, one in which the instructional materials are developed from lectures and readings culled from actual university courses, as well as a "task-based" one, organized around a sequence of tasks taken from these same content courses.

Content-Based Instruction

In the model of content-based instruction (CBI) used in the EAP course I am describing, units are based on videotaped lectures and accompanying reading assignments from general education undergraduate courses on our campus. However, unlike in the regular university course, the content material does not race by at a breakneck speed; rather, it is presented in shorter segments with focused attention on academic language and skills.

Two areas of concern for EAP instructors of content-based courses include (1) their possible lack of expertise in the content focus of the unit and (2) the difficulty of providing a systematic treatment of grammar within the content materials. With regard to the first concern, the difficulty of any given content depends not only on its linguistic complexity but also on the background knowledge of the reader or listener. Since the content for the EAP units I develop is taken from real courses, lectures were chosen that either occurred at the beginning of the term or were relatively self-contained, not requiring much specialized background knowledge. Neither the instructor nor the students need "fear" the content; it is the necessary vehicle through which academic language proficiency is acquired.

A second major concern of many content-based instructors is that language instruction gets lost once we start focusing too heavily on content ideas, information, and concepts. So, how can grammar be incorporated systematically into this type of course? When we address grammar within a content-based syllabus, we can use the following four areas as points of departure.

The content input we give our students, that is, the lectures and readings

> *What type of grammar instruction can prepare students for the linguistic demands of the content?*

The tasks and assignments we set

> *What grammar will students need to complete the task?*
> *How can thinking about the language demands of a task help us to frame assignments better in the first place?*

The output or product we get from our students in speaking or writing

> *Are there patterns of errors in student output?*
> *Can any particular linguistic tools or strategies help them to revise?*
> *In retrospect, was there any preassignment language instruction that would have helped that we did not predict?*

Skills and strategies to promote autonomous language learning

> *How can we make students aware—within the context of language instruction—of their own learning process and of efficient learner strategies to adopt?*

By incorporating grammar instruction in these four ways, we can continue to use content without losing sight of the language.

Objectives

The overall aim of this EAP course is to help students become "academically proficient." By the end of the course they should have gained skills necessary to be able to function more competently in mainstream university courses. More specific objectives can be divided into the following categories.

Reading

> to distinguish main versus supporting information
> to understand the function of discourse markers and cohesive devices within a written text

Vocabulary development

> to guess meaning by using context clues and analyzing word parts
> to learn basic academic vocabulary related to the genres of summary, report, explanation, and description

Writing

> to learn basic organizational patterns for academic writing
> to learn strategies for synthesizing source material to compose an academic essay
> to revise written work through giving and receiving feedback

Listening and note-taking

> to note the main idea and key points of a lecture
> to understand how discourse markers, intonation, and pauses convey meaning
> to develop a personal note-taking system indicating relationships between ideas

Speaking

> to learn to ask for repetition, clarification, and elaboration
> to gain fluency in both small group and whole class discussions

Grammar and editing

> to analyze grammatical structures in reading passages
> to edit for grammar in one's own writing

These skill objectives are integrated through the unifying content focus of each unit.

Syllabus Design

The design of the course syllabus derives from both content-based and task-based models. Simultaneously, the points of departure are the content of a university lecture and readings as well as the kinds of academic tasks assigned in the university course. The advantage of this meshing of content-based and task-based approaches to syllabus design is twofold: (1) the tasks are those that students grapple with each day; thus, they have strong face validity; (2) the content provides necessary unity and is a natural vehicle for EAP pedagogic tasks to exist within.

The resulting syllabus consists of two units, each of which is based on

> a single videotaped lecture (one to two hours) from an introductory general education course
> the course readings assigned for that day's lecture
> the types of tasks assigned in the course

In designing the EAP course, it was necessary to discover what real world tasks undergraduate students are asked to perform, to examine how student performance is evaluated, and to re-create the academic tasks as closely as possible in the ESL classroom. Thus, the professors of the videotaped lectures were consulted regarding sample writing assignments, essay questions, test formats, supplementary activities, and grading criteria. Observing authentic discussion sections taught by graduate teaching assistants (GTAs) provided additional information on speaking demands and how lecture material is handled in smaller groups.

The EAP pedagogic tasks within a unit come in two stages: (1) processing the content input and (2) using the content knowledge to perform academic tasks. Each of these two stages has both a skills focus and a language focus. In the first stage, digesting the content, students learn skills such as understanding a lecture, taking effective notes, and extracting important points from a reading. Language tasks highlight the actual language used in the lecture and readings, such as noting what discourse markers the lecturer uses and how they function or discovering how key terms are defined in the text.

In the second stage, application of the content to academic tasks, students learn skills such as summarizing source material, analyzing and responding to an essay question under time pressure, and writing a paper in several drafts. Language tasks focus on learning to use vocabulary and structures appropriate for academic discourse and on editing language errors in one's writing. Throughout both stages, processing the content and applying it, students reflect on how to transfer what they are learning to other university courses in which they are enrolled concurrent with the EAP course.

Activity Types

Analyzing Course Syllabi

One of the important skills at the university level is understanding the expectations of a particular professor. To this end, students analyze not only the syllabus for the EAP adjunct course and the syllabi for the two content courses we work with (e.g., sociology and history) but also the syllabi for their *other* university courses. If any aspect of these other course syllabi is unclear, we practice ways to approach their GTAs or professors about it. In addition to providing information about our students, this activity also lends credibility to the tasks performed in the EAP course. For example, in the sociology syllabus, the grading criteria are as follows.

Take-home midterm	20 percent
Final essay examination	30 percent
Active section participation	10 percent
Homework	10 percent
Ethnographic research project:	
Observations	10 percent
Analysis	20 percent

Active section participation is defined as coming to class having already completed and reflected on the assigned reading(s). Students are also expected to (*a*) connect readings, lectures, and observations in thoughtful ways; (*b*) answer and pose questions as part of in-class discussions; and (*c*) respond supportively to other students' comments (Matthews 1990). Noting this and the fact that 30 percent of the grade is based on an in-class essay (the final) and 50 percent on out-of-class papers lends credibility to the tasks performed in the EAP course.

Journal Writing

Weekly journal assignments focus on digesting content input, making connections between the lecture and readings, and posing questions about unclear points. In addition, students are asked to illustrate ways in which they are transferring the skills and strategies learned in the EAP course to their other courses. Sample journal assignment topics include the following.

> What connections do you see between the chapter from William Golding's *Lord of the Flies* and the sociology concepts we have been studying?
>
> (Midquarter) Discuss the activities and atmosphere of this course. What do you hope for in the next five weeks? Also, discuss the workload and difficulty of your other courses. What have you learned in this ESL class that has helped you in your other university courses?

Video Lecture: Beyond Note-taking Guides

In this activity type, the video lecture we work with for each unit has been edited into multiple segments, each with its own note-taking work sheet or task. Segments at this level usually run 8 to 10 minutes, depending on locations of natural breaks between subtopics in the lecture. During the first listening, students take notes on a blank sheet; then they use these notes to fill out an instructor-generated note-taking guide. For the second viewing, students listen specifically to fill in gaps on the note-taking guide. Finally, students respond to some "application and review" questions that can be answered either by referring to the reading passage or by applying personal knowledge. (See Internet app. 15.1 for an illustration.)

This activity emphasizes the importance of interacting with academic content material in order to understand and apply it more effectively. Internet appendix 15.2 features an additional work sheet designed to help students deepen their understanding of content material by applying it to new contexts. For this activity, students categorize a variety of groups using sociological concepts they have learned about, first as a homework assignment, then as a group consensus activity.

Video Lecture: Comparing One's Notes to a Model

Here, students compare their own notes with two model sets of notes tied to a particular lecture segment. In this way, learners are exposed to different note-taking strategies, abbreviations, and symbols. One objective is for learners to realize that even the two model sets of notes do not necessarily highlight the same pieces of information in the same ways but that both capture the essential information featured in the video segment.

Getting into the Content

A schema-building task for getting into the content involves small group discussion. Following Johnson and Johnson (1987), specific tasks are outlined for the roles of discussion leader, timekeeper, and note taker within a group of three or four students at a table. Each group has the same packet of six to eight discussion questions written on separate cards and placed facedown on the table. At the very beginning of the unit titled "The History of the American Family," in which the lecturer discusses the American family ideal, students begin by discussing their *own* concept of an ideal family. For example,

> In your opinion, what is the ideal role for the husband and/or father in a family?
> Is this view changing in your culture? If so, how?
> How has family life changed from your grandparents' time, to your parents' time, to yours?

To begin, the discussion leader for the first round picks up the top card, reads it aloud, and makes sure each member understands the question. The discussion leader then either answers the question or calls on another member to participate. The timekeeper allows a predetermined amount of time per question per round (usually three or four minutes). At the end of a round, the students' roles shift, and a new discussion leader picks up the next card on the pile. At the end (groups usually finish at around the same time because of the imposed time limit per question), I elicit the main points from each group's discussion on the board and highlight those points that will contribute most to clearer understanding of the upcoming unit. (For further details, see Goodwin 1997.)

Whole Class Discussion

To jump-start a class discussion of an assigned reading, I write 15 to 20 key terms from the reading out of order onto an overhead transparency. I then take a seat at the back of the room and begin with an introductory question, such as, *Can anyone explain one of the terms?* Since many of the terms are related, an explanation for one term may involve using one or two others. Students are asked to provide examples to illustrate the term and to indicate whether they agree with a classmate's explanation. Having the technical vocabulary on the transparency minimizes the need to memorize the terms and helps students explain challenging concepts in their own words. By providing their own examples, students learn ways of interacting with information to remember it better. By practicing turn-taking strategies in the larger group, they gain skills for participating in the discussion sections of their other courses, which are usually conducted with the support of a GTA.

Text Analysis: Paraphrasing Connectors in the Reading

One text analysis activity is to highlight the connectors used by the assigned reading's author to relate one idea to another. For example, in one sociology paragraph, we find the following discussion.

> Groups are not tangible things; rather, they are products of social definitions—sets of shared ideas. As such they constitute constructed realities. In other words, we make groups real by treating them as if they were real. (emphasis added) (Vander Zanden, *Sociology: The Core*, 1990, 93)

Students work in pairs to come up with an acceptable paraphrase of each underlined connector. This activity highlights the critical importance not just of understanding the author's ideas but of understanding how these ideas are related to one another.

Text Analysis: Understanding Cohesion within a Paragraph

This activity is an adaptation of the well-known "strip story" procedure. First, the sentences of a single paragraph from the reading are retyped onto a sheet of paper that can be photocopied and cut into individual strips of paper with a random letter assigned to each strip. Each group receives a packet of sentence strips that they are to sequence into a unified paragraph, recording their sequence of letters on the board. Each group must be able to explain how they determined that one sentence came before or after another. Using the same sentences on OHP transparency strips, we come to a group consensus about the sequence, which can be verified in the textbook reading. However, before checking with the text, the members of the class discuss whatever they were taking into consideration while performing the task and how their reasonings and understandings relate to a knowledge of paragraph structure and cohesive devices (e.g., connectors, pronoun reference, cataphoric reference, anaphoric reference).

Peer Feedback: Paragraph Cohesion

Having explored how cohesion works within a paragraph from the reading, in this activity students apply what they have learned to their own writings. They take a paragraph from one of their own papers and put each sentence onto a separate strip of paper. In class, students exchange strips with a partner, try to put their partner's paragraph in order, and then compare solutions. If either partner has difficulty, the reader and writer exchange ideas on how to make connections between sentences easier to recognize. Even though no explicit judgments are made about the writing, peer feedback of this nature emphasizes the importance of cohesion and taking the reader more directly into consideration.

Peer Feedback: Read-around Technique

In the read-around technique (Gossard 1987), each member at a table contributes a current draft of her or his paper (with no name, just an identifying number) in order to create a paper-clipped packet of four drafts. The teacher passes each packet to a new table round by round in a circle around the room. When the teacher says, "Begin," each table unclips their new packet and distributes one draft to each person to begin reading. After a predetermined amount of time (40 to 60 seconds), the teacher signals, "Pass your draft to the right," until all four drafts in the packet have been read by all group members. Although many drafts will not be read completely by each member, the idea is to get students to read more quickly and to gain an overall idea of the clarity of the writer's ideas. Groups then have one minute to agree on which draft is the best (I intentionally don't define "best" for them in advance) and record the number on a list. At the end of a round, the group reclips the packet of drafts, and the teacher passes it to another table for the next round. Based on time limitations, the teacher can decide how many rounds to have. In my course, I have five groups and thus can do four rounds (a group *never* judges the best of their own packet of drafts!) However, I might stop at three rounds if I'm running out of time. You need at least three rounds to reach consensus of opinion on which are the best drafts. At the end, I elicit the results for all rounds in a grid on the board. After the grid is complete, any instances of repeated numbers are circled. The repeated numbers signify that the same draft was judged to be the "best" at more than one table. Then, the teacher says, "You were able to judge the 'best.' Now, what are some of the writing features that distinguish more effective drafts?" Responses are elicited and put on the board. This list contains what the students themselves consider to be the qualities of a good paper. If any single draft was selected three or four times, I read it aloud, and we discuss how it exhibits the traits on the board. Finally, students complete a brief quickwrite.

> After reading your classmates' papers, what have you learned that can help you to improve your own paper?

Grammar Editing: Pair Activity

As feedback on in-class writings and the second draft of the out-of-class papers, I identify error types in the right margins of the lines in which they have occurred, neither correcting them nor pinpointing the exact location within the lines. In class, students work in pairs to locate the errors and correct them. I make sure they work together on only one of their papers at a time, rather than exchanging papers. The goal is to share their knowledge verbally while problem solving by correcting language errors. At this level, I restrict the types of errors I highlight to those that we have worked with in class or that I can reasonably expect students to recognize from previous instruction.

Writing a Limited-Time Essay

In both in-class and out-of-class compositions, I emphasize the following: (1) summarizing, paraphrasing, and citing source materials; and (2) applying concepts from source materials to personal knowledge or to information from a literary text. Because limited-time essays are common in academic courses and often stressful for ESL learners, practice of this kind is central to the writing component of the EAP adjunct course. Emphasis is placed on examining writing prompts carefully, organizing one's response in advance, and self-editing one's work at the end. For example, in connection with William Golding's (1959) *Lord of the Flies,* a writing prompt might be as follows.

> Of the three main characters in chapter 1 (Ralph, Piggy, or Jack), which one would you choose to be your leader? Discuss why you would choose that person using concepts from the sociology chapter to explain and justify your choice.

By doing three or four such essays, students gain confidence in their ability to decode a prompt and target their response.

Writing a Multidraft Paper

The sociology unit of my course contains an observation and analysis task that is similar to an ethnographic research project assigned in the mainstream sociology course. Students are asked to observe a group they are familiar with and analyze it according to sociological principles they have been studying (see app. 15.1 for the prompt). In the actual sociology course, students only submit one draft; in the EAP course, the papers in both units involve multiple drafts with peer feedback, teacher comments, and conferencing to support the revision process.

Writing Conference

Following the second draft of a paper, students attend a 30-minute writing conference. They bring with them both drafts and all feedback from peers and instructor. In preparation, students are asked to

> highlight the thesis statement in the latest draft
> write down the main idea of each body paragraph
> revise language errors labeled in the margin of their paper
> formulate a list of questions they have about teacher feedback or any aspect of the paper they are having difficulty with
> mark with a highlighter pen any ideas that are not their own, that is, those that come from a source text

When students arrive this well prepared, I find they are better equipped to initiate, participate in, and sustain a more substantive interaction. The goals are for students to take ownership of their writing, to learn the value of revision, and to gain a better sense of audience.

Learners' Roles

As they sit facing each other at tables, learners interact from the moment they greet each other until the final bell rings. Through a series of pair, table, and whole class activities during the lesson, they take on a variety of roles, including audience member, problem solver, teacher, ethnographic researcher, and informant.

In the role of *audience,* learners listen to a peer rehearse an oral presentation, making suggestions for improvement and asking questions of clarification or elaboration. When reading a draft of a partner's paper, the peer reader provides feedback by analyzing the structure, pointing out unclear points, and asking for more explanation when it is needed. As *problem solvers,* students work together to complete a task, such as ordering sentences into a cohesive paragraph or locating and correcting grammar errors in each other's writing.

In completing the paper in the sociology unit, students also become *ethnographic researchers.* Their task is to observe a group with which they are familiar, take notes, and analyze the group according to the sociological categories they have been studying. By relying on more than personal knowledge, through guided/focused observation students begin to understand the process of data collection and analysis, a task they will encounter often in subsequent stages of their college careers. A final role is that of *informant.* Students inform both teachers and classmates in many ways. In this course, they provide a window to the wider university by bringing their own experiences in mainstream courses to bear on the skills they are learning in ESL. The connections they voice supply a constant reminder of one of the course's foremost goals—to help them achieve success in their other university courses.

Teacher's Roles

As a *facilitator,* the teacher defines the tasks, sets up a favorable climate for interaction, and then monitors and guides the progress learners are making. Through reflective journal and discussion topics, the teacher is also a *guide,* helping students to take control of their learning. For example, after completing a paper, students look over the series of drafts they have written and compare their first and last versions. I ask students to discuss what they consider the most significant changes between their first and last drafts and to reflect on what they learned by writing the paper. As we examine together "what was learned," it is an impressive list, one in which learners can take justifiable pride. The teacher in this type of course also functions as a *bridge*, laying the groundwork for making connections between what students are learning in the course and how to apply those same skills across the curriculum. Finally, the teacher takes on the daily role of *manager*, navigating the preplanned lesson while remaining responsive to learners' questions, efforts, and errors.

Instructional Materials

Due to the localized nature of this course with units based on UCLA lectures, instructional materials are collated in a course packet that students purchase. The packet includes the sociology and history textbook readings (Vander Zanden 1990, chap. 4; Leslie and Korman 1989, chap. 10), the first chapter from Golding's (1959) *Lord of the Flies*, reading and vocabulary work sheets, note-taking guides, syllabi and course descriptions for the EAP course as well as for two content courses (Introduction to Sociology and History of the American Family), the out-of-class writing assignments, a peer feedback form for each paper, oral presentation guidelines and assessment forms, work sheets on in-class essay exams, writing assessment forms for ESL compositions, UCLA grading information, and a listing of campus resources.

Although grammar is incorporated within the course through analysis of assigned readings and the editing of students' errors, students are required to buy an additional grammar review text, Lane and Lange's (1999) *Writing Clearly: An Editing Guide.* Recommended textbooks include the Longman *Dictionary of American English* (1997) and Hacker's (1995) *A Writer's Reference.*

Lesson Particulars

In the fourth week of class, I begin the lesson by having each table discuss a homework assignment that required them to rate the three main characters of *Lord of the Flies*, Ralph, Piggy, and Jack, according to various character attributes.[1] I start off by saying:

> What I would like you to do is to discuss at your table where to put Ralph, Piggy, and Jack. I going to give each table one transparency and one pen, and

---

1. This discussion is based on videotaping and transcriptions by Irene Koshik, a former UCLA Ph.D. student in applied linguistics and TESL.

self-confidence	LOW --- HIGH
intelligence	LOW --- HIGH
tolerance	LOW --- HIGH
sensitivity	LOW --- HIGH
aloof	LOW --- HIGH
empathetic	LOW --- HIGH

Fig. 15.1.   Character attributes in *Lord of the Flies*

I'm going to ask you at your table to come to some kind of consensus or agreement about where you would place Ralph, where you would place Jack, and where you would place Piggy for each characteristic. And I'd like you to be able to justify your choice. I know you've read this story very carefully—I can tell that from what you've said until now.

I then distribute a transparency and one washable OHP pen to each table. The transparency is identical to the original homework exercise and contains character attributes in the left-hand column, each of which is followed by a continuum line from low to high. The task is to put a letter for each boy (*P* for Piggy, etc.) at an appropriate location on each line according to one's judgment of the boy's character (see Collie and Slater 1987).

One group near the front consists of three Vietnamese students, Ban, Vinh, and Thang, and one Chinese student, Lee.

Ban: (*picks up the pen*) OK, now we do it. The first one is self-confidence. Piggy—low Piggy.

Vinh: (*looking at Lee*) Did you do this yet?

Ban: (*All four table members are looking at the transparency in the center of the table. As Ban says each name, he writes the initial on the transparency.*) Piggy on the left, Jack in the middle, and Ralph on the right.

Thang: (*looking back and forth from his homework to the transparency*) What? Self-confidence? No! Jack first, then Ralph, and then Piggy.

Ban: (*points to the right side of Thang's homework sheet, where the word high is written*) No, high! (*Ban begins moving his hand to the left side of Thang's homework sheet.*) Them are high!

Through gesture and talk, Ban has clarified an oversight on Thang's part, namely, that the continuum line moves from low to high and not vice versa. Once this misunderstanding about the work sheet format is solved, members continue with the task at hand.

Another group is beginning to discuss the term *aloof*. Students at this table include one Korean, one Japanese, one Thai, and one Vietnamese individual.

Trinh: OK, how about the next one?

Yoon: Aloof?

Trinh: I think Jack is the highest.

Joop: I don't really understand this word. What is the meaning?

Trinh: OK, like they doesn't want to get along. They doesn't want to stick together. That's the meaning of the word.

Joop: They they . . . (*still looks puzzled*)

Trinh: OK, like all of us we work together in the table, right? (*gestures in circular motion*) So all of us want to get along, want to get things done. (*gestures with hands cupped in circle*) But, for example, me? (*gestures toward self*) I don't want to be a team; I don't want to get along with you guys. I just let you do whatever you want. (*gestures toward others*) I want to be separate. That's the meaning of the word . . . aloof. (*The rest of the students nod.*)

Joop: Um, and what do you think who is the highest?

In a third group, the table consists of five female students from Japan, India, Hong Kong, Taiwan, and Vietnam. One student is looking up the word *empathetic* in their table's dictionary while another leans over to look at the dictionary definition.

Anita: It's different?

Tu-uyen: (*reading from the dictionary*) The power of imagining oneself to be another person and so sharing his or her feelings. (*Anita continues to look at the dictionary definition; Tu-uyen looks across the table at Vivian's paper.*) What did *you* put down?

Vivian: Huh?

Anita: Want to see? (*Anita picks up the dictionary, holds it up for Vivian to see, and rereads the definition.*)

Vivian: Ask her? (*Vivian looks toward me and puts her hand halfway up.*)

Teacher: Can I answer a question?

Tu-uyen:	Yeah. We don't really understand the meaning of this word. (*points to* empathetic)
Teacher:	OK, and when you look up *empathy*? (*I see a few nods; then I take the dictionary and look up* empathy.) It's right here: The power of imagining oneself to be another person and so being able to share his or her feelings.
Anita:	So is it positive or negative?
Teacher:	Oh, it's positive. It's the idea of—
Anita:	(*interrupts*) You consider the other person?
Teacher:	Yeah. You probably know the word *sympathy* better. I think it's a more common word in English. (*I begin flipping through the dictionary.*) OK, let's look up that one just so we can compare them because they're similar, but they're not exactly the same. (*I begin reading the dictionary definition.*) OK, *sympathy* is the expression of pity for the sufferings of other people. OK, so when I feel sorry for somebody like (*with visible affect*) "Oh, golly, that's too bad!" that is a *form* of empathy. But empathy isn't restricted to just feeling sad for somebody . . . or feeling pity for somebody. Empathy is the ability to feel *all kinds* of emotions that other people feel. It's like if you're really happy, then gosh, I can be happy with you. I can feel just as happy because I can understand *why* you're happy and *how* you're happy, OK? So, *empathy* is kind of a broader term, and *sympathy* is a little more specific. OK? (*I leave the table.*)

This lesson highlights the use of cooperative learning within a problem-solving task. Together, the students clarify the task, share knowledge, negotiate meaning, and debate answers. When consulted, I try to approach the group as a knowledgeable coparticipant, another resource among many available to students.

Caveats/Final Thoughts

The materials development aspect of a course as localized as this one can be overwhelming to teachers with limited time and resources. The investment to create video-supported units is indeed significant, but I am convinced of its value in preparing second language students for the formidable academic challenges they face in university settings. Furthermore, by attempting to move beyond our sometimes insular orbit as ESL teachers into the wider university arena, we begin forging links with other departments and across disciplines (see Benesch 1996). Not only do we discover what the students on our campus actually need to *do* beyond settings of ESL courses, but we sometimes are able to transform these links into a dialogue where university colleagues share ideas and strategies for making subject matter courses more accessible to ESL learners.

Prompts for Discussion and Reflection

1. Think about an experience you have had as a foreign or second language learner, especially if you have studied outside your home country. What skills or strategies did you need most to succeed in your studies? Compare your needs as a language learner to those of the ESL students for whom this course was designed.

2. In order to design this course, the EAP teacher observed and interviewed professors and graduate teaching assistants of undergraduate lecture courses. What is the value of such preparation activities? In what ways might the time invested be justified?

3. In what ways does Goodwin's method of teaching reflect any of the general ELT principles listed in table 2.4 of chapter 2?

4. The students enrolled in this university ESL course also participate in two or three other university courses at the same time. In what ways might this broader context of students' learning experiences impact the design of an ESL course? How might the nature of Goodwin's course, and students' responses to it, differ from the nature of and students' responses to a preuniversity intensive ESL course?

5. The core materials for the course (videotaped lectures and related readings) are taken from actual undergraduate courses rather than from a published ESL textbook. What are the pros and cons of such a "real-life" materials choice? Would you consider such an option in a course you (might) teach? Why or why not?

6. The author presents four points of departure she considered when designing grammar instruction. What are they, and how do they relate to your own idea of how grammar should be taught? Consider possible connections to other discussions of grammar teaching with which you are familiar or others included in this book (e.g., chap. 18, by Dana Ferris and chap. 19, by May Shih).

7. Unlike some EFL learners, who may have little immediate use for English outside the classroom, ESL learners often have pressing language

needs beyond the language classroom. How might the course model Goodwin describes be adapted to address the language needs and objectives of learners you have taught or hope to teach in the future? Compare how your (future) students' needs might compare to the needs of students described in the chapter.

8. While teaching, the author explains that she functions as a facilitator, bridge, guide, and manager. What evidence does she provide to support such self-descriptions? Do they seem justified and accurate? How do such roles fit with your own self-image as a language teacher?

9. This course purports to be simultaneously *content based* and *task based*. How would you define these terms? To what principles of syllabus design do they apply? Do you agree that the design of Goodwin's course addresses both of these aims? If so, does this dual-focus course structure result in a coherent plan for teaching, in your opinion? Why or why not?

10. The learners in the course come from a diverse array of majors and will take a great variety of courses during their university studies. Thus, it is impossible to target a lecture and readings from any specific course that a given student might take in the future. When choosing which lectures to videotape for such a course, what do you think are appropriate criteria to consider? Which types of courses or content seem to you to be most appropriate?

Miniprojects

11. The guiding principle of the course described in this chapter is to have a clear understanding of learners' target language situation. You may or may not be planning to teach university EAP students. For a context in which you are teaching, or might be planning to teach in the future, design a needs assessment plan for investigating the needs of those learners. How would you begin? What would you do?

12. Check through a college catalog and ask permission to observe a typical undergraduate lecture course on your campus or at a local college. If possible, try to obtain a syllabus and course description and make arrangements to discuss the course with someone who teaches it. Following the observation, interview the course instructor regarding such things as the tasks and assessment of students. (Alternatively, interview one of the students.) Prepare a brief summary report for your classmates and discuss the suitability of this course as the basis for an EAP unit such as the one described in this chapter.

Appendix 15.1

Writing Assignment 1: Sociological Research

1. *Identify* a group other than your family that you either belong to or have access to (in terms of observation). Examples of such groups include

fraternity/sorority	musical group
sports team	service organization
youth group	club
Bible study group	a group of colleagues at work
choir/chorus	a very *small* department

2. *Observational research.* Observe the group you have chosen over a period of days. Try mentally to become an "outsider" so that you can look at this group and its members objectively. Take notes on the group's behavior, paying particular attention to the two main concepts of this chapter.

   a. Group relationships
      (*for example: primary and secondary groups, in- and out-groups, and reference groups*)
   b. Group dynamics
      (*for example: group size and leadership*)
      What are the important features to look for in each of the above aspects of groups?

3. Write a paper analyzing the group you have chosen on the basis of relationships and dynamics.

What are your rst ideas on ways to organize this paper?

Chapter 16

A Theme-Based Literature Course: Focus on the City of Angels

Donna M. Brinton

As her chapter suggests, Donna Brinton loves the city of Los Angeles, California. Though students who take the course featured in her chapter may not end up as fond of the city as she is, they will have richer appreciation for its history, cultural contributions, and people. Traditional literature courses for advanced ESL students usually include a sampling of "great works" of literature written in English. These works are read either in their entirety or as excerpted materials. This chapter presents Brinton's attempt to design an alternative ESL literature course around a single extended theme: the city of Los Angeles. The genres she incorporates in the course include essays, autobiographies, short stories, poetry, novel, and film. In all of the works selected, the city of Los Angeles takes on dimensions of a "character" and exerts a powerful influence over plot, theme, and character development.

After describing the setting for the course, Brinton explains her rationale for using sustained content in an advanced ESL course. She then discusses immediate course goals, highlighting the importance of a language-based approach to teaching literature. Integral to the course are activities that engage learners in analyzing the literary work along traditional lines (e.g., with reference to plot, character development, use of irony). However, equally important are activities that use literature as a vehicle for advanced study of language features. Among the course components Brinton describes are systematic use of instructional media, minilectures on literary style and techniques, guided group discussions, e-mail response journals, and in-class as well as take-home assessment measures. Brinton traces the evolution of these various components to her own view of learner and teacher

I am grateful to Christine Holten for the many hours she spent with me consulting on pedagogical issues concerning the teaching of ESL 109 and to Chris LaBelle for his assistance on the course website. I am also grateful to Janet Goodwin for her help in writing this chapter.

roles and the role of instructional materials. She highlights other innovative features of the course such as use of a course website to post class handouts and an on-line glossary that clarifies many of the course readings' cultural references. It is worth mentioning that Donna Brinton is a colleague and collaborator of Janet Goodwin, who is the author of chapter 15. (They both work in the same ESL program.)

The use of literature in second/foreign language programs enjoys a rich and long-standing tradition. In foreign language classes, students are often rewarded for their semesters of basic language study by reading literary works in the original language during subsequent terms. In such contexts, especially for students majoring in a foreign language, the ability to read and analyze great works by well-known authors is one of the culminating goals of the curriculum. In English as a second/foreign language classes, the role of literature is somewhat different. Our students seldom major in literature, but they need English for a wide variety of other purposes. To the extent it is incorporated within the ESL curriculum, literature serves as a vehicle for language and cultural enrichment (see Lazar 1993). Students of English in second/foreign language contexts may be exposed to poems, short stories, and other extracted forms of literature in the general English curriculum; they may also, depending on the context, have the option of taking an elective course where literature is the main object of study. In the latter case, high intermediate or advanced level language proficiency is usually assumed, and the class tends to attract (1) students who want more exposure to literature written in the English language (and the authors associated with its literary tradition) or (2) students who hope to gain more insight into the culture of the English speaking world. ESL 109, the course described in this chapter, is such an elective class offering.

Setting

The University of California, Los Angeles (UCLA), is a large urban campus serving a highly diversified student body. At the undergraduate level, a large percentage of students are nonnative speakers of English who have completed some portion of their education in the United States and who intend to remain in the United States upon completion of their degrees. As my colleague, Janet Goodwin, explained in chapter 15, UCLA also attracts a large number of international students, most of whom are pursuing advanced degrees and intend to return to their home countries. The characteristics of these two populations, along with their linguistic and academic needs, differ radically.

Due largely to the nature of the mixed population and student needs, which relate closely to their academic courses of study, the curriculum of the ESL program's service courses can best be described as English for Academic Purposes (EAP). In addition to the four-course required multiskills course sequence, a range of skill-specific elective courses is also offered, thus providing students with additional support in the areas of reading, composition, grammar, literature, and oral communication.

ESL 109, Introduction to Literature for ESL Students, is a four-unit advanced level elective. Its prerequisite is completion of the university's ESL requirement (either via ESL course work or exemption by examination). The course is offered once a year and attracts a mix of undergraduate and graduate students. Most students choose 109 as an elective to further expand their knowledge of literature, the English language, and cultures of the English speaking world. The students' writing proficiency levels vary from Intermediate-High (i.e., generally comprehensible to natives used to the writing of nonnatives) to Advanced (i.e., showing remarkable fluency and ease of expression) on the American Council on Teaching Foreign Languages (ACTFL) (1986) proficiency scale for writing (see Internet app. 16.1 for student writing samples).

Conceptual Underpinnings

As background to describing the conceptual underpinnings of the course, I should mention that I first "inherited" teaching this course from a colleague in the late 1970s. At the time, I taught the course in a rather conventional manner, using a literature anthology as the main source text and covering a variety of genres from well-known British and American authors (e.g., short stories by William Faulkner and Shirley Jackson, poetry by Emily Dickinson and Robert Frost, a play by Arthur Miller).

After a 10-year hiatus, during which period another colleague taught the course, I decided to teach it again, bringing to bear my own background and interest in theme-based instruction (see Snow and Brinton 1997). Specifically, I was interested in redesigning the course around the extended theme of Los Angeles in literature and film—in the process exposing students to essays, excerpts from autobiographies, modern multicultural urban poetry, short stories, a novel, and films (see app. 16.1 for the course readings). In this case, I chose works in which Los Angeles figured centrally, taking on the dimensions of a character and exerting a powerful influence over the work's plot and characters. I was also interested in applying work I had done with the California Literature Project, applying a language-based approach to teaching literature. Finally, I wanted to design the course in keeping with my background and belief in the use of instructional media for language teaching purposes.

In keeping with these principles, three main conceptual underpinnings drove the design of the course: (1) a theme-based approach to language teaching, (2) an interactive language-based approach to teaching literature, and (3) a media-infused approach to teaching language.

A Theme-Based Approach to Language Teaching

Theme-based instruction, in which a theme or themes serve as the unifying principle of the course, is part of the larger content-based approach to language teaching in which content (in the form of themes, topics, or academic subject matter) drives the language curriculum. The following characteristics are usually present in theme-based instruction (Brinton, Snow, and Wesche 1989; Stoller and Grabe 1997).

Topics are chosen to be of high interest to students and may either cover a variety of topics or treat one topic more in depth.
The units incorporate multiple skills (listening, speaking, reading, writing, grammar).
The teacher presents the topics as a vehicle for language development—that is, teaching language (not content) is the main goal.

ESL 109 displays all these characteristics—in other words, it is centered around a broad topic of high interest to the students (Los Angeles), addresses multiple skills, and has as its primary goal language development rather than topic mastery. Further, its choice of literature as content finds rationale in the work of Holten (1997), who argues convincingly that literature is the quintessential content of a theme- or topic-based course and can serve as a crucible for advanced language study in an English for Academic Purposes context.

An Interactive Language-Based Approach to Teaching Literature

Advocates of a language-based approach to teaching literature (Carter and Long 1991; Lazar 1993) espouse a close integration of language and literature in the ESL/EFL classroom. By using techniques such as an "into, through, and beyond" framework (see Brinton, Goodwin, and Ranks 1994), teachers guide students toward the discovery of meaning in a text, helping them to approach it (into), interact with it (through), and respond analytically to its content (beyond). Activities in the language-based literature classroom span the spectrum from using literature primarily as a vehicle for language practice to helping students arrive at a deeper appreciation of the literary work via an in-depth analysis of the language and stylistics involved. The ultimate goal of such an approach is to provide students with the language tools they need to arrive at the meaning of the text.

In keeping with this approach, ESL 109 includes numerous tasks designed to focus on language (especially vocabulary choice and stylistic considerations) and literary analysis (discussion of the importance of theme, setting, character development, etc.). It also includes numerous interactive tasks to assist students in their understanding of the course readings and to enhance their appreciation of literature.

A Media-Infused Approach to Teaching Language

An indispensable feature of my own classroom teaching has always been the use of multimedia in the classroom. In Brinton 1991, I note:

> Whatever the approach, language teachers seem to universally agree that media can and do enhance language teaching, and thus in the daily practice of language teaching we find the entire range of media (from non-mechanical aids such as flashcards and magazine pictures all the way up to sophisticated mechanical aids such as video cameras and computers) assisting teachers in their jobs, bringing the outside world into the classroom, and, in short, making the task of language learning a more meaningful and exciting one. (454–55)

In light of this belief, I use a variety of noncommercial and commercial media materials to enhance my way of teaching ESL 109. These media resources include sticky-backed notes, butcher paper and poster board, colored markers, maps, postcards, magazine pictures, and photos of Los Angeles in the 1930s and 1940s (for further discussion, see the activity types section).

These three conceptual underpinnings of theme-based instruction, a language-based approach to teaching literature, and a media-based approach to language instruction work in harmony to provide the course its direction and rationale.

Syllabus Design

The syllabus for advanced literature courses for ESL students is often genre based, that is, it contains discrete segments devoted to the reading and explication of targeted literary genres. Thus in a 10-week course, 1 week might be devoted to an overview of literary tradition, 2 weeks to the short story, 2 weeks to the essay, 2 weeks to poetry, and 3 weeks to drama. Within the discrete subsections of the course, students learn about the literary conventions of a specific genre and read works by major authors representative of it.

I choose to retain the genre-based organization of the syllabus, although I expand the traditional genres covered to include autobiography and use film in lieu of the more traditional drama. We begin with the essay and (in order) cover the genres of autobiography, poetry, short story, novel, and film. My rationale for this sequence has more to do with the interconnection of themes across works than with the level of difficulty or accessibility of a given genre and/or work. In other words, I begin with the essay since the essays I have selected present an excellent overview of themes that are continuously recycled throughout the course.

Goals/Objectives

In keeping with the UCLA catalog description of the course, which states that it is designed to "introduce non-native speakers of English to . . . literature," to "reinforce language skills," to help students "gain an understanding of the cultural contexts of . . . writing," and to "provide a substantive basis for discussion," I describe my goals in the course syllabus in the following fashion.

> The primary aim of this course is to expose you to interesting and provocative works of literature. Its secondary aim is to provide you with effective approaches to reading and appreciating literature. To achieve both these aims, we will review techniques that deepen your understanding of literary texts and your appreciation of them. Since literary authors use the English language in interesting, novel, and beautiful ways, we will also examine issues of style and vocabulary. As an end objective, it is my hope that reading carefully crafted literature by writers whose use of English is rich and varied will improve your overall range of English proficiency.

Because the course is a standard part of the curriculum, I do not carry out a specific needs analysis in order to arrive at these goals. Rather, I base my decisions on my previous experience teaching the course and on consultations with any instructor who has been teaching it more recently. By the end of the course (i.e., as a result of having participated successfully in it), students should be able to demonstrate mastery in the following skill-specific areas.

Speaking

> perform oral (dramatic) readings of key passages
> exchange impressions and ideas with peers about the literary works read
> participate in discussions and debates about key incidents, characters, and literary devices

Reading

> explore and identify key ideas
> do a close analytical reading of key passages to determine their meaning and relationship to the larger work of literature in which they are found
> recognize the moral conundrum implicit in a given piece of literature
> perform a close stylistic analysis of the role of word choice and usage
> better understand the cultural dimensions of literary works
> identify point of view and the significance of plot, theme, and symbols

Writing

> express personal judgments and assess the actions of literary characters
> argue a point of view, using evidence based on the works read in class.

Activity Types

The course follows a lecture/discussion format. Class activities include instructor minilectures; guided class discussions; interactive group activities; media-based activities; in-class explications of text; e-mail "inksheds" (defined subsequently; also see app. 16.2); an analysis of a film/novel (with student products posted to the course web page); and a take-home final examination. Details of these activity types are included here.

Minilectures

One of my primary goals in planning lessons is to divide class time appropriately between teacher-fronted, more traditional classroom presentations and interactive tasks that enable students to work out the meaning of the literary works for themselves. To this end, I condense the lecture format of the course into "minilectures" on various features of literary text that I believe to be most relevant to students' understanding and appreciation of the works. During each class meeting, I present one or two minilectures, using overhead transparencies for reinforcement. During such segments, I stress that students should listen, rather than take notes, as the minilectures will be posted to the course website and can be printed out for closer examination. Selected topics of the minilectures include point of view, persona in literature, tone and voice, poetic devices, setting, and theme (see Internet app. 16.2 for a sample minilecture).

Guided Class Discussions

At the end of each class period, I distribute discussion questions for the assigned readings (see Internet app. 16.3 for sample discussion questions). These serve a dual purpose as guide questions to assist students in their reading of the literary selections and as a discussion stimulus during the follow-up class period.

Interactive Group Activities

Each class period contains one or more interactive group activities evolving from the works read. These collaborative activities cover a wide range of activity types, involving students in tasks such as writing poetry, creating collages, charting a plot time line, and writing advice column letters and responses about character conflicts in the literary works being analyzed. What the activities have in common is that they engage students in problem solving and require them to use evidence from the text to argue their solutions. (See Internet app. 16.4 for a poem written collaboratively in one such group activity.)

Media-Based Activities

As described in the conceptual underpinnings section, I frequently use instructional media to assist students in their understanding of the literary works we are reading. For example, to help students make sense of the Helen Hunt Jackson excerpt from "Ramona" (which uses the literary device of the flashback throughout), I recently prepared two sets of sticky-backed notes to use in class. On the large yellow notes, I listed key historical events in the work (e.g., *California under the rule of Spanish and Mexican viceroys, the restoration to the Church of all Missions south of San Luis Obispo*). On smaller green sticky-backed notes, I listed key personal events in the characters' lives (e.g., *the general dies in battle; Señora Moreno erects huge wooden crosses on her lands*). The students' task was to work in small groups to create parallel time lines of the historical events and the personal events in the main characters' lives and then to display these time lines on the whiteboard. In this manner, the students are able to work out connections between historical and personal events. I also used mounted magazine pictures of people to have the students do "character casting" for a proposed film version of Budd Schulberg's novel *What Makes Sammy Run?* requiring students to justify their casting decisions. In addition, I brought in old magazines and had students create "LA collages" representing the different essayists' views of the city. Finally, I used the classroom itself as a medium, posting students' products (such as the LA collages, the collaborative poems they had written, etc.) on the bulletin board at the back of the class. To help students locate the various geographical references, I brought in a large colored map of greater Los Angeles and its attractions to enhance the bulletin board display. With colored yarn and pins, I located any references we had read about and, whenever possible, purchased postcards of these sites to pin up around the edges of the map.

In-Class Explications

For each genre covered in class (i.e., essay, autobiography, poetry, short story, and novel), students write an in-class response to questions about the works read. These responses take approximately 30 minutes of class time and are open book in format. Students are graded on their ability to demonstrate a close reading of the passage and to determine its meaning and relationship to the larger work of literature.

Inksheds

Inksheds, or e-mail interactive reaction journals between instructor and student, are due in alternate weeks during the term. Students are asked to select one work that interests them (e.g., one poem, one short story) and respond to some aspect(s) of that work. They are also encouraged to pose questions to the instructor in the inkshed and to use these written exchanges as opportunities to further explore the meaning of the work (see app. 16.2 for a sample student/teacher inkshed dialogue).

Analysis of Film or Novel

Outside of class, students view a film or read a novel in which Los Angeles plays a central role. They then write a short (maximum 250-word) analysis of the way in which the setting impacts the work (i.e., affects the characters, the plot, and/or the theme) and post this analysis to the class website.

Final Take-Home Examination

The final take-home examination provides an opportunity for students to synthesize and explicate the themes and motifs that they encounter in the course readings. It presents two options: in 10 pages or less, they should (1) respond to selected controversial statements about Los Angeles and/or its inhabitants and argue their point of view on these statements, using evidence based on the works read in class; or (2) write the text of a panel discussion between selected authors on the state of the city today (see app. 16.3 for sample final exam prompts).

Learners' Roles

The role of the learner in the second/foreign language classroom has undergone considerable redefinition in recent years—primarily in response to teachers' growing acceptance of principles of communicative language teaching (see, e.g., Candlin 1981; Littlewood 1981). It has also been greatly influenced by cooperative learning (Kagan 1988; Kessler 1992), a learner-centered approach emphasizing the importance of student cooperation rather than competition. In cooperative learning, students often form a "team" to assist each other in achieving learning goals, thereby learning not only from the teacher but also from other students.

Partly in response to such contemporary orientations, the passive role of students in traditional ELT classrooms has given way to more active, social roles (Lee and VanPatten 1995) involving interactive learning, negotiation, information gathering, and coconstruction of meaning. Richards and Rodgers (1985) and Nunan (1989b) characterize some possible roles played by students in communication-oriented classrooms as follows: recipient/ listener; planner, interactor, and negotiator; tutor of other learners; and evaluator/monitor of her or his own progress.

In ESL 109, all of these learner roles come into play. Students continue to assume the "recipient" role in those segments of the class where I deliver minilectures on literary tradition, provide information on the authors, or explicate cultural references in the works we are reading. However, in a considerably larger percentage of classroom activities, they serve more active roles.

Learner as Planner, Interactor, and Negotiator

A role that combines planner, interactor, and negotiator dominates those portions of the course in which students engage in the literature-based interactive activities. For example, in an activity where students were asked to depict a given essayist's portrayal of Los Angeles in a collage, they collaboratively planned which visual images would best portray the designated author's point of view and negotiated the overall purpose and design of the collage. Similarly, in an activity where they were to transform an essayist's point of view into a poem, they planned the poetic style and images they wished to include, and in their collaborative construction of the poem they actively negotiated which ideas, words, and phrases to include.

Learner as Tutor of Other Learners

The role of tutor, which reinforces the principle that the teacher is not the sole source of information in the classroom, is also a central one in ESL 109. It dominates those segments of the class where learners work out answers to discussion questions and is also present during interactive activities. As I monitor group work in both these activities, I often notice one student in the group taking charge and explaining, with a great deal of authority, what other students in the group might not have noticed. For example, the student might be explaining how Julian and Kit, both secondary characters in the novel *What Makes Sammy Run?* serve as foils to Sammy, the protagonist. Or a student might be explaining how in the poem "Down Central Avenue" the phrases "mustard-plastered," "jazz fog," and "sweat of the moon" refer to the mist encountered by the poet's taxi as he drives down the abandoned Central Avenue, once a center of the jazz movement in Los Angeles.

Learner as Evaluator/Monitor of Her or His Own Progress

This role surfaces primarily in connection with the students' e-mail ink-shed responses. In this activity, students are encouraged to probe their own understanding of the work being explicated and to pose questions to me to confirm any hypotheses or predictions they have made about the work's character development, plot, theme, and so on.

Teacher's Roles

Harmer (1991) delineates the various roles of the teacher as follows: controller/facilitator, assessor, organizer, prompter, participant, resource, tutor, and investigator [*editors' note:* cf. table 4.3 in chap. 4]. No doubt in any class period teachers perform almost all of these roles; however, depending on the focus and goal of the course and/or particular lesson, certain roles may be more dominant. In ESL 109, my role as teacher falls predominantly into the following five categories, listed in relative order of importance.

Teacher as Resource

This role of the teacher is an especially important one in elective literature courses. Not only is the teacher expected to be a resource where language issues are concerned (as in ESL/EFL classes generally), but the teacher is also expected to have expertise and to serve as a resource in the areas of literary tradition and theory. Also, because of the very embeddedness of cultural values within the literature that students are reading (see the section on culture, which follows), the teacher also serves as an informant to explicate cultural references or explain actions or situations within the literary works that may be culturally motivated.

Teacher as Controller/Facilitator

Harmer (1991) presents this role of the teacher as falling along a continuum from teacher as "puppet master" (i.e., controlling all class activities) to teacher as facilitator of student-centered activities (i.e., where the teacher maintains a low profile, allowing students to take center stage in the classroom). My role in ESL 109 shifts between these two ends of the continuum, with a modicum of teacher-fronted activities where I might be, for example, delivering an interactive lecture on literary devices. In this case, teacher talk dominates, with students simply posing clarification questions and providing examples when prompted. More frequently, however, I find myself serving as a monitor or facilitator (e.g., of pair or group work activities, debates, creative writing activities, etc.). In such cases, student talk dominates.

Teacher as Organizer

This role is closely related to the preceding one in that during times when I move away from my controlling role, I nonetheless retain my role as teacher by (1) clearly outlining for students the tasks they are to do, (2) modeling or otherwise initiating the task at hand, (3) circulating throughout the room to insure that students are on task, and (4) providing feedback to students upon completion of the task.

Teacher as Prompter

Given the priority in the course placed on peer/peer interaction and the adoption of an inquiry-centered or "into, through, and beyond" approach to teaching literature, many of the class activities require students to problem solve, that is, to collaboratively discover evidence to support their analysis of the work (e.g., its narrative structure, its character development, the significance of themes and symbols). During these activities, students work at tables in groups of three or four. I move around the room probing students' knowledge and providing further clues to solving problems. For instance, I might prompt students to reread certain paragraphs of the work or to examine closely the significance of lexical choice and/or repetition.

Teacher as Assessor

In this role, the teacher makes judgments about students' performance and/or command of the material and provides formal and informal feedback. I build in elements of informal assessment and feedback to students in the form of discussion questions and interactive tasks that are a part of our daily classroom routine. Additional informal feedback is provided in my replies to student inksheds, where I encourage students to venture opinions. These inksheds prove to be a valuable clue to student understanding of texts and inform my classroom practice to the extent that in subsequent class sessions I am able to clarify misunderstandings that have surfaced. Finally, in terms of formal assessment measures, I evaluate student performance on the biweekly in-class explications and on the take-home final examination. To provide feedback to students on the in-class explications, I make it a practice to compile "best responses" to the various questions (taken from actual student responses) and distribute these when returning graded student products (see the lesson particulars section for a sample "best response").

Instructional Materials

The primary instructional materials for the course consist of the course reader (containing the shorter works of literature), the novel *What Makes Sammy Run?* the film *The Player,* a recommended dictionary of language and culture, a recommended glossary of literary terms, and the course website. Supplementing these primary instructional materials are media resources (such as magazine pictures, realia, and photos) and bulletin board displays. These materials are described here.

The course reader: Because no appropriate commercial anthology is available to teach a course on the literature of Los Angeles, I have compiled a course packet/reader containing the shorter works (e.g., autobiographical excerpts, poems, and short stories) that I want students to read.

What Makes Sammy Run? This novel, which represents one of the quintessential works on Hollywood and the entertainment industry, is available in paperback form.

The Player: Chosen to parallel the themes in *What Makes Sammy Run?* the Altman film is shown in class and is available for additional viewing in the university's multimedia library.

The course website: As a relatively new requirement, undergraduate courses in the School of Letters and Sciences at UCLA are required to have an "e-campus" course website, for which students pay a minimal instructional fee. Course management software along with graduate student technical support is provided for all instructors to encourage instructional innovation in the use of computers for pedagogical purposes. The course management software has built-in features such as a course calendar, Internet links, an electronic bulletin board, and on-line chat. It can also be tailored more specifically to the instructor's course needs. I make use of these resources to create a variety of minisites for my students to investigate outside of class time. For example, I post all course lecture materials and discussion questions to the course "e-campus" site. I have also integrated into this website an on-line "cultural glossary" with active links to relevant topics (e.g., the Chumash Native Americans, Greene and Greene architecture, the Zoot suit riots, the Hollywood blacklist, *Dragnet, Leave It to Beaver,* the Sunset Strip, Dana Point surfing, etc.) to help students with cultural difficulties that they might encounter in their reading (for additional detail on the cultural glossary, see the culture section, which follows).

Although the e-campus environment can only be accessed by registered UCLA students, the cultural glossary is available for viewing at <http://www.humnet.ucla.edu/humnet/TESL/esl-curriculum/donna.html>.

Culture

Early on in my teaching of the course, it became clear that a major barrier to students' understanding of the selected works was their lack of exposure to, and knowledge of, relevant aspects of North American culture. Specifically, the authors whose works we were reading made many incidental references to people, places, and things that they presumed as the shared cultural knowledge of their targeted native speaker readers. Passages like the following from Candice Bergen's autobiography *Knock Wood* (1984), in which Bergen describes her "privileged" childhood, are heavily loaded with cultural references and require more than cursory explanation.

> Our fantasy lives were shaped by movies like those of other kids of our generation, but it was our parents who made the fantasies, who cherished childhood more than we. Hollywood, for them, was the Sea of Dreams where they set their silver sails and filled their nets with magic. Our parents were Ivanhoe and Moses, Spartacus and Shane. They fought lions, roped stallions, slew dragons, rescued maidens; they healed the sick, sang in the rain, woke up in Oz and got back to Kansas. Snapped their fingers—it snowed in summer. Sent a memo—it rained indoors. (59).

My students had no knowledge of the Hollywood subculture and the many celebrities and classic films Bergen was alluding to. Nor had they ever heard of Betty Boop, the Manson Gang, *Father Knows Best,* Jack Webb, the Donner party, Helen Gurley Brown, or the myriad of other cultural references sprinkled throughout the works we read. Even when they *did* possess relevant cultural knowledge, it often misguided them in their interpretation of the works. For example, on encountering the phrase "we're not in Kansas anymore, Toto" in one of the essays, one of my students asked why the author was referring to the rock band Toto.

My reaction to this quandary was (1) to devote more time than originally intended to explicating cultural references and (2) to establish the previously discussed on-line cultural glossary with links to external sites where students, in their free time, could delve more deeply into these references.

Creation of this cultural glossary was very time and labor intensive, as it required that I spend hours "surfing the net" to locate appropriate websites, to upload the glossary entries to the course website, and to insert appropriate links. It is clear from the end-of-course anonymous student evaluations, however, that this aspect of the course was greatly appreciated.

> I really liked the idea of learning new term/vocabulary that is specific to LA on American Culture and can't be found in a dictionary such as "we're not in Kansas anymore, Toto" and I wish we would have more of these.

Lesson Particulars

The following "snapshot" of a recent class in action presents the activities and events occurring during the first day of the eighth week of instruction. Classroom instruction takes place in one of two departmental classrooms, well configured for ESL instruction, with six movable tables, lots of bulletin board and whiteboard space, built-in video playback equipment and monitors, and cupboards containing overhead projectors and high-quality audio playback equipment.

As is typical in this 8:00–10:00 A.M. class, students arrive somewhat sporadically, still a bit bleary eyed from the early hour of the day or frustrated from their commute and the heavy traffic. By the beginning of class, only five of the nine students enrolled are present, seated around the tables in their preferred seating arrangement (e.g., two linguistics majors seated together at the same table, two Russian students seated at another table, and a Vietnamese student seated alone at yet another table). Nonetheless, I begin the class on time by reminding students that their inksheds about the novel *What Makes Sammy Run?* are due later that day. I pass back the graded in-class explication number four, encouraging students to read over my comments. Some students somberly read over the comments amid a buzz of Russian from my more vocal students. As this is happening, several of the perennially late students wander in and take their seats, bringing the number of students present up to seven. I hand back the papers to these latecomers with the same instructions, that is, to take a few minutes to look at my comments. To reward those students now present, I distribute three pages of "model" answers, compiled (albeit slightly edited by me) from the students' own answers.

> Excerpt from "Model" Answers
>
> A literary symbol is a word or an image that takes on a larger significance within the work. Select a work and discuss the primary symbols within that work.

Brown carpet in "Over the Hill" symbolizes Jessica's emotional turmoil. Jessica, who is extremely dependent on her husband, is experiencing marital difficulties and is contemplating divorce with her husband. However, the husband, who is abusive, tries to keep Jessica in bondage, warning her that if she separates from him, she will be living in an apartment with brown carpet in the San Fernando Valley. So Jessica is worried that she may lose everything, such as her children and her support from her husband, after her divorce.

Students almost literally devour these model answers, and again the class is abuzz with students claiming responsibility for portions of the model answers.

I allow students five more minutes to look over and discuss the model answers, circulating among the tables and checking that they are on task. Some students are actively comparing their own answers with the model answers; others are simply studying the model answers or (in the case of those students whose answers I have used as the model) comparing my edited version of the answers with their own. I field a few questions on English grammar from one of the Russian students and use this time to ask a few personal questions of students. "Did you get your hard drive fixed yet, Danny?" He shakes his head and launches into a diatribe against the computer company where he has left the computer to be repaired. I empathize, having had both the C and A drives of my office computer crash less than one year after its purchase. I continue in this vein, moving around the class and also using the opportunity to set up an overhead projector for the next class activity.

[*8:20 A.M.*] As usually happens, I now move into an interactive minilecture on a new aspect of literature. For today's lecture, I have picked the topic "Satire, Irony, Sarcasm, and Parody" since these elements are omnipresent in the novel we are reading. I project the overhead lecture notes (see Internet app. 16.2) on the screen at the front of the class and move over to the side. I extemporize from the notes, pausing for emphasis and checking student faces for signs of comprehension. Another student arrives, apologizing that she overslept, and joins the table with her fellow economics major. Intermittently, I ask students to provide examples: for instance, "Which characters in *Sammy* are the main butt of Schulberg's satire?" "Can you think of another example of irony in the chapters we just read?" or "Who said, 'I come by way of Boulder Dam?' Can you explain the context of this quote?" Students provide me with additional examples of Sammy's sarcastic remarks and thumb through their copies of the novel looking for some of their favorites. One student chimes in that in the discussion questions I had distributed the previous time, she found it easy to identify the quotes from Sammy because of his sarcastic tone. Another student asks me how soon the minilecture will be posted to the class website since he wants to download it in preparation for Thursday's in-class explication. I assure students that it will be posted no later than this evening.

[*8:30 A.M.*] I then ask students to take out the discussion questions pertaining to part II of the novel (see Internet app. 16.3), which were distributed during the previous class period. I reconfigure the students to four different tables to better distribute native languages and to control for student ability levels. Each table is assigned one roman numeral on the handout to discuss since time is short and I want to finish this activity by the end of the first hour. I intentionally assign questions II and IV to the tables where the slightly more proficient students are seated and circulate to monitor group activity and answer questions. At the tables assigned to questions II and IV, disagreement as to the correct answer evolves. I stress to the students involved that these are opinion questions rather than factual questions and that with adequate evidence from the text they might conceivably be able to argue either answer. "Will this question be on Thursday's quiz?" asks one student. I deliberately ignore the question, and she then says, "I bet it will." (She's right. It is!) About this time, a final class member arrives (no apologies), bringing class attendance up to 100 percent. She joins a table but clearly hasn't read or prepared the materials for the day's discussion, so she doesn't take an active part in the class.

[*8:45 A.M.*] Upon sensing a lull in the groups' discussions, I check with them to see that they are nearing the end of the task. "Have you chosen a reporter yet?" I ask each group. They commence negotiating who will report their group's answers, and fingers get pointed at the usual suspects. "Choose someone other than Yefim, this time," I tell one group. "He's always the one picked." The remainder of the first hour is taken up with a lively reporting session. Students from the other tables listen attentively to the student who is reporting and often take notes on their handouts—no doubt in preparation for the upcoming in-class explication. The discussion goes over our normal time for break, and students negotiate with me to return five minutes later than usual from break. I agree, telling them, "No later than 9:05!" Predictably, they stretch the break a bit, arriving back just before 9:10.

My lesson plan for the next activity reads as follows.

Location scout—Pick three or four photos that would work well as "locations" for the film adaptation that you are doing of *What Makes Sammy Run?* Describe which scene you would film in this location, which characters would be present, and which actions would take place.

To prepare for this activity, I have mounted 13 black and white photos of Los Angeles in the 1930s and 1940s on colored construction paper. In my own mind, I have chosen certain photos for certain key scenes in the novel, though I am curious to see what students will decide.

[*9:10 A.M.*] I prepare students for the activity by writing the term *location scout* on the board and asking them to tell me what a location scout does. Living in Los Angeles amid the influence of the entertainment industry, they are easily able to articulate this. I then tell them that I want them to stay in their previously arranged groups, and I explain the game plan while spreading the photos out on an unoccupied table. The students rush to pick out photos, obviously intrigued. (They take quite naturally to this activity since in the previous week, we did a similar "casting agent" activity using magazine pictures.) They return to their tables with several photos each, unable to make an immediate, definitive decision. They begin discussing and thumbing through their novels. Five minutes into the activity, students from one table approach another and effect a trade of photos. Although I hadn't anticipated this twist on the activity, the negotiation goes smoothly, and both groups appear satisfied with their transaction.

[*9:25 A.M.*] I circulate, asking students which location they have chosen, which scene they will shoot there, and which characters will be involved. I'm pleased with the results. Most groups pick exactly the same scenes and locations I had envisioned when creating the activity, confirming my intuition that they have a good understanding of the novel and enjoy reading it. I ask each group to choose a reporter (different from the person who previously served in this capacity) and ask for volunteers to begin.

[*9:35 A.M.*] One by one, the groups present the results of their "location scouting." Some additional off-topic (but ultimately culturally relevant) discussion takes place as students ask me where certain buildings are located (e.g., Mann's Chinese Theater, the Bradbury Building, Paramount Studios) and if they can visit them.

This activity takes up most of the second hour of class time. I had initially planned an additional "character sketch" activity in which students would (1) individually select one character from the novel that they wanted to portray and (2) answer a series of questions to help them get into the frame of mind of that character. However, due to lack of time I save this activity for another day and instead distribute the discussion questions for the third part of the novel, reminding students—per their syllabus—that they should read pages 198–234 for next time. Students waiting for their 10:00 A.M. class are already entering the classroom to take their seats; my students have loaded their belongings into their backpacks and are poised to exit the classroom. I end class quickly by reminding students that the in-class explication will take place during the first hour of our next class and will cover the entire novel up to page 234.

Caveats

I only recently redesigned this course and have had just one chance to teach it as outlined in this chapter. Therefore, any thoughts I have about its success are somewhat preliminary. However, I can say that as an instructor, I vastly prefer the sustained-content and theme-based organization of the course to the prior scenario of reading works of literature based on their literary merit and predicted interest level. My students, though initially somewhat confused about why I had not chosen to have them read great works by well-known writers, eventually recognized and appreciated my rationale. As one student in the end-of-course evaluation commented:

> It was very nice of her making all her efforts to show us how Los Angeles is portrayed in literature. I learned not only American literature, but also culture of California. I really appreciate the way she approached her class, concentrating issues on Los Angeles. I didn't actually expect that it would be this much fun to learn literature.

Ultimately, what I believe a sustained-content and theme-based structure for the course offers is a coherent thread that students can trace from work to work, continually expanding their knowledge base about both the theme itself and the works of literature written around the theme.

The decision to structure an advanced ESL literature course around a sustained-content theme is not, however, without its drawbacks. For one, the choice of literature is limited and in some cases difficult to find. In my selection of literature for the course, I was often torn between choosing lesser works by well-known authors (e.g., the short story "Crazy Sunday" by F. Scott Fitzgerald) and works with more literary merit by less-known authors. Ultimately, I compromised by including the Fitzgerald story but used a majority of works by lesser known authors. I also had difficulty finding poetry in which Los Angeles figured prominently, though ultimately I was able to find a volume of poetry by ethnic LA poets that served my purpose. Because of the more restricted range of literature that I could select from, the course was weighted more heavily toward contemporary literature. This turn of affairs had the additional drawback that much of what I surveyed initially for inclusion did not appear appropriate due either to its stylistic difficulty or very bleak thematic orientation. Though I exercised discretion in my choice of literature and discarded many works that I thought students would find too bleak, they nonetheless complained that the portrait of Los Angeles drawn by many of the writers was too depressing, and they requested that I include works by authors with a more uplifting outlook. As one student in her end-of-course evaluation commented:

> For me personally, I would have liked to see good sides of Los Angeles or the stories about people who were involved or contributed their money or knowledge [skills] in LA development. For example: Getty, Grifith, Malholand, etc.

The next time I have an opportunity to teach the course, I will be more sensitive to this reaction and conduct a wider search to include a more balanced literary portrayal of Los Angeles in the assigned readings. Other than that, however, my recent experiences with the course have encouraged me to continue teaching it much in the same manner described here.

Prompts for Discussion and Reflection

1. According to the author, what are the primary goals of the course? How are speaking and writing activities integrated into the course?

2. Due to the dual ESL population at UCLA, the author notes that the "characteristics of these two populations, along with their linguistic and academic needs, differ radically." Discuss what types of linguistic and academic needs you would expect a teacher working in Brinton's setting to encounter, how students' needs might differ, and how these needs might color students' attitudes toward an advanced ESL literature course.

3. Brinton notes that students enrolling in the course have two main goals: (1) to gain more exposure to literature written in the English language or (2) to gain insight into the culture of the English speaking world. In your opinion, which of these two goals does the course best fulfill? Why? If you were interested in better balancing them out, how might you structure the course differently?

4. The author describes a number of techniques using instructional media to generate student discussion about the selected works of literature. Which of these appealed to you most? How might you modify this technique to use with a work of literature you select to teach? What alternative ways of using instructional media might you suggest?

5. Brinton describes creating an electronic "cultural glossary" to help explicate references that might impede students' comprehension of

the literary texts. (Consider visiting Brinton's "cultural glossary" on the Internet for yourself.) How might you modify this technique to get students even more involved in the process?

6. This course is taught in a university setting to matriculated students. Consider the settings in which you have taught/intend to teach. What changes might you need to incorporate to build upon Brinton's model for your local teaching situation?

7. This chapter illustrates that language teachers are always participating within a context of teaching and learning considerably larger than many teachers may realize. It reminds us as language teachers that we need to be aware that the courses we teach are part of a larger system. Discuss ways in which the institutional setting and region of the world where Brinton teaches influence the course and how she teaches it. For more extended discussion (or a possible miniproject) compare how Brinton's context and setting influence her work with parallel influences in one of the following chapters: chapter 10, by Anne Burns and Pam MacPherson; chapter 14, by Lindsay Miller; chapter 17, by David Mendelsohn; chapter 18, by Dana Ferris; or chapter 22, by Janet Graham and Susan Barone (and/or with some other teacher and course with which you are familiar).

8. Brinton describes a course in which reading literature is the primary focus. Such a course does not exist in all programs or settings. What do you consider to be the potential (or an appropriate role) for using literature in ELT? Tie your position to two or more of the general ELT principles listed in table 2.4 of chapter 2.

9. Students in this class view the film *The Player* and discuss its thematic connection to the novel *What Makes Sammy Run?* Describe the use of film in courses you have taught (might teach). What advantages does this medium offer? If you have the opportunity, watch the video of *The Player* and report on its potential for prompting either language work or meaningful discussion with English language learners.

10. One component of the course is for students to respond to the works they have read by sending the teacher e-mail "inkshed" responses. The teacher then responds in kind. What do you believe the author's rationale for this practice is? What benefits might it have for both parties? Can you comment on any possible connections between your understanding of the issues involved and some of the general ELT principles listed in table 2.4 of chapter 2?

11. In the lesson particulars section Brinton mentioned that one

student arrived almost 45 minutes late and that the student "clearly hasn't read or prepared the materials for the day's discussion, so she doesn't take an active part in the class." Given the participatory nature of the course Brinton describes, what are some of the issues suggested by this turn of events? How do you envision learners' responsibilities to the course, their peers, and the teacher with respect to attendance, preparation for class, and participation? Discuss how you would handle such circumstances in your own teaching.

Miniprojects

12. Brinton lives and teaches in Los Angeles, California, and she describes using literary works around the topic of that city to organize her course. Pick a sustained content around which you would like to organize an advanced ESL literature course. For example, for the part of the world where you live (or see yourself serving as an ELT teacher in the future) what might be some of the literary works around that part of the world (e.g., city, locale, region) you might be able to incorporate into a course along the lines Brinton describes? Brainstorm genres you would wish to include and works of literature that might be appropriate for your course focus. What would be your criteria for selecting specific works of literature?

13. The author describes several activities (e.g., "character casting," "location scout") using magazine pictures to deepen students' understanding of the literature they have read. Read the final take-home exam essay prompt that follows (or see the complete prompt in app. 16.3) and examine the three first paragraphs from student essays that follow it. Rank these three student products according to how well they appear to address the prompt. Compare and contrast them on such dimensions as the writers' uses of language, the content they present, both of these considerations, and/or any other concern about their writing you may have. First, here is the original final exam prompt: "*Throughout this course, we have encountered variations on the name 'Los Angeles' that connote a value judgment of the city and its inhabitants. Select four of the nicknames below and discuss the opinion that is portrayed. . . . Provide specifics on how this value judgment is expressed. . . .*"

Student essay 1: "I remember that a friend of mine who was raised in California once told me in cynical way that to survive in Los Angeles I should have much knowledge of three things which are movies, restaurants, and fashion because what the people in Los Angeles like to talk about are mainly those three issues which is fairly true, I think. Throughout this course I have learned how Los Angeles are portrayed from writers by reading all different literature. Each work of the literature showed the significant images and the role of Los Angeles by looking at the city and its inhabitants. However, Los Angeles is referred to by derogatory nicknames such as La La Land, Los Angeles, City of Fallen Angels, and City of Angles. These negative value of nicknames are represented in each work of literature, and they provided how this value of the Los Angeles is expressed . . ."

Student essay 2: "All of the essays, biographies, and poems that we have read about Los Angeles present a certain vision of this city. Each of the works speaks with a different voice. But the overall picture that emerges of Los Angeles is one of a somewhat confused city, a city whose identity is so multifaceted that it is almost schizophrenic. Because Los Angeles is a constantly moving and diverse mixture, any given body examined separately in the context of the chaos around it tends to appear lost. Hence, all of the nicknames given to Los Angeles are somehow suggestive of loss. "La La Land" is a nickname that suggests an existence so surreal that contact with reality is lost. "Seismic City" suggests volatility and perpetual but invisible movement that threatens to swallow you up at any given moment and this uncertainty contributes to a feeling of being lost. Babylon, according to the *Dictionary of Phrase and Fable,* is the "embodiment of luxury, vice, splendor, and tyrrany." What is lost in this case is the (metaphoric) favor of the Gods. It is a loss of purity, a loss of innocence, even a loss of humanity, And finally, "Lost Angeles" is a nickname that takes all of the city's lovely, and not-so-lovely, absurdities and comments on them collectively . . ."

Student essay 3: "Throughout the entire course, we have encountered a lot of portraits of the city that we are living in—Los Angeles. Los Angeles is a city of diversities and varieties, we can know this by looking at both the positive and negative sides of Los Angeles. Each of the authors has different feelings and opinions about Los Angeles. Through their literary works, they express their thoughts. From these varieties of works, we can find a lot of nicknames of Los Angeles. Right now, I would like to discuss four of them. Out of the four nicknames, two of them—La La Land and Land of Fruits and Nuts are positive; the other two—Boulevard of Broken Dreams and City of Fallen Angels are negative. These give us a roundabout image of Los Angeles. They can fully bring out the theme of 'Diversities' and 'Varieties' of Los Angeles. . . ."

Appendix 16.1

Course Readings

Essays

Michael Chrichton's "Sex and Death in L.A."
Joan Didion's "Los Angeles Notebook"
Sandra Tsing Loh's "My World: A Defense, White Trash"
Al Martinez's "City of Angles"
Susan Orlean's "Scene Making"
Jack Smith's "Los Angeles the Magnificent"
Peter Theroux's "Seismic City"

Autobiographies

Candice Bergen's *Knock Wood*
Mike Rose's *I Just Wanna Be Average*

Short Stories

T. Coraghessan Boyle's "Sinking House"
F. Scott Fitzgerald's "Crazy Sunday"
Helen Hunt Jackson's "Ramona"
Kate Braveman's "Over the Hill"

Poetry

Akilah Nayo Oliver's "shit talk on the venice boulevard bus heading
   east one summer's night"
Steve Effingham's "Hot Day"
Sue Caylor's "Line 471 Downtown LA, empty silhouettes"
Georgiana Valoyce Sanchez's "Chumash Man, Fat of the Land"
Mark Colasurdo's "Down Central Avenue"
Henry J. Morro's "Winter, Los Angeles"
Christine Choi Ahmed's "Eating"
Sam Shepard's "Motel Chronicles"
Tom Clark's "Things to Do in California (1980)," "Priests of Newport,
   Manhattan & Laguna," "The lost hard 'g' in Los Angeles"

Novel

Budd Schulberg's *What Makes Sammy Run?*

Film

Robert Altman's *The Player*

Appendix 16.2

Sample Student/Teacher Inkshed Dialogue

Student

A poem "Hot Day" was written by Steve Effingham around 1960s. It is contemporary piece because the strong relationship with present time is shown. The author's purpose of writing this poem is descriptive. To the viewer author presents his one-day observation of people action. The action takes place in Downtown Los Angeles.

Steve Effingham shows us the real Downtown life. From the beginning of the poem, he starts with phrase "Hot Day," which gives us a sense of unpleasant environment. The author leads us through "the 5th street of Main which is behind Greyhound Station." The Greyhound station is a bus station which is old and ugly. The author is "wandering." That is walking without purpose. The author shows a small part of history of Downtown comparing the Downtown before and after. But, again the picture is not happy. There is none improvements. We, readers, follow the author and see people who are on the street. The reality is sad and hopeless "50 blacks mill in small groups, card games business meetings, gesticulating hands emphasizing minute data, muscular youths sweating, men on curbs heads in hands, crazed bug-eyed holy fool . . . "

The author in the poem rich his purpose by showing the vivid picture of homeless and desperate section of humanity.

Teacher

Thanks for responding to Steve Effingham's poem "Hot Day."

I agree that the intent of the poet is descriptive. Notice that besides all the detail about things you can SEE in this depressed area nearby the Greyhound Bus station, the author also appeals to other senses:

Sense of smell—"piss stink"
Sense of hearing—laughter, radio jazz, babbling
Sense of motion—cop car moves slowly down street
                                    gesticulating hands
                                    mill in small groups
                                    swaggers struts dances staggers

I felt that by appealing to these other senses, the visual images that the author presents (50 blacks, card games, muscular youths, men on curbs, etc.) conspire to present a very bleak image of a depressed area inhabited by "strange abandoned humanity."

In your response, it would have been good to show how the author uses various literary devices (image, theme, language, stylistic devices) to achieve his purpose. Notice, for example, how he uses largely sentence fragments rather than complete sentences to compose the poem. This fragmented sentence style helps to support his theme of strange, wandering individuals who have no connection to life and its meaning. In many cases, he uses only single words (laughs, plots, threats) as well. I'm glad you liked this poem. I thought it was very powerful.

Appendix 16.3

Final Examination Prompt

Your take-home final examination is due to me by 5 P.M. on Monday, March 23. No late papers accepted! Please provide me with double-spaced, typed hard copy of your answer. Maximum length is 10 pages. Your essay will be judged on its content, organization, language, and rhetorical style.

Choose *one* of the two options below.

Option 1

Throughout this course we have encountered variations on the name "Los Angeles" that connote a value judgment of the city and its inhabitants. Select *four* of the nicknames below and discuss the opinion that is portrayed with reference to the works we have read. Provide specifics on how this value judgment is expressed in each work that you choose to discuss. For each nickname, you should discuss at least two different works from two different genres (i.e., in total, you should discuss at least *eight* different works and at least *four* different genres).

La La Land	Land of Fruits and Nuts
Babylon	City of Fallen Angels
Boulevard of Broken Dreams	City of Angles
Lost Angeles	Seismic City

Option 2

A panel of eight distinguished authors who have written about Los Angeles has been convened to discuss the state of the city and its inhabitants. Your task is to write the script for this panel discussion. Please write this in dialogue form, selecting eight of the authors whose works we have read to participate in this "state of the city" discussion panel. Their comments should reflect the views we have read in their works. Identify the authors at the outset of the paper by name and work they have written.

Chapter 17

Canadian Language and Culture: A Course for Nine Academic Credits

David J. Mendelsohn

In this chapter, David Mendelsohn describes a two-semester course offered to ESL learners for academic credit at York University in Toronto. Although those who take the course have been admitted to the university as matriculated students, tests of language proficiency indicate they are in need of the kind of continued ESL support Canadian Language and Culture (CLC) is designed to provide. The course is offered in multiple sections each term and has been a vital component of York's undergraduate curriculum for many years. Mendelsohn discusses several of the course's distinctive features. First, CLC is an advanced level English for Academic Purposes course designed for lower-division undergraduate students enrolled in their first year of academic study. Second, those teaching the course use authentic, specifically non-ESL, materials and make sure the materials selected are comparable in length, level of difficulty, and sophistication to materials used in other (non-ESL) freshman year courses. Third, CLC students are taught the kinds of academic skills they will need to master in order to succeed at the university.

Mendelsohn adopts a strategy-based approach to teaching CLC and draws inspiration for his way of offering the course from literature on strategy instruction. Students are taught how to read a challenging academic article, give an oral presentation, participate in seminar discussions, ask lecturers for clarifications, and write academic essays along with other targeted tasks. In addition, CLC is a content-based course that includes a substantial body of social science and humanities material for students to learn. Since those who complete the course earn nine academic credits that are applied toward their undergraduate degrees, its content is not only treated as a vehicle for language learning but is given major prominence.

Sincere thanks to my colleague and friend Nicholas Elson for his valuable comments on an earlier draft of this paper and to all of my colleagues at York University for their insightful contributions to the continuing development of CLC.

Finally, CLC is a *foundations course*, a term used to signal a series of humanities and social science courses designed to enhance the first-year undergraduate experience of everyone who attends the university.

––––––––

Setting

Canadian Language and Culture (CLC) is a first-year credit-bearing ESL course offered through York University's Faculty of Arts. York University occupies an urban campus in Toronto with over 40,000 students, most of whom commute to school. Students in CLC are either immigrants who have recently settled in Canada or international students on student visas. International students comprise less than 15 percent of CLC's student body; therefore immigrants represent the majority of CLC students. While recent course sections include increasing numbers of students from Eastern Europe, for the past decade the largest group of students has come from Hong Kong along with smaller numbers of students from Taiwan, Japan, Korea, Israel, and Iran.

Students receive 9 academic credits (equivalent to three single-semester courses) that may be applied toward the 90 credits required for a three-year Ordinary degree or the 120 credits for a four-year Honors degree. While CLC carries regular credit and final grades are factored into the students' grade point average, such an ESL course credit structure is relatively rare in Canadian universities. Nonnative speakers of English planning to enter York University are required to complete an English proficiency test. Based on test results, those admitted to the university with relatively weak English language skills for university standards are required to take CLC. The proficiency levels of students who enter CLC average Intermediate-High in speaking and listening on the American Council on the Teaching of Foreign Languages (ACTFL) scale. Although the majority of the students in the course are enrolled because of the requirement, most of them appreciate the opportunity since CLC not only yields academic credits but meets a general education requirement in the field of humanities as a *foundations course.*

CLC is a 104-hour course meeting 4 hours per week over the 26 weeks of a full academic year. In 1999/2000 there were 19 CLC course sections of 25 students each. Some of the facilities available to support the course are a multimedia language learning center, a computer-assisted writing center, and reference librarians available for instruction in how to conduct library searches and other related activities.

Conceptual Underpinnings

Canadian Language and Culture integrates language instruction with academic and cognitive skills development. The course has three distinct dimensions. First, it is an advanced level English for Academic Purposes (EAP) course designed to yield improvement in students' overall production and understanding of English. The language improvement features of the course are rooted in explicit strategy instruction. Second, CLC can be described as a content-based course since there is a substantial body of material to be learned. This second feature ensures that the course merits academic credits and resembles other academic courses offered by the university. A difference between CLC and other credit-bearing courses at York is that all of the students taking CLC are second language speakers of English. Third, it is a *foundations course,* a term our university uses to signal courses designed in part to teach learners the kinds of academic study skills every first-year student is expected to acquire.

CLC and EAP

CLC is designed on the premise that students enter the course at the equivalent of an Intermediate-High ACTFL proficiency level, that is, with a reasonable level of competence in general English. By general English I mean English for social and basic interpersonal communication purposes as opposed to academic purposes (for further discussion of such differences, see Cummins 1981). Most CLC course participants need considerable support in reading, writing, and academic purposes oral communication. To these aims, I use a strategy-based approach to teaching CLC (see Mendelsohn 1994; Mendelsohn and Rubin 1995). In earlier decades, what passed for language teaching in our field was having the student "do" a lot of the skill in question. In a reading skills class, for example, students might have been asked to read through a prose passage and then answer a series of questions designed to check comprehension. This approach assumes that if ESL students had enough practice, their reading abilities would improve, but it fails to constitute much in the way of teaching since learners experience little more than a series of loosely related test-like questions. What is missing is the teacher to have explicitly taught students "how to" manage learning tasks in the target language, for example, how to learn, how to read, how to listen, how to give a presentation, how to tackle a difficult article, how to handle difficult questions, how to discuss what they have read, or how to structure a verbal report.

I believe that teaching how to manage authentic learning tasks is one of teachers' fundamental responsibilities in any language program. A teacher assigned to teach an ESL course should use some type(s) of needs analysis in order to determine the learning tasks students are unable to manage upon entering the course but should be able to manage by its completion. With such information in hand, the teacher needs to decide how to provide sufficient opportunities for learners to acquire the needed skills. In CLC course sections I offer, I use a strategy-based approach to teaching. When the focus in on reading, some "reading-to-learn" strategies included in the lesson could be any of the following: how to preview chapter headings to activate relevant schemata, find the main idea of large sections of discourse, differentiate fact and opinion, recognize important details, locate answers to specific questions, make inferences about content, adjust reading rate relative to the purpose of reading and difficulty of the material, skim for important ideas, monitor one's degrees of understanding, take reading notes, arrange reading notes in a hierarchy of importance, summarize and paraphrase longer texts, and critically evaluate content (for further discussion of the kinds of reading strategies that need to be taught in EAP courses, see Gunderson 1991; Shih 1992).

There is nothing revolutionary or unique about a strategy-based approach. In fact, I believe it is fundamental to most effective language pedagogy. Students need to be able to handle and complete relevant tasks and to accomplish goals while using the target language. Since students in the CLC course need to be able to demonstrate understanding of academic articles and lectures in English, one way of assisting them is by providing strategy instruction designed and sequenced to achieve these goals. This approach serves as the basis for the language instruction components I incorporate within the CLC course.

The Academic Content of CLC

CLC is an academic course with a focused body of content. While more traditional EAP courses tend to be "university preparatory" in nature, one of the special features of CLC at York is its status as a full-fledged university course. This distinction is reflected in both the approach to instruction and the content included in the course. Rather than using a set of ESL or EAP materials designed to practice strategies and skills needed for academic English, CLC features authentic and substantive content from social science and humanities source materials. Early in the course I spend more time directly teaching and providing opportunities for students to practice using academic study skills and strategies. Then, to increasing degrees as the course develops, I am able to integrate the development of these skills and strategies into the content of what becomes a regular academic course. Since a single area of content is sustained for a full 26 weeks, the structure of the course allows students to develop deeper understandings not only of the academic contexts in which they are functioning but of themselves as university students and as second language learners. The fact that taking CLC meets one of the degree requirements for undergraduate students in the Faculty of Arts provides students with significant extrinsic motivation. In addition, the departmental faculty's way of structuring and offering the course gives the ESL program enhanced respect and status within the wider university community.

Goals and Objectives

CLC's goals and objectives can be categorized in two ways: in terms of the macro learning skills and in terms of the language abilities to be improved. Within each of these broader categories, I will make references to specific microgoals and objectives. By the end of the course, all successful participants are expected to have developed the following macro learning skills.

1. critical skills (thinking, reasoning, and problem solving)
2. abilities to cope with demanding content
3. abilities to read critically and communicate to others orally and in writing what they have read
4. research skills (including library searches)
5. abilities to retrieve and manage information from different sources
6. abilities to propose and test a hypothesis and defend a thesis with supportive evidence presented in appropriate format

Beyond the goals of the university's other foundations courses, additional macrogoals of the CLC course are to enhance students' (1) understandings of the societal and academic contexts in which they are living and learning, (2) understandings of Canadian society and culture, (3) self-confidence in academic settings, and (4) academic learning skills. CLC goals and objectives in terms of language abilities focus on reading, writing, and speaking for academic purposes, as well as related enhancement of academic-discourse vocabulary.

Reading-to-manage content. Using the body of readings assembled for the course—articles in the area of social science, plus Canadian short stories and a Canadian novel—students are taught how to read academic material critically. As mentioned previously, critical reading abilities are developed through strategy instruction. Students are taught, for example, to use such strategies as looking at the heading of an article and predicting what the author will discuss in the article. Lessons are devoted to practicing different reading strategies and then applying them to course materials. As an important part of their reading experiences in the course, students are taught to conduct library searches for academic material.

Academic writing. Time is also devoted to teaching students how to write an academic essay/paper of substantial length. Explicit instruction is allocated to teaching students how to narrow a topic; how to write a strong, clear thesis statement; how to organize supporting argumentation; how to synthesize and incorporate material they have researched themselves; how to cite other people's work; and how to examine their own writings from a reader's perspective. In addition, they learn to use computers for academic purposes—to use word processing programs and conduct Internet searches.

Speaking. In terms of enhancing learners' speaking abilities, students are taught how to give oral presentations in academic settings, including how to field questions from the audience and how to participate in seminar discussions. By taking part in oral presentations and discussions they learn to analyze/critique academic material and to organize what they want to say in intelligible ways with appropriate support. Oral communication instruction covers issues such as the inclusion of substantial, but not overwhelming, amounts of content; how to organize an oral presentation; how to ask relevant questions of others; how to respond to others' queries; and how to handle paralinguistic dimensions of EAP speaking such as body posture, voice quality, volume, eye contact, pace of speech, gesture, and enthusiasm.

Vocabulary. In the course I provide opportunities for students to develop tools for expanding their vocabularies. Key lexical items from texts are identified and worked on in and out of class. In addition, I teach students strategies for how to learn new lexical items, how to set priorities for vocabulary study, and how to cope with unfamiliar words.

Syllabus Design

Like most other features of CLC, the syllabus for the course has evolved over many years. During the 26 weeks of the course, I incorporate approximately 10 academic articles, 4 to 6 short stories, and one novel. This corpus of academic reading material serves to anchor the course. As a result, students are always involved in learning to manage reading tasks. Based on their reading experiences at any given point in time, I provide subsequent written or oral work, through which we practice targeted reading strategies. In addition to the teacher-selected course topics, students prepare at least one of their major presentations on a topic unrelated to the required readings and another presentation that necessitates original library research. To support such tasks, the course features an orientation to library resources and frequent opportunities to consult with library personnel.

The CLC course reflects many features of what Long and Crookes (1992) term an *analytic* syllabus type. Their description of this syllabus type indicates that

> analytic syllabuses are those which present the target language whole chunks at a time, without linguistic interference or control. They rely on (a) the learners' assumed ability to perceive regularities in the input and to induce rules and/or (b) the continued availability to learners of innate knowledge of linguistic universals and the ways language can vary. (29)

The CLC course is both content based and strategy instruction based to significant degrees. Coupled with the ways in which learners interact with and learn to manage content materials, these features are clear indications of the course's analytic syllabus type.

Activity Types

Classes in CLC are held twice weekly in 120-minute blocks. In keeping with my strong belief that variation in classroom activities is motivational, each lesson contains a range of alternative activity types. I make every effort for each lesson's format and sequence of learning activities to differ from the previous lesson while studiously avoiding a set pattern for adjacent lessons. A broad range of activities is used for all the skills integrated within the course.

In the speaking component, students learn to give academic oral presentations. I begin with a consciousness-raising activity and ask students to brainstorm about the necessary elements of such a presentation. We list students' ideas on the blackboard and then attempt to group them into categories such as content, organization, manner of delivery, body language, language, and so on. The end result is a feedback checklist used by students throughout the course as a reference point when preparing their own presentations (see app. 17.1). Since they are part of preparation activities, these efforts serve to foster active listening behaviors during both teacher-led and student-led presentations (Mendelsohn 1991–92).

At the start of this learning process, I teach students how to organize academic oral presentations, in particular what to include and what to exclude. Then on a microlevel, the discussion shifts to focus on paralinguistic features such as voice projection; body language; facial expression; manipulation of voice quality, gesture, and the like; and how to use such features to one's advantage when presenting or contributing to seminar discussions. Having been taught how to make such a presentation, and after having developed a class-constructed feedback instrument and explored the requirements and procedures for an oral presentation, one or two students from the class are asked to give "mock" presentations for which everyone is aware that no grades will be assigned. These test runs are videotaped and analyzed by the whole class (in even more detail than the formally evaluated presentations students will be making later in the course). Students learn to complete peer feedback sheets, which together with their notes on the same will be used in group analysis of every presentation throughout the course.

The speaking part of the course also includes practicing what I refer to as "transcoding"—the conversion of a statistical table, chart, or graph into an accessible oral presentation. Students are taught how to analyze a statistical table, to extract its most salient feature(s), and to turn their interpretation into an oral presentation that captures the essentials of the data without overwhelming the audience with details. Many students report that they find the transcoding activities we used in CLC challenging but extremely valuable for application in other academic courses.

For the writing component, students are taught how to write expository academic essays of various genres (e.g., compare/contrast, define, justify a position). In addition to the writing skills, students are given extensive practice opportunities prior to being asked to write anything for a grade. The class studies models of different genres prior to analyzing their peers' work. Students are taught, for example, how to write (*a*) a good introduction, (*b*) a clear, strong thesis, and (*c*) an effective conclusion and are also taught (*d*) the importance of using appropriate discourse markers. They practice strategies tied to these and other features of effective writing before being asked to compose whole essays.

CLC's writing component includes how to format an academic essay according to writing and citation conventions of the American Psychological Association (APA) and the Modern Language Association (MLA), and students practice using reference handbooks for these systems. Following course tasks for which students conduct library and database searches, they learn to synthesize information gained from library research in order to produce a coherent piece of written discourse that reflects a student's own voice. The course includes considerable discussion of plagiarism concerns as exemplified in the context of ESL instruction by Pennycook 1996. Grammar points that come up in the students' own writing are dealt with as needed. In one teaching strategy learners seem to appreciate I extract typical and recurring grammatical errors learners have been producing in their writing and (without identifying any students by name) put them on a handout or on a transparency for analysis by the whole class. In addition, I use such illustrations of students' grammatical errors as sources for planning minilessons in this area.

In the reading part of the course, I teach reading strategies and how to handle extensive reading assignments. Such instruction usually begins with consciousness-raising and guided activities, followed by having students apply what they have learned to the core reading material of the course. Students are taught a range of strategies for tackling an extended academic reading text. Students' experiences in CLC often represent their first encounters with reading passages of significant length. To address their needs as readers, I teach explicit strategies for learning to manage the content of longer selections.

Prereading activities such as class or group discussions always precede reading in the classroom in order to activate and discuss appropriate schema. An example of a helpful strategy students are trained to use is that of predicting using the title, abstract, subheadings, and other rhetorical/ organizational conventions of academic prose. When there are no subheadings students try to get at the essence of a text through other means, for example, by seeking out the thesis statement of the whole text plus the topic sentences of selected paragraphs. Close readings of texts are seldom if ever done in class, as these are the kinds of reading experiences students should be attempting alone while applying some of the strategies practiced in class. Other frequent prereading tasks include handouts with key vocabulary items and questions that students are asked to study before reading a specific article. In class, after the reading and work sheets have been completed or assigned, I implement various types of group activities based on the scheduled reading. These opportunities require each group to complete different tasks in order to fill genuine information gaps and to facilitate meaningful exchanges of information between groups during culminating phases of lessons. While I provide opportunities for students to practice strategies in the contexts that they are presented, many of these same strategies can be applied to other CLC course tasks.

Learners' Roles

Students in CLC are expected to be active in virtually all phases of every class. In fact, 20 percent of their final grade is determined by their active and sustained participation. Much of what is done in the course is cooperative, requiring much negotiation and team effort. The frequent use of group work requires students from different backgrounds and cultures to work together to answer questions or prepare responses to something in the reading and also to relate what they have read to their own life experiences. As long as they are well structured, learning through the interactive negotiations of meaning made possible through group work helps to ensure team efforts and, at the linguistic level, increases opportunities for student talk. Furthermore, students' more extended oral presentations are given in pairs—an arrangement requiring cooperation and a substantial degree of team effort (cf. Murphy 1992; *editors' note:* also Tim Murphey, chap. 11 in this volume).

Students in CLC serve at different times as writers, readers, assessors, presenters, researchers, teammates, and collaborators. An additional learner role is that of peer-coach. For example, when students are learning to organize an extended piece of writing, I involve them in pair or group editing and planning of a writing assignment. Particularly when working on a very long article or one heavily laden with information, different groups of students analyze and present the various aspects of whatever the issue in question might be.

In speaking, I consider peer feedback to be central to the learning process. I spend a substantial amount of time at the beginning of the course creating the ground rules for providing appropriate affective support and feedback on classmates' oral presentations (see Mendelsohn 1991–92). Since students often come from very traditional educational systems, I prepare them for the idea that their peers can serve as effective sources of constructive feedback—some of which initially may seem negative—while reminding them that these are valid learning opportunities and that they are important. It takes time for students from many cultures to learn to respect and value their peers' comments, as opposed to their teacher's, in ESL classroom settings. Exploring ways of getting everyone involved in feedback processes is an essential role of the teacher in the CLC course.

In the second semester of the course when we study a novel, most class meetings take the form of seminar discussions. Students are required to read the novel over the vacation between the two semesters of the course. Early in the second semester I divide students into groups of two or three and assign them discussion topics. Using examples from Paci's (1982) *Black Madonna*, some topics I assigned recently are "Discuss the importance of eating in this novel," "Compare the relationship between Joey and Annalise to the relationship between Richard and Marie," "Discuss the symbolism of the Hope Chest," and "Discuss the priest's analysis of Italian immigrants." As the second semester of the course progresses, virtually all discussions of the novel become student led. I facilitate, monitor, and, where necessary, steer, but most of the novel work in CLC is peer taught and genuinely student driven. Such a discussion format plays a prominent role throughout the course's second semester.

Teacher's Roles

Part of my role as teacher is to make students feel at home. I make every effort from the first day of class to be as informal as I can and to create a relaxed environment in the class. At the same time, I draw the lines clearly and spell out my expectations firmly. I believe it is possible to successfully walk that tightrope of being relaxed and informal without conveying a message that "anything goes." This is one area in which I feel at an advantage because of having offered the same course over many years. I have found that confidence in teacher decision making associated with classroom management strengthens with time and opportunities to reteach the same course. Another important role for the teacher is to serve as the facilitator of the lesson. After all, ultimate responsibility for what goes on in a course rests with the teacher. Therefore, I always have a lesson plan for every lesson, however many times I may have taught the course, the article, the unit, or even the specific language point in question. Lesson plans at this stage of my teaching in the CLC course are not overly detailed. They usually take the form of sketchy notes that provide a reminder of what I plan to cover and in what order.

Despite never entering a class without a lesson plan, I find it is essential to be ready to deviate from such a plan if changes seem necessary. Finally, I do not have a preplanned grammar syllabus from which I teach. My preference is to pick up and teach grammatical points that arise out of students' illustrations of their own interlanguage forms and patterns.

Affective Concerns

Because it is rather large, York University can be somewhat impersonal, particularly for first-year students. I believe in learning environments in which students feel relaxed enough to take risks but also feel challenged to try hard. At an institution the size of York, second language speakers of English can feel intimidated in large classes and may be reluctant to take the kinds of risks necessary when pursuing an English-medium university degree. Part of the supportive atmosphere I aim for entails an environment in which the CLC class becomes something like the students' homeroom in secondary school. I make sure that everyone knows each other in the class, and in opening lessons, I spend considerable energy getting students to feel comfortable with their peers as well as with myself. After all, a course like CLC should be their safe harbor, a place where it is safe to try things out even at the risk of not succeeding. At the beginning of the course, we discuss openly the need for learners to be supportive of each other (see Mendelsohn 1992). When we develop the feedback checklist, I make a point of teaching the sociolinguistic rules of softening negative comments, and I make sure that such softeners are used in the provision of any negative feedback. I encourage students to call me by my first name if they feel comfortable doing so. They know that my door is always open to them, and I remind them to visit me in my office if they have questions or problems. Last but not least, following the teachings of Korczak (1967) I make deliberate efforts to treat students with the utmost respect (see Mendelsohn 1999).

Culture

As the title implies, culture is a central focus of the course. The content is tied to culture-specific themes and understandings and is designed to cover topics related to language, to Canada as a nation, and to Canadian culture. In addition to being informative for new Canadians and international students, the content featured in the course helps to foster an atmosphere of intercultural tolerance, awareness, and understanding. For example, there is a major unit on immigrants and immigration in Canada. In the unit we study Canada's immigration policy and how it has changed over the years. Featured topics include Canada's legislated policy of multiculturalism, the degree to which this policy has been successful, immigrant experiences as they are reflected in Canadian immigrant writers' literary works, the status of women in Canadian society (particularly in the workforce), and issues concerning Canada's native peoples. There is also a unit on French Canada and the unique situation of Quebec in comparison with other provinces [*editors' note:* cf. Brian Morgan, chap. 8 in this volume].

I usually have students focus at least one of their larger writing assignments on comparing the immigration trends of two different immigrant groups and their successes in acculturating to life in Canada. Such assignments fit well with Kumaravadivelu's (1994a) discussion of the importance of raising cultural awareness in ESL classrooms. The cultural themes of the CLC course are relevant to the students' interests as residents of Canada, and many students respond enthusiastically to the fiction and nonfiction selections included in the course.

Instructional Materials

Course materials of CLC consist of a readings kit, a Canadian novel, and handouts. The readings kit consists of a series of social science–type articles for the different units of study, excerpts from Hacker's (1996) reference text on how to enter citations and references using the APA and the MLA systems of citation, plus a selection of Canadian short stories. The articles, selected and updated each year by a team of CLC instructors, are grouped into the following sections.

research, essay writing, plagiarism
language, communication, gender
culture, identity, multiculturalism, immigration
Canada's aboriginal peoples
economics and work

Examples of the 34 items currently included in the kit are the following: Crawley's (1991) "Gender Relations" and Steckley's (1997) "Aboriginal Peoples." Two of the short stories are Emily Carr's (1992) "Sophie" and "Canadian Experience" by Austin Clarke (1990). One Canadian novel is selected from the list by the instructor and purchased by students. Examples of two of the novels I have chosen in recent years are Culleton's (1992) *In Search of April Raintree* and Paci's (1982) *Black Madonna*. All the reading materials have to be Canadian or directly related to Canada; all selected fiction has to be written by Canadian authors. We try to find novels that are interesting to students, that are not too long, and that fit in well with the major themes of the course.

Additional course materials include a large number of handouts with supplemental material and activities we use throughout the year. These handouts include sheets of common language errors; work sheets of specific tasks for different groups; and charts, tables, and diagrams serving as a basis for transcoding. I also hand out subsidiary language practice sheets, notes on referencing and organizing essays, and additional readings that are germane to those included in the kit (e.g., from the current daily press). I encourage students to buy a monolingual dictionary plus a reference grammar. Recently I have found the Collins *Cobuild English Dictionary* and its companion *Cobuild English Grammar* (London: Harper-Collins, 1990) to be helpful resources for the students.

Assessment

Because CLC is a credit-bearing course that is counted in the students' official grade point average, my colleagues and I realize we need to attend carefully to assessment. In sections I offer, grades for the yearlong course are determined as follows.

two large research essays (25 percent)
two major oral presentations based on research (20 percent)
a large number (around 12 to 15 pieces of work in this category) of
    small oral and written assignments (together worth 25 percent)
an in-class, end-of-course final examination (10 percent)
participation (20 percent)

Great care is taken to make all assessment tasks/procedures opportunities to learn and to provide students with detailed written and oral feedback. In connection with oral presentations, extensive peer assessment and feedback also take place (see app. 17.1).

Lesson Particulars

Rather than attempting to present a typical lesson, in this section I will provide some details of what portions of a representative CLC lesson are like. The following describes a 100-minute lesson that took place about halfway through the academic year in which the course's 25 students had been asked to read for homework Palmer's (1976) article "Mosaic versus Melting Pot? Immigration and Ethnicity in Canada and the United States." I place explanatory comments in italics and some of the ideas described earlier in the section on teacher's roles between brackets.

This particular lesson began with an oral presentation by two students titled "Fostering a Child." [*The topics, pairs, and dates of presentation—all determined randomly—were assigned very early in the course. Students are expected to do some library research on the topic and to present for about 10 to 15 minutes, followed by a question period.*] During the presentation, I sat among the students and made notes on the feedback sheet along with the rest of the class. Two students not presenting were specifically required to have questions ready for the presenters, and the rest of the class was expected to ask additional questions as well. A question period followed the presentation. [*I promise students that I will have finished with my own assessments prior to the question period so the rest of the class will not be hesitant to provide feedback, lest it should influence my grading decision.*] Finally, a class discussion took place on the strengths and weaknesses of the presentation. [*Students are discouraged from making vague, general comments like "The organization was good" and instead are required to be specific in what they say.*]

[A shift in focus] I returned an essay the students had written on an aspect of the previous article we had been working on. [*The essays have corrections on them.*] Students worked in pairs looking over and discussing the corrections I had made to each of their papers, and they called on me to help them where necessary.

[A shift in focus] I then handed out a photocopied sheet containing key language points from the set of essays and used this as a basis for some explicit grammar teaching. [*I have the students save these sheets. I am always careful to include some points that have reoccurred in the hope that some of the students will identify the problem. Moreover, I point out two or three of the most recurrent and useful points on the sheet and ask students to look for and work on those points explicitly in their next piece of writing. For example, I might ask them to reread while looking specifically for run-on sentences or subject-verb inconsistencies.*]

[A shift in focus] We moved on to discuss the article "Mosaic versus Melting Pot? Immigration and Ethnicity in Canada and the United States," which is an academic article analyzing the professed difference between Canadian and U.S. immigration philosophies. [*Students had been asked to read this article at home.*] I asked the class if there were any points/words that were unclear and then held a discussion as to what the author's primary thesis was. [*This is a sophisticated and long piece of writing, and defining the thesis is not simple.*] I then handed out a detailed work sheet containing 22 key questions arising out of the text (see Internet app. 17.1) and had the students work in four groups. [*They worked on three or four questions I selected for each group. Presenting considerable challenges, these questions required students to manage different segments of the reading and to synthesize their answers from several places in the text.*] Each group was required to prepare a verbal report on their questions to the class. Before students had finished with these tasks, time had run out. The next step, which took place in the following class, was to have each group present their answers and to use their contributions as a basis for an analysis of the article.

Caveats/Final Thoughts

CLC is a course that has existed for a long time. Its objectives have changed and evolved considerably over the past decade. While this period has witnessed an increasing focus on the development of spoken English for Academic Purposes, more recently I have begun conducting research into students' EAP listening needs in order to contribute to enhancement of CLC. Both language and content-area courses should be scrutinized, assessed, and updated to suit the needs of students for whom they are being fine-tuned. As well as my being pleased to be able to share at least some facets of my work with other teachers, the ever-changing nature of the CLC course seems an appropriate theme on which to close this discussion.

Prompts for Discussion and Reflection

1. Describe the setting for this course, who the students are, and what is expected of them. What is the course preparing them to be able to do?

2. How do the instructional features of CLC correspond with your understanding of either strategy-based or content-based teaching?

3. Review table 2.4 in chapter 2. Identify any connections you may infer or recognize between features of Mendelsohn's course and some of the English language learning and teaching principles featured in chapter 2. Rank order what you think Mendelsohn's top five principles from table 2.4 might be. Finally, compare your rank ordering with someone else's and be prepared to support your decisions.

4. In the section on syllabus design, Mendelsohn explains that he deliberately tries to vary the format and sequencing of lesson activities to include as much variety as possible within and across classroom lessons. How important is it for teachers to vary their ways of teaching in language classrooms? Consider that following established routines in teaching sometimes may facilitate language learning. From your perspective

as either a language teacher or learner, discuss any related issues you recognize.

5. To what extent is the author's discussion of what he does in the classroom, how students are assessed, and the shape of the course in general reflective of what he describes as the course's theoretical underpinnings? Identify and discuss instances in which you were able to find any clear connections and/or inconsistencies.

6. If you were asked to teach a course similar to CLC at another institution (but with parallel characteristics such as class size, number of hours, level, credit, etc.) what aspects of the course would you adopt and why? Discuss any aspects of the course and how Mendelsohn teaches it that you believe would need to be modified to fit your own teaching style, personality, and/or philosophy.

7. Mendelsohn states that he handles grammar through pointing out features that are recurrent problems and teaching them as they come up. In other words, he does not have an explicit, preplanned, and systematic grammar syllabus. How do you feel about this in terms of the widely discussed role of a "focus on form" in ELT? What are some alternative ways of structuring the course?

8. How are vocabulary learning and teaching incorporated in CLC? Compare Mendelsohn's way of handling vocabulary instruction with other approaches familiar to you. Or, compare how this area of ELT is handled by other contributors to this volume, such as Brian Morgan (chap. 8), Janet Goodwin (chap. 15), Donna Brinton (chap. 16), Dana Ferris (chap. 18), Joy Janzen (chap. 20), or Carol Numrich (chap. 21). What is your reaction to Mendelsohn's—or any of these other teachers'—ways of handling vocabulary teaching?

9. What roles does reading instruction play in CLC? How is it handled? Discuss any strengths and weaknesses you see. How does Mendelsohn's discussion of CLC's reading component fit with other contemporary approaches to teaching reading?

10. Midway through the section on the role of the teacher, Mendelsohn mentions that he always has a lesson plan ready for each class, though his daily plans are not overly detailed. What issues do his comments in this section raise? How do you envision the role of lesson planning in ELT? Compare and contrast what you perceive as possible differences between beginning teachers and more experienced teachers with respect to lesson planning.

11. Assessment is a matter of paramount importance, particularly

in a nine-credit course, where a grade becomes a part of the student's transcript and GPA. Moreover, the weight assigned to the different aspects of the course by definition dictates the nature of the course itself (i.e., the "washback" effect). How would you handle assessment issues if you were designing a similar course? What assessment options would you plan to include? Why?

Miniprojects

12. The readings in CLC are selected to fit the Canadian context. They are distinctly and deliberately Canadian, in keeping with the course title and goals. If such a course model were adopted for purposes of some other ELT program with which you are familiar, what might become the course's major themes? What would be the content focus? What readings might you include? Begin developing a syllabus plan for such a course.

13. Several years ago, the author of this chapter published in *TESOL Journal* a classroom-focused article entitled "Instruments for Feedback in Oral Communication" (Mendelsohn 1991–92). For this project, locate and read the article to see if it is consistent with the instructional philosophy outlined in this chapter. Discuss with others any points of similarity or contrast between the two discussions. Alternatively, compare also Mendelsohn 1992, "Making the Speaking Class a Real Learning Experience."

14. Imagine you are a member of a committee that is planning a series of workshops. You have learned that David Mendelsohn is available as a presenter but that he prefers it if workshop organizers are clear with respect to the topics they would like to see discussed. Which aspects of what you read in the chapter might you propose to him as workshop topics? Begin to make a list of these. Which aspects of CLC would you like to see further developed? Initiate plans to draft a letter of invitation in which you outline what your committee would like to see as the focus of his workshop.

Exhibit 1: Feedback Instrument for Group Interactions

I. Background Information

1. Students' names: _____
2. Date: _____ 3. Task: _____
4. Relationship between speakers: _____
5. Place where discussion takes place: _____
6. Other: _____

II. Appropriateness of Language

1. Level of formality of speakers: _____
2. Choice of language, given the setting: _____
3. Directness, indirectness, tact: _____
4. Use of "softeners": _____
5. Level of politeness: _____
6. How well did the participant "attend" when not speaking?
   a. Lets speaker finish: _____
   b. Response shows he/she was attending: _____
   c. Behavior shows he/she was attending: _____
7. Other: _____

III. Conversation Management

1. Interrupting:
   a. How did the speaker interrupt? _____
   b. When did the speaker interrupt? _____
   c. How often did the speaker interrupt? _____
   d. How effectively did the speaker interrupt? _____
2. Preventing interrupters from taking over:
   a. How did the speaker do this? _____
   b. How effective was he/she? _____
3. Signaling that they wanted to speak:
   a. How did the speaker do this? _____
   b. How effective was he/she? _____
4. Signaling the end of the speaker's "speech":
   a. How did the speaker do this? _____
   b. How effective was he/she? _____
5. How much did the speaker talk? _____
6. Moving the discussion in a new/different direction:
   a. How did the speaker do this? _____
   b. How effective was he/she? _____
7. Other: _____

IV. Fluency And Hesitations

1. Speed of speech: _____
2. Hesitations: _____
   a. How appropriate were they? _____
   b. How frequent were they? _____
3. Other: _____

V. Body Language and Use of Voice

1. Eye contact: _____
2. Hand movements: _____
3. Facial gestures and smiling: _____
4. Body movement: _____
5. Loudness and softness: _____
   a. In general: _____
   b. Variation for effect: _____
6. How enthusiastic did the speaker sound? _____
7. Other: _____

VI. Effectiveness + Content

1. Did the speaker introduce good, new points? _____
2. Were the speaker's comments persuasive? _____
3. How clearly were the points made? _____
4. Did the speaker signal the different parts of what he/she was saying (e.g., signaling the start of a new idea, signaling that an example was to follow, signaling that clarification was to follow)? _____
5. Was the speaker forceful? _____
6. Did the speaker use humor? _____
7. Did the speaker seem enthusiastic and committed to the topic? _____
8. How "alive" was the speaker? _____
9. Other: _____

VII. Pronunciation of Individual Sounds, Stress, and Intonation

_____
_____
_____
_____
_____

VIII. Grammar and Language Use

_____
_____
_____
_____
_____

IX. Vocabulary

_____
_____
_____
_____
_____

From Mendelsohn 1991–92, 27. Reprinted by permission of *TESOL Journal*.

Chapter 18

Teaching "Writing for Proficiency" in Summer School: Lessons from a Foxhole

Dana R. Ferris

Dana Ferris describes an academic "writing for proficiency" course she taught during a six-week summer session at a large university in the United States. This upper-division course is required of undergraduate students who have failed the university's Writing Proficiency Examination. For many students in the ESL course section Ferris discusses, this was the final requirement they needed to fulfill to receive their university degrees. Failure in the course could mean dismissal from the university. Thus, the class is strongly influenced by two critical factors: (1) students' relatively "high stakes" motivations to succeed and (2) the course's condensed six-week time frame.

Ferris explains that the general design of the "writing for proficiency" course is shaped by both a process approach to teaching writing and an English for Academic Purposes instructional paradigm. She presents her views about several specific pedagogical issues, including the following: (1) the importance of teacher feedback, (2) potential benefits of peer response, and (3) the value of helping students improve the accuracy of their writing through systematic, selective error correction and in-class grammar instruction. Ferris describes the process of her decision making in selecting course goals, choosing a text, and designing the syllabus, noting especially how institutional constraints shaped many of the choices she made. She also characterizes the syllabus type as "task based," with multiple-draft essay projects serving as the primary unit of organization.

As Ferris describes it, the course is student centered, with whole class teacher-led instruction comprising less than a third of total class time. The chapter's lesson particulars section describes a three-day sequence as students prepared for their final exam and completed course portfolios. Ferris concludes by describing the outcome of the class (an encouraging pass rate) and some significant lessons she learned while teaching it. Specifically, she reports becoming more efficient in presenting reading and writing strategies to students and showing more patience when she recognizes that students are struggling to keep up with course demands.

Setting

The Institution

The course described in this chapter is offered at California State University, Sacramento (CSUS), a large urban four-year public university in northern California. All students in the California State University (CSU) system must satisfy the Graduation Writing Assessment Requirement (GWAR), which is implemented in different ways on the various CSU campuses. At our campus, the GWAR may be satisfied in one of two ways: (1) by obtaining a passing score of 8 out of a possible 12 on the Writing Proficiency Examination (WPE) or (2) passing an upper-division English course (109) entitled "Writing for Proficiency." The passing level for the WPE and for English 109E is roughly equivalent to a score of Intermediate-High to Advanced in relation to the ACTFL writing proficiency guidelines. If a student never passes either the WPE or a 109 course, she or he will have to leave the university without a degree.

The Course

English 109E is the GWAR course offered for nonnative speakers (NNSs) of English. It is a three-semester-unit, letter-graded course that does not offer credit toward graduation (though the grade counts in overall GPAs). English 109E is taught only by TESOL-trained and experienced instructors, who may be either part-time lecturers in the English department or full-time (tenured or tenure-track) faculty. The course described in this chapter was taught by the author during a six-week summer session in June–July 1998. It met four times per week (Monday through Thursday) for an hour and 35 minutes in the early afternoon. The final examination was administered on Wednesday morning of the sixth week; thus, there were 22 class meetings in total. Students had standard American university resources available to them (library, computing facilities, e-mail accounts, Internet access). In addition, tutorial support was available to all 109E students through the University Writing Center and from volunteer tutors enrolled in a summer session of a graduate (MATESOL) seminar entitled "Teaching ESL Writing." The instructor was also available in her office for several hours after each class meeting. All 109E students who requested individual tutoring were accommodated through one or more of these support resources.

The Students

The 21 students (7 men and 14 women) in the 109E class were all juniors, seniors, or graduate students at CSUS. All of them had failed the WPE at least once and most twice, but only one was taking the 109E course for the second and possibly final time. While some of the students had taken courses in CSUS's ESL composition sequence, others had entered CSUS as junior year transfers with credit for freshman composition and had not taken any prior English or ESL courses at our campus. Course participants came from 13 different countries: Japan (3), Mexico (2), Hong Kong (3), China (2), Malaysia (2), Laos, Cambodia, India (2), United Arab Emirates, Thailand, Vietnam, Taiwan, and Poland. All were at advanced levels of English proficiency, had strong aural/oral skills, and generally functioned well in their other courses. As they entered the course, both their oral and written abilities ranged from Intermediate-Low to Intermediate-High levels on the ACTFL proficiency scale.

Conceptual Underpinnings

The 109E course as I taught it may be characterized as a hybrid of a process approach and an English for Academic Purposes (EAP) approach to teaching writing (Ferris and Hedgcock 1998; Reid 1993; Silva 1990). Components of a process approach included prewriting/idea generation activities for all essay assignments, emphases on multiple drafting and revision, frequent and extensive peer response activities, teacher feedback on intermediate essay drafts (rather than solely on final drafts), and postponement of editing concerns until final stages of the writing process (Zamel 1982). On the other hand, an EAP focus may be observed in consistent emphases on writing from and about other textual sources, awareness of the demands of academic audiences (especially the audience that would be reading the students' exit examinations and their final portfolios), preparation for timed essay examinations, and strategy training for building students' critical evaluation and editing skills. Further, in discussing the topic "Structure of an Academic Essay," key terms from the "current-traditional" composition framework (Ferris and Hedgcock 1998; Johns 1990; Silva 1990) were utilized (e.g., thesis statement, topic sentence, introduction, conclusion). However, there was no suggestion that students follow a rigid order of presentation, produce a minimum or maximum number of paragraphs, or write according to specific rhetorical modes such as description, comparison and contrast, and so on.

In addition to the conceptual underpinnings provided by these historical approaches to teaching ESL writing, I was guided first and foremost in the design and teaching of the course by identification of learner needs (Long and Crookes 1992). These are discussed in some detail in the goals/objectives and syllabus design sections later in the chapter. Further, the available literature on several specific theoretical issues informed the planning and teaching of this course. First, I operated on the assumption that thoughtful, well-executed teacher feedback is critical to the success of students in the course (Ferris 1995a, 1997; Ferris and Hedgcock 1998; Zamel 1985). Second, the class provided numerous opportunities for peer feedback. As discussed in Ferris and Hedgcock (1998), carefully designed peer response activities can have a variety of important benefits for student writers. Though there is some disagreement in the literature about the best ways to implement peer response activities, I followed the highly structured methods advocated by Mittan (1989) and Ferris and Hedgcock (1998): students were given training and practice in giving feedback to a sample essay before evaluating their peers' writing; they were given concrete and specific peer feedback forms both for written feedback (completed out of class) and for in-class discussion; and they were held accountable in various ways for taking the peer response activities seriously, whether as a giver or receiver of feedback.

Another principle guiding the design of English 109E was that students need a great deal of help in improving the accuracy of their written texts, including specific, individualized feedback about their errors; focused instruction on specific problematic grammar points; and strategy training on how to edit and proofread their finished texts (Ferris 1995b; *editors' note:* also see May Shih, chap. 19 in this volume). Though Truscott (1996) argues that error correction is useless and even counterproductive in L2 writing classes, I have argued elsewhere that students benefit from carefully constructed error feedback and editing strategy training and that the absence of such input may not only frustrate students but may also ensure that many students never become self-sufficient in editing their own work (Ferris 1995b, 1999). However, I do agree with Truscott that different types of errors (lexical, syntactic, morphological) represent distinct types of linguistic knowledge and require different strategies for error correction. This understanding was critical to how I approached error correction throughout the course.

Goals/Objectives

The course objectives shown here were listed in the course description given to students on the first day of class.

During this course you will learn to

1. improve in your ability to understand readings and apply them effectively to your writing;
2. write clear, well-organized essays in which you (*a*) take a position and support it and (*b*) incorporate and analyze ideas from other authors;
3. effectively edit your writing for any serious and frequent problems in grammar, word choice, punctuation, and other mechanics;
4. improve in your ability to self-evaluate and revise your work;
5. develop and apply successful strategies for taking timed essay examinations.

The first three objectives were based upon my knowledge of and experience with the English 109E grading criteria (see Internet app. 18.1). These criteria would be applied to students' final examinations. The fourth was based upon my firm conviction that writing students should learn strategies for managing their own learning in ways they may continue to apply long after the writing class is over. The final course goal was stated to assure students I took their needs seriously—and understood that their most pressing need was to pass the exit examination at the end of the course. The most obvious measurable outcome of these goals would be students' abilities to produce a passing final essay and/or a passing portfolio of their collected work at the end of the six weeks of the course.

I assessed the probable needs of the student population both during the course design phase (before instruction began) and after the class started. In the first phase, I gathered information about program-wide goals, procedures, and grading criteria for English 109E; borrowed syllabi and materials from the two instructors who had taught the course during the previous summer; discussed the course informally with several spring semester instructors; and participated in the group grading of the 109E final examinations at the end of spring semester. Second, during the first two days of the course, I obtained background information about students entering the section of the course I would be teaching (through a questionnaire) and had them produce a 50-minute diagnostic writing sample. I analyzed their writing samples for content, organization, and types of errors made. The diagnostic essay analyses, together with specific information about students' first language backgrounds, prior experiences with composition instruction, and perceptions of their own strengths and weaknesses as writers, helped me to fine-tune my lesson plans and materials and to select grammar points (specifically, noun errors [plurals or articles], errors in verb tense or form, and errors in word choice or form) that were most salient to cover in and out of class.

Syllabus Design

The syllabus design followed directly from the course goals discussed in the previous section. (A portion of the course description is shown in Internet app. 18.2.) Since a good deal of the structure of the course, including its methods and criteria for assessment, was predetermined by the English department, neither the students nor the instructor had much control over a number of its key aspects. In designing the course syllabus, I had the following "givens" to consider: (*a*) the program-wide grading criteria for English 109 (see Internet app. 18.1); (*b*) the group-graded final examination at the end of the course; (*c*) the portfolio requirement. At the end of the course, students were required to submit a portfolio of their best work with a cover letter. In addition to being a significant portion of the final course grade (see Internet app. 18.2), portfolios could be submitted by 109E instructors to a portfolio appeals committee if students failed the final examination. Students had to receive a passing score of "4" or higher (equivalent to a score of Intermediate-High to Advanced on the ACTFL writing proficiency scale) on the six-point grading scale on either the final examination or the portfolio appeal in order to pass the course. The first "given" (the grading criteria) helped me to identify the aspects of composition on which I should focus during the six-week period. The second and third factors led me to spend a great deal of time helping students to prepare for essay examinations and to compile their portfolios.

The general structure of the syllabus was fundamentally task based (Long and Crookes 1992), with the major essay assignments being the primary units of organization around which all other activities clustered (see table 18.1).

The textbook used for the course (Smalzer's [1996] *Write to Be Read: Reading, reflection, and writing*) was selected for its suitability with regard to student needs and course goals (see the instructional materials section, which follows). Though students completed most of the readings and many of the activities, and all of the writing assignments were based upon the textbook, the textbook served to support and anchor the syllabus, rather than being the starting point for it. The textbook units, readings, and activities

TABLE 18.1. Task-Based Structure of the Course

Week of Class	Tasks
Week 1	Diagnostic essay written in class Essay 1 (out of class) assigned Readings completed for Essay 1
Week 2	Essay 1 submitted; peer feedback Preparation for Timed Writing 1 Essay 1 returned with teacher feedback
Week 3	Essay 1 revision submitted Timed Writing 1 returned with holistic score and feedback Essay 2 assigned; prewriting for Essay 2
Week 4	Essay 2 submitted; peer feedback Preparation for Timed Writing 2 Essay 2 returned with teacher feedback
Week 5	Essay 2 revision submitted Essay 1 revision returned with holistic score and feedback Timed Writing 2 returned with holistic score; peer feedback and teacher-student conferences In-class revision of Timed Writing 1 or 2 In-class drafting of portfolio letter
Week 6	Portfolio submitted Preparation for final essay examination

were not covered in the original order as presented by Smalzer but as they fit the tasks I had identified and designed for the course. In the task-based syllabus framework, the course design represents a blend of both the "Type A" (i.e., preplanned) and "Type B" (i.e., negotiated) syllabuses discussed by Long and Crookes (1992). The English 109E course is primarily Type A in that it is "other-directed, determined by authority . . . and assess[es] success and failure in terms of achievement or mastery" (29). On the other hand, this particular class also embodied some Type B characteristics in that some of the course-specific objectives, lessons, and activities were "determined by a process of negotiation between teacher and learners after they meet, as [the] course [evolved]" (29).

Activity Types

A wide variety of activity types and interaction patterns was included over the six-week period. The most frequent configurations were individual and pair work, followed by small group (four or five students) discussions and by whole class discussion or teacher-led instruction. To reiterate, the course activities themselves were determined by the course goals previously discussed and included the types discussed subsequently (writing, peer response, reading, rhetorical strategy instruction, and grammar and editing).

Writing. The students did a good deal of in-class writing, including their 50-minute diagnostic essay, two 2-hour in-class practice examinations, in-class revision of one timed essay, and in-class drafting of their portfolio letter. In addition, they completed various written prewriting, revision, and grammar activities in class.

Peer response. Peer response activities were included in 6 of 22 lesson plans. They included structured responses to whole completed essay drafts, editing for errors, responses to each other's summaries, outlines, and reactions to assigned course readings. In each case, students were given explicit instructions, with handouts, about what to focus on in giving peer feedback (see Internet app. 18.3; and table 18.2, which follows in the section on lesson particulars).

Reading. With a couple of exceptions, most assigned readings were done outside of class for homework or as preparation for scheduled essay examinations. In class, we discussed general strategies for approaching an assigned text, and principles and mechanics of summarizing, paraphrasing, and quoting another author's ideas. Students also worked individually, in pairs, and in small groups on various textbook exercises related to the assigned readings. Finally, we talked about strategies for reviewing readings in preparation for an essay exam. This discussion was followed by several student-led brainstorming sessions about the main ideas of the readings and possible exam questions that might proceed logically from those readings.

Rhetorical strategy training. I provided whole class instruction, based upon examples and activities from the textbook, about paragraph and essay structure, introductions and conclusions, different types of support for a thesis (definition, examples, etc.), and strengthening a persuasive essay by anticipating and refuting possible counterarguments. These teacher-led presentations were followed up with textbook exercises and/or applications of the principles to either essays students were working on or texts they had already completed. For example, my in-class presentation on the topic of providing various types of support for a thesis was supported by the sample paragraphs shown on pages 48–53 of Smalzer's (1996) text.

Grammar and editing instruction and practice. We completed a wide variety of individual, pair, and whole class activities related to grammar and editing skills. These activities included presentation and discussion of an editing strategies checklist, grammar minilessons on selected topics (based upon the results of the error analyses of the diagnostic essays), completion of in-class and homework grammar exercises (with answer keys) from the textbook, peer and self-editing exercises, and an activity I call "editing under time pressure," in which students were given a sample student essay and asked (with guidance) to find and correct as many errors as they could in a 20-minute period. The purpose of this last activity was to simulate what they would need to do with their own essays during the two-hour essay examinations.

Though the preceding activity types have been separated by subheadings here for the purposes of elaboration, it is important to note that for the most part, one activity type was seamlessly connected with another, while focusing on the primary unit of organization, the major in- and out-of-class essays written for the course. Activities selected were carefully and intentionally connected to the five major course goals listed previously. The "Reading," "Writing," and "Rhetorical Strategies" activities addressed the first two goals (applying reading material to one's own writing); the "Grammar/Editing" activities were designed to meet the third objective (editing); "Peer Response" and in-class revision activities addressed the fourth goal (self-evaluation and revision); and the three in-class writing sessions, together with three lessons on the topic "Essay Exam Strategies" (one before each of the three exams), were planned to meet the fifth objective (strategies for timed essay exams).

Learners' Roles

Despite the aforementioned top-down (or Type A) organization of the course, it was the students themselves who made the course function. I delivered relatively little teacher-led, up-front instruction. The vast majority of class time was spent in individual, pair, or small group work. Students' cooperation in completing essay drafts and other homework assignments and their participation in discussions of readings and peer feedback activities were essential not only to the smooth execution of lesson plans I developed but also to their own progress as writers.

I made it clear from the beginning that "we are all in this together"—trying to make a lot of progress in a short period of time—and that they needed to cooperate with me and with each other for an important common goal: to prepare as many of them as possible to pass the course. During the 1998 summer session, I was fortunate to have a serious-minded and agreeable group of students who seemed to trust that I had their best interests at heart and believed I knew what I was doing. As a result, they were extremely involved and cooperative with most of the activities I designed for them. For instance, several times I asked them to bring to class two copies of their current essay draft, one to give to me and another to give to a partner for peer feedback. In previous composition courses I have taught, students consistently forgot to bring their extra copies even when reminded to do so. Yet this group of students was different. Each time I asked them to bring two copies of an essay, 100 percent of them complied! This sign of their serious commitment to the course not only amazed me but my colleagues in the English department as well.

As previously discussed, the course included a great deal of peer feedback as well as other types of pair and small group interaction. Students took the peer response activities seriously, and most did a fairly good job of giving their partners feedback and carefully considering the comments given by peers in constructing revisions. In addition, students were given several structured opportunities to engage in self-assessment, most notably during an in-class revision session and during the composing of the portfolio letter.

Somewhat to my surprise, students made no objections to either peer or self-evaluation activities, apparently accepting my explanations of the importance of developing autonomy and critical evaluation skills. Examination of student portfolios, homework folders, and essay folders showed that most had put a great deal of thought and energy into these activities and that they appeared to be beneficial in developing various analysis and writing skills.

Teacher's Roles

As may be clear from the foregoing section, my typical persona as a writing teacher is that of facilitator or conductor rather than strong up-front presence. However, I regularly gave whole class presentations and/or led whole class discussions, usually as a lead-in to individual or small group work. For instance, during a presentation on quotation use, I spoke from a four-point outline that was up on an overhead, accompanied by a student handout with the same four points plus examples of properly integrated quotations from texts they had already read. This presentation was followed by a homework exercise in which students selected quotations from two essays to which they were about to respond during an in-class examination.

A different type of teacher-led activity occurred when we were reading and discussing a poem by Kahlil Gibran entitled "On Friendship."

Following a warm-up activity on the topic (conducted in small group discussion format), I read the poem aloud to the class twice. We then discussed the main idea of the poem, worked through the meanings of several stanzas, and compared the tone and content of the poem to a *Psychology Today* article on the topic of friendship that students had read previously (both readings are featured in the Smalzer 1996 text).

Generally speaking, I lead whole class discussions by posing open-ended questions to the whole class and waiting for volunteers to respond (I rarely call on individual students). I follow up on volunteers' comments or questions by repeating the student contribution and asking the other students to react or answer the questions. If students fail to respond or if one or two students are dominating the discussion, I will cut the whole class discussion short, make a few summary comments of my own, and move on to the next activity. Though I have faced such group dynamic problems in previous writing classes, they did not arise in this particular summer course.

Though teacher-fronted activities never consumed more than 20 to 30 minutes of a 95-minute class session, the students clearly perceived me as in control of the class. All individual, pair, and small group work was tightly structured as to what students were supposed to do and how long each phase of an activity should take. I tried to be consistent and conscientious in monitoring student work by circulating to see whether they had questions, needed assistance, or were "on task."

Finally, I believe the students saw me as an involved teacher because I spent so much time providing written and oral feedback on their writing, both inside and outside of class. Over the six-week period, I spent close to 100 hours providing various types of responses (including error correction) to student writing. In constructing this feedback, I attempted to be (*a*) clear; (*b*) selective, prioritizing the most important issues for each student and each text; (*c*) constructively critical, giving both comments of encouragement and suggestions for improvement; and (*d*) text specific, consciously giving praise and suggestions in terms unique to the student's particular paper (Ferris and Hedgcock 1998).

Instructional Materials

I used one textbook, which students were required to purchase, in teaching the 109E class. I selected the textbook, *Write to Be Read* (Smalzer 1996), after searching for several months. I was not satisfied with the materials that had been used for 109E during the academic year, and as soon as I was assigned the summer course, I began looking for a replacement. A review in the *TESOL Journal* (Liu 1998) alerted me to the features of Smalzer's text, and in a happy coincidence, I already had it on my shelf. After examining it carefully and consulting with several spring semester 109E teachers, I decided the book was compatible with the goals of the 109E course and students' needs.

In particular, several textual features appealed to me. First, the book contained eight thematically organized units with two to three readings each that were of about the right length and challenge for students in the course. Though the 109E assignments must all be based on readings, I did not want to allot too much class or homework time to working intensively with other authors' texts, preferring rather to focus primarily on students' own writing. Thus, I looked for readings that would be interesting for students to write about but that were not so long or difficult that students would be bogged down. The readings represented a variety of text types, including popular magazines and newspapers, scholarly journals, fiction, and poetry. There were also a number of related student-authored essays scattered throughout the text. The units included such topics as "Birth Order," "Friendship," "Work," and "Courtship," which seemed generally accessible and interesting to a diverse young adult population.

I was also impressed with the wide variety of reading and writing support activities that the text included. The writing topics included all of the major issues I had identified as important for the course (see the preceding course goals section), including summary, paraphrase, and quotation of other authors' texts; essay organization; developing and supporting an opinion; and writing persuasive essays. Finally, each unit included what seemed to be effective grammar explanations and exercises, with additional "grammar and punctuation guidelines" and activities included in an appendix. Answer keys to the exercises were available in the instructor's manual. A final quality of the book that pleased me was that it was relatively small and inexpensive. I knew we would be able to cover most of the text within the six-week course, and indeed, we utilized nearly all of the readings and many of the exercises.

By the end of the course, I continued to be extremely pleased with the textbook, as were the students. They found the readings accessible and interesting and the subsequent writing assignments motivating. We were all pleased with the clarity, helpfulness, and practicality of the supporting exercises.

However, no textbook matches students' and a teacher's needs and expectations perfectly. I supplemented the Smalzer text with a wide variety of handouts and other instructional supports. These included materials on strategies for reading, editing, and preparing for and taking essay examinations, as well as specific essay assignment sheets, peer feedback forms, and an "essay evaluation checklist" that I used for my own feedback as well as for peer response. I also created a number of homework assignment sheets and accompanying handouts, some of which were adapted from materials in the textbook. Finally, I regularly used overheads for in-class presentations; students were also given hard copies of all of my overhead transparencies.

Lesson Particulars

In this section, I will describe a three-day lesson sequence from week 5 (or days 17 through 19 out of our total of 22 class meetings) of the course that involved peer response and revision of an in-class timed writing. The goals for this three-day sequence were for students to (*a*) reflect critically on their peers' and their own writings; (*b*) provide peer feedback to help their partners decide which of the two timed writings to revise and what changes they might consider; (*c*) plan their revisions taking peer feedback, teacher feedback, and self-assessment into account; (*d*) spend substantial time in class working on their revisions with opportunities to gain access to on-the-spot feedback from me; and (*e*) complete focused self-editing activities to work on grammar trouble spots before they finalized their revisions. On Monday of week 5, students arranged themselves into pairs and exchanged in-class essays they had written at the previous class meeting (Thursday of week 4). They then were asked to complete the following activities.

1. 20 minutes: Read partner's essay, assign a score from the 109E grading criteria, and complete the Essay Evaluation Checklist. Both the grading criteria and the checklist (shown in Internet app. 18.1) were already familiar to the students.
2. 20 minutes: Distribute peer feedback discussion questions (see Internet app. 18.3); pairs spend 20 minutes discussing their reactions (about 10 minutes per paper).
3. and 4. Rest of class period: Partners read each other's papers again, completing the peer editing work sheet (see table 18.2). When they have completed the work sheet, they return the paper to its author; students spend the remainder of the class time editing and correcting their papers.

TABLE 18.2. Timed Writing 2: Peer Editing Workshop

Instructions: Read your partner's Timed Writing 2 again, this time looking for any errors in grammar, vocabulary, punctuation, or spelling. <u>Underline</u> any errors you find but *do not* write any corrections! When you have finished, complete the chart below.

Error Type	No. of Errors Found
Spelling	
Wrong word or word form	
Noun endings or article errors	
Verb tense or form errors	
Sentence structure errors (missing words, extra words, run-ons, fragments)	
Punctuation errors	

During the peer and individual work, I sat at the front of the room responding to questions as students called me over or came up front to talk to me. The nature of the questions and my feedback varied over the three-day period depending upon which stage of revision and editing students were focusing on. For instance, during day 1, students asked me for clarification about my feedback and peers' feedback about the timed writing they had done during the previous class, so that they could understand where they might have gone wrong. On day 2, students would make content changes to their drafts and ask me if I thought the changes solved previous problems and improved the draft. During day 3, the focused editing stage, students came to ask me specific grammatical questions. At the end of the first class period, I went over the following homework assignment with the students (given on a handout).

> Read both of your Timed Writings again. Decide which of the two you will revise for the last out-of-class assignment. Read the teacher and/or peer feedback you have received for the Timed Writings. Then write several paragraphs (no more than one page, total) in which you respond to the following questions.
>
> 1. Which of the two papers will you revise, and why have you selected that one?
> 2. What are the problem areas in the paper you will need to work on as you revise it?

3. What are your revision plans? What steps will you take to make sure your revision is an improvement over the first draft?

Students were reminded to bring both Timed Writings, plus their completed homework, to class the next day. The next two days (Tuesday and Wednesday) proceeded as follows.

1. Students completed an outline form that showed how their revised Timed Writing would be structured (30 to 40 minutes).
2. Students began drafting their revisions on Tuesday (for about one hour); the revisions were collected at the end of the class period.
3. Students spent about another hour on revisions on Wednesday.
4. They then completed a self-editing activity similar to the peer editing exercise as presented in table 18.2.

Students then took their completed revisions home to type, polish, and further edit them. The original in-class version, the handwritten in-class revision, and the typed out-of-class revision were all included in the students' final portfolios submitted the following week.

Caveats/Final Thoughts

This class went extremely well. At the end, exactly two-thirds, or 14 out of 21 students, passed the course. In our program this proportion is a high pass rate for English 109E, especially during the summer session. I attribute the success of the class equally to my careful planning (including my textbook selection), the energy I expended in giving substantive feedback throughout the six weeks, and the very agreeable and hardworking mix of students enrolled in the course. In addition, the availability of high-quality tutors was of great benefit to many of the students. Further, it is possible that because the class took place during a summer session (so students had to pay extra for it), they took their work more seriously. I am also convinced that the summer session, despite its brevity, offers one significant advantage over the regular academic year: students (and teachers) have fewer distractions and concentrate more efficiently on the task at hand.

Because the course was relatively short, I did a number of things differently than I typically would. Most significantly, I "front-loaded" a lot of information, giving students summary sheets during the first week on effective strategies for reading, developing essay structure, and editing. Normally, I would introduce these strategies more gradually over a number of weeks, allowing students to experiment and discover whatever approaches they might like best. During the summer of 1998, I opted for a quicker and probably more expedient approach: "Here's what you need to do to succeed in this course. Now we'll spend the rest of the six weeks practicing it." In addition, I was a good deal more lenient about late papers and homework than I normally would be. I had trouble keeping up with the workload myself; I did not have the heart to come down too hard on students who seemed to be having similar problems. Usually, I do not tolerate overdue assignments except in cases of dire emergency. As a result of these two major accommodations to the short session, I was at once a more efficient, tightly focused teacher and a kinder and gentler one. Since "necessity is the mother of invention," I may have stumbled upon some better strategies for teaching my writing classes *all* the time and not only in a condensed, summer session version of the 109E course.

Prompts for Discussion and Reflection

1. What is the setting of the course described in this chapter? Specifically, what were the institutional requirements and constraints that helped to shape the class?

2. The author emphasizes feedback as a primary teaching and learning tool for academic writers. What connections do you see between the principles she presents to support this emphasis and the specific choices she made in teaching the class? Do you recognize connections to any of the general ELT principles listed in table 2.4 of chapter 2?

3. The author argues for the importance of helping students improve the accuracy of their written products. How do her course goals, major activities, and specific tasks in the sample lesson illustrate this stated value?

4. The course Ferris describes was designed for a 6-week intensive summer session. How do you think the intensive nature of the class might have affected how it was taught? If you were to teach a similar course at a more relaxed pace (e.g., either a 10- or 15-week course) what might you do differently? What characteristics would you retain? How might a longer version of the course differ from the 6-week version?

5. The students in Writing for Proficiency seem highly motivated because they had to pass the course in order to graduate from the university and because they had paid extra money to take the summer course. If you were teaching an academic writing class for which neither of these external motivation issues was a factor, how do you think it might

change the dynamics of the class? What might you need to do differently to motivate the students to succeed? Discuss any insights you could provide on such issues.

6. As Ferris's discussion implies, there is some controversy in the ESL writing literature about whether peer response activities are beneficial for second language students. Yet the author drew heavily upon peer response and in-class writing and revision activities to structure class sessions and accomplish course goals. Thinking about ELT courses you have taught (or a writing course with which you are familiar), do you think these types of activities would be effective in other settings (e.g., in your teaching setting)? Why or why not?

7. This writing course included error feedback and grammar/editing instruction as key components. Are you aware of any principles of second language acquisition that appear to support this focus? Any that would argue against it? Compare with table 2.4 in chapter 2.

8. When you have had a chance to examine both chapters, compare the error feedback and grammar/editing features of the course Ferris describes with May Shih's discussion of similar topics in chapter 19. Are their instructional philosophies compatible? Discuss any differences or similarities you may notice between them. Who do you think would have an easier (or a more difficult) time: (*a*) Dana Ferris, if she were charged to teach the course May Shih describes or (*b*) Shih, if she were asked to teach Ferris's course? Why?

9. The author notes that a relatively small amount of class time was "teacher fronted." What principles of English language teaching would seem to support this approach to structuring class sessions? How else was the class organized?

Miniprojects

10. The author describes her selection of William Smalzer's (1996) text *Write to Be Read* and explains how the characteristics of the text matched her course goals. Make arrangements to examine this text (or some comparable ESL writing text). If you were going to teach a course similar to the one Ferris describes, under similar circumstances, would you use Smalzer's text (or the other text you located)? Are there some other texts you might prefer? Bring whatever ESL writing texts you find to class and in a 5- to 10-minute presentation, explain why one of them might be a good fit for the course Ferris describes or why some other text would be even better. What are some of the text characteristics you are looking for and value?

11. Make arrangements to interview two or more teachers of ESL composition about their use of feedback in writing classes. Create a list of 5 to 10 questions that aim to elicit their philosophies and approaches toward teacher response, peer feedback, error correction, and revision. For one of the questions, show them Internet appendix 18.1 from this chapter and explain that the author adapted it from course grading criteria and used it consistently for both teacher commentary and peer feedback. Ask the teachers what they think of such an approach. Be sure to ask about their perceptions of the benefits of their own feedback and peer response in helping students to revise texts and improve their writing skills over time. Prepare an oral presentation or a poster presentation or write a three- to five-page paper in which you present and synthesize your respondents' answers, comparing them to the ideas presented by Ferris in this chapter.

Chapter 19

A Course in Grammar-Editing for ESL Writers

May Shih

May Shih teaches in San Francisco State University's undergraduate ESL program. She discusses a grammar-editing course of her own design. Most of the students in the course are long-term U.S. residents who are required to take grammar editing due to persistent errors in their writing. The goals of the course are to increase understanding of general grammar rules, to enhance awareness of weaknesses in their writing, and to strengthen self-editing abilities. Students are expected to apply what they learn to writings they are generating for other courses taken concurrent with the grammar-editing course. By the end of the semester, learners should be able to locate and self-correct many of their most frequent errors.

As Shih structures grammar-editing, students write several short compositions that they edit with attention to general grammar points and to their more personal trouble spots as writers in English. Over time, they develop a repertoire of general and error-specific strategies to assist in locating and correcting errors. Some of the general strategies Shih teaches include time management, strategies to focus attention on written forms, and structured reviewing for editing in purposeful cycles. Error-specific strategies include editing specific types of errors at word, sentence, and discourse levels. Shih posits that second language writers of English require principled feedback to help them become more effective self-editors. To this aim she makes maximum use of indirect feedback and requires students to keep personal grammar notes on past errors. Through these and other procedures, students become actively involved in self-editing. From time to time, Shih conducts one-to-one grammar conferences with students to provide individualized diagnosis, instruction, evaluation, goal setting, and encouragement.

For ESL writers, an important part of the writing process is editing. Ferris (1995b) defines editing as "finding and correcting grammatical, lexical, and mechanical errors before submitting (or 'publishing') a final written product" (18). In process-oriented composition classes that give priority to higher order concerns such as focus, content, and organization, teachers and students often find it difficult to give editing time the systematic attention it deserves. ESL students whose writing is heavily marked by error benefit from separate courses focused specifically on improving the grammatical accuracy of their writing (Kroll 1990). One option is to offer a grammar-editing course taken concurrently and in a coordinated manner with a composition class. This chapter describes just such a course.

Setting

Grammar for Writing (G/W) is a one-unit, credit/no credit (pass/fail) adjunct course in the undergraduate ESL program at San Francisco State University (SFSU). Part of the California state university system, SFSU is a public institution of over 27,000 students. The course focuses on increasing students' awareness of common ESL errors and personal grammar weaknesses and on improving their editing skills. G/W students are required to take the course as a result of previous ESL instructors' determinations that their writing contains persistent and frequent errors. Concurrent with G/W, students are enrolled in a three-unit composition course at one of three levels and are expected to apply the skills they learn in the G/W course to their writing in the composition class. Some students retake G/W (for credit) if their grammar continues to be unacceptable based on end-of-term summative assessments by both their G/W and composition class instructors. Each section of G/W normally has a class size of 20, and the class meets twice weekly, for two hours per week, over a 15-week semester. The typical classroom has movable tables and chairs and is large enough to permit students to move around for pair and group work. Chalkboards, screen, and overhead projector make it easy to present visual material in class.

Most of the students who take the class are long-term U.S. residents. In a recent semester, 90 percent of the students in one section were permanent residents, and 10 percent were international students on F-1 visas; most were from mainland China, Hong Kong, and Vietnam, with the remainder from Korea, Japan, and the Philippines. All had been in the United States from three to nine years. Many of the students have part-time jobs and lead very busy lives. G/W students are at all class levels at SFSU (freshmen through seniors), though a majority are studying in their junior or senior years. According to the ACTFL proficiency guidelines (writing), their English proficiency level is Advanced; they exhibit "an ability to write narratives and descriptions of a factual nature of at least several paragraphs in length" but still make "frequent errors in producing complex sentences." Although all of the students have previously taken at least one formal grammar course, they do not readily apply their knowledge of grammar to editing their own writing. Most seem to have forgotten many previously studied rules of English grammar. Many of their easy-to-address errors are mistakes that they are able to self-correct, but other errors reflect gaps in linguistic competence and misconceptions about forms and rules.

Conceptual Underpinnings

The pedagogical approach of the G/W course is based on assumptions and principles derived from theory and research in second language acquisition (e.g., Ellis 1994b) and ESL composition (e.g., Ferris and Hedgcock 1998).

Second Language Development

According to SLA theory, the development of proficiency in a second language is "a process that involves both acquisition (the subconscious incorporation of linguistic forms primarily through reading/listening) and learning (the conscious assimilation of rules and forms through individual study or classroom instruction)" (Bates, Lane, and Lange 1993, 7). The long-term U.S. resident students who enroll in G/W have developed much of their proficiency through immersion in an English speaking environment. Their writing commonly exhibits developmental errors (due to incomplete learning of rules) that reflect ear learning (i.e., reliance on aural input) (Reid 1998). In the G/W course, they need to make a concentrated effort to fill in knowledge gaps as well as to unlearn misconceived forms and rules that underlie habitual and persistent ("fossilized") errors. On the other hand, the short-term international students in the G/W course have learned English mainly through formal classroom study. Because of limited exposure to English beyond classroom settings, they often have problems with idiomatic language. They also lack experience composing academic papers in English and therefore, like immigrant learners, need plenty of practice applying rules for purposes of editing their own writing.

Second language learners need feedback to help them to form and revise mental hypotheses about rules. Without such feedback, incorrect hypotheses may result in stabilized (fossilized) errors in a learner's developing system of rules (interlanguage) (Bates, Lane, and Lange 1993). For maximum impact, feedback on errors in student writing should be selective because dealing with an excessive number of errors can be overwhelming and discouraging for both student and instructor. Some guidelines are to give priority to more serious errors that hinder communication of ideas; recurring errors; and errors on grammar points appropriate to a student's proficiency level, course goals, and the type of paper (Frodesen 1991; Raimes 1991; Ferris and Hedgcock 1998). Use of minimal feedback (i.e., indirect feedback such as Xs in the margin of the page or comments on errors, rather than direct correction) stimulates students to become more actively involved in analyzing their own errors, as a "discovery" process (Corder 1967; Bates, Lane, and Lange 1993), and helps to shift the burden for dealing with errors from the teacher to the student (Ferris 1995b). In the G/W course, I provide selective feedback in order to help learners develop awareness of their individual grammar strengths and weaknesses and to stimulate habits of self-correction. Improvement in grammatical accuracy is slow and variable.

> The process of language acquisition is not a matter of simply aggregating one structure after another in linear fashion. The process is a gradual one; and even when learners appear to have mastered a particular structure, backsliding may occur as their attention is diverted to a new learning challenge. (Celce-Murcia and Larsen-Freeman 1999, 8)

Learners need repeated "spiraling" of grammar rules (Byrd 1998), occasional guided recycling and reexamination of rules, and time to absorb and apply information about English grammar. In G/W lessons, I reexplain and expand upon rules as needed and constantly seek ways to condense rules to essentials that can be easily accessed during the editing process. Each new grammar point studied is added to a cumulative checklist for which students are held accountable when they edit their own papers.

Optimal moments for learning about language are times when learners' attention is drawn to linguistic features, including errors in their own utterances, while engaged in interactive communicative tasks.

> Negotiation work . . . elicits negative feedback, including recasts, that is, corrective reformulations of a . . . learner's utterances that preserve the learner's intended meaning. Such feedback draws learners' attention to mismatches between input and output, that is, causes them to focus on form. (Long and Robinson 1998, 23)

Very similar observations have been made in L2 composition research; ESL student writers' active negotiations of meaning during teacher-student writing conferences result in effective revisions in their writing (see Goldstein and Conrad 1990; Nelson and Murphy 1993). In G/W, one-to-one writing conferences provide opportunities for student writers to gain access to form-focused feedback and rule explanations in the context of their attempts to communicate ideas in writing.

Composing and Editing in ESL

A process approach to teaching composition helps student writers to build a variety of strategies for

prewriting (e.g., defining the task with consideration to purpose and audience, exploring ideas, finding a topic and a focus, and selecting and ordering supporting material)

drafting (structuring ideas into a linear piece of discourse)

revising (reviewing a draft and adding, deleting, reorganizing, and refining material to make the content and structure fit (*a*) the writer's intentions and (*b*) the reader's expectations for clarity and logical order)

editing (making surface corrections and improvements in grammar, vocabulary, mechanics, and style in accordance with rules/conventions)

Students are given ample time to explore and refine their ideas. During revising and editing, writers shift their attention from articulating ideas for themselves (producing writer-based prose that may be rambling, repetitive, messy, and error filled) to preparing their writing for an audience, that is, transforming it into reader-based prose that is coherent and easy for others to understand, with precise and clear language.

The teacher provides support, feedback, and assistance throughout the writing process. She or he serves as a reader (audience) for students' writing, a diagnostician who helps students to identify problems in their writing, a resource person who responds to questions and problems on work in progress, a coach who gives comments on what has worked well and what needs further work, and a counselor who listens for what might be derailing students' efforts and who offers advice and encouragement (Harris 1986).

In process-oriented composition instruction, teachers guide student writers to set different goals as they work on successive drafts of a piece of writing, reflecting a hierarchy of priorities (attention first to content and focus, then organization, then grammar and mechanics). Editing is a "lower order concern" (Keh 1990). The shifting priorities are reinforced by the type of feedback provided. Writers first receive feedback on focus, development, and organization of ideas, and only after these aspects have been resolved is attention turned to grammar and mechanics.

Research and experience in the classroom have shown that inexperienced writers compose more efficiently if they delay consideration of grammatical and mechanical details until they are satisfied with the content and organization of a paper, so that premature editing does not disrupt their thought process (Jones 1985). If writers understand that they will have a chance to repair and perfect their current draft before readers actually see it, they will be free to concentrate on ideas and not worry about form (Shaughnessy 1977). Another reason to treat editing as a separate step is that it is a very different cognitive process from reading for comprehension. "Normal" reading is a process of anticipation and prediction that is too rapid and selective for the reader to see details; effective editing, on the other hand, requires suspension of this anticipation and an ability "to attend to the text closely and deliberately—looking specifically at each word and mark of punctuation, carefully noting not only what is there but also what is not there" (Harris 1987, 464).

The G/W course works on developing students' editing strategies in a manner consistent with the shifting priorities of a process approach to writing. For short G/W papers, I allow sufficient time for students to gather and refine ideas and to write a first draft. Then I encourage careful editing by scheduling editing steps into the time line for paper revision, allotting class time for editing, modeling editing strategies, and providing form-focused feedback. When students edit papers from their composition and academic content courses, they have already spent considerable time working on content and organization before they are asked, in G/W, to turn their attention to editing near-final drafts. In the G/W course, students' sense of audience is heightened. They come to appreciate how errors can cause readers to become confused and distracted and to realize that editing is an essential part of the process of preparing a document for an outside audience.

ESL writers whose writing is heavily marked by error need to develop their knowledge and skills in several areas, including (1) time management, (2) commitment to an editing habit, (3) awareness of what to look for when editing, (4) grammatical knowledge, and (5) a repertoire of general and error-specific editing strategies to assist in locating and correcting errors (Shih 1998). These are the areas of focus in the G/W course.

Objectives

The main goal of the course is for students to improve the grammatical accuracy of their writing. To this end, lessons cover common ESL errors and rules that underlie them such as typical problems with count/noncount nouns, articles, subject-verb agreement, verb forms and tense, sentence structure, fragments and run-together sentences, logical connectors, parallel structure, verbals, relative clauses, word forms, and pronoun reference and agreement. Rule explanations allow students to reactivate their understanding of grammar rules (often previously studied but forgotten) and to apply such knowledge to editing their own writing. Grammar discussions also help individuals to fill in gaps in their linguistic competence and to correct misconceptions about forms and rules. By the end of the course, successful students have an increased understanding of rules underlying common errors and an enhanced awareness of their personal grammar strengths and trouble spots (recurring errors). They are able to find and self-correct many of their most frequent errors.

In the course, students are expected to improve their editing process by developing a repertoire of general and error-specific strategies to assist in locating and correcting errors. General strategies include effectively managing one's time (allowing plenty of time for revising and editing, with lengthy breaks between rereadings); being alert to potential grammar problems given the type of writing and to personal trouble spots; using strategies that counteract the normal reading process and focus attention on form (e.g., reading the paper aloud, using a finger or pencil to look at each word and punctuation mark); and editing in purposeful cycles (scanning and checking a paper for one grammar point or error type [or related error types] at a time) (Madraso 1993; Shih 1998).

Error-specific strategies include accessing relevant forms and rules (from memory as well as from sources such as learner dictionaries and grammar reference charts) and using the information to solve certain types of grammar problems (e.g., word form, whether a noun is count or noncount, whether a verb is followed by an infinitive or a gerund). The students build a repertoire of strategies for avoiding and editing specific types of errors ("self-help strategies" for specific grammar points as in Lane and Lange 1999). They learn to edit at the discourse level (examine successive sentences); to find certain types of grammatical problems (verb tense consistency and sequencing, person and number consistency, pronoun reference, choice of connector); to edit at the sentence level for other errors (missing subject or verb, errors in subject-verb agreement, adjective/adverb clause structure); and to focus attention at the word level to find morphological errors (missing and incorrect word endings) (Shih 1998).

Syllabus Design

Selection and Coverage of Grammar Points

The G/W course reflects a structural syllabus. It focuses on rules that underlie common ESL errors rather than comprehensive grammar study. The syllabus builds on basic grammatical knowledge students are assumed to have; with only two class meetings for a total of two class hours a week, the coverage must be selective. Units are chosen from the textbook, *Writing Clearly: An Editing Guide* (Lane and Lange 1999), based on judgments of students' needs. The selection of grammar points is both preplanned (predictive), based on instructors' experiences in previous semesters, and (especially during individual conferences) responsive to needs that emerge. The most recent time I taught G/W, I selected and sequenced grammar topics as follows: count and noncount nouns; number and determiner agreement; subject-verb agreement; verb forms and tenses; sentence structure/clause types, fragments, and run-together sentences; conjunctions, logical connectors, and punctuation of clauses; parallel structure; gerund and infinitive complements; relative clauses and participial phrases; word forms; pronoun reference and agreement.

Design of Composition Assignments

Students write several short compositions and edit them with attention to grammar points that have been covered in class (this list of points grows over the course of the semester) and personal trouble spots. They are also expected to apply the skills they learn in the G/W course to their writing in their composition class. The compositions I assign include three in-class essays written during separate class periods and with a two-day break in between. Sample topics include the following.

> Describe (with examples) a women's rights problem (or some other social problem) in your country of origin.
> State whether in the future you will be staying in the United States or will return to your native country to live and work (be sure to discuss your reasons).
> Give descriptions of sights in a city (or other region) and advice for

travelers from other parts of the world who might be interested in visiting the part of the world where you grew up.

Ideally, G/W writing assignments resemble the kind of tasks students do in their composition and academic content courses. However, the students are enrolled in composition courses at any of three levels in the ESL program, and their assignments for those courses vary from writing grounded by personal experience, to summarizing and responding to readings, to writing research papers. Due to time constraints, the one-unit workload, and the editing focus of the G/W course, I typically use assignments on familiar topics that do not demand a great deal of prewriting preparation. Some sample topics for short compositions done at home include the following.

Describe desirable characteristics (with concrete supporting details) of either your future career or your future spouse.

Summarize and give personal reaction to a brief newspaper article on changes in immigration laws.

By the middle and end of the course, students are far enough along in their composition and academic content courses to have drafts of papers in progress for those courses. I then shift attention to having students edit these papers, and G/W becomes more of an "adjunct" course. Flexible due dates are necessary to fit in with the times when students are working on near-final drafts.

Editing Strategies

In addition to reviewing grammar rules that underlie common ESL errors, an important part of the G/W course content is presentation, modeling, and practice of specific editing strategies. Figure 19.1 includes examples of condensed rules and accompanying strategies I have taught, in order to edit for verb tense choice and consistency.

Activity Types

Lessons consist of review of grammar rules, modeling of editing strategies, and practice editing exercises. I find the most valuable kinds of exercises for developing editing skills to be ones that have students examine their peers' writing and edit for a particular error type. Students move from correcting errors in exercises to correcting them in their own writing.

Rules

1. Each sentence needs (auxiliary verb(s) +) a main verb.
2. Past tense (simple, progressive, perfect) indicate past, completed events or situations.
3. Simple present tense is used to comment and generalize.
4. Present perfect describes something that began in the past and continues/ is still relevant.
5. Future tenses are used to state events or situations that are expected to take place in the future.

Editing Strategies

Ask yourself general questions about each section of the paper and determine the logical time frames. Overall, which tenses are needed? Then, find and check the main verb in each sentence. You can ignore verbals. Fix sentences without clear main verbs. Check your verb forms to see that the appropriate tenses are correctly signaled (with verb endings, auxiliary verbs, time words). At places where you switch time frames, is there a good reason to switch? (Consider signaling it to the reader—e.g., by using a time word/ phrase: *last week, now, in the future.*)

Fig. 19.1. English grammar rules and editing strategies

Exercises to Sharpen Student Perception

Before assigning an exercise to edit for a particular language problem, I review the relevant formal rules and conduct an exercise or two to sharpen students' perception and understanding of how the form/structure works in context. For example, many students have difficulty perceiving word endings; they can be given exercises in which they must mark a particular type of ending in a passage, for example, noun plural -*s* in one color of pen and verb singular -*s* in another color (Shaughnessy 1977). Students identify all instances of the targeted form/structure (e.g., all verbs in present perfect tense, all participles, all adjective clauses and their head nouns) and analyze their use.

Modeling and Practice of Editing Strategies

After students are familiar with a structure and can manipulate it, the class is ready to work on finding and fixing errors. To model an editing strategy

---

My Weakness in Locating Errors

When it's time for me to proofread my essays before I turned it in, I'm not doing a good job as I wanted. All of my English teachers asked me to proofread my essays more carefully before submitting the papers. I always have grammar mistakes throughout my writing and I wish that I can correct most of the errors by the time I graduated from this university.

Before I turn in my paper, I read over the paper two to three times to see if there are any errors that I can correct. My weakness is that I can't find mistakes on my paper so I turned it in to the teacher. A week later when the teacher returned my paper, there are the teacher's marks and comments all over the paper. I was surprised that there were so many grammar mistakes that I couldn't catch on my own. Sometimes I felt that I didn't spend enough time on proofreading.

Fig. 19.2.   A sample of student writing

for students, I use a student's composition displayed on an overhead projection. (I sometimes create a composite piece blending excerpts from several students' compositions.) While reading out loud for the class, I verbally "think aloud" and visually demonstrate the editing process [*editors' note:* cf. Joy Janzen on strategic reading, chap. 20 in this volume]. For example, when we discuss verb tense choice and consistency, I have the class examine the following piece of writing, which is full of incorrect verb tense shifts. Thinking aloud while underlining the verbs on the OHP transparency, I say something like the following.

> Let's see, in this essay I'm talking about how to edit my papers. I'm describing my usual procedures. . . . That's a repeated action, and it's still true now. So, I should mainly use simple present tense, and if I shift to another tense, I better have a good reason (like giving an example of a past situation or future goal), and I should give some kind of signal to my reader when I shift. O.K. The first main verb is *it's*—present tense, fine. *Turned* is past tense. Why past tense? That's wrong. These things are still true. I need to keep this in present tense. [*I continue checking main verbs.*]

Next, I typically ask students to practice editing strategies on another paper containing similar problems. They compare and defend their answers, in pairs or groups of three, and sometimes I have them show their editing changes on an overhead transparency. I lead a whole class discussion and answer questions. Finally, I encourage students to apply the same or similar strategies when editing their own papers.

One-to-One Conferencing

Because students' editing abilities and problems vary widely, one-to-one conferences are an ideal way to address individual students' questions and concerns and to provide diagnosis, feedback, explanations, assessment, goal setting, and encouragement to each student (Harris 1986; Shih 1998).

I conduct short (20 to 30 minute) individual grammar conferences at least three times during the semester. The conferences provide information about students' editing process, including reasons behind poor editing (e.g., not enough time spent on editing, editing too fast, lack of awareness that a dictionary can answer certain editing questions). They provide chances to follow up on a problem, perhaps having a student try out a strategy. A second benefit conferences offer is that one-on-one discussion reveals errors students produce but cannot self-correct due to misconceptions about grammar rules and competence gaps. I can immediately follow up with a mini grammar lesson, using the student's own sentences as contextualized examples. Finally, conferences are a way to encourage students to take initiative for their own grammar learning. Students ask me many more questions than during class. We can review rules as many times as needed and go beyond the course syllabus. I encourage students to show me papers they are working on for their other classes and answer grammar questions.

Lesson Particulars

During conferences, I ask students to bring specific questions they would like to discuss (e.g., on what was covered in class, grammar problems they have on a specific paper, error feedback they would like clarified). I also ask them to edit sections of their papers for selected grammar points, with immediate feedback. I explain grammar rules with contextual and visual support such as time lines, labeling of sentence parts, formulas for grammatical patterns. Finally, we set goals for the immediate future and evaluate progress on previously stated goals.

The following is an example from a 30-minute conference I conducted in a recent semester. This was the second conference of the semester for Hyun (a pseudonym), conducted at midterm (week 7). Our discussion includes the kinds of tasks identified by M. Harris (1986) as typical of conferences:

getting (re)acquainted, diagnostic work to assess needs, instruction, evaluation, and goal setting.

Getting reacquainted. I ask Hyun how he's doing in his classes, and he tells me about his work in progress for his ESL composition class. I offer encouragement.

Diagnostic work. I return the first in-class midterm essay. I ask Hyun about his editing process for this paper. He tells me he had spent 25 minutes checking for all of the points on the G/W checklist; he had edited the paper three or four times but had run a little short of time. I ask him to edit the paper one more time on the spot (some errors are marked with X's; these are errors I think he should be able to self-correct). The following is an example.

> My home country has less crime and better health care system. Even don't have to experience the racial discrimination against the minorities like blacks, Hispanics and Asians. After getting married, if I have children, I better live in Korea. Because I could raise them in a better health care system and less crime society. Even my future children doesn't have to struggle with the racial discrimination if I live with them in my native country.

Hyun successfully corrects some errors (such as the number and subject-verb agreement errors with *children*) but misses the *because* clause fragments and errors with the use of *even*. I decided to address these points. I ignore the fact that the sentences are repetitious and could be revised to be more concise, choosing instead to deal with the intersentential connector problems.

Instruction. When I ask Hyun about his use of *even*, he tells me he uses *even* to emphasize an idea (i.e., as a sentence connector rather than as an intensifier). I tell him that *indeed* is more appropriate in such cases, and I provide some sample sentences showing *even* used in phrases like *even more*, *even so*, and *even* + NP. I also reveal some of my confusion as a reader: "racial discrimination" seems to be a new point added to "less crime" and "better health care" (rather than emphasis of an idea already stated), so a connector to signal an additional idea (such as *in addition to* or *also*) seems more appropriate. I refer to these phrases as listed on a conjunction/connector chart I'd given out in class. (See Internet app. 19.1.)

With prompting, Hyun remembers that *because* introduces a dependent clause, which cannot stand alone as a sentence, and corrects the error. I remind him that when editing, he can make a special point to find all the sentences where he uses *because* and to check that a main clause is attached.

I ask Hyun if he has other grammar questions. He seeks my advice on his many lexical collocation ("word choice") errors. I suggest that he make a point of noticing unfamiliar word collocations in his reading and taking notes on them. I also answer Hyun's questions about some constructions he wants to use in his paper in progress for his composition class.

Evaluation and goal-setting. Summing up, I praise Hyun's successful error corrections on the midterm. (I had asked that editing changes be made in a different color ink, and Hyun had made many.) Nevertheless, his midterm had been graded "✓−" (minimally passing), and we review the error types he needs to check more carefully in the future. We add "use of *even*" and "dependent clause fragments" to Hyun's personal editing checklist. Finally, we discuss his need to watch his time more carefully during the second in-class midterm exam. Hyun's conference illustrates how one-on-one discussions can serve to diagnose, teach, address individual questions/ concerns, and offer encouragement.

Learners' Roles

G/W aims to guide students toward becoming more independent self-editors. To reach this goal, students must study error feedback conscientiously and make a concentrated effort to edit their papers. They must be open to changing certain habits. For example, they have to work on time management so as to allow sufficient time (with lengthy breaks between rereadings, if possible on different days) for revising and editing. I have observed that successful learners use active learning strategies to expand their knowledge of English grammar and lexicon, for example, keeping notes on interesting usages in their concurrent readings and taking time to study teacher feedback on errors. For this reason, in the G/W course, students keep personal grammar notes on note sheets.

During class meetings, it is the students' responsibility to ask clarification questions as needed. When called upon to propose editing changes, students must not only identify errors and provide corrections but must explain underlying grammar rules. ("Why?" is a question they must frequently consider.) Students are encouraged to answer each other's questions and to share individual editing strategies and problems, during pair and group work as well as during class discussions.

Teacher's Roles

The teacher has a variety of roles in the G/W class. The teacher serves, first of all, as an informant on the English language. To reactivate, build, and fine-tune students' understanding of grammar rules and to connect this knowledge to error correction, a portion of most lessons is devoted to formal teaching of grammar and answering students' questions. I try my best to explain forms and rules concisely, using charts, diagrams, and examples in handouts and on the chalkboard. I prefer an inductive approach (i.e., "illustrations first," from which learners are provided opportunities to infer patterns), and whenever possible, I elicit forms and rules from the class rather than lecture. Because it is hard to be selective when explaining grammar, and responding to students' many questions can use up a great deal of time, I try to make efficient use of the limited class time. Two strategies for using class time efficiently are to hold students responsible for reviewing grammar information from the textbook on their own and to address individual problems during conferences.

The teacher is also an experienced writer who models editing strategies. For teachers like myself who are native speakers of English, the most difficult part of this role is getting inside the head of an ESL learner and understanding which strategies are realistic. To keep in touch with learners' perspectives, after modeling an editing technique, I ask students to comment on whether or not it could work for them and how they might modify the technique. I also keep notes from conferences on strategies that students actually use and find to be productive.

In the classroom, I conduct grammar presentation and error correction exercises at a fairly rapid pace, with frequent checks on students' understandings of the rules. To keep students mentally engaged in "editing-as-problem-solving" and to give them practice articulating rules aloud, I often have them work on editing exercises in pairs and small groups. In keeping with a process-oriented approach to teaching composition, the G/W instructor serves as a reader of students' writing; a diagnostician who helps identify editing strengths and problems; a resource person who can respond to grammar questions and problems; and a coach who offers assessment, advice, and encouragement.

Affective Concerns

Occasionally, some students seem less motivated to spend time and effort on editing. I have had students tell me that their other instructors do not care about grammar and do not mark them down for it; consequently, they are less committed to improving their editing skills. To build intrinsic motivation, I demonstrate with compositions displayed on an overhead projector (or handout) how errors can (1) cause a reader to misunderstand a writer's ideas, (2) distract the reader from paying attention to content, and (3) even lead to stigmatizing inferences about the writer. I also try to get students motivated in finding and correcting their own and peers' errors, as a kind of problem solving.

Some students are discouraged by their past failure to reduce errors. They are frustrated when they receive papers back with general (non-specific) admonitions such as "You need to work harder on editing," when in fact they had tried their best to find and correct errors. I am aware of how easy it is for students to lose motivation, since improvement sometimes seems slow and gradual (see Larsen-Freeman 1991) and hard to detect; as papers get more complex, errors may increase. Students seem to do much better work when editing short compositions for G/W than they do on longer, more complex papers for their concurrent composition course and other content courses. In my role as a writing coach, I remind them that improvement takes time and constant effort. When providing written feedback, I use check marks and positive comments in the margins to praise students on grammatical structures used well.

Conferences are the best time to boost morale. When talking to students one-on-one, I use every argument I can think of to keep them working on editing. I stress that the ultimate goal is not error-free writing (which is, of course, unlikely) but reduction of errors to make their writing easier for others to read.

Instructional Materials

The instructional materials in the G/W course consist of Lane and Lange's (1999) *Writing Clearly: An Editing Guide* and a variety of supplementary reference materials. *Writing Clearly* is used both as the core text for G/W and as a reference in the students' concurrent ESL composition courses. Using the same text throughout our composition program helps to ensure that there is some consistency in terminology and marking symbols used by different instructors in different courses. I find *Writing Clearly* an appropriate textbook because its content and approach are consistent with my way of organizing the G/W course. Each unit explains one category of common ESL errors, offers selected grammar rules and "self-help strategies" for controlling the forms/structures, provides sentence-level and paragraph-level editing exercises, and gives tips on applying what students have learned to writing assignments in other classes. The emphasis is on leading learners to become independent self-editors by making them responsible for charting their errors to raise consciousness of their most frequent error types.

In addition to the textbook, G/W students need both a good ESL dictionary as a necessary reference tool (e.g., for checking count/noncount nouns, transitive/intransitive verbs, verb complements, and certain collocations) and a monolingual native speaker dictionary (to consult for definitions and usage of less-frequent words and expressions not found in a learner dictionary). In class, I use a variety of supplementary materials.

1. Handouts with charts summarizing forms and rules for students to use as aids when editing
2. Materials for short composition assignments (e.g., readings to provide data and to stimulate thinking on a topic)
3. Supplementary editing exercises (e.g., recognition exercises and sample pieces of writing for editing practice)
4. Diagnostic charts (expanded version of the error awareness sheet in *Writing Clearly*) and grammar note sheets

Assessment

In the G/W course, specific, personalized error feedback helps students build awareness of their grammar strengths and weaknesses and to remedy misconceptions and gaps in their knowledge of rules. However, students are easily overwhelmed and discouraged by papers with all errors indicated. Written feedback on errors needs to be selective, prioritized, and clear. Thus, I begin by holding students accountable for only a few error types (verb tense choice, verb forms, subject-verb agreement) and then add to the checklist over the course of the semester. I explain my marking system to students when I return the first set of papers. I use minimal, indirect feedback (Xs in the margins) to indicate the general locations of error types the class has studied; students are expected to find and to self-correct these errors and turn in their papers one more time for me to reexamine. When I review their papers a second time, I provide further, direct feedback (error code words, abbreviations, and/or explanations) for undiscovered, miscorrected, or newly generated errors, specifically because errors that remain are likely to reflect gaps in linguistic competence. I rely on conferences to provide expanded oral feedback on errors and mini grammar lessons tailored to individual needs.

To help students become more aware of their most frequent errors and to let them observe progress (or lack of progress) in reducing errors, they keep a diagnostic chart on which they tally their errors in different categories for each composition returned to them. To help them remember rules that underlie past errors, students take notes on personal grammar note sheets, in particular on certain idiosyncratic points that can not be learned by general rules: count versus noncount nouns, problem prepositions, verb complements, word forms, and past spelling errors. During conferences, we look over the diagnostic charts along with their note sheets and use them to help set goals and evaluate progress. I use the following symbol system to grade all papers.

✓+ (= good),   ✓ (= O.K.),   ✓– (weak),   NCr (no credit)

I indicate the number of errors on points studied in class, which students should be able to edit, with a number: – _____ (e.g., –5 if the paper has five errors). To receive credit for a writing assignment, students must fulfill the stipulated content, length and other requirements, and they must also demonstrate a level of grammatical accuracy that I determine by means of the simple error count. I count a repeated, identical error only once and weigh global errors more heavily than local ones. As papers become longer and more complex, I allow for more errors per page; in general, the goal in G/W (the criterion level used in assessing the in-class midterms and final) is no more than three errors per handwritten double-spaced page, on grammar points studied in class. To pass G/W, students must do satisfactory work editing their writing in their concurrent composition course. At the end of the semester, the two instructors together determine if a student passes G/W or might benefit from retaking it.

Caveats/Final Thoughts

A one-unit adjunct course may be adequate to assist and prompt students who already have a basic foundation in English grammar to edit their writing more systematically. However, in our program we have begun to see more and more students who do not possess these basics, for whom two class meetings per week are not enough time (and one unit not enough work and credit) to meet their needs. Therefore, we recently expanded G/W into a three-unit, graded course. The increased contact time and workload permit more in-depth study of certain grammar topics for which students need a stronger formal foundation at a slower pace. Students get more time and practice in producing structures and editing their writing with attention to these structures.

Prompts for Discussion and Reflection

1. What are some of the reasons why ESL writers might have difficulty finding errors in their own writing? From your own teaching and/or language learning experiences, can you shed any light on such difficulties?

2. Although this chapter focuses on grammar-editing in connection with the teaching of writing, discuss possible implications you may infer from Shih's discussion for the teaching of speaking in ELT. Can you envision an ESL oral communication course designed in any ways parallel to Shih's Grammar-Writing course?

3. Current theory, research, and pedagogy in ESL reading and composition give a lot of attention to building effective strategies. Define what the word *strategy* means in this context. Give some examples of grammar-editing strategies or more general writing strategies. What are some of the examples of strategies Shih discusses? Make a list of three to five editing strategies you use as a writer. Get one or more of your colleagues to do the same. Then compare your strategy listings.

4. Generate a brief listing of what you believe to be Shih's conceptual underpinnings. With a partner, discuss possible connections between these underpinnings and the list of general ELT principles in table 2.4 of chapter 2.

5. Imagine you are a member of a language program's curriculum committee. Discuss some of the arguments the committee might provide in favor of offering a separate course in grammar-editing. Try to build a convincing case. Be sure to acknowledge and plan responses for counterarguments.

6. In the field of ESL composition, a great deal of discussion and research has focused on the very controversial issue of feedback on error. What are some of the issues involved? Read some of the published literature on this topic and formulate your own opinion. See relevant sections of any methods book, for example, chapter 7 of Ferris and Hedgcock 1998 or some other comparable resource. If you are already familiar with such resources and discussions, how do you conceptualize the role of error correction and feedback in the teaching of writing?

7. What are some examples of editing strategies ESL writers might use to identify and correct errors in their papers? How might less experienced student writers learn such strategies? What procedures might you use to teach editing strategies in your own courses?

8. An important feature of the G/W course seems to be one-to-one

conferencing. Why are teacher-to-student conferences of this kind worth doing? What do you think can be accomplished during such conferences? If you are interested in using such conferences, list ideas you would like to remember for making them productive. If you do not think conferences are (will be) feasible for the particular context you are (will be) working in, what could you do, instead, to address individual students' varying grammar and writing needs?

9. In designing and teaching a grammar-editing course, possible problems are that emphasis on editing may shortchange the rest of the composing process (in particular, prewriting) and that editing may not be integrated into students' writing process very well. In what ways can the teacher of a G/W course encourage student writers to integrate editing into their writing practices, especially for papers they work on in other academic content courses?

10. Although many ESL writers can benefit from instruction focused on helping them to improve the grammatical accuracy of their writing, some of the features of the G/W course Shih describes may be difficult to implement in some teaching contexts. For example, editing is often taught in more broadly focused composition courses (not as a separate course), and one-to-one conferencing may not be practical due to large class size and lack of time and office space. Think about an ESL program with which you are familiar. If you were teaching in this program, which features of Shih's G/W course would you adopt and which might you modify? Why?

11. Identify a specific ESL class (specify students' proficiency level and background) that you now teach (or may teach in the future). In responding to whatever might be the forms of writing students produce, what procedures would you use to provide feedback on grammar errors? Which of the procedures described in this chapter would you adopt, and which might you modify? Explain.

Miniprojects

12. May Shih's 1998 article in the journal *College ESL* is titled "ESL Writers' Grammar Editing Strategies." Locate a copy of that discussion and compare its themes to Shih's discussion of her teaching as reflected in this chapter. Do the two discussions seem consistent? Once you have examined both sources, report to your colleagues on similarities and any differences between them.

13. Speak with an L2 writer of English about a final draft of a paper in progress or recently completed. Find out about her or his editing

process and preferences for error feedback. Alternatively, consult with one or more ESL writing teachers and ask about what forms of error feedback they provide to learners. What are some of the principles and procedures these teachers follow for providing feedback on errors? If possible, speak with both an ESL teacher and an L2 writer of English in order to compare and contrast their perspectives on such topics.

14. Follow through on one or more of the following three tasks: (*a*) Examine an ESL composition textbook that uses a process writing approach. How is grammar-editing (or proofreading) taught? Evaluate the materials and procedures. How, if at all, might you supplement the text if you were teaching with it? (*b*) Examine an ESL grammar-editing textbook. How are grammar rules presented? What editing strategies are taught, and how do students practice these strategies? Consider locating a copy of the Lane and Lange (1999) *Writing Clearly* textbook Shih mentions in this chapter. (*c*) Examine an ESL learner dictionary. Give examples of grammatical information that is provided in the dictionary that ESL learners can use when they edit their papers.

Part 5
University-Preparatory Courses
(Non–Credit Bearing)

Chapter 20

Strategic Reading on a Sustained Content Theme

Joy Janzen

Joy Janzen is a fan of modern cinema. As will be clarified in the body of her chapter, she has found a way to weave this passion into her teaching. She describes a reading course focused on developing students' abilities as skilled, strategic readers. Jansen believes that, to become more proficient readers, ESL students must learn how to use a variety of reading strategies, as well as how and when to apply them depending on the kind of text they are reading, the task at hand, and background knowledge they possess. She outlines five features of course syllabus design: (1) explicit discussion of what reading strategies are, along with where, when, and how to use them; (2) teacher modeling of strategic reading behaviors; (3) student reading-and-thinking-aloud while practicing targeted strategies; (4) classroom discussion; and (5) adoption of a sustained area of content for the course. To realize these primary design features, Jansen works to find a balance between advance planning and instructional flexibility. Advance planning includes identifying strategies to be introduced in class and preparing scripts as a resource for presenting strategies to students. Flexibility requires recognizing/responding to student needs and being ready to adapt class activities and assignments as necessary. In the absence of requisite levels of guidance and support from reading teachers, Janzen finds that many ESL readers tend to overuse a narrow range of strategic options.

In addition to the role of explicit strategy instruction, Janzen suggests that selection of an appropriate content area and text to use in the course is central to curriculum planning. When examining possible texts for course adoption, teachers need to give careful consideration to the (1) level of difficulty, (2) potential for sparking students' interests, and (3) incorporation of sustained content. A course text must be sufficiently challenging to prompt learner activation of a range of strategies. However, if the text selected is too difficult, even persistent use of reading strategies will result in frustration. Finally, Janzen claims that the adoption of sustained content within a strategic reading course enables ESL students to develop essential reading-to-learn abilities.

———

Setting

The reading course described in this chapter is part of an Intensive English Program (IEP) at a midsize public university in the United States. The general purpose of the IEP is to prepare students for academic study. The core of the IEP's overall curriculum is an integrated-skills class with a content-based syllabus. Supplementing the content-based core is a group of courses focusing on discrete skills. The reading course introduced here is one such supplementary course emphasizing reading for academic purposes with a focus on strategic reading. The primary texts used in the course are nonfiction. During the 15-week term, Strategic Reading (SR) meets twice a week for an hour and 50 minutes with a short break in the middle of each class period. The first half of the class is devoted to group activities, while part or all of the second half is occupied by Sustained Silent Reading (SSR) (Gunderson 1991).

While students in the IEP come from a range of first language backgrounds, in recent years students from Asian countries have tended to be in the majority. Based on ACTFL guidelines, the students' reading proficiency levels range from Intermediate-Low to Advanced, although most students are at an Intermediate-High ACTFL reading level. Because the IEP is small, classes are not divided into more precise proficiency levels, and most course work is geared toward the Intermediate-High level. Most students plan to pursue academic study in either undergraduate or graduate programs after satisfying the university's TOEFL requirement (500 for undergraduate work; 570 for graduate). ESL students normally spend one or two semesters in the IEP before moving on to degree study. Once they have exited from the IEP, students enter a variety of programs at the university.

The room used for Strategic Reading is large and attractive with plenty of light. The front wall is covered by a large blackboard, and one side wall contains several rows of windows. Two remaining walls are filled with student work; posters relating to local activities; and displays connected to the core, content-based class. Movable tables and chairs are arranged in the middle of the room. For the reading class, tables are formed into a square. Students sit on the outer perimeter so that all the members of the class can see each other clearly.

Sets of reading materials are available in the classroom during the class period. A table covered with a variety of magazines is along one wall of the room. Because the classroom is open during the day, it is not feasible to leave an extensive reading library permanently in the room. Instead, most of the resources used for individualized reading are kept on a cart stored in a nearby closet and that I push to class each day. On the cart is an array of books, magazines, and graded reading texts, most of which are non-fiction and academic in orientation. The classroom reading materials are sufficient to meet most students' needs, but learners also have access to the university library and a local public library. The core textbook used in the course is *Special Effects in the Movies* (Powers 1989).

Conceptual Underpinnings

The design of this course is based on two interlocking themes: the characteristics of skilled readers and strategic skilled-reading instruction. In this section, I will briefly discuss some features of skilled reading behavior, particularly the use of reading strategies, and then consider properties of strategic reading instruction that encourage the development of targeted reading behaviors. The properties of instruction to be discussed include direct instruction, modeling, feedback, student engagement with the text, the use of instructional conversations, and a sustained content base.

Skilled reading is a complex affair that entails a variety of bottom-up and top-down competencies, from the ability to automatically recognize words to extensive knowledge of vocabulary and syntax (Grabe 1991). An effective reader is a strategic reader, one who commands an array of reading strategies that include local actions such as paraphrasing as well as more global actions such as connecting one text to another (Pearson et al. 1992; Pressley and Woloshyn 1995). Skilled readers, however, do not use discrete strategies in a serial fashion. They use strategic behaviors as a package and read actively to construct meaning from the text (Gunderson 1991).

> [Skilled readers] . . . are selectively attentive. They sometimes make notes. They predict, paraphrase, and back up when confused. They try to make inferences to fill in the gaps in text and in their understanding of what they have read. Good readers intentionally attempt to integrate across the text. They do not settle for literal meanings but rather interpret what they have read. (Pressley and Afflerbach 1995, 79–80)

Enabling students to reach these heights of reading behavior is clearly beyond the scope of a single-semester course. However, students can begin to read more successfully by utilizing particular reading behaviors. In the course described here, the aspect of successful reading that receives the most attention is strategic reading. A traditional method of teaching reading—where the students activate their background knowledge about a text topic, review relevant vocabulary, read the text, and answer comprehension questions—will not elicit the kinds of behaviors that distinguish effective readers. Increased self-awareness of one's process of reading is needed for students to make more efficient use of a wider range of strategic behaviors (Chamot and O'Malley 1996; Pressley and Afflerbach 1995). By developing awareness of the reading process, students may also learn to read more quickly. This awareness may assist them in transferring abilities they already possess in first language reading to their second language.

Extensive research has been carried out to identify types of instruction that are effective in developing students' strategic reading behaviors (e.g., Pressley et al. 1994). According to this research tradition, programs in which strategic reading is taught effectively exhibit several common characteristics. First, they provide explicit instruction about reading strategies: what they are, why they are helpful, and how they can be used. Second, the teacher models targeted reading behaviors, demonstrating what skilled readers do through reading-and-thinking-aloud. Third, students are assisted in reading strategically through access to principled feedback techniques. This feedback can take several forms, such as giving praise for using strategies, interacting with readers while they explain why they use certain strategies, prompting students to use particular strategies, or simply acknowledging verbally that students have used appropriate strategies while reading (Pressley and Woloshyn 1995).

Direct instruction, modeling, and feedback are important in encouraging learners' awareness of the reading process and in developing their reading proficiencies (Casazza 1993). Such techniques are needed due to the sheer complexity of knowledge about reading that students must assimilate. Providing students with opportunities to develop as strategic readers entails short-term goals as well as the long-term one of furthering skilled behavior (Brown et al. 1996). One important short-term goal is to comprehend the text being read at the moment. Through strategic behaviors, students can make sense of what they are reading and begin to arrive at degrees of understanding that are the hallmark of skilled reading.

In strategic reading instruction, students are not pushed to arrive at a meaning of the text that has been predetermined by the teacher. Instead, they learn to engage with the content through the use of strategies. To facilitate this engagement, the teacher must act as a participant, not as the sole source of knowledge in the classroom. As with constructivist views of learning, students are assumed to be the possessors of information that is central to completion of reading tasks (Brooks and Brooks 1993). The teacher's role is to assist students to reach their full potential in using strategies to grasp the meaning of the text. Tharp and Gallimore (1991) refer to classroom interactions that arise when the teacher assists learners in such ways as "instructional conversations." Features of instructional conversations include a challenging but nonthreatening atmosphere, teacher responsivity, general student participation, and promotion of discussion in contrast to an excessive focus on correct answers (Rueda, Goldenberg, and Gallimore 1992).

A final feature of effective strategic reading instruction is the use of a sustained content base for a significant portion of the course. A content base sustained over time is an important part of developing students' reading abilities (Pally 1999) for a number of reasons. Success in reading beyond novice levels of proficiency is largely dependent on the reader's knowledge of vocabulary and background information. Sustaining a single content theme for an entire course makes it more probable that such knowledge will increase. Strategies are used in a content environment to interpret a particular text being read for an authentic purpose. For example, in the course I am describing we use reading strategies to discover new information, not merely to practice strategies as ends in themselves. Last, a sustained content base for a whole reading course is also an opportunity to introduce students to written genres that are central for academic success. Here, students can learn about the discourse and format features typical of textbooks within a given discipline.

Goals/Objectives

The central goal of the course is to expand students' expertise in reading in terms of strategic behaviors, fluency, and vocabulary acquisition. Through class participation, students develop a repertoire of strategic behaviors that assists them in increasing comprehension, managing the reading process, and repairing breakdowns of understanding. They also become capable of more fluent reading and acquire tools for expanding their vocabularies. These goals are determined partly by the nature of skilled reading but also by the demands students may expect in academia. As students enter post-secondary education, they are expected to derive a high proportion of new content information from reading; as a corollary, the amount of reading they are required to do is challenging. Helping second language students to expand their vocabularies, to read quickly, and to read independently are three crucial objectives in this English for Academic Purposes course. By the end of the course, students are expected to have increased self-awareness about the ways they read. This self-awareness includes a better understanding of the complexity of skilled reading, for example, the variety of available strategies and the knowledge types (vocabulary, grammar, content, text structure) good readers control. Learner objectives include increasing ability to monitor comprehension while they read and taking steps to repair lapses when they occur. Upon successful completion of the course, participants should be able to identify and use independently most of the array of reading strategies introduced, discussed, and practiced in class.

Syllabus Design

The nature of strategic reading and effective reading comprehension strongly influences how the reading course is organized. Successful readers use background knowledge extensively to understand texts they read (Pressley and Afflerbach 1995). In the class under discussion, students build on their own background knowledge while reading. Because the students have diverse academic interests, the course cannot focus on one content area all of them will be studying in the future. Instead, the principal course book was selected because its topic, *special effects in the movies*, is one with which every student has some familiarity. By using the same book for most of the course, students deepen their comprehension of the text through an ever-expanding knowledge of the topic. The syllabus, then, is grounded in a sustained content theme, which means that the largest proportion of class time is devoted to reading within one content area. In addition, most of the vocabulary discussion arises from questions students have about words appearing in the text. The textbook, in effect, serves as a primary resource for organizing the syllabus.

In the Strategic Reading course, the choice of the text and the method of delivery are thoroughly planned in advance. Exhaustive lists of strategic reading behaviors can extend to well over 100 strategies (Pressley and Afflerbach 1995). In a 15-week course only a few can be introduced, so it is important to choose the most valuable strategies, specifically those applicable to a variety of situations. (For an extended discussion of strategy choice, see Janzen and Stoller 1998.) In the first weeks of class, I introduce a narrow range of strategic options: asking questions, predicting, checking predictions, summarizing, and connecting background knowledge to what is being read. These specific strategies are important to introduce early because students who use them are better equipped to monitor their comprehension, note when this comprehension has broken down, and repair their grasp of targeted text meanings. As part of my planning efforts, I compose detailed scripts and handouts for initial class sessions (see Janzen 1996). The example that follows is a version of a script I use to introduce students to the course and to the concept of reading strategies.

> The purpose of this class is to help you to learn to use reading strategies. . . . Strategies are actions you take to help you understand when you are reading. Examples of strategies are asking questions while you read; asking questions of yourself, of the book, or of the writer of the book. Guessing what the author will write next or what comes next in the text is also a strategy. Another strategy is checking to see if your guesses are correct and connecting what you are reading to what you already know. . . . For example, when you read about movies you think about movies you've already seen.
>
> There are several reasons why we talk about strategies in this course. The first is that efficient readers always use strategies when they read. This is what good readers do. Also, strategies will help you to become a better reader and will help you to understand what you are reading.

While planning the course, I carefully consider the types of homework and class activities that support discussions of strategic reading. Once the class gets under way, however, my aim is to be responsive to students' needs. The topics of my lesson plans and homework assignments are affected by what actually happens in class. If I notice that the class seems to lack awareness of a particular strategy that could help them, I introduce it either at that point or soon thereafter and use the text to provide opportunities to practice it.

Homework assignments are designed to reinforce classroom activities related to strategic reading. For example, asking questions, summarizing, and predicting are all strategies we discuss in class. Outside of class, students are prompted to write questions about the material they read, to summarize content, and to predict what the author will write about next. The students are also required to keep reading logs listing everything they read, strategies they are using to understand the material, and other strategies they might be using spontaneously on their own without direct instruction.

Activity Types

In this section I discuss four activity types featured in the Strategic Reading course: (1) group reading (used to focus on developing strategic behavior), (2) reading strategy posters, (3) Sustained Silent Reading, and (4) vocabulary work. During the first segment of each class, we read the same text together. In the second segment our focus varies. Sometimes group reading is extended into this part of class; more often, however, the class works on vocabulary or the students read individually. The creation of strategy posters is an occasional activity, something we do approximately once every three to four weeks.

Group Reading

Group reading is the course's core activity type. The reading tasks used change somewhat over the term. During group reading at the beginning of the semester, we move through the following sequence: (1) general discussion of reading strategies, (2) teacher modeling, (3) review of strategies introduced through teacher modeling, (4) student reading, (5) review of strategies used by students while reading, and (6) feedback from the teacher and peers on student strategy use. In the first step, I explain what reading strategies are and why they are important, as well as what individual strategies are and how they can be used. As the class becomes more familiar with the concept of strategic reading, the teacher explanation phase turns into group discussions in which students share their own views on reading and reading strategies. By the end of the semester, group reading discussions become much less frequent.

After discussion or explanations of strategy use, I model reading-and-thinking-aloud, using the strategies that have just been reviewed. Before I begin to read aloud, I ask the students to note which strategies I use, and after I read, we discuss the strategies they have noticed. As the course progresses, my modeling grows less frequent, and more time is spent on students reading-and-thinking-aloud. Over several iterations of the course, I have found reading-and-thinking-aloud an effective way for the class to stay focused and keep together. Most students seem very comfortable with the reading-and-thinking-aloud responsibilities and related classroom activities.

Before asking a student to read aloud, I prompt the whole class to use particular strategies. At other times, I wait until a particular individual reads and direct my prompting specifically toward this reader, who may, for example, be overrelying on a narrow repertoire of strategies. While reading-and-thinking-aloud, a student may refer to the comments of a past reader, checking that reader's predictions, for example. Usually a student covers only one or two paragraphs per turn to ensure that at least three people will have opportunities to read aloud during this phase of a lesson. After each student finishes a turn, we discuss what strategies have been used. At this point, I, along with one or more students, give feedback, praise successful use of strategic behaviors, and/or suggest alternate behaviors for the future.

From the beginning of the term, work on strategic reading is blended with discussions of textual meanings. We ordinarily read only a portion of a text chapter in class with the rest of the chapter assigned for homework. As a result, students come to class with questions about the portion of the chapter read at home. As we read in class, comprehension breakdowns sometimes occur, and we use a range of different reading strategies to work through them. For example, when a student doesn't understand a word, she or he may ask questions or keep on reading. Either the designated reader or someone else may look the word up in the dictionary, paraphrase the sentence, or guess the meaning from context. To a great degree, the depth and length of our discussion, as well as the pacing of this lesson phase, are determined by students' contributions.

Reading Strategy Posters

Another activity tied directly to strategic reading is the development of posters that list and explain reading strategies. The task of creating and adding to these posters is important since we frequently refer to the posters during class discussions. The first poster session occurs several weeks into the course when the students have had some time to develop familiarity with a spectrum of strategies. We begin by brainstorming a list of strategy types that I write on the blackboard. A recent list included the following: evaluating the text, asking questions, predicting, checking predictions, previewing, rereading, paraphrasing, summarizing, reading for a purpose, and connecting ideas being presented through the text to what the reader already knows (for discussion of these and related strategies, see Gunderson 1991). Then the class is divided into pairs, and each pair selects a subset of the strategies listed on the board. The posters have three columns: *what, when,* and *why.* The student pair is asked to list the strategy and describe when as well as why it might be used. As their posters take shape, students arrange the strategies in an order that seems logical to them. Previewing, for example, may be connected to predicting what text content will be about. When the posters are finished, each pair provides rationale for their work. Through discussion, students articulate how and why strategies are interconnected. We expand and add new strategies to the posters as the course progresses.

Sustained Silent Reading

Other class activities are not as directly connected to goals of strategic reading. These are Sustained Silent Reading (SSR) and vocabulary work. In SSR, students silently read material of their own choice. While they read, I join them by reading silently myself. For the most part, the students engage in pleasure reading for this part of the course, usually fiction or magazine articles. In SSR they are not asked to complete any follow-up exercises or activities. Some students, however, select nonfiction materials for which comprehension checks in the form of questions and tasks are provided. In these instances, I lend assistance as needed.

Vocabulary Work

A final set of frequently used activities in the course involves work with vocabulary. Most students enjoy learning about words and find that the attention they pay to the process is worthwhile. As part of homework, learners identify and define words new to them in their reading of the content-area text. Then, as a class, we choose some of these words for in-depth study. I prioritize words nominated by more than one student. We apply various techniques for making word meanings clearer and more memorable. For example, we often list five or six words on the board, define them, and then attempt to create sentences that highlight connections between at least two of the words. Sometimes we devise extended stories or dialogues with all of the words. At other times, I model semantic mapping, and we draw semantic maps for individual words. We use a cline or continuum to compare words of related meanings and to understand the relative intensities of words with similar meanings. As homework activities, students are asked to develop semantic maps and write sentences using the words they have selected from the text. In addition, we regularly recycle previously introduced vocabulary so that meanings of words are not lost for lack of use.

Learners' Roles

An important goal of the course is to develop learner autonomy in reading. At the start of the course, I am largely responsible for leading class discussions. I explain the nature of strategic reading, the goals of the class, and my expectations. Once these issues and course structures are clarified, the students are, for the most part, eager to take on more central roles during the reading-and-thinking-aloud phases of lessons. Part of this eagerness may be a reflection of their status as fairly competent readers in their first languages. Many students already possess a fund of background knowledge about the reading process. Through discussion about reading in both their first and second languages, new information and insights constantly emerge. Based on student input, strategies and perspectives on reading behaviors are added to the repertoire we discuss and use in class.

In addition to acting as sources of knowledge about reading behaviors, students are also responsible for identifying what they understand or may have trouble understanding in the book we read together. In class, we devote a portion of group reading time to using reading strategies as resources for working our ways through difficult points in the text. Students' responsibility for identifying trouble spots is reinforced through homework assignments. For example, they are asked to write down questions they have about assigned readings. In a sense, homework topics provide opportunities for student choice, as the assignments contain no direct comprehension questions about the text. Rather than having to answer predetermined questions, students are required to explore their understanding of textual meanings through active use of reading strategies. Student input plays a part in determining how we spend time in class in other ways as well. Activities that the students say are beneficial, such as vocabulary work, are emphasized. More time is spent on group reading if learners say they prefer to read together in class rather than being required to finish a significant portion of the text at home.

Teacher's Role

In the conceptual underpinnings section, I discussed how the varied nature of strategic reading instruction—direct explanation, modeling, and feedback—is combined with a type of instructional conversation in which the teacher participates in classroom interaction rather than dominates it. The teacher plays several roles in the classroom: model of proficient reading behaviors, facilitator of discussion, provider of feedback on student behavior, and source of knowledge about the English language. While two characteristics of strategic reading instruction are teacher responsivity and increased learner autonomy, a great deal of planning is required to fulfill these aims. Before teaching the course, I write out plans for the class as a whole, including instructional rationale. These plans and rationale are expanded versions of points mentioned earlier. As will be explained in the section on instructional materials, I tried out two different nonfiction textbooks as potential course material in a pilot study. One of these was the *Special Effects in the Movies* (Powers 1989) text that I now use in the course. I also piloted the scripts briefly illustrated in the syllabus design section. In the scripts, I explain the nature of strategic reading and the value of reading strategies. I center my planning time and decisions on the primary focus of the course: introducing and providing ample practice opportunities for using reading strategies. Although the content focus of the Powers text serves as a useful carrier topic and facilitates strategy instruction, mastery of text content is not my primary concern in the course.

To model the "how" of reading behavior effectively in class also takes preparation and rehearsal on the teacher's part. I practice alone with the text in preparation for most classes and make notes to be better able to demonstrate strategies I plan to discuss. For example, if I am planning to model the strategy of predicting, I want to make sure that I can exemplify predictions at least once as I read aloud for the class. As the term progresses, I allow my thinking aloud responses to the text to be more spontaneous; I want to give a more "natural" demonstration of skilled reading behavior. Sometimes, I use modeling to reinforce feedback on strategy use, as when students seem to find difficulties in incorporating use of a particular strategy during the think-aloud process. In the excerpt that follows, used early in the semester, I am asking and answering questions and predicting. The words in italics signal the textual materials the class is reading.

> *"I Think We Got a Big Problem."* So who is "I" and what's the problem? *Steven Spielberg knew exactly what he wanted.* "I" must be Steven Spielberg, but what does he want? And what does he want it for? *The young movie director's 1984 film,* Indiana Jones and the Temple of Doom, *would open with a spectacular stunt involving an out-of-control airplane.* So this must be his problem, how to do something spectacular and amazing with an airplane. *The stunt would be difficult, and perhaps dangerous, to film.* So Steven Spielberg knows what he wants for his film: he wants a dangerous stunt with an airplane. So I think the next thing the author will talk about will be a description of the stunt and what special effects were used to film it [**Predicting**].

Feedback and facilitation of discussion are part of what I see as the responsive aspects of teaching. In carrying out these tasks, I keep the nature of strategic reading in mind. Since skilled readers use a variety of strategies, I would like my feedback to help students move away from a narrow range of behaviors. The notes I keep on what strategies we have used in class and which ones have yet to be introduced help me make decisions about feedback on strategy use.

In leading discussions about textual meanings, I am aware that students need to develop their own understandings of the text. In practice, this means that I frequently encourage students to continue a class discussion, working through the text, rather than expecting me to simply resolve a misunderstanding through a direct explanation. However, this tactic does not prevent me from probing student comprehension by regularly asking questions and assessing whether there is a lack of understanding. These inquiries are particularly important since proficiency levels vary in the class and the most vocal students tend to be the more proficient readers. I try to be as careful as possible and use such probes judiciously in order to attend to the needs of the quieter, less overtly participatory members of the class.

My final role is as a source of information, both about the English language and about the content of the course text. Since the whole group reading activity type is theme based, I have to bring to our discussions an understanding of the content not limited to the Powers text alone. While much of our discussion surrounding the *Special Effects in the Movies* text is focused on language issues such as vocabulary meanings, answering other questions requires a considerable degree of background knowledge. Though students soon realize I am not a specialist in the area of cinematic special effects, as a movie enthusiast I delight in providing supplementary information when I can. As gaps in my own knowledge become obvious to students, I promise to research whatever the topic might be and let them know as soon as possible what I have found. In most cases I am prepared with relevant information for the next class. When my outside searches are less successful, I discuss the situation in a straightforward manner with the class and move on.

Instructional Materials

In teaching strategic reading, I am convinced that the choice of instructional materials is extremely important. A book aimed at too low a level will not provide readers with material challenging enough for them to engage in deliberate use of strategic options. Alternatively, even conscientious use of potentially useful strategies will not enable a reader to comprehend an excessively difficult text. The core textbook was selected through review and analysis of several alternatives. While planning the class, I examined and discussed with colleagues a range of possible textbooks. From these, I piloted two potential course books with a group of IEP students. Both of the books piloted were written for native English speakers, one for high school students and one for college students. I conducted the textbook trial through a series of short lessons. I used the trial to determine which book presented an appropriate level of challenge to students without overwhelming them and, in addition, which one appealed more to their interests. The book that seemed best suited to the group's range of understanding and interest was the high school text. By the end of the first term I offered the full 15-week course, students and I agreed that it had been a very appropriate choice. All of the students reported they had appropriate background knowledge to connect with the topics treated in the book. Their comments convinced me that they found learning about content tied to special effects in cinema both engaging and intrinsically motivating.

Lesson Particulars

The central instructional feature of the course is group reading. This activity represents the phase of the lesson when students are focused directly on developing as strategic readers. As mentioned earlier, the way the members of the class and I carry out this task changes somewhat over time. It also varies from session to session depending on students' responses to the text being read. The class session I describe here occurred in the eleventh week of a 15-week term. At that point in the course, I was concerned with finding a way to make students more aware of text structure, a type of knowledge that is important for efficient reading (Pearson and Fielding 1991). Using knowledge about text structure was not a strategy the group seemed to be transferring from their first language reading abilities. Since we were about three-quarters of the way into the course, students were already comfortable with the group reading procedures and with each other.

On this day, we were looking at a portion of the text that described how actors can be set on fire using special effects. I began the session by quickly eliciting what strategies could be used in the reading. The lesson started with summarizing to remind the students of what they had already read and to enable them to predict effectively. Prediction, in turn, was intended to sharpen their perceptions of text material and to help them monitor their comprehension. In this case, one student summarized and three others predicted, largely basing their predictions on their awareness of text structure. In the following example of prediction, the student speaking is referring to an earlier part of the chapter where the text topic had been special effects used with gunshots.[1]

---

1. All the excerpts in this section come from an audiotaped class session that has been transcribed and then edited slightly to make it more comprehensible. Names given to the students are pseudonyms. S stands for a student whose voice from the audio recording could not be identified.

Yukio:	I remember the text structure. Last time you predict that usually the author said a general idea and then, how can I say, the narrow?
T:	More specific?
Yukio:	More specific information. And then maybe the last part of the text the author talk about general idea again. But I remember, gunshot just general idea and then talk about the specific example and that's it. They don't say about general idea again.
T:	So you expect . . .
Manuela:	Yeah, maybe fire also, the same structure.

Then another student, Kazami, read aloud, checking the predictions the group had made as she progressed through the text. After this I asked if the group had understood the word *inferno*. My question led to an extended discussion about this word and several other words and phrases in the text: *flames, towering,* and *sucked out of a high window.* A short example follows of the discussion about the meaning of *inferno.*

T:	Do you remember this word, *inferno,* we talked about it before?
Michiko:	I forgot.
T:	Can someone say?
Manuela:	Hell.
Michiko:	Hell, oh, yeah. How about frames? Uh, flames?
T:	Oh, okay. What are flames?
Manuela:	This. (*Manuela gets out her cigarette lighter and shows the flame to Michiko.*)
George:	Smoke.
Manuela:	This is a flame.
George:	Flame is the smoke.
Manuela:	Flame is just light, the light.
George:	Oh, just light. Oh, okay.

At the end of the discussion, the group quickly reviewed what strategies the reader had used, in this case, checking predictions. Before the next student (Michiko) read, she asked Kazami to restate the prediction she had made at the end of her turn reading. After Michiko started reading, I prompted her to use strategies more overtly since she was reading the text out loud but was not articulating her thinking process. After prompting, she asked a question about a phrase used in the text, *falls off a building*. Her question led to others by another student about the difference between *falls off* and *falls down*. As we discussed the vocabulary, attempting to visualize what the text was saying, I wrote our conclusions about word meaning on the blackboard.

When Michiko was finished reading-and-thinking-aloud, I asked the class to consider the paragraph just read in terms of what we knew about text structure. I asked, "Was it focused more on generalities or on specific examples?" A student then wondered whether it had a similar function to a section earlier in the chapter. To answer this question we looked back in the book and compared the two sections. After this, we again reviewed the reading strategies we had used.

Manuela, the next reader, asked Michiko to repeat the predictions she had made at the end of reading. During her own turn as the class reader, Manuela checked Michiko's predictions, made some of her own, and guessed the meaning of, or asked questions about, several words in the text as illustrated in the excerpt that follows.

> I think the next paragraph is about an example of a movie because they write the name of a movie and what they use to make these special effects [**Predicting**]. *In The Towering Inferno, the stuntman doubling for Susan Flannery had to wear several layers of protective clothing.* The prediction was right [**Checking Prediction**]. *Next to his skin he wore long, fireproof underwear.* So, he's explaining the kind of clothes that the actor has to wear to be safe [**Summarizing**]. *Over this he wore a "silver suit," the same kind of aluminum-based fire protection worn by race car drivers.* This is all the description about his clothes [**Summarizing**] and I don't know what is silver suit, but if it is similar to the race car driver's I guess it's a pants and also sweater together [**Guessing Meaning and Using Background Knowledge**]. I think the next paragraph is about, still about the description of this kind of clothes [**Predicting**]. *The stuntman's outer clothes were made of flame-resistant material, and he wore asbestos gloves.* Okay, the predictions were right [**Checking Prediction**]. I guess asbestos gloves were on the same material as aluminum, but I don't know [**Guessing/Asking Questions**]. I think, the next sentence, we are looking in detail at what the actor, not the actor, the stuntman is wearing so maybe the next sentence is again about a complete dress [**Predicting**]. *To protect his face, he wore a flame-proof mask (like a ski mask) underneath a mask that had been molded to look like Susan Flannery's face.* Oh, so that mask protect his face and also it looks like the face of the actress [**Summarizing**]. I wonder in which material is this mask? [**Asking Questions**] Flame-proof mask, maybe it's the same material, aluminum, I don't know. I'm asking [**Asking Questions**].

As with Michiko, Manuela's last question led to another. While the class discussed the meanings of words such as *asbestos* and *underneath,* they used strategies, that is, breaking words into parts and consulting the dictionary. At the end of the discussion the class reviewed what strategies Manuela had used.

The fourth reader, George, was one of the weakest in the class. He struggled to understand the paragraph he was responsible for, and the class discussed his difficulties, using strategies.

George: *As the stuntman took his flaming leap the camera crew knew that they had only twenty seconds to record the shot.* Um, okay, how is the flaming leap? Is the flaming leap to cause fire? The fire? Their clothes have a fire, something like that [**Asking Questions**]?

Manuela: I don't know what is a leap.

T: Okay, what is a leap? Anybody know?

George: Is a material [**Guessing Meaning**]?

T: No, it is not. It's an action.

George: Action.

T: What strategy could we use to understand this part of the sentence?

S: We could keep going.

Manuela: Ask.

S: Check the dictionary.

The students reviewed what strategies the reader had used, and more questions emerged about the meaning of another sentence in the paragraph.

Manuela: *Other stuntmen would rush in and extinguish the fire.* I just wonder why other stuntmen, is the scene, it must be real dangerous? I just wonder how come it's dangerous enough to use the, how do you say the people who put the fire out [**Asking Questions**]?

T: Firefighters.

Manuela: Why do other stuntmen do that [**Asking Questions**]?

At this point, I suggested that the class try the strategy of "continuing to read" to see if their difficulties would become more clear.

The last reader for the day, Viviana, began by referring to Manuela's question; next she summarized what we had read so far; and then she read part of the paragraph. While Viviana was reading, another question came up.

> *Viviana:*   Maybe in the next paragraph we'll find the answer for Manuela's question [**Making Prediction**]. So in the last two, three paragraphs the author is explaining about the use of fire and the techniques of stuntpeople [**Summarizing**]. I have a question here, if Manuela's prediction is correct, maybe we will find out how many seconds a stuntman can be in a scene or a shot without danger [**Making Prediction**]. *The top stuntpeople prefer to have other stuntpeople, rather than fire-fighters, handle the fire extinguishers. They say that only someone who has been lit on fire himself can appreciate the danger of the situation.* This is the first part of your question [**Finding Answer to Question**].

Eventually, Manuela and Viviana reach a resolution for Manuela's question about why stuntpeople extinguish fires when the scene isn't over.

> *Manuela:*   That means they pay more attention for that person.
> *Viviana:*   They have experience. They know how is the job, the work. They know how.
> *Manuela:*   Okay.

At the end of Viviana's reading, I asked the class if there were aspects of the text they didn't understand. Michiko asked about the meaning of the word *threat*. Manuela suddenly scowled menacingly, pretending to threaten her, and the class erupted into laughter.

There were no further questions, so we talked about the text in terms of structure, comparing it to earlier parts of the text. The students identified what features seemed to be the same—types of specific examples and also another feature that seemed to be different—the author ended one section with a discussion of a specific movie but had not done so in several other sections. The group reading activity came to a close with students explaining why they thought it was valuable to think about text structure.

Assisting ESL students to develop as strategic readers presents challenges to both learners and teachers. To gain the full benefits from instruction, students need to sustain a habit of thinking and reading over a long period. Teachers must prepare extensively before class starts and continue planning during instruction. However, strategic reading instruction can be the solution to a central issue in education: how to go beyond the teaching of content alone to teaching content and the learning process together.

Prompts for Discussion and Reflection

1. Review the description of skilled reading in the conceptual underpinnings section. According to this description, what does skilled reading entail? What aspects of reading are emphasized in this section? Discuss any elements of skilled reading that you believe might be missing.

2. In this course, the teacher has used *special effects in the movies* as the sustained content theme. Discuss pros and cons to this topic selection. What alternative content areas would you suggest? What kinds of alternative texts might you use?

3. Near the end of the section on teacher roles, Janzen mentions that she sometimes responds to students' questions about cinematic effects by saying, "I don't know." Discuss some of the complications in language classrooms that might arise when teachers are unable to answer students' questions. Give an example from your own experience as either a language teacher or learner.

4. How is the nature of skilled reading reflected in the classroom interactions and in the teacher's choice of activities? What are the students expected to be able to do after completing this course?

5. Janzen states that extensive planning is needed for effective teaching of strategic reading. If you are already a classroom teacher, how extensively do you plan your lessons? What do you do with your plans before, during, and/or following class? What suggestions would you give to a novice teacher? Compare Janzen's ways of generating and working with lesson plans with ways of planning lessons as discussed by other contributors to this volume, such as Terdahl, Ruhl, and Armstrong (chap. 6), Lindsay Miller (chap. 14), Janet Goodwin (chap. 15), David Mendelsohn (chap. 17), and Carol Numrich (chap. 21), or other teachers whose work is familiar to you.

6. In the conceptual underpinnings section, Janzen mentions several features of reading instruction that have been shown to be effective in developing students as more strategic readers. What are these features? Identify ways in which this class resembles other reading classes with which you are familiar. Relate the gist of your discussion to any of the general ELT principles listed in table 2.4 of chapter 2.

7. The majority of the activities in this course are related to one theme.

How does the teacher's discussion of the content focus of *special effects in the movies* compare to other chapters in this book in which sustained content or themes were used (chap. 8, by Brian Morgan; chap. 14, by Lindsay Miller; chap. 15, by Janet Goodwin; chap. 16, by Donna Brinton; chap. 17, by David Mendelsohn)? What rationale is provided?

8. In the conceptual underpinnings section, the teacher suggests that several features of classroom interaction should be goals in a reading class. These features include explicit explanations of reading strategies and strategic behavior and also include a type of interaction called an "instructional conversation." How are these goals reflected in activities used in the classroom? Discuss ways these goals might be mutually (in)compatible.

9. Janzen states that encouraging students to use strategies in independent reading is one of her explicit goals. Transfer of strategy use to reading beyond the classroom is facilitated through homework assignments and class discussion designed to increase student awareness of their reading processes. Beyond the activities suggested in this chapter, how else could students' use of reading strategies be reinforced outside the classroom?

10. The course described here is supposed to prepare students for general academic work. How could this course be modified for an English as a Foreign Language context, for an English for Specific Purposes context, or for some other context with which you are familiar?

11. The reading class in this chapter is essentially a single-skill course. How could the approach and activities used in the reading class be modified to fit more directly within a multiskill environment? What sorts of activities do you use in your classroom to make connections between reading, writing, listening, and speaking? What else could Janzen do in her class?

12. Recent discussions of teaching ELT have placed great emphasis on the use of sustained content. How would you define the phrase *sustained content language instruction?* How does this course embody such current pedagogical trends? How does it differ from other thematically oriented or other content-based courses? Find several sources that will enable you to further explore these topics.

Miniprojects

13. Janzen has suggested that developing prepared scripts for introducing and discussing reading strategies in class is important. Write a sample script for introducing ESL learners to the topic of reading

strategies or for introducing a specific reading strategy, such as asking questions, summarizing, or predicting. Compare your script with one written by someone else on a similar topic. How might you be able to use such a script in your own teaching? Would you? What purposes might scripting of this kind on the part of a language teacher serve?

14. The author of this chapter has two earlier publications on the topic of strategic reading instruction in ELT (Janzen 1996 in *TESOL Journal*; Janzen and Stoller 1998 in *Reading in a Foreign Language*). For this project examine at least one of these earlier discussions in order to compare it/them with the chapter you have just completed. In what ways are they similar or different? Prepare to discuss with colleagues points of comparison and contrast between Janzen's discussions of strategic reading.

15. Working cooperatively in a group, select a reading passage from a content-area book of interest to everyone (but from a section you have not previously read). Emulating Janzen's suggested procedures, take turns "reading-and-thinking-aloud" while applying some of the reading strategies Janzen mentions such as predicting, checking predictions, summarizing, checking understanding, asking questions, and so forth. Continue working this way for at least 10 minutes. Afterward discuss your impressions of the procedure as well as its potential for strategic reading instruction. (If you are teaching a language or reading course, try out the procedure with your class and afterward discuss what it was like.)

Chapter 21

Theme-Based Instruction: Fieldwork in a Small Connecticut Town

Carol Numrich

――――

Carol Numrich prepares learners in English for Academic Purposes at Columbia University in New York. She designs instruction for students to learn through meaningful practice and for language acquisition to take place while learners are engaged in the study of challenging content. Consistent with these beliefs, Numrich organizes her syllabus around theme-based lessons arranged to give students provocative content to think, read, speak, write, and debate about.

Her chapter features discussion of an instructional unit centered on the development of gambling casinos on Native American reservations in North America. She and the members of her class explore topics that are embedded within this theme, such as casinos, money, gambling, addiction, economics, racism, government policy, ethnic survival, and cultural adaptation. In contrast to the students described in most chapters in this collection, Numrich's students tend to be well traveled and well educated, and some have already been accepted into one of Columbia University's academic programs. As might be expected, many of Numrich's students have high expectations for the course and bring opinions and assumptions about both the topics and classroom procedures she introduces. Her chapter features a sequence of several activity types: listening comprehension and vocabulary work, contextualized grammar practice, ethnographic fieldwork, and preparation tasks for essay writing and oral reports. Numrich gives considerable attention to the fieldwork component of the Native American gaming unit. As a group, students visit an out-of-state Indian museum, tour an Indian-owned and -operated gambling casino, and survey residents of a neighboring town. On returning to class, students organize data, pool information, summarize findings, and prepare for oral reports. As her chapter illustrates, theme-based instruction offers students multiple exposures to content, provides contextualized language practice, and gives opportunities for EAP language learners to develop abilities for academic success.

――――

Setting

This chapter's centerpiece is an English for Academic Purposes (EAP) course at Columbia University's American Language Program (ALP). Columbia is a large private research university located on New York City's Upper West Side. Students in the ALP receive 20 hours of English language classroom instruction per week. The ALP's curriculum is similar to that of many other Intensive English Programs (IEPs) throughout North America. It offers intensive and part-time ESL courses, specialized courses for professionals, credit-bearing college composition courses for international students, and pedagogy courses targeted to international teaching assistants (ITAs) from a range of academic disciplines. The number of students in the ALP ranges from approximately 300 to 750, with highest levels of student enrollments during summer sessions. The ALP's teaching philosophy is founded on the concepts that students learn language through meaningful comprehension/expression and that language acquisition happens when learners are engaged in the study of content at a cognitively challenging level. For 30 years, an academic, thematic, integrated approach to teaching ESL has guided curriculum decisions for the ALP. Each of the program's levels is taught by teams of three teachers who meet weekly to plan curriculum, discuss student progress, and review related concerns.

The course discussed in this chapter targets learners at the seventh level of proficiency out of a total of 10 levels in the ESL program. In reference to ACTFL descriptors, Level 7 students' speaking and listening proficiency levels range from Intermediate-Mid to Advanced. Recently, Asian students in the course have tended to be closer to the Intermediate-Mid level in listening and speaking, while European, South American, and other non-Asian students seem closer to the Intermediate-High level in these areas. Just the opposite tends to be the case with respect to reading and writing proficiency levels. Asian students tend to enter the course as stronger readers and writers and closer to ACTFL's Intermediate-High reading and writing levels. Usually, a small number of students perform at Advanced ACTFL levels in one or more of these areas. Level 7 students are, for the most part, academically oriented, though their motivations for academic study may vary widely within and across different sections of the same course. Typically, between 17 and 20 students enroll in the 12-week "theme-based EAP course." Twenty students participated in the course section featured in this chapter.

Most of the students who enter Columbia's ALP are well traveled, and a majority enter the program having benefited from strong educational opportunities prior to coming to the United States. Some students are extremely motivated to succeed in academia and have already been accepted into one of the university's academic programs. These students are awaiting completion of their ESL requirement for general admission to the university and tend to be very serious about their English language studies. A larger number of students in the Level 7 course may have less clearly defined goals and are unsure of whether they want to return to their home countries or study at an American university upon completion of their study in the ALP. Still others are casual learners who have come to the metropolitan area to experience what New York City has to offer while studying English in a university setting. Such a heterogeneous mix is typical of the Level 7 course.

Goals/Objectives

A primary course goal is for learners to acquire language skills necessary for successful participation in content-area university-level courses designed for native speakers of English. In listening, Level 7 students should comprehend approximately 70 percent of a radio report or an academic lecture on a topic for which they have some background knowledge. In speaking, students should produce oral language at the Advanced level of ACTFL proficiency. The reading objective of the course is for students to be able to read any nontechnical, authentic text dealing with current events and issues without significant difficulty. Level 7's writing objective, which is the most important of the course, is for students to produce, in a two-hour exam, a well-developed essay demonstrating some originality of thought and a clear thesis with supporting details, as well as some use of academic vocabulary and complex structures with only occasional lapses in syntax and diction. The essay must exhibit some development of ideas and content in all paragraphs and even fuller development in some paragraphs. There should be topic sentences with supporting examples and illustration, use of effective cohesive devices, and parallel structure.

To achieve these goals, the students study several themes through a variety of integrated-skills exercises. To enhance the students' writing and self-editing abilities, the course covers at least 10 grammar points throughout the semester, such as adjective and noun clauses, mixed conditionals, modal perfects, negative inversions, participles, subjunctive forms, and mixed verb tenses. Class lessons each week build toward a two- to three-page take-home essay to be completed over the weekend, the culminating product of each unit of study. Students are expected to revise their writing and turn in a second, and in some cases a third, draft for each of these weekly essays. Both midterm and final essay exams are given to assess progress and in part to determine end-of-term promotions, which are based on a holistic evaluation completed by at least two teachers on the Level 7 team.

Activity Types

Some of the recurring classroom activity types of the Level 7 course include the following: information gap and listening comprehension tasks, practice with inference statements, preparation for out-of-class assignments, and fieldwork. I try to recycle activity types for each of the course's thematic units. Later sections of this chapter give attention to grammar instruction through contextual analysis and structured grammar practice. The lesson particulars section is devoted to a fieldwork-based lesson.

Most of the activities I use in the course are organized around a series of thematic units. By focusing on meaningful themes and authentic language use, I find that the teaching of listening, speaking, reading, writing, and cultural awareness may proceed in an integrated fashion. I look for controversial themes as a means to provide students with something substantive to think, talk, and disagree about during language learning activities. I also try to find themes that expose students to new ideas and information. The thematic unit described subsequently, and featured throughout this chapter, focuses on the gambling industry on Native American Indian reservations in the northeast region of the United States. The unit is titled "Indian Gaming."

In the course, I use the theme of Indian gaming as a basis for students to learn about and discuss many contemporary topics including gambling, addiction, economics, racism, ethnic survival, and cultural adaptation. These themes and subthemes offer opportunities to present new information to international students, who may have little knowledge of Native American people, their history, or roles they are playing in current events of Canada and the United States. Individual lessons within the Indian gaming unit provide students with background knowledge, skill work, vocabulary practice, and opportunities to study grammar. Student work in the unit is designed as preparation for an ambitious fieldwork assignment: an ethnographic study conducted by the students in the small community of Uncasville, Connecticut, a town bordering the "Mohegan Sun" casino. The Mohegan Sun is Native American owned and operated.

Before discussing the many issues associated with the gaming industry and Native American populations in the United States, I begin the course by assigning students different background information, statistics, and facts to research on the Internet. For example, students search for different pieces of information relating to the following topics: states that allow the establishment of casinos on Indian reservations, revenue brought into nearby (non-Indian) communities because of Indian casinos, and the effects of casinos on Native American families and their social life. Following their Internet searches, students come together in groups of three or four to interview each other about their research. Together, they fill out a chart, creating a "big picture" of facts related to the phenomenon of Indian gaming. Students respond to two or three general questions requiring them to summarize and reflect on social and economic issues tied to Indian gaming and their implications for societal changes as they understand them. Students then go on to discuss whether or not they think the Indian gaming industry might be a helpful resolution to the unsettling history of indigenous people in North America.

The primary source material for the lesson is based on a single Public Radio International (PRI) report on the topic of Indian gaming. I have divided the longer audio recording into four sections. Each section is supplemented with written instructional materials of my own design. As presented in class, the individual sections consist of prelistening vocabulary work, intensive listening comprehension exercises, and grammar work (for illustrations of instructional materials of this type, see Numrich 1995, 1997, 1998). I lend assistance as the students become more familiar with the vocabulary anticipated in the listening materials. Then they engage in tasks designed to develop their listening comprehension abilities.

One activity I frequently use in both reading and listening comprehension work involves inferential *true/false* statements. In the Level 7 course students can more easily deal with interpretive levels of meaning than at lower levels in the ALP. They can "listen between the lines" and begin to understand what a speaker means, even when the meaning is not explicitly expressed. For example, after listening to a recently widowed woman talk about patronizing an Indian-run casino, students evaluate *true/false* statements such as "The woman has found her happiness in gambling." Some students answer that the statement is true if they listen to her words only at a surface level. Other students disagree, pointing out that her tone of voice and hesitations communicate very different feelings; they are more likely to answer that the statement is false. I like to create *true/false* statements that require students to listen for such subtle purposes as tone, feelings, and indirect meanings because students at this level are ready for relatively challenging listening tasks.

Whenever possible, one of my goals in the course is to provide opportunities for students to use language for genuine communication by getting them out of the classroom and involving them in fieldwork assignments. These assignments take the form of investigative work related to what we have been studying in class. In the Indian gaming lesson, I arrange for the class to travel by bus to the Mashantucket Pequot Indian Reservation in Connecticut—a two and a half hour bus ride from our campus. Once there, students visit the Mashantucket Pequot Indian Museum, where Native Americans give us a tour and present their history. We then continue our tour through the Foxwoods casino built on the Pequot Indian reservation, before just a brief visit to the more recently opened Mohegan Sun casino, which is located not far away on the Mohegan Indian reservation.

Prior to our field trip to Connecticut, students spend a considerable amount of time preparing in class. Our goal during the Indian gaming fieldwork activities is to investigate through the use of survey questionnaires the attitudes of a sample of people living in the local community. During the week preceding the trip, small groups of students collaborate to design several different questionnaires. In whole class formats, we discuss possible topics, anticipated responses, and ways of keeping track of what community informants might have to say. The questionnaires focus on residents' attitudes toward the U.S. government's policies on Indian gaming, the economic influence of the casino on the local community, and current social life of Indians and non-Indians in the area.

On the day of the field trip, students are well prepared to gather information when we arrive in the small town of Uncasville, located just outside the Mohegan Indian Reservation. For several hours, pairs of students go into shops, restaurants, and parking lots in the town. There, they interview local residents about any changes that may be affecting their community since the opening of the casino. During their fieldwork conversations with Uncasville residents, students learn about local history and the impact of the casinos.

In the classes following our fieldwork activities, students analyze the data from their surveys and anecdotes from their conversations with the Connecticut residents who served as their informants. In groups, they discuss and tally their information and prepare oral reports for the class. In writing their essays and in preparation for oral reports, students are asked to derive their own conclusions about Indian gaming and possible effects it may be having on local communities in the United States.

Lesson Particulars

In the class following their field trip to Connecticut, Level 7 students reunite with the same group members with whom they had prepared their questionnaires. In one group, a student immediately starts calling out the number of *yes/no* responses she received to her group's first question. The other three students in her group ask her to slow down as they try to get themselves organized. Some of them are still looking for their own completed questionnaires. One student volunteers to tally everyone's information on her own sheet so everyone will be able to examine in one place all of the information the group has gathered. As her classmates read off their responses to the first question, they try to make sense of something one of their informants said. In response to the question, "Do you think Indians deserve the special privilege to own casinos?" a member of the group reports that her informant had answered, "I really don't care." The students wonder out loud: "Should we count this as a negative or a positive?" Initially they can not make up their minds but they continue discussing several possible solutions. Finally, and without my assistance, they resolve to create a new category they decide to call "neutral."

In a different group off to the left of the room, one student, Monica, reports a comment made to her group's survey question, "Have you ever gambled in the Mohegan Sun?" One of her informants' responses to this question was surprising, and Monica seems excited to talk about it. A local Connecticut resident had told her that not only had he gambled at the Mohegan Sun but he had won $5,000 on his first visit playing blackjack! Then the man pointed to a car parked right outside the Dunkin' Donuts where Monica and her partner had been conducting their interviews, and he went on to explain that he had bought the car with his winnings. The other members of Monica's group react in amazement with "Ah!!" and "Really?" For quite some time after the members of the group return to their task of continuing to analyze data, I continue to hear such exclamations as "Oh. . . . Interesting!" "He must have made that up," and "I can't believe that really happened!" Not only in connection with Monica's anecdote but for other students' contributions, too, the members of the class continue to express their surprise and excitement at the differing opinions and pieces of information they have collected.

At one point, a third group of students calls me over to help them interpret one of their respondent's answers. When asked whether or not she thought the U.S. government was doing enough to help Indian society with its casino policy, a female interviewee had replied, "Well, it really depends on the tribe now, doesn't it?" The students say they are confused about this answer and ask me why the policies for tribes should differ. I remind them of information we had learned from the lecture at the Mashantucket Pequot Indian Museum the morning of the field trip. One of the tour guides had discussed the considerable degree of negotiation that must go on between individual Native American tribes and the U.S. government for any single tribe to obtain permission to open a casino on a reservation. My reminder stimulates more questions from the other three students in the group about policies toward Native Americans, and we spend about four minutes discussing related aspects of U.S. history. I then look around the class to see whether any students are beginning to complete the analysis of their data, and I tell them that their oral reports will begin in about 10 minutes. The pace of students' collaborations picks up a bit as they proceed to choose and divide up roles for their presentations. One group member offers to introduce the details of the group's survey (e.g., where the interviews took place, how many people were interviewed, unsolicited or surprising pieces of information they learned about); others choose to present their data and related comments offered by the Connecticut informants; a final person chooses to summarize what they learned by examining the survey results from everyone in the group.

After about 10 more minutes have elapsed, I begin to bring the class together. I ask them to rearrange the configurations of their seats out of the format of small groups and to face the front of the room in preparation for oral presentations. Having participated in similar activities before, students know that they should take notes on each other's reports. They prepare themselves to do so. As a motivator, I encourage them to take effective notes by reminding them that they will be able to use each other's data, not just their own, as source material for the composition I will be expecting them to work on over the weekend. The first group presents the results of its surveys and shares a few more stories about the people who served as their informants. As they speak, the students make several errors in grammar and pronunciation. Some of these errors interfere with intelligibility, but I choose not to correct their errors at this time. Instead, I make notes about several of their more severe errors for possible error treatment work in our next class.

As the last group presents its results, I realize that in their reporting many students have suggested that some of their informants may have answered somewhat less than truthfully. Some students suspect the interviewees had additional feelings and perceptions about the casino industry or about Native American people that they had been reluctant to reveal. I remind them that in reporting survey data, they should try to remain true to what their informants actually said and avoid the temptation to interpret what they might now believe to be their respondents' hidden attitudes. Several students nod their heads in apparent agreement; others seem less convinced.

After the reporting has been completed, we review all the class materials from the lessons that led up to the fieldwork assignment. I assign two essay topics (they select one) relating to the themes we have studied, and we spend a few minutes brainstorming about what might be helpful sources to consult in preparation for writing an essay on the Indian gaming topic. Some example resources students mention, and ones that have been used in earlier classroom activities, include the following: the Public Radio report on Indian gaming, an excerpt from Louise Erdrich's (1994) novel *Bingo Palace*, articles from the *New York Times* reporting controversies over the building of casinos in Connecticut, statistics found on the Internet, and the survey results from their fieldwork. We then review themes discussed during the week related to Indian gaming that include gambling, gambling addiction, racism, wealth, and poverty. Finally, I remind students of the vocabulary and grammatical structures (inverted conditionals, noun clauses, "*would* + base verb" to describe repeated past actions) from recent lessons and encourage them to incorporate examples of these target language forms in their written essays. As the class draws to a close, I am relieved that no one seems panicked about the essay they are expected to write over the weekend and hand in on Monday. I feel satisfied that their discussions today have served their intended purpose: to provide a shared background experience as preparation for a related writing task. (For discussion of a comparable set of fieldwork tasks and related in-class pedagogic activities, see Montgomery and Eisenstein 1985.)

Conceptual Underpinnings

The story of my teaching recounted in the preceding section illustrates what I believe to be the heart of theme-based instruction. The preparatory activities, fieldwork experiences, and in-class opportunities to share and pool information provide rich and sometimes surprising opportunities for students to deal substantively with ideas while they are involved in the process of language learning. Unlike many approaches to ELT that may focus more directly on language learning activities, theme-based instruction focuses on content-rich instructional units. The underlying philosophy of theme-based instruction is that knowledge will be less fragmented when presented in contexts of shared experiences. Consequently, ideas can be explored with more breadth and depth, creating sustained interest among students. When language is presented in short self-contained lessons, students may be left with the impression that the teacher is merely reaching into her or his bag of tricks to teach another lesson. Experience teaches that with theme-based instruction learners tend to feel they are on a journey of discovery with the teacher. They have a sense of where they are going because the focus is on meaning. Under such conditions, some aspects of language learning may even become incidental (Lipson, Valencia, and Peters 1993; Scarcella and Oxford 1992).

Research on how the human mind operates also provides support for theme-based instruction (see Caine and Caine 1990, cited in Gianelli 1991; Wolfe and Brandt 1998). Smith (1978, 1990) observes that the human brain engages in a constant search for meaning, is characteristically curious, and at the same time, strives to fit new material into the already familiar. Theme-based learning provides both novelty and familiarity; students are able to assimilate many new ideas because new information is being presented within familiar contexts. One of the reasons I enjoy using a theme-based approach in the Level 7 course is because of the recycling of language and content it provides. Students are generally unable to reproduce new language, such as vocabulary or grammatical structures, after studying it only once. They require multiple exposures to new language features, within a variety of contexts, before they seem ready to internalize them for later production. In fact, many ESL programs have recognized the need for multiple exposures, reorganizing their curriculum efforts in order to provide requisite degrees of recycling and looping back within and across courses (Stoller and Grabe 1997). Such programmatic structures help develop fuller understandings, more efficient internalization of new content, and better language control.

In a thematic approach, students have access to multiple exposures to content as well as formal properties of language. They might study a particular theme through integration of language skills by (1) reading an article or essay, (2) listening to a radio report or interview, and/or (3) watching a television news broadcast on the same or a similar theme. Similar concepts, vocabulary, and even grammatical structures tend to reoccur through these multiple exposures. Moreover, in theme-based instruction, students often guess meanings more easily, even when confronted with unknown language forms, since new meanings are being presented within increasingly familiar contexts. As Smith (1978) suggests in connection with reading experiences, "a reader's comprehension of the whole can contribute to comprehension of the parts, and even to the learning of words that are unfamiliar" (17–18). With themes as the foundation of language lessons, I try to select universal, intrinsically motivating, content-based themes that will best fit students' needs and interests. Topics that will not become dated in the near future and that offer "powerful ideas" (Routman 1991, 277) usually form the basis of my lessons. When presented with multiple perspectives on a sustained theme, students can comprehend more challenging concepts, can reflect on issues more deeply, and are better prepared to reach conclusions independently.

Because Level 7 students tend to enter the course with an interest in American culture, I usually select themes from North American history and literature, as well as sociopolitical topics with an international appeal. Novelty is important for stimulating student interest and motivation, and the perspectives I introduce in the course are planned to be fresh and less familiar for international students. Yet, with novelty, it is also necessary to present students with some background knowledge to provide them with security. Therefore, I usually preteach certain cultural or historical concepts before presenting students with completely new topics, themes, and materials. In developing a particular theme, I try to find materials that depict marginal points of view or views that I, as the teacher, do not necessarily share. When students have to grapple with unfamiliar ideas representing less commonly held point of views, they are better able to engage in what Freire (1988) calls the "dialogue of critical thinking."

In addition to a theme-focused syllabus, grammar instruction plays an important role in the Level 7 course. Many adult students expect to be able to refer to a rule-based system when making self-assessments of their oral and written production of a second language. Moreover, contemporary research signals the effectiveness of grammar instruction for some types of learners (Larsen-Freeman 1991; Pica 1994a; Yorio 1994). In theme-based instruction, I teach grammar within the context of selected themes. Specific grammatical forms that appear in authentic texts can be made salient for the purpose of instruction. Alternatively, grammatical forms may be taught when they can be integrated into discussions on a particular topic.

While grammar plays an important role in my lessons, I try to give equal emphasis to fluency and accuracy in order to help students develop their oral production. At times, such as in debates or role plays, students are concerned more directly with presenting their ideas and developing oral fluency. Interrupting them to correct errors during such lesson phases would only disrupt their train of thought and communication flow. At other times, however, such as in small group discussions or pair work activities, teacher interventions are both useful and necessary. During these latter communication exchanges, I find I am better able to provide accessible cues to learners on how to modify their errors.

Syllabus Design

Two colleague-teachers and I collaborate closely to design the syllabus and learning objectives for the Level 7 course. Over a 12-week semester, the class studies as many as 16 different themes. During the semester highlighted in this chapter, the themes included were the following: New York City, ethics in science, heroes, witch hunts, success, privacy, westward expansion, AIDS, animal rights, Indian gaming, Frank Lloyd Wright's architecture, and euthanasia. Some themes, such as Indian gaming, extend as long as a two-week period. Some may be taught by more than one of the teachers working at Level 7. Other themes might be covered within a short four-hour segment by one teacher alone. However they are presented in the course, the themes drive the design of the course syllabus, and features of language to be covered are derived from the content being studied. Materials chosen for developing listening or reading abilities all deal with related themes, as do written texts used to model specific rhetorical patterns in writing.

In preparing lessons for the course, I plan out some of the themes I want to teach ahead of time but do not give students a fully elaborated syllabus at the start of the term. As the course progresses my colleagues and I invariably suggest additional themes since we all bring our own expertise and interests to the course. Because collegial collaborations between teachers are one of the course's key features, I find it necessary to keep the syllabus plan somewhat open. In addition, some students may have already studied, or may be disinterested in, particular topics. Consequently, adjustments to the syllabus often need to be made. In an effort to get the students to contribute to the content of the course, I also try to develop materials during the 12 weeks of the semester that accommodate students' goals and personal interests. Even though the course's themes are somewhat flexible, many of the language skills presented and reviewed are preplanned. Having taught the course many times, I can usually anticipate which grammatical structures and elements of writing need to be introduced or reviewed to enhance students' writing, and these points, too, are covered in the course.

Instructional Materials

A textbook committee meets twice a year to select textbooks for all levels in the ALP. Aquilina's (1993) *Timely Topics* is the text used currently in the Level 7 course. Because the themes are interesting, the sections on vocabulary study are well planned, and the grammatical exercises are extensive, the Aquilina text has consistently been well received and highly rated by Level 7 students and teachers. I use it more as a supplementary text than as a core one, covering 6 of the text's 10 chapters during the 12 weeks. Because students usually respond well to these topics, I include chapters on the themes of immigration, education, parents' rights, reproduction technology, Americans' obsession with pets, and women and the family. In addition, a very practical reason I like working with these themes is that I have collected an array of supplementary materials to accompany them. Generally, I assign no more than half the exercises the author provides in each chapter, and students complete many of them as homework assignments. The students read each of the three reading selections featured in a single chapter and complete the accompanying comprehension exercises. In some cases, I organize the various reading selections into information gap activities by asking three different groups of students to read only one of the chapter's selections each. Then, in class, students pool their information with other members of the class who have been responsible for reading one of the other selections.

In most of the lessons I teach, some direct attention is given to language forms. Level 7 students expect to be taught efficient ways of making their means of self-expression more sophisticated and nativelike. One of the ways I try to do this is by providing explicit, form-focused grammar instruction and practice activities. We study grammar in the context of thematic material already incorporated into our discussions.

In the Indian gaming lesson, one of the grammar points we focus on is the use of "*would* + base verb" for repeated actions in the past. In the PRI report, we hear people talk about common events that happened in a small town in Minnesota whose population was composed of both Indians and non-Indians. In one excerpt, the speaker makes frequent use of "*would* + base verb" to describe what the Indian women used to do (e.g., "They would sit around the store and chat and talk and visit . . . and they would nurse their babies"). In this lesson, I ask students to focus on one piece of the speaker's description in which he makes extensive use of this form. We discuss how, when, and why the form is used. Then the students examine a written transcript of the segment in which all the verbs have been changed to "simple past." The students' task is to change all the verbs that potentially could be changed to "*would* + base verb," after having considered whether or not a particular verb is describing a repeated past action.

Learners' Roles

One of the roles I expect Level 7 students to assume is that of risk taker. At this level, it is particularly easy for students to take in new language without ever having to "make it their own." Students may learn to recognize new vocabulary, grammatical, and rhetorical patterns in their reading and listening comprehension, but unless they force themselves to try out new structures in their own oral presentations and writings, the new language may never enter their production level. I expect students, especially when writing essays, to push themselves to integrate, in fairly structured ways, the use of new language forms. In fact, I often ask them not only to use but to highlight in their written essays (sometimes with a colored marker) new vocabulary words and structures we have studied during a previous week's lessons.

I also expect students to develop as critical thinkers. Because I have classes of mixed cultures and mixed proficiencies, I try to encourage students to question their own assumptions, biases, and presuppositions about issues, and I remind them to be tolerant of other students' beliefs.

Finally, the third role of a Level 7 student has only become apparent in recent semesters, but it a very important one: I expect Level 7 students to become "learner-researchers" in their study of English. I believe that what they learn in the course should take them on an exploration outside the classroom. Thus, field assignments such as the Indian gaming unit discussed earlier are becoming an increasingly significant component of my teaching. During such assignments, students sometimes forget they are learning English because they are using language as a means for exploring the world around them. In addition, when students ask their own questions and come to their own conclusions about current issues in a local community, I feel they are more fully engaged in the learning process and are more likely to make progress in their dual roles as language learners and language users.

Teacher's Roles

My first role in teaching a theme-based course is that of syllabus designer. Because many of my lessons are teacher made from authentic materials, I spend considerable time choosing and designing materials that are appealing to a young, relatively well-educated audience (see Numrich 1997). From these materials, I must also design skill-building and grammar-focused activities. In addition, I try to develop units and material that will last over time, because I would like to be able to recycle and use them in future sections of the course. Another important role of a teacher is that of motivator. I see my role as one in which I challenge students and present them with high expectations. The process of setting and maintaining high expectations is necessary if students are to succeed in the university upon completion of ESL studies.

Throughout the course, I also try to serve as a supportive bridge between students' background knowledge and the class materials. One of the reasons students enroll in Columbia's ALP, when there are so many other English language programs available in New York City, is that they are interested in academic studies and the kind of exposure to American culture they perceive a private university is well equipped to provide. They are interested in learning about American values and attitudes through studying history, literature, culture, and current events. I try to provide learning opportunities by creating links between what students already know and the new content I include in the course. I attempt to help learners build their own bridges by getting them to share their knowledge and experiences with the class. For this reason, our lessons often begin with prediction or values clarification activities.

Another way I try to serve as a bridge in the classroom is to make salient the students' various strengths. In the course, I want students to both learn about and learn to respect the strengths of their peers. Often in the Level 7 course, European and South American students' spoken fluencies seem stronger than those of many Asian members of the class. Though this is an uncomfortable topic to acknowledge and discuss, European and South American learners sometimes seem to resent studying alongside Asian peers because they perceive the Asian students' oral capacities in English to be lacking. However, Asian students' control of writing in English tends to be stronger than that of the European and South American students I meet. A technique I have found useful for breaking down some students' negative perceptions is to present portions of Asian students' written essays as models for in-class analysis. As the class examines these essays projected on an overhead transparency, the non-Asian students are often stunned by the Asian students' command of written English, and the result often leads to a stronger appreciation for what Asian students are able to contribute within our learning community.

In addition to creating increased awareness of what students bring to the classroom, I also take on the role of challenger. I try to ask provocative questions and to push students toward a deeper analysis during class discussion. I try to pose inferential or interpretive questions related to reading or listening texts we study in order to encourage students to "read or listen between the lines" and to delve into the gray areas of comprehension. I believe such abilities are essential for successful academic study. As often as I can, I pose open-ended questions that have no definite answer. This strategy can be disturbing to some students, especially those from very traditional systems of schooling. However, dealing with inferential levels of interpretation is especially important for students who plan to begin university studies and who come from cultures where educational practices tend to be more didactic and where answers to teachers' questions are expected to fall within clear parameters.

Finally, I consider it very important to provide students with feedback, not only on their written essays but also in their oral work. The students expect to be corrected and perceive cuing for error modification as one of the ESL teacher's more important roles. To meet this dimension of learners' expectations, I try to focus attention on oral errors judiciously, with good humor and personal tact, while being conscientious in trying to avoid overwhelming students with too many interruptions, too much cognitive feedback, or too little affective support. There is a delicate balance between providing learners with the degrees of grammatical, pragmatic, and pronunciation feedback they expect in language classes while simultaneously searching for ways of encouraging meaningful expressions of ideas.

Caveats/Final Thoughts

In spite of its benefits, a theme-based approach, like any other approach to second language instruction, has limitations. The two greatest limitations I encounter are a possible lack of student interest in a theme or themes I might choose to teach and insufficient time and opportunities to provide what might be even more appropriate degrees of structured skill practice. To develop effective thematic lessons that engage learners' interests and enthusiasms, I need time to research relevant topics, find and prepare materials, and lend assistance in organizing field trips and planning field itineraries. Because of these responsibilities, I usually organize new units of materials within the short periods of time between terms when I am not teaching. Hence, most of my planning efforts take place before I have opportunities to meet students who will actually be participating in the course. Consequently, what I assume to be an interesting topic may not necessarily match the needs or interests of a particular group of students. One way I attempt to deal with this drawback is to give students as many choices as I can and negotiate with them about which themes they would prefer to examine during the semester as a class. Yet, regardless of these efforts, there will always be *some* students who are not interested in *some* themes.

An additional drawback I have encountered is that a focus on content sometimes means controlled and guided practice opportunities are underrepresented in the course. For example, I am often reluctant to take the time to give explicit attention to pronunciation. I attend to pronunciation issues if they interfere with students' attempts at expressing meaning. However, I find it difficult to incorporate much in the way of pronunciation support within the lessons I teach. In an effort to continue to grow as a teacher in this area, I have set as one of my short-term goals to examine several sets of recent professional development resources that target speech-pronunciation teaching (e.g., Celce-Murcia, Brinton, and Goodwin 1996; Greenburg 1997; Morley 1994b).

With these caveats in mind, thematic approaches such as the one described in this chapter offer important learning opportunities for students interested in entering university study. Theme-based language teaching provides requisite contexts and experiences for students to acquire tools of self-directed learning as well as the control of vocabulary, syntax, and discourse structures they need to succeed in meeting academic goals. A focus on meaningful thematic content provides clear contexts for learning language and for increasing learner self-confidence because the instructional approach engages students in substantive negotiations of ideas. Finally, when I am able to focus on interesting thematic units, I have a better chance of inspiring students to become excited about the challenging task of learning a second language.

Prompts for Discussion and Reflection

1. What are the goals and objectives of the Level 7 course as described in this chapter? Discuss ways in which these goals and objectives do (or do not) fit within the setting and student needs Numrich describes. Discuss further specifications of such learners' needs.

2. What do you think this teacher's students will be able to do more competently after completing the lesson on Indian gaming? What specific skills in that lesson might transfer to the larger goal of learning English for academic work?

3. Do you recognize any activity types described by this teacher that reflect theoretical principles described in her discussion of conceptual underpinnings? Which activities seem to support which principles?

4. What research literature, or principles of L2 learning, can you point to that may support the forms of teaching described in this chapter? Of the 14 ELT principles listed in table 2.4 of chapter 2, discuss any that seem (in)compatible with Numrich's chapter.

5. Are there teaching activities described in this chapter that you might incorporate into your own teaching? How might they transfer to other teaching contexts? How might they be adapted to fit programs that are not necessarily theme based?

6. In the lesson particulars section, the author describes the final stage of the Indian gaming lesson, which finishes with a review and preparation for a weekend essay assignment. How might this culminating lesson phase be organized differently if it were geared to learners who were studying English for more general purposes and not for academic purposes?

7. Given Level 7's focus on themes, what additional ways might this teacher explore for incorporating even more of a "focus on form" in her teaching?

8. The teacher emphasizes the benefits of getting students out of the classroom for language study by describing her fieldwork assignment tied to the Indian gaming theme. Can you envision any benefits to fieldwork activities in ELT? Have you used any fieldwork assignments in your teaching? What suggestions might you make for planning such activities?

9. What are some of the social, (inter)cultural, institutional, pragmatic (or other) issues involved when a language teacher becomes interested in organizing field trips for students? Collaborate with someone else to make a list of what some of these issues or concerns might be. Discuss ways of reviewing such considerations with learners. What are some of the policies in place in an ELT program you know of to guide teachers interested in organizing field trips? How would you advise a teacher who seemed enthusiastic about such efforts?

10. In the lesson particulars section, the teacher describes a synthesizing activity in which students work independently in small groups to compile data and organize oral presentations. How would you organize such group work activities in your own teaching? What kinds of support would learners need? What problems might you anticipate? How would you address them if they did arise?

Miniprojects

11. In the section on activity types the author lists three ESL classroom textbooks she has authored during the past decade (Numrich 1995, 1997, 1998). For this miniproject locate and examine one or more of these sets of teaching materials and see if the ESL textbooks Numrich publishes are consistent with any of the plans for teaching or conceptual underpinnings discussed in this chapter. Are there connections between her textbook(s) and discussion in this chapter you are able to recognize or infer?

12. Numrich emphasizes the importance of "recycling of language and content," claiming that theme-based teaching is an ideal context for taking advantage of such recycling. What other words, phrases, or concepts could be substituted for Numrich's use of the word *recycling* in this context? What does she mean? How might such features be facilitative of language learning? To what general ELT principles in table 2.4 of chapter 2 might they apply? For a miniproject activity, review syllabi that are not organized by theme (or other forms of teaching familiar to you) and try to determine the amount of "recycling of language and content" that exists in other types of syllabus design.

13. In this chapter, the teacher describes a field project that contributed to the students' understanding of gambling casinos on Indian reservations as well as related topics such as addiction, racism, and cultural adaptation. Design a comparable fieldwork unit that includes survey or interview questionnaires on a theme that you could develop for your own teaching. Generate a listing of related topics that might be explored. What might be some possible locations to visit?

Chapter 22

Academic Speaking: Learning to Take "Longer Turns"

Janet G. Graham and Susan M. Barone

In this chapter Janet Graham and Susan Barone describe a course titled Academic Speaking (AS) they offer at Vanderbilt University. The course is geared toward graduate students, international teaching assistants (ITAs), and other academic professionals. It focuses on enhancing their intelligibility as speakers of English in academic settings. Since AS students participate in academia as seminar discussants, lab assistants, and course instructors, they need to be able to express themselves through relatively extended speaking turns. Producing longer stretches of discourse—to deliver a reasoned argument or provide detailed information as part of a seminar discussion—represents an even greater challenge for language learners than maintaining a social conversation. The goal of AS is for students to be able to speak more confidently, effectively, and intelligibly in what are relatively "high stakes" academic situations. To reach this goal, Graham and Barone explore ways of maintaining a balance between accuracy and fluency concerns. Their course is designed to (1) encourage learner independence, (2) incorporate pronunciation instruction, (3) feature structured exercises and communicative practice, (4) provide instruction in communication strategies, and (5) highlight relevant cultural knowledge. One of the strategies they discuss is to promote automatic use of conventional formulaic constructions that are very common in academic speech. Graham and Barone propose that if students learn such preset chunks of language to the point where they can produce them automatically, they will find it easier to attend to other dimensions of academic speaking such as pacing, volume, rhythm, accuracy, rhetorical planning, word choice, specific audience adaptations, and content management. Graham and Barone explain that activities such as oral presentations, debates, and roundtable discussions are powerful motivators for improving intelligibility and managing the complex process of academic oral communication.

Setting

Academic Speaking (AS) is a course designed to be useful to graduate students and other scholars who need to do the following: communicate orally in academic or professional contexts, converse with colleagues, participate in scholarly discussions, and make both formal and informal oral presentations. The course is offered through the English for Academics and Professionals (EAP) program at Vanderbilt University, a research university located in Nashville, Tennessee. While it is open to Vanderbilt graduate students, faculty, and staff, most students in the course are graduate students. Enrollment in the course is limited to no more than 12; 11 students participated in the course section featured in this chapter.

Students in AS come from a variety of language backgrounds. Those who wish to enroll must pass a screening process in which we examine tape recordings of extended stretches of their speech, both prepared and extemporaneous, as well as single sentences. In terms of the ACTFL scale, the students' speaking proficiencies in English range from Intermediate-High to Advanced Plus. The Advanced Plus participants take the course primarily for public speaking instruction and practice.

The students' needs are first of all linguistic. While all AS students have extensive English language backgrounds, with TOEFL scores ranging from 550 to well over 600, they want to be able to speak in a range of different academic situations with greater fluency, accuracy, and comprehensibility. In the course, students attain greater command of conventional expressions (lexical phrases) used to perform common functions in academic speech, functions such as introducing a topic, providing clarifications, or presenting an opposing point of view. Most of the students need some instruction and practice in pronunciation, and all need opportunities to obtain specialist feedback on aspects of their speech.

In addition to linguistic needs, the course highlights sociocultural information relevant to the academic and professional environment of North America. Students need to know, for example, (1) appropriate registers and body language in various circumstances and (2) culturally appropriate styles for public speaking and argumentation. Units on sociocultural information also introduce organizational patterns of extended academic discourse common in North America.

AS students come from a range of disciplines, including the physical sciences, engineering, the social sciences, and, less often, the humanities. A few are teaching assistants who are required to take the course, but most of the students are not teaching assistants and take the course voluntarily.

Those who are not teaching assistants take the course to prepare themselves for one or all of the following: (1) to make presentations in graduate seminars, (2) to defend dissertations, (3) to give papers at scholarly conferences, or (4) to make presentations as part of job interviews. Motivation is generally high, even though the course does not carry academic credit. Because students recognize that AS is tailored to meet their needs, they tend to appreciate the relevancy and usefulness of its lessons and materials.

Classes meet two times a week for 12 weeks, with each class lasting 90 minutes. The classroom is set up with conference tables and movable chairs to facilitate pair and group work and is equipped with an overhead projector and several writing boards. A videocassette player and a high-quality video camera are available, and we use them as integral parts of the course. In addition to classroom resources, the students have access to a language laboratory for both whole class and individual pronunciation instruction and practice. They also have access to the university's several libraries and to the Internet as research resources for their oral presentations.

Conceptual Underpinnings

Academic Speaking is an English for Academic Purposes (EAP) course designed specifically for graduate students and other scholars. It fulfills what Robison (1991) posits as two salient criteria of English for Specific Purposes (ESP). First, the course is directed at a goal other than general linguistic proficiency—the goal of oral communication effectiveness in academic settings—and, second, it is based on analysis of learners' needs.

Like most ESP practitioners, we are not tied to a particular theoretical position as to how adults learn second languages. Along with many others, however, we believe that learning a language requires not just acquiring linguistic knowledge but acquiring communicative competence as well. "Competence" as used here refers both to knowledge and to skill in using that knowledge. We take communicative competence to mean grammatical competence, sociolinguistic competence, discourse competence, and strategic competence (Canale 1983). The AS course attempts to build learners' competencies in these four areas.

We see language learning as a highly complex phenomenon that is far from being fully understood. Ellis (1985) is one of many scholars who discusses its complexity. Among the many hypotheses he offers, the following in particular are reflected in our teaching: (1) motivation affects learning; (2) interaction with an interlocutor, along with language input, is necessary; (3) communication strategies aid learning by encouraging comprehensible input; (4) learners form hypotheses about a language and test them while using language; (5) learning formulaic speech plays a role; and (6) automatization is part of the process. These last two points, the role of formulaic speech and automatization, are especially important for an understanding of the AS course we offer.

Both research (Peters 1983; Nattinger and DeCarrico 1992) and our own experience as language learners and teachers convince us that learning "chunks" of language is an essential part of the language learning process. Language chunks, which we call "lexical phrases," are prefabricated, formulaic, and conventional (see Nattinger and DeCarrico 1992). They can be completely fixed or can have slots that need to be filled in. Memorized lexical phrases can, with practice, become automatic, thus significantly freeing a speaker's mind to think about the ideas needing expression and to self-monitor her or his speech. Mastering certain lexical phrases is particularly useful in connection with academic discourse because academic speech, both formal and informal, is full of prefabricated patterns (Nattinger and DeCarrico 1992). We believe mastery of commonly used lexical phrases not only improves syntactic accuracy, fluency, and comprehensibility but can also improve the content of learners' extended speech production.

In teaching spoken academic discourse, it is helpful to understand the concept of extended discourse or "long turns" (Brown and Yule 1983, 16). Extended discourse consists of utterances of more than just one or two sentences and tends to be transactional, rather than interactional. Transactional language, language whose purpose is to transmit information (Brown and Yule 1983), requires greater precision and clarity than interactional language. It is the lifeblood of academic discourse. From our testing of high intermediate and advanced English learners, we have been able to document that students who can converse competently in "short turns" often fail to produce clear and comprehensible longer stretches of discourse, presumably because doing so is a more cognitively demanding task.

No single theory of language instruction has dominated our teaching. Academic Speaking can be classified as a communicative course in that it takes into consideration not just grammatical and lexical content but "everything required to assure communication," including the learners' goals, their social roles, the situations where they will use the language, and the necessary discourse and rhetorical skills (Yalden 1983, 87). However, although the course is communicative in scope and purpose, we do not limit ourselves to "communicative" activities, as will become clear subsequently. Along with Hammerly (1991), Morley (1994a), and Murphy (1991), we believe that both fluency and accuracy are necessary for a high level of communicative competence and that use of communicative activities alone favors the development of fluency, sometimes at the expense of accuracy. For this reason, we strive for a balance between activities designed to foster fluency and those designed to foster accuracy (see Harmer 1991, 41–42). In fact, content, methods, and teaching strategies are chosen with principled eclecticism (Hammerly 1991) and depend on the particular objective being addressed.

In virtually every choice we have made and continue to make in planning the AS course, the issue of relevancy is foremost in our minds. Relevancy is, of course, an inherent attribute of any ELT course based on an analysis of learners' needs. We believe it is exceptionally important when teaching graduate students and scholars, who, like other busy adults, have little patience with language instruction they perceive as incidental to their immediate goals. In addition, relevancy is important because having spoken some variety of English for years, our students may be somewhat resistant to change. For change-resistant learners, relevancy seems to be especially important, not only for motivational reasons but also because teaching experience indicates that while it may be very hard to bring about global improvement for such learners (see Acton 1984), significant improvement may often be achieved in specific types of oral discourse (Graham 1994).

Goals and Objectives

The overarching goal of Academic Speaking is to prepare students to speak English more effectively in academic situations. This goal means, first of all, that they will speak comprehensibly. We know that few, if any, will acquire native speaker–like pronunciation, but we expect them to have good control of the basic sounds and to have a good command of the suprasegmental system of English—in particular the rhythm, intonation, stress, and emphasis patterns that are critical to communication among English speakers.

By the end of the course students will be speaking more comprehensibly with more accurate sounds, better control of stress and rhythm patterns, and increased self-confidence, as well as with fewer grammatical and lexical errors. They will learn (even overlearn) lexical phrases typically used in academic settings and will be able to produce them with improved precision, resulting in greater overall accuracy in their speech. Enhanced automaticity in the production of both generic and discipline-specific academic words and phrases will allow learners to monitor their speech more effectively. Strengthening their control over common discourse patterns of academic speech (e.g., the structure of process descriptions) also serves to enhance the intelligibility of their speech. In addition, students increase their understanding of communication processes, communication patterns, and other cultural norms characteristic of college and university classrooms in the United States and Canada.

We expect students to be able to participate actively and confidently in discussions and debates by the end of the course. We also expect that they will be able to produce clear, extended informative speech within small groups and to deliver well-planned oral presentations of their own design to the entire class.

Syllabus

In planning a course called "Academic Speaking," we first needed to decide what we meant by the term. Our working definition is the type of speaking that characteristically takes place in the classroom during instruction, in the science lab, in the seminar, or at a scholarly conference. We exclude from our definition discourse styles that occur purely for social purposes. Academic speaking can be formal or informal, but in most academic disciplines it consists of extended informative or argumentative discourse, that is, informative or argumentative discourse that consists of long turns. Our syllabus is constructed in deliberate but flexible ways. We think of the syllabus as a general plan, but not a specific blueprint, for the content and structure of the course and as a guide for the planning of individual classes. The AS syllabus remains somewhat open ended because the composition of student groups varies from semester to semester and we adapt the syllabus accordingly.

As with EAP courses generally, our design for the course is based on our ongoing analysis of students' needs. We rely on published research reports such as surveys of academic faculty, on our own experience as participants in academic life, on observations of graduate research presentations and classes, and on students' self-expressed needs. Time constraints prevent us from conducting a completely new needs analysis each time we offer the course, but we always ask students to fill out detailed questionnaires at the beginning of each course (see Internet app. 22.1). We have concluded that students' most important needs are to be more comprehensible and fluent in their speech, more culturally appropriate with respect to examples and kinds of supplementary topics they talk about in class, more skilled as communicators, and more self-confident in public speaking.

Thus, our syllabus includes attention to five areas: lexical phrases, pronunciation, intercultural issues, communication skills, and presentation skills. Each week we work on most of these areas. The approach is layered: for example, we will use certain lexical phrases, such as those for explaining cause and effect (e.g., *X brings about/results in* and *It has nothing to do with X but rather*), as the linguistic content to perform a language function (explaining cause and effect) and then practice performing the language and function through communicative activities. These activities provide practice not only in language but also in using communication principles that have been previously presented to the students in class.

The academic lexical phrases in the syllabus are predetermined (see app. 22.1 for categories and examples), but the amount of instruction and practice required for the various categories remains flexible and is determined by the needs of the particular class. The lexical phrases we cover include the language of numbers and mathematical functions, description and position, process, classification and analysis, cause and effect, discourse signaling, and interaction.

In teaching this primarily functional language, careful attention is given to pronunciation. For example, when presenting a phrase such as "x is divided by y," we model it and point out both the phrase's distinctive rhythmic structure and the additional syllable to mark past tense after the final /d/ of "divide." (For explanations of rhythm patterns and other suprasegmental features of English, see Celce-Murcia, Brinton, and Goodwin 1996; Gilbert 1993.) We further support pronunciation instruction by assigning individualized practice activities from the textbook and accompanying audio recordings included in Orion's (1996) *Pronouncing American English* instructional package. We assign specially targeted sections from the Orion materials to individual students because the text is very useful for self-instruction. In addition, we include culminating activities such as group presentations that require students to work together, research a topic, create an outline, and speak to the rest of the class.

J. D. Brown (1995) has identified seven types of syllabuses, or "ways of organizing courses and materials": structural, situational, topical, functional, notional, skill-based, and task-based. He recognizes, however, that very often these types are "mixed" or "layered." Using Brown's system, our syllabus can be classified as "mixed" since it is organized primarily by functions but also takes tasks, skills, and topics into consideration.

Activity Types

The learning activities we incorporate into lessons are designed to encourage students to use lexical phrases we specify; to practice pronunciation;

and to develop cultural, communication, and presentation skills within a meaningful context. These activities vary according to the area being highlighted. We try to keep them mostly, but not entirely, communicative in nature.

The lexical phrase focus of the AS course provides ample opportunity for group, pair, and individual activities. First we introduce the phrases to be studied, explaining their function and modeling their pronunciation. We try to establish the importance of being able to use such phrases fluently and accurately. Our initial activities are highly structured, but we attempt to create realistic, relevant contexts and situations so that students can use the phrases aptly and meaningfully. We ask students to produce sentences tied to content from their fields of specialization. At this early presentation and practice stage, we often provide pictures and other graphics, such as charts and tables. We then proceed to more communicative tasks. When learning lexical phrases of definition, for example, we have used an "information gap" crossword completion activity where students work in pairs. Both students have the same crossword puzzle, but each student has only half the answers filled in. The clues (definitions) for the answers are not provided. Each student has the answers that the other does not have. The task for each student is to define her or his answers so that the partner can fill in the missing words. This activity provides practice with the lexical phrases of definition and of clarification, as well as promoting pronunciation and fluency development.

Another communicative activity for practicing lexical phrases is based on an activity adapted from *Look again Pictures* (Olsen 1984). We have two nearly identical pictures of a science laboratory. Partner A and Partner B receive different versions and do not see each other's pictures. The task is for each partner to describe her or his own picture and ask questions about the partner's picture until the pair can come up with a complete list of differences. This information gap activity provides excellent practice in the lexical phrases of description, location, comparison, questioning, and clarifying, as well as providing pronunciation and fluency practice.

We use role plays both to practice language and to illustrate cultural information. For example, one role-play activity has students, again working in pairs, playing the role of either a teaching assistant or an undergraduate. A slip of paper is given to the "teaching assistant" with a description of a situation and an instruction, for example, "A student who normally turns papers in on time has requested a deadline extension, which is strongly against the professor's assignment policy. What do you do in this situation?" The "student" is given a slip such as the following: "Plead with the teaching assistant for a deadline extension. Give reasons why you should be granted the extension. Be insistent and somewhat aggressive." Pairs develop and practice their role play, and selected pairs may be asked to present their role play to the entire class for observation and discussion.

Group activities include debates and roundtable discussions to give students opportunities to experience group dynamics; to practice communication strategies we have presented, such as turn taking or preventing interruption; and to practice lexical phrases for agreeing, disagreeing, asking for clarification, and restating.

Students work individually on homework assignments. Frequently, homework includes listening to pronunciation cassette tapes that accompany the Orion text, which are lent to students chapter by chapter. Students also make recordings on their personal tapes. These recordings generally give the students an opportunity to prepare carefully and to refine their production of specific lexical phrases, with attention to pronunciation and accuracy. For example, when teaching the lexical phrases used for talking about graphs or tables, students might be asked to record themselves explaining a graph they have selected from their own field. The graph must be handed in along with the tape. The teacher provides feedback on the same tape by modeling, correcting, and commenting. Sometimes, feedback is given more graphically. For example, when teaching lexical phrases of description, students are asked to describe pictures they have previously drawn. The teacher then draws the pictures exactly as the students describe them. Subsequently, comparisons are made between the original drawings and the version produced by the teacher. Individual activities taking place in the classroom include brief extemporaneous talks and prepared oral presentations that require use of these same or similar phrases.

Lesson Particulars

AS differs from many other speaking courses in English language teaching in that it prioritizes mastery of lexical phrases common to academic speech. The following is a description of a class that reviews a set of lexical phrases and provides progressively less structured (and more extemporaneous) practice opportunities. We generated the description with the support of a video recording of the entire lesson. As teaching colleagues and coauthors, we viewed the video recording together repeatedly while attending closely to the lesson events it captured.

Prior to the beginning of our description, the teacher had engaged everyone present in some small talk, taken attendance, and collected homework audiotapes the students had generated. After class, she would listen to the students' recorded materials and provide feedback on the quality of their work by recording comments and advice in her own voice onto the students' individual tapes. The students' other homework had been to practice lexical phrases introduced in the previous class—phrases expressing classification and differences—and to try to commit the phrases to memory. They were asked to practice these phrases with content from their own fields, to be prepared to be able to use them in class, and to prepare a brief minipresentation on a topic from their disciplines that would incorporate the phrases.

(*The teacher puts a transparency with the classification lexical phrases on the overhead projector.*)

Teacher:	Let's just review them here. (*reading from the overhead transparency*) "X can be categorized on the basis of . . . " do you remember these? . . . and "x can be classified according to . . . ," and so on. Can you read that all right? (*affirmative murmurs*) (*pause*) Let's try it with medical colleges, with the information we just got from Shi Yu, okay? What can we say? (*pause*) Everybody. (*prompts*) Medical colleges . . . (*pause*) Medical colleges . . .
Class:	(*slowly and carefully, looking at the transparency*) Medical colleges . . . can be categorized on the basis of . . . whether or not they belong to a university.
Teacher:	That was really good. Wasn't that good? This is what I want you all to be able to do, is just have this language automatic, because it's so useful in academic speaking. That was very well done. Let's do the same thing using one of the other choices here. Medical colleges . . .
Two students:	Medical colleges . . . may be classified . . . according to whether they belong to a university or not.
Teacher:	(*asking the rest of the class*) Is that correct?
Some students:	(*tentatively*) Yes.
Teacher:	Yes. (*then she repeats, to model phrasing and intonation*) Medical colleges may be classified according to whether they belong to a university or not. (*adds*) That's very interesting. . . . I didn't know that was true. See, I never

knew that was a basis for classification . . . and now I do. (*moves on to a new portion of the lesson*) All right, we've reviewed some of the language, and now remember I asked you to prepare some sentences using concepts or items in your field. (*She places a transparency with the lexical phrases for classifying [with empty slots] on the overhead projector.*) Let me ask you for sentences from your own field. Use any one of these [lexical phrase frames] . . . you choose one. (*long pause*)

Ilgar: Fields of chemistry can be . . . are . . . grouped into four categories: physical, organic, inorganic, and analytic. (*Each other student follows with a statement of classification.*)

Teacher: All right! (*She puts another transparency on the projector.*) Did anyone come up with differences between classes?

Huafeng: Visible light and . . . ultraviolet light differ, differ from . . . their wavelength.

Teacher: All right, try saying that again.

Huafeng: Visible light differs from their . . . (*long pause*)

Teacher: You don't want to . . . what you might want to say is "Ultraviolet light differs from . . . " Say that.

Huafeng: Ah-ha. Visible light differs from ultraviolet light in that . . . in that its wavelength is longer.

Teacher: That's perfect. (*looks around at the class*) Who can repeat that? (*prompts*) Visible light . . . (*Teacher and class slowly repeat the statement together. The teacher asks for other statements of difference.*)

Young-Ruk: (*very softly*) In a perfectly competitive market there are enough sellers and buyers of a good [goods] while in a monopoly there are not.

Teacher: Okay. You have some very interesting information there. Let's say it again. (*Young-Ruk repeats his statement, more confidently.*) Okay. That was a good structure to use there, comparing the perfect market and monopolies. Thank you. (*Kerim then volunteers.*)

Kerim: Conventional lasers are . . . ummm . . . let me see . . . Ah, conventional lasers use atomic or molecular electrons to give out energy while a free electron laser uses electrons that are free.

Teacher: That's wonderful. Again I can't repeat it, (*laughter*) because it's too long. But that sounded very good. You made the distinction clear, and the form was good. Very good. (*Several other students give their prepared statements to the class.*) Okay, we're going to move on to the next part of our class, and in this part we're going to divide into groups of three, and you're going to give your minipresentation to other members of your group which will deal in some way with classifications in your discipline. And you have to be very clear, because after the activity is over, I may ask someone else to explain what you said.

The students divide into groups of three and give their minipresentations. One student talks confidently, and for a bit too long, about microeconomics and macroeconomics. The teacher steps in.

> *Teacher:*   Young-Ruk, you're running overtime. Can you wind it up now?

Another student talks shyly and softly about acids, which can be divided into two categories. The teacher walks from group to group, listening, questioning, occasionally supplying a word or phrase. After the activity is over, she asks two students to summarize what they learned from someone else's minipresentation.

As a final activity, the teacher calls on two students to represent their minipresentations to the entire class. Wei-Wei of the physics department goes first. She is visibly tense and speaks carefully and clearly.

> *Wei-Wei:* Physics consists of two categories. One category is theoretical physics. The other one is experimental physics. The experimental physics differs from theoretical physics in that the experimental physicists use relatively large equipments, while theoreticians use computers, and paper and pencils. (*She sits back and smiles with relief. Some of the students chuckle.*)
>
> *Teacher:* Okay. Very good. Thanks. Do you have any comments, the other physicists in the class? Do you agree with her classification? (*some laughter*) Huafeng: Yes. It's one kind of classification.
>
> *Teacher:* (*to Wei-Wei*) Well, thank you very much.

The second student to speak is Milene, from the Department of Human Resource Development. She speaks quite smoothly, and her speech is very comprehensible.

> *Milene:*   Some of the things I was saying was that human resource development in the organization can be classified on the basis of whether the programs are training, education, or development. And then I was saying that training differs from education in that it's focused on the present job and the immediately results, while education is not focused on the job, it's focused on future position and cannot be evaluated as much as training. I also said that development differs from education in that it's not possible to be evaluated and sometimes, you never know the results about it. That's more or less what I had to say . . . a lot of information. . . .
>
> *Teacher:*   Mmmn. That's very interesting . . . and good classification. . . . I never knew the difference before. So that's a very useful classification.

Learners' Roles

We use "role" to refer to the "part that learners and teachers are expected to play in carrying out certain tasks as well as social and interpersonal relationships between the participants" (Nunan 1989a, 79). In AS, our adult students are expected to cooperate with the teacher but at the same time to be independent thinkers actively involved in their own learning. Not all students, of course, fulfill their role completely, but it is always the case that our students respond eagerly to a questionnaire given toward the beginning of the semester that asks them to explain their own goals and evaluate their own strengths and weaknesses (see Internet app. 22.1).

The questionnaire also helps them to gain insight into their own learning styles (cf. Oxford 1990). Self-awareness of learning styles is useful because the students' role is to take responsibility for their learning, knowing that we cannot "give" them the language and communication skills they need. Rather, they must acquire such skills through their attention and actions. An example of the students' active role is that they often assist in designing some of the communication tasks they are asked to perform. While we might describe tasks in general, the students often provide the content from their own disciplines and refine the tasks to make them even more meaningful and relevant to their own disciplines. For example, the task might be to speak to their group, comparing and contrasting two concepts from their fields. The students themselves select the concepts and choose the style they wish to practice: formal or informal, speaker fronted or interactive.

The students' relationship with the teacher is such that they address her by her first name. They are expected to participate enthusiastically with their peers in group and pair activities, cooperatively or competitively, depending on the task. Something that has surprised us over our years of teaching the course is that most AS students particularly enjoy competitive tasks. During oral presentations their role is to listen attentively to their peers, fill out evaluation sheets [*editors' note:* cf. Mendelsohn 1991–92; and the same author's chapter in this volume, chap. 17, especially app. 17.1] and give both encouragement and constructive criticism.

Teacher's Roles

Teacher and student roles are interdependent. If students are to be independent and active in their learning, the teacher must adopt a complementary role (Nunan 1989a). We see our primary role as that of facilitator; that is, we believe that our major responsibility is to set up the conditions for learning to take place. We attempt to do this in a number of different ways: by planning our classes carefully; by finding or preparing the best possible materials; by providing clear explanations and directions; by pacing classroom activities so that interest and attention are maintained; by providing opportunities for controlled, guided, and extemporaneous practice; by providing appropriate feedback; and by reminding students frequently of the relationship of what they are learning to their own lives and desires.

Although our major role is that of facilitator, we also assume various subroles. At times we assume the traditional role of teacher as authoritative dispenser of knowledge. For example, we give brief lectures on such topics as the meaning of various intonation and stress patterns in American English (see Celce-Murcia, Brinton, and Goodwin 1996) or on role expectations in the American classroom. We also act as informants. We attempt to answer questions they might have about customs and practices within the academic world. We certainly act as coaches, evaluating, motivating, and shaping student performance. Sometimes we act as judges, assessing progress and performance. Finally, we know that, whether we like it or not, we are role models. When we present information to the class, our students may very well learn more from our example than from our precepts.

Instructional Materials

We have developed most of the teaching materials for the AS course over a number of years. The originals are kept in file folders, and selected handouts are distributed during class periods depending upon their suitability for particular sections of the course. We will not necessarily use the same handouts for every group of students because, within the broad outlines of the course, we want to remain flexible, customizing instruction to the degree we can. Our materials include handouts with the lexical phrases to be learned, by category, together with examples of their use. Once these phrases have been introduced, we often use accompanying overhead transparencies as prompts for guided practice in using them. We also distribute informational handouts dealing with communication theory, communication strategies, cross-cultural issues, and public speaking. In addition we have a variety of drawings, graphs, and other visuals for activities and games. We also use index cards with prompts or information for pair and group activities.

Our only textbook is the one we have selected for individualized pronunciation instruction, Orion's (1996) *Pronouncing American English*. Some possible alternatives to the Orion text include Dauer 1993, Grant 1993, Hahn and Dickerson 1999, Hewings and Goldstein 1998, and Miller 2000. We also own a commercially prepared set of audiotapes titled *Stress and Intonation, Part 1*, by ELS (1967) that we find valuable for stress and intonation practice in the language lab, with teacher supervision. We use blank audiotapes for student recordings and teacher responses, and occasionally we use a commercially produced videotape that demonstrates vowel and consonant articulation (Novey and Cowin 1991). Finally, blank videotapes play an important role. Student presentations are videotaped, and students review them individually, or in pairs, with their teacher [*editors' note:* cf. Tim Murphey's contribution, chap. 11 in this volume].

Assessment

Assessment of students' performance and progress is frequent and integral. Before classes begin, students will have taken a recorded oral test to give us samples with which to assess their pronunciation, fluency, accuracy, and their ability to communicate information in extended speech. These tests require students to read selected passages aloud and respond orally to specially designed prompts. At the end of the course, students take a similar test. We use the pretests to help us plan classes, and we use a comparison of the pre- and post-tests as reference points to help us when we write evaluations of the students' progress once the course is over.

We design many of the course's homework assignments to be completed via audio recordings. This format provides students with additional opportunities in using the language structures and functions that have been modeled, studied, and practiced in class. After students complete and hand in their audio recorded homework assignments, we listen to their recorded voices in order to assess the quality of their speech for various features, including pronunciation, grammatical accuracy, appropriate use of functional language, aptness of word choices, and fluency. We respond at the end of the recorded segments by recording our own comments directly onto the students' individual tapes. We also make written notes and keep them for a cumulative profile for each student.

When we review the *video*taped recordings of students' classroom presentations with individual students, we talk with them one-on-one about their strengths and weaknesses. We also make written notes of our impressions. We give a copy of our written feedback to the student and keep the originals for a cumulative profile. These profiles are invaluable for assessing students' progress at the end of the semester.

Listening to and responding orally to the taped homework assignments is time consuming for the teacher but definitely is valued by students. Over the years many students have said they appreciate contrasting their speech to that of the teacher and gain a lot from the individualized feedback, as well. Similarly, reviewing videotapes with each student is time consuming, but we continue to do it because students invariably rate this activity as the most useful one in the course.

In addition to the teacher's assessments of students, students are asked to assess their own videotaped oral presentations using a questionnaire we have designed as a guide (see Internet app. 22.2). Finally, students always assess the course itself. Sometimes we ask for midsemester (formative) appraisals, especially if we sense that interest or motivation is flagging. We always have them complete final (summative) course evaluations in which students rate the usefulness of the various components of the course and provide suggestions for improvement. Changes that resulted from course evaluations are that we now spend more time on the lexical phrases of agreeing/disagreeing, and we practice them in contexts of panel discussions and academic debates.

Caveats/Final Thoughts

Ferris and Tagg (1996a and 1996b), from their surveys of faculty at four California tertiary institutions, concluded that traditional formal oral presentations were not as common, even in the graduate schools they surveyed, as is generally supposed. Learning of this finding gave us pause. It prompted us to reconsider whether the time spent on public speaking in our course (perhaps one-fifth of class time) was justified. After reflection, however, we decided that in fact it was. First of all, we have reason to believe that presentations are more common at Vanderbilt University than at the schools included in the Ferris and Tagg surveys. Second, most of our students are approaching the time when they must defend their dissertations, present at professional conferences, or make presentations during the job application process. Third, the presentations provide a communicative context for meaningful practice of all that the students have been working on in the course: language, communication skills, and cultural knowledge. And finally, the oral presentation component is one of the facets of the course most highly rated by the students on both their formative and summative course evaluations. Our students believe that making effective oral presentations is important, not only during their years as graduate students but in their professional careers as well.

Prompts for Discussion and Reflection

1. Describe and discuss what you perceive "Academic Speaking" students' needs to be. Try to be specific: What should students be able to do by the end of this course? Do the teachers' expectations as presented in this chapter seem achievable? How would you modify your expectations to fit a longer time frame for such a course (e.g., two semesters rather than just one)?

2. Discuss the role of assessment in the course. Who and what are evaluated; under what conditions does the evaluation occur; who does the evaluating; and when are evaluations done? What are the purposes of such assessments?

3. What are the underlying principles and concepts that support the teachers' beliefs about language learning? List specific examples of how these principles and concepts are reflected in the course. Can any of them be related to the general ELT principles presented in table 2.4 of chapter 2?

4. How do these teachers attempt to balance attention to both accu-

racy and fluency in their construction of the syllabus and design for teaching? In their assessment procedures? In their choice of classroom activities?

5. How are technological resources used in the course? Would this type of course be possible without the use of such technologies? What changes would have to take place in order for the course to remain successful?

6. Why do you think these teachers choose to use a language lab in this course? What kinds of practice can a language lab provide that might be helpful for improving speech comprehensibility? What are some of the ways such facilities are currently being used that contrast with earlier eras of ELT?

7. Are you familiar with the use of video- or audiotape recordings with ELT learners? What type of preparation is necessary before video-taping students? How can you explain the authors' purpose for using this tool? What strategies might you use in order to minimize student anxiety? Discuss options for providing feedback on learner performance if working with such recordings. Compare with Tim Murphey's discussion of "videoing conversations for self-evaluation" (chap. 11 in this volume).

8. In Academic Speaking, students evaluate each other's presentations as part of the course. What theories/principles support this type of activity? How useful do you think it is to students? In the classroom, how would you explain the benefit of such activities to students? How else would you prepare them?

9. In contrast to the authors' opinion, some language specialists do not believe that focusing on individual linguistic components (such as lexical phrases) is a necessary precursor to participation in communicative language tasks. With which view do you agree and why? What are some of the issues and related points of controversy on this issue?

Miniprojects

10. Make arrangements to listen to a nonnative English speaker at an intermediate level of proficiency delivering a five-or-more-minute stretch of uninterrupted extended discourse (preferably on audio- or videotape). Identify any features of the discourse that you suspect might interfere with comprehensibility. Consider organization of ideas, discourse signaling, word choices, pronunciation, syntactical problems, pacing, and any other features you think affect comprehensibility. Consult with others about your findings. How could you address any of the interfering features you find in an AS-type classroom? Or, in your own classroom?

11. Make arrangements to observe and audiotape a native English speaker delivering an academic lecture or a professional presentation. Tape 5 to 10 minutes of the talk and then write at least a partial (selective) transcript of the excerpt. How formal is the speech? What types of lexical phrases are used? What discourse markers? Does the speaker tend to use a variety of lexical phrases and discourse markers, or are the same ones used repeatedly? How might your findings affect ways you might teach an Academic Speaking course?

12. If you know of someone who offers a course along the lines of the one described in this chapter, ask her or him about that course. Find out as much information about the course and its students as you can. How does this teacher's course differ from the one Graham and Barone describe?

Appendix 22.1. Lexical Phrase Categories for Academic Speaking

1. Verbalizing mathematics

   Examples: *a* is to *b* as *c* is to *d*
   X divided by Y equals
   plus or minus (number)

2. Describing objects—shape, size, amount, orientation, location

   Examples: X is_____ in height and_____ in width.
   close together/far apart
   in the upper/lower right hand/left hand corner

3. Giving instructions

   Examples: the first thing you have to do is
   make sure you remember to
   the final thing to do is

4. Defining, classifying, analyzing, comparing, and contrasting

   Examples: by X I mean
   X is made up of
   X differs from Y in that

5. Expressing causality

   Examples: due to the fact that
   it has nothing to do with
   keep/prevent/stop_____ from (VERB + -*ing*)

6. Explaining research—purpose, results, graphs and tables

    Examples: <u>the purpose of this research/study/investigation was to determine</u>
    <u>the results seem to show/suggest that</u>
    <u>the *x/y* axis represents</u>

7. Discourse signaling—introducing and shifting topics; summarizing; exemplifying; showing relationships; evaluating; qualifying; making asides (DeCarrico and Nattinger 1988)

    Examples: <u>what I'd like to do is</u>
    <u>so let's turn to</u>
    <u>take (say) *X* (for example)</u>

8. Interacting—asking for information, asking for clarification, comprehension checks, rephrasing, hesitating, avoiding, interrupting politely, preventing interruptions, giving opinions, agreeing, disagreeing

    Examples: <u>I wonder if you could tell me</u>
    <u>you have a point, but</u>
    <u>Let me put it another way.</u>

Chapter 23

English through Web Page Creation

Heidi Shetzer and Mark Warschauer

In this chapter, two early adopters of technological innovations in ELT collaborate to describe a course they both teach. English through Web Page Creation is offered five hours per week for 10 weeks in an Intensive English Program in the United States. Through instruction in how to use the Internet for purposes of web page creation (including HTML authoring and Java scripting) as well as language learning instruction in oral discussion and presentation, reading, research, and writing, the course develops both language learning and multimedia production skills. Shetzer and Warschauer design the course around a process syllabus that allows students' learning needs, interests, and proficiency levels to be reflected in class activities. With generous amounts of explicit instruction, guidance, and teacher support, students complete three projects. Each one culminates in the creation of a website. The first project is a travel essay that students work on individually. The second project is a restaurant review that students work on collaboratively in small groups. For the final project students work individually on a topic of their choice. Over time, fewer teacher interventions are needed as students learn to work more autonomously and begin to integrate a range of both technical and language skills. In the course section featured here, the instructor (Shetzer) plays the role of web developer, technical trainer, troubleshooter, task monitor, editor, respondent, discussion facilitator, and language specialist. The coauthors agree that the course is a challenging one to teach. They also agree that English through Web Page Creation succeeds in helping ESL learners develop and extend a variety of essential language skills while learning to communicate effectively both about and through this important new medium.

Setting

English through Web Page Creation (E-Web Page) is a course offered in the 10-week Intensive English Program (IEP) at the University of California,

Santa Barbara (UCSB) Extension. The IEP currently includes one integrated skills course that meets two hours per day, five days a week, and two elective courses that meet one hour per day, five days a week. E-Web Page is an elective course among several choices, ranging from Film Talk to TOEFL Preparation. The IEP offers one section of E-Web Page every quarter with typical enrollments of 15 students. The section detailed in this chapter took place from March to May of 1998 and was taught by Heidi Shetzer, though coauthor Mark Warschauer has taught similar courses in the recent past.

UCSB's IEP enrolls 150 to 200 students per semester with approximately 46 percent from Asia, 28 percent from Europe, 23 percent from Latin America, and 3 percent from other areas. Almost all students are between 19 and 35 years old, with the majority in their early 20s. Some students are en route to full-time university study, many are on a temporary hiatus from jobs in their home countries, and others come as temporary exchange students. The IEP students' English proficiency levels range from Intermediate-Low to Intermediate-High on the ACTFL proficiency scale. Students' oral proficiency levels tend to be somewhat higher than their writing proficiency levels.

The setting for the E-Web Page course is a 15-station, networked computer laboratory with Pentium PCs including several writing and communication programs (e.g., Microsoft Word, Microsoft PowerPoint, and Netscape Communicator), a whiteboard, laser printer, and full Internet access. Located at the front of the room, the instructor's computer is linked to a projector that displays the screen of the instructor's monitor on the wall.

All students in the English program are provided with e-mail accounts and web space. IEP students can use the computers in class and during the two hours of open access per day. There is a lot of competition to get a seat in the lab during open access time since there are 30 student computers and nearly 200 students wanting to use them. Due to these circumstances, homework requiring a computer is avoided.

Conceptual Underpinnings

This course reflects principles of content-based language instruction (Brinton, Snow, and Wesche 1989; Flowerdew 1993; Mohan 1986; Spanos 1987). Content-based instruction involves the use of substantive subject matter over a sustained period of time for second language teaching purposes. As Widdowson (1978) notes, integrating language and content "not only helps ensure the link with reality and the pupil's own experience, but also provides us with more certain means of teaching language as communication, *as use rather than simply as usage"* (16, emphasis added). Through content-based instruction, students can be pushed toward understanding language use in complex contexts and delivering messages that are appropriate from the point of view of both content and language (Snow 1991). Spanos (1987, 229, cited in Flowerdew 1993, 123) suggests five conditions that content-based language teaching should fulfill. An analysis of how these five conditions are reflected in the course illustrates how principles of content-based instruction inform our teaching in the E-Web Page course:

1. *Language teaching should be related to the eventual uses to which the learner will put the language.* People in the United States and other developed countries are experiencing one of the most rapid shifts in literacy processes in human history—from the literacy of the page to the literacy of the screen (Lemke 1998; Warschauer 1999; Shetzer and Warschauer 2000). The World Wide Web is becoming a primary means of publishing and locating information for businesses (Gartner 1998), and government training programs are shifting rapidly from textbooks to computer-based multimedia sources (Lanham 1993). Some 95 percent of U.S. college students are using the World Wide Web (Diederich 1998), with an increasing number developing their own home pages to assist them in career development (Heiberger and Vick 1998). Knowing how to develop web pages is not yet a mandatory skill, but it is a valuable asset for personal, occupational, vocational, and academic purposes. Many students will be able to apply this skill through the design of websites for themselves or for their institutions, organizations, and employers.

2. *The use of informational content tends to increase the motivation of the language learner.* Our previous research (see Warschauer 1996) has indicated that second language students find learning about computer use highly motivating. This motivation is magnified when students have the opportunity to publish their own work on computers for their classmates, and others around the world, to see (Warschauer 1999). In this course, we take advantage of students' general motivation about learning computer skills with the intrinsic incentive that comes from self-publishing opportunities. Such motivation helps guarantee that students pay close attention to language content so they can master the skills necessary to do top-notch work.

3. *Effective teaching requires attention to prior knowledge, existing knowledge, the total academic environment, and learners' linguistic proficiencies.* The course uses a flexible learner-centered syllabus that allows it to proceed based on the background knowledge, existing knowledge, and linguistic proficiency of the students as expressed through a needs analysis, formal and informal feedback sessions, and samples of their writing. Allowing student flexibility

in designing and carrying out their projects also helps ensure that their work corresponds to their own proficiency levels. At the same time, the web techniques covered in the course, and the background articles assigned for reading, are carefully selected based on the changing role and use of the Internet and World Wide Web in academia, business, entertainment, and related electronic media.

4. *Language teaching should focus on contextualized language use rather than on sentence-level usage.* Students in E-Web Page are immersed in contextualized language use as they read course materials, listen to the instructor's demonstrations, discuss projects with their classmates, and compose texts for their web pages. More language-specific instruction is tied directly to the language students use in particular contexts, in particular, the written texts for their web pages and their oral presentations about those pages.

5. *Language learning is promoted by a focus on significant and relevant content from which learners can derive cognitive structures that facilitate the acquisition of vocabulary and syntax as well as written and oral production.* Partly because the course is an elective among other alternative course offerings, its content focus on the Internet and web page creation is perceived by students who enroll in the course as being highly relevant to their interests, needs, and future career goals. It provides a direct basis for students' writing and oral production. Students acquire new vocabulary and syntax through their attention to course readings and lectures and through their own writing, revision, and presentations of web pages.

Finally, it should be noted that the goal of content-based instruction is not only to use content to teach language but also to use language to teach content. As Flowerdew (1993, citing Mohan 1986) explained, content-based instruction "has the advantage of not only helping students to learn a language, but also teaching them how to use the language to learn" (122). The Internet provides a powerful medium for autonomous, lifelong learning. Using the Internet to its full advantage requires accessing and publishing information in English, which at the present time is the Internet's international lingua franca and is expected to remain such for many years (Graddol 1997). Thus, the E-Web Page course attempts (1) to provide motivating content on which to base language learning activities while also (2) teaching language skills necessary for students to fully exploit the power of the Internet as a lifelong tool for learning, communication, and self-expression.

Goals/Objectives

E-Web Page has five specific objectives that include expanding upon or learning computer skills, content, and language—and the use of language to present products of one's learning to others. First, by the end of the course students should be able to create and maintain websites on the Internet. The three projects in the course are designed to guide students toward achieving this objective. Second, upon completion of the course, students should understand several of the sociopolitical issues related to Internet use such as copyright, censorship, privacy, and corporate influence. This goal is accomplished through reading and discussion assignments. A third objective is for students to improve their writing and develop a better understanding of effective writing processes. This purpose is accomplished by having students plan, write, and revise multiple drafts of their writing that focus, in order of priority, on content, organization, and mechanics. A fourth objective is that students develop their speaking and presentation abilities. This aspect of the course is accomplished through frequent group discussions and through planning and delivering presentations at the end of each project. Fifth, the course aims to develop autonomous learners. The syllabus proceeds from teacher-directed to student-directed projects, with the goal of empowering students to plan and implement their own projects to help them reach personal and professional goals.

Syllabus Design

The syllabus for the course incorporates tasks from two subject areas: language learning and computer training. In order to guarantee that students' background knowledge and personal learning goals are taken into account, a *process syllabus* is used that evolves throughout the course (see Candlin 1984). Long and Crookes (1992, 38) explain that the focus of a process syllabus

> is the learner and the learning processes and preferences, not the language or language learning process. [Breen and Candlin] argue that any syllabus . . . is constantly subject to negotiation and reinterpretation by teachers and learners in the classroom. . . . Both Breen and Candlin claim that learning should be and can only be the product of negotiation, which in turn drives learning:
>
>> A Process Syllabus addresses the overall question: Who does what with whom, on what subject-matter, with what resources, when, how, and for what learning purpose(s) . . . (Breen, 1984, p. 56)

Before the course begins, a rough sketch of a syllabus is prepared to plan out the content material to cover. The first day, the teacher conducts a needs analysis to determine the prior knowledge, skills, and interests of the students in the class (see Internet app. 23.1). The course has a basic skeletal structure comprised of three projects. Each project incorporates flexibility to meet student needs as identified in the needs analysis or during informal and formal feedback sessions. What happens in the course is tracked in a daily electronic schedule. Eventually, the electronic schedule becomes a retrospective, a posteriori course syllabus. In other words, the syllabus is not organized a priori around predetermined linguistic items, functions, or genres but is negotiated by learners and the teacher interactively and is organized in response to the language and computer training needs that emerge as necessary to fulfill the goals of the course.

Two types of tasks are included in the syllabus: language practice tasks and web page creation tasks. The language practice tasks involve speaking and writing in the target language. Students write independently in the first project, collaboratively and individually on the second project, and independently once again for the third project. The web page creation tasks are ordered from basic Hypertext Markup Language (HTML) instruction in the first project, to web page creation software instruction in the second, to a combination of the two for the third project. HTML is taught in order to give students a foundation in the underlying structure of websites. Equipped with this foundation, students can then learn how to use cut-and-paste JavaScripts to make their websites more interactive. Most students want to add some "bells and whistles" to their websites, such as digital clocks and button rollovers. They access websites like Earthweb, <http://www.earthweb.com/earthweb/cda/home.jhtml>, to find scripts to copy and paste. These are added bonuses and by no means required fare. Besides use of HTML and JavaScript, other technical skills integrated into the syllabus include learning how to digitize photos using a scanner and how to create original graphics using graphic design software.

Activity Types

Five types of activities take place in the course: technology training activities, group work and negotiation activities, writing and research activities, reading activities, and speaking/presentation activities.

Technology Training Activities

A variety of training activities to meet web page creation goals are used. In the first project, students come to class with a prepared travel essay to type into the computer. The focus is usually on a place to visit in the students' home countries, a topic that encourages some cross-cultural sharing early on in the course. Once their work is entered and saved onto a diskette, students learn basic HTML through step-by-step instructions on paper and an instructor-led demonstration of how to create a web page with HTML. Students either follow the teacher's demonstration closely or move at a quicker pace by reading ahead on the handout. This same type of interaction occurs whenever new computer tools are introduced. For example, the process is repeated when the class discusses how to create graphics and add them to web pages and when the class discusses how to use the File Transfer Protocol (FTP) program to move a copy of the finished web page to the World Wide Web. At times, students demonstrate web techniques they have learned on their own. For instance, a student recently showed his classmates how to copy and install a web page counter.

Group Work and Negotiation Activities

The second course project has students form teams and negotiate the research and design of a collaborative restaurant-review website. First, groups are formed of students from different native language backgrounds in order to encourage interaction in English. Once arranged into teams, students decide which restaurant to visit; when they will get together outside of class to go for a meal; and what they will look for, listen for, and taste during the meal itself. Once back in the classroom, they reconvene with their groups in the computer lab to decide how they will organize collaborative construction of their restaurant-review website. Minimally, each student is required to create one web page that provides links to the pages created by other members of the group.

Writing and Research Activities

The writing approach taken in the course is simultaneously communicative and process based (Reid 1993). Students are given feedback on the content, organization, and mechanics of their writing in feedback sessions with the teacher. During the course, students continually revise and change their websites, possibly adding pictures, colors, or other layout features as well as revising the text.

The research activities for the course take place in the community and on the Internet. Community research is featured as part of the restaurant-review project. One class session is devoted to developing strategies for interviewing people at the restaurant, assessing the quality of restaurant services, and writing restaurant reviews. Internet research is featured as part of the travel guide project and in the final course project, which is a site based on the students' interests. In the travel guide project to find links to websites relevant to their writing, students use search engines such as Yahoo <http://www.yahoo.com>, AltaVista <http://www.altavista.com>, Google <http://www.google.com>, and Dogpile <http://www.dogpile .com>.

Reading Activities

Assigned readings are from two sources: a web page creation textbook and newspaper and magazine articles about the Internet. The textbook (Shelly, Cashman, and Repede 1998) we use is a reference book about Netscape Composer, the software made available in the computer laboratory. Students are assigned specific chapters to read before their in-class training.

Articles discussing the Internet and World Wide Web make up the other assigned course readings. Since technology changes quickly, these articles are used once and then replaced in subsequent offerings of the course with new articles from newspapers, computer magazines, and online Internet periodicals. Students read the articles for homework and discuss them in class on the following day. Our discussions usually follow a large group, whole class format facilitated by the teacher.

Speaking and Presentation Activities

The last type of activity used in the course is formal presentations. At the end of each of their three projects, students come to the front of the class and formally introduce and discuss their completed websites. Students are given feedback on their site, as well as on the content and language used in their presentations. The presentations are videotaped once per quarter so students can review their presentations for further self-study. Video recording encourages students to prepare themselves and give more thoughtful presentations. In addition, it provides a tangible record for reflection and self-analysis on presentation style and delivery [*editors' note*: cf. Tim Murphey's contribution, chap. 11, and Janet Graham and Susan Barone's chap. 22 in this volume].

Learners' Roles

Based on the different activities taking place in the course, students assume various roles such as writers, computer users, planners, negotiators, discussion participants, and presenters. As computer users, learners develop extensive technical skills during the course. Many students become so focused on the primary medium of the course (the computers and software programs we use), that at times it is difficult to shift their concentration to other course features. When necessary, the teacher brings the class to another room to draw their attention away from computer screens and to other matters such as listening to a presentation given by another student or discussing a reading assignment.

Students interact as planners and negotiators for the second project required in the course. They need to speak with other students to determine who will write which subsection of the restaurant-review website. In most cases students are successful at working together to determine the content and design of their collaboratively constructed websites. Some groups struggle with the task of finding a comfortable balance between creative autonomy/independence and group collaborative responsibilities. When a group of students is having trouble, the instructor will intervene to suggest possible solutions.

During class discussions about Internet issues, students are expected to assume the roles of either discussion participants or active listeners. Some students participate in the discussions more actively, while others listen attentively but rarely contribute. Generally, students are not forced to speak if such is their preference. At the end of each project, students formally present their work to the class. During this culminating phase, they become public speakers, an opportunity that gives them practice (1) speaking in the target language, (2) using their own visual aids, and (3) learning to field unplanned questions from an audience of their peers.

Teacher's Roles

Like the learners whose multiple roles were described previously, the teacher assumes different roles depending on the type of activity. The instructor is a course developer and webmaster, trainer, technical troubleshooter, task monitor, editor/feedback provider, discussion facilitator, and language teacher. As course developer and webmaster, the instructor continually updates a master schedule and resource pages on the course website, for example, adapting the schedule to make up for unexpected delays or problems and adding new tools and resources. When students are learning how to use the computer as a tool for website construction or research, the teacher assumes a role akin to that of a trainer. Whenever one is teaching with technology, unpredictable problems are bound to emerge. Thus, the E-Web Page teacher has the responsibility of solving most technical problems that arise during class sessions.

When students are working on project tasks and/or negotiating the content and design of their sites, the teacher begins to assume the role of task monitor. At such times, the teacher visits each student or student group to make suggestions and lend support as needed. Specifically, the teacher listens in when students are discussing their projects in groups and tries to help confused students devise realistic plans for their projects. Throughout the course, students are turning in drafts of their writing, usually in hard copy form. It is essential for the teacher to read the students' work in a timely manner in order to provide prompt feedback on the content, organization, and mechanics of their writing. After students give formal presentations about their websites, the teacher provides feedback (usually in private) on their spoken English as well.

The students realize that the teacher uses information about their presentations to assess their progress in the course both at midquarter and at the end of the course. As students are giving presentations, the teacher takes detailed notes on the following: (1) organization, (2) delivery, (3) any serious pronunciation errors that interfere with intelligibility, and (4) whatever might be more salient grammatical errors. The teacher compiles information in these categories for each student and uses it in private consultations with them. Rather than using any preprinted assessment instruments during their oral presentations, it is more efficient to use plain paper with the names of the four category headings written across the top of the page.

Organization   Delivery   Pronunciation   Grammar

This way students receive customized, qualitative feedback. The teacher also responds to questions students pose about their language use and develops short-term minilessons on formal features of language as needs arise. In some cases, students might ask how to write or say something "correctly." When this happens during phases of lessons focused on other areas, the teacher responds as thoroughly as time will allow. On other occasions the teacher holds off responding until a subsequent class, a strategy that gives extra time to consult outside sources, to generate illustrations of the targeted language point, and to prepare more complete explanations. Finally, the instructor of E-Web Page is a discussion starter and facilitator. The days following reading assignments about Internet issues such as copyright, privacy, or censorship, the teacher initiates and facilitates whole class discussions on the topics.

Instructional Materials

Materials used in the E-Web Page course are training handouts, a web page creation reference textbook (Shelly, Cashman, Repede 1998), current articles from newspapers and computer magazines, and a website with links to on-line resources <http://www.newtierra.com/ucsb/>.

Training Handouts

Whenever a new tool is introduced in the course, students are given written directions explaining specific procedures to accomplish different tasks, such as how to use File Transfer Protocol (FTP) to move a web page onto a web server. These handouts are created and revised by the instructor. Students are told to practice the procedures outlined on the handouts, which are also used as instructional tools. The teacher demonstrates the procedures in front of the class at a relatively slow pace. As mentioned earlier, students who want to work at a faster pace are encouraged to do so. Web addresses for several of the handouts used in this implementation of the course are listed here.

> How to create a basic web page with HTML:
> <http://www.newtierra.com/tags.html>
> How to create a basic web page with Netscape Composer:
> <http://www.newtierra.com/composer/>
> How to upload your website to a server using FTP:
> <http://www.newtierra.com/ucsb/ftp.html>

Web Page Creation Textbook

The course uses a computer reference book written for native speakers of English (currently Shelly, Cashman, and Repede 1998) that teaches, in a visual manner, how to create web pages using Netscape Composer. Students are assigned chapters to read in this book when a new procedure is upcoming in the course. The Netscape Composer book is also used as a reference text in which students can look up answers to their own questions that come up when they are using the software. Rather than having to come to the instructor whenever they have a question, they can turn to the appropriate chapter in their textbook.

Newspaper/Computer Magazine Articles

Articles from current newspapers and computer magazines are other materials used in the E-Web Page course. Topics discussed include copyright, privacy issues, economic issues, social issues, educational issues, and others that deal with the Internet, web page creation, web design, web searching, and the promotion of websites. These articles provide students authentic reading material that is related to technology and current events. This course feature vividly illustrates to students that the topics they are studying in class are relevant to themes discussed in daily newspapers and contemporary magazines. It also informs them of sociopolitical issues related to the work they are doing, thus helping students become better informed and more thoughtful online publishers.

Articles from the PC Novice Guide series as published by Smart Computing on the Web at < http://www.smartcomputing.com> are also used. One issue of particular value is titled "Guide to Building WebSites." The students purchase these "magazines" for around $8 by using an 800 publisher's telephone number. In addition to these longer publications, the Smart Computing on the Web site includes shorter articles that are available without charge.

To meet the needs of students with varying levels of computer proficiency and to manage teaching with online resources, the course has its own website. An example can be found at <http://www.newtierra.com /ucsb/>. Like earlier versions, this current site combines links to useful information on the web about the course and its resources.

Lesson Particulars

This section describes one class in the E-Web Page Course that was devoted to HTML training. The goal was to teach students how to convert their written homework into a basic web page using HTML, Notepad, and Netscape Navigator. The agenda was fourfold: (1) to add basic and intermediate HTML tags to the students' Notepad documents to convert them into web pages; (2) to view the HTMLized Notepad documents in Netscape Navigator, the web browser; (3) to make changes to the Notepad document to add more HTML tags; and (4) to view those changes once again using the Netscape Navigator browser.

To prepare for the class session, the teacher (Heidi Shetzer) created and revised three handouts. First, she revised a travel essay she had written about Chicago. Then, she added basic HTML tags to the essay, including required HTML tags, an e-mail link, hyperlinks, a bulleted list, a centered title, and paragraph breaks. She printed a copy from Notepad to show an example of a web page with HTML tags and a copy from Netscape Navigator to show what the web page looks like in a browser. (See Internet apps. 23.2 and 23.3 for copies of these handouts.)

Besides those two handouts, she created a handout that lists, step by step, the following procedures: how to open up a document created in Notepad and edit it, how to add basic HTML tags to a Notepad document to convert it into a basic web page, how to view HTML documents in Netscape Navigator, and how to find more HTML tags and web resources to enhance work done so far.

When Heidi entered class, she returned students' first drafts of their writing that she had collected the day before. Overnight, she had made comments on the content and organization of their writing. Students then worked quietly on their individual pages for 15 minutes revising their work. Afterward, Heidi reviewed how to open up their writing document using Notepad. She circulated around the room to help students who were having problems.

Heidi then gave a brief lecture about the relationship between web pages and their HTML source code. She opened up her sample web page about the city of Chicago and displayed it to the class in Netscape Navigator. Then she selected View—Document Source and showed the underlying HTML tags. She wrote some of the tags on the board and discussed the difference between the beginning tags < > and the end tags that have a slash </>. Next, she gave students a handout explaining the procedures used to create a web page with HTML. The students then copied the required HTML tags directly around their essays, while she moved around the room examining students' screens to monitor how well they were following through with the task. If students were having trouble following the procedure correctly, she explained or discussed needed changes with them. The students worked for about 20 minutes and then took a 10-minute break.

After the break, Heidi showed students how to reopen their Notepad essays, so they could continue adding HTML tags. They worked quietly for about 10 minutes while she continued to check their work. Some students worked at a faster pace than others. One student who was ahead of the others changed the background color of his document before Heidi had a chance to mention this feature. He also accessed the recommended resources she listed at the bottom of the handout, which were links to more HTML tags. The same student then managed to copy and paste an image into his web page. Unfortunately, he had copied it without securing permission to do so from its source website on the Internet. After noticing this sequence of unplanned events, Heidi decided that copyright restrictions and ethical concerns should be on the lesson agenda for the next day's class.

Finally, Heidi distributed two remaining handouts: the Chicago web page with the HTML tags visible and the Chicago web page as shown in Netscape with the tags hidden. On the whole class screen, she demonstrated some intermediate HTML tags that were on the Chicago HTML handout, and took three to four minutes to demonstrate how to make an e-mail link, a procedure also explained at the bottom of their handouts. Students then worked to make e-mail links for five minutes, while Heidi consulted with individuals. She then returned to the instructor station and demonstrated how to establish and present a hyperlink to another web page and again assisted individual students in doing it for themselves. Finally, she explained how to make numbered and unnumbered lists on web pages. Every new tag she demonstrated during the class was included on the Chicago HTML handout.

The particulars of the lesson just described illustrate a combination of course features: instructor lectures and modeling, demonstrations, individual work, instructor visits to students' individual computers, interactive discussions with learners on what they are trying to accomplish, the need to keep track of what students might be attempting on their own, and the essential role of high-quality handouts. Several students commented at the end of the class that time really seemed to have passed quickly. From a teacher's perspective, the lesson went well because all students managed to complete the assigned tasks without an excessive degree of teacher intervention.

Caveats/Final Thoughts

Teaching a course such as E-Web Page is challenging and enormously time consuming. Designing and teaching the course require an instructor willing to stay current on tools, resources, and techniques related to web page creation and the Internet, while simultaneously finding ways to both extend and stay true to sound principles of second language instruction. The teacher continually needs to keep learning and redeveloping the course as technology changes. During class periods, the teacher sometimes has to manage technical breakdowns, while also managing the disorder that often emerges in decentralized student-centered classrooms. Thus, the E-Web Page course is not for all teachers, just as it is not for all students. But teachers who are willing to dedicate the substantial time and effort the course requires will gain the satisfaction of learning about an exciting new communications medium, while empowering students to take advantage of this still growing medium for creative self-expression and publishing.

Finally, while the results of the course have been quite positive, we feel there is definitely room for improvement. In particular, it seems that the most worthwhile and relevant project is the final one, in which students have free rein to develop websites corresponding to their own needs and interests. Currently, we are considering ways to reorganize the course to allow students greater time to work on a project of their own choosing with less time and effort devoted to the two preliminary teacher-defined projects. A challenge will be to incorporate sufficient scaffolding into the process so that students can begin a complex project even earlier in the course without feeling overwhelmed while learning English through web page creation.

Prompts for Discussion and Reflection

1. In the conceptual underpinnings part of this chapter, the authors analyze connections between the E-Web Page course and content-based language instruction. Review the five points made by the authors and analyze what you see as the course's connections to them.

2. E-Web Page aims to engage students in authentic tasks they might find in the real world outside the classroom. According to Shetzer and Warschauer, which tasks described were relevant at the time the chapter was written? Would you consider these tasks "authentic" in terms of your context and experience? How do you think they might have evolved, even for the coauthors, since the time of the chapter's composition?

3. The conceptual underpinnings for the course are grounded in content-based language teaching. What other language learning or educational philosophies do you observe (or might you infer) in E-Web Page? Discuss any connection(s) there may be to any of the 14 principles listed in table 2.4 of chapter 2.

4. A process syllabus is used in this course. Describe what you believe a process syllabus entails. How are process syllabi generally

manifested in ELT writing courses? In your opinion, was a process syllabus an appropriate choice for the course Shetzer and Warschauer describe? Please explain.

5. Technology changes fast, and it has changed in significant ways since the time of this chapter's composition. What would you update or change in this course to bring it up to date? What would you keep? What would you discard?

6. The course is organized around three projects: a travel project that students work on individually; a collaborative, restaurant-review website created by groups of students; and a final project done by individual students on a topic of their choice. Discuss what you perceive to be the rationale for sequencing the three course projects in this order and not in some other progression. From your perspective, how would you modify or change this organization if you were teaching such a course?

7. A needs analysis (shown in Internet app. 23.1) is given to students at the beginning of the course to determine their proficiency with computers. The language proficiency for the students in the course ranges between ACTFL Intermediate-Low and Intermediate-High. Besides this variance in language abilities, students come to the course with varying degrees of computing proficiency. What are some of the ways in which these learner differences might impact the course? What challenges would they present to the teacher? If you were teaching a course like E-Web Page, how would you design activities to meet students' needs?

8. Is a course like E-Web Page the type of course you might find in your current or future teaching context? If yes, how would you adapt the course to match your context? If no, explain what an even more useful course that integrates language learning, computer use, and the Internet might be like.

9. Compare Shetzer and Warschauer's way of organizing and teaching their E-Web Page course to one of the following as you might envision them: (*a*) an ESL writing course with full access to personal computers but without a focus on Internet use, (*b*) a writing course where ESL learners have access to computers for word processing outside of class but not inside the classroom, (*c*) a writing course that does not feature computer use at all.

Miniprojects

10. If possible, observe a language course that integrates the use of technology. Afterward, compose a "lesson particular" journal entry in the style presented in this chapter. Or, if you are currently teaching a course

that integrates technology and language learning, write out the day's teaching/learning events in this fashion. Try to do so immediately following the class since our memories of such events fade quickly. Once completed, share and discuss your "lesson particular" entry with others.

11. Take a look at a current technology news section from a source such as the New York Times Online <http://www.nytimes.com>. Write down a list of the current technological issues that appear in the section. Now, choose one issue and devise a language teaching activity using it.

12. Training handouts play an important role in the technology training component of this course. Take a look at Internet appendixes 23.2 and 23.3. Also, take a look at these and additional course materials as Shetzer makes them available on the Internet at <http://www.newtierra .com/ucsb/>. Explain what is useful in these handouts, and then suggest ways to improve these handouts or suggest entirely new handouts you think would be even more effective.

Chapter 24

Looking Forward:
Connectivity through the Internet

John Murphy and Patricia Byrd

In the age of the Internet, possibilities for communication exist that could barely have been imagined only a few years ago. In contrast to the static nature of relationships between authors and readers in the past, we would like to provide a forum for interactive discussion between readers, the editors, and other contributors to the *Understanding* collection. Our hope is to move beyond the information-transmission styles of communication that predominate between authors and readers of printed books. Through an interactive Internet site serving to support this book, the editors and contributors provide a setting for continuing communications with teachers and others interested in the teaching of English to speakers of other languages. With the support of the University of Michigan Press and Georgia State University, we have created an Internet site at <http://www.gsu.edu /~wwwesl/understanding/> with the following features.

Additional information about each chapter in the book
Resources to support teachers who use the *Understanding* collection within preservice or in-service teacher education courses
A system through which readers can share their reactions to materials in the book and develop and receive feedback on descriptions of their own courses using the *Understanding* framework for discussion of English language teaching

Section 1 of the *Understanding* Website:
Additional Information about Each Chapter

By combining Internet materials with a print publication, we are able to offer additional information beyond the space limitations imposed by the printed textbook. In the first section of the *Understanding* website, we offer the following additional resources.

1. Tables, figures, and appendixes promised in individual chapters of the printed text through notes that prompt readers to find certain sources of information on the *Understanding* website
2. Additional supplementary materials (e.g., course handouts, other instructional materials, samples of student writing, updated course syllabi) provided by each of the local-perspectives-chapter authors and used in the course as the contributor teaches it
3. A list of the references cited in the chapter for readers who might find a chapter-specific bibliography a useful complement to the unified bibliography that comes at the end of the printed book
4. Additional suggested resources for further reading tied to each chapter
5. Links to sites on the Internet that provide supporting information on the content of each chapter

Section 2 of the *Understanding* Website: Suggestions for Using the *Understanding* Collection for Purposes of Preservice or In-Service Teacher Training

In this section of the website, suggestions are made to teacher educators who plan to use the *Understanding* collection in teacher-training or teacher-education courses. Initially, these suggestions will be based on John Murphy's and Pat Byrd's efforts while using the *Understanding* chapters and related materials in courses they teach at Georgia State University. For example, we will post web versions of course syllabi used to incorporate the book into MATESOL courses along with guidelines and suggestions on how to work with the collection in both preservice and in-service settings. Over time, additional ideas and resources will be gathered from other teacher educators and their students who would like to contribute to this section of the website. Eventually, these materials will serve as an instructor's manual for using the book but with this difference: teacher educators and other readers of the collection will be able to contribute to, suggest changes to, and expand the resources made available. For example, one plan is to expand each chapter's listing of discussion topics and mini-projects to give teacher educators an ever-growing range of choices for their courses. Some readers may be interested in providing the following.

study guides

chapter outlines

lists of key words and terminology for pre- or postreading tasks

summaries of discussions with colleagues about individual chapters

firsthand reports by readers who try out in their own classes some of
the ideas discussed by one or more of the contributors

more personal reflections tied to individual chapters for posting on
the web

further suggestions of journal articles, book chapters, or Internet sites
related to topics featured in one of the chapters

Anyone who would like to contribute to this section of the website should
communicate with John Murphy at <jmmurphy@gsu.edu>.[1]

Section 3 of the *Understanding* Website: Communication to Respond to Chapters and Discussion Materials Provided at the End of Each Chapter

In addition to providing information to expand and extend the content of
each chapter and to support teachers who use the *Understanding* collection
in teacher-training courses, the website will have interactive features that
will allow readers to communicate with the editors and other contributors
to the book. This section will encourage communication between the editors, chapter contributors, and readers in two ways. First, the e-mail addresses for editors and chapter contributors are provided so that readers
can address questions and comments directly to them for the purpose of
engaging in individual discussions about particular issues raised in the
chapters. If teacher educators would like to arrange for course participants
(e.g., pre- or in-service teachers, MATESOL candidates, other degree candidates) to communicate with the editors or other chapter contributors,
arrangements can be made prior to the beginning of the course to make such
communication easier and more effective by ensuring that the editors/
contributors understand the purpose for the communication. A schedule
might be set up, for example, to facilitate substantive exchanges more con-

---

1. Since e-mail addresses sometimes change, these will be updated on the *Understanding* collection's Internet site. Check there if problems arise with any of the e-mail addresses cited in this chapter.

veniently via a threaded e-mail discussion list available on the web to any-one interested. Second, readers can post their responses to the various dis-cussion topics and miniprojects provided at the end of the chapters. To post these longer contributions to the website, individual readers should com-municate with either John Murphy at <jmmurphy@gsu.edu> or Pat Byrd at <patbyrd@gsu.edu>. After discussion and possible revisions, the editors will arrange for reader contributions of appropriate quality to be posted on the *Understanding* collection's website. Instructors of teacher-education courses who would like to make use of this website feature for their courses would communicate with John or Pat ahead of time to make arrangements to have course participants' materials posted on the web.

Section 4 of the *Understanding* Website: Addition of New Course Descriptions Based on the *Understanding* Chapter Framework

We envision this fourth section as the most exciting and potentially the most important feature of the *Understanding* collection's Internet site. In-dividual teachers are invited to provide descriptions of their own courses using the *Understanding* framework (as introduced in chaps. 1–5 and illus-trated in chaps. 6–23) to guide their thinking and writing (see also table 1.1 in chap. 1). After e-mail discussions with the editors and possible revisions of the course descriptions, teachers will be able to follow through with arrangements to have their descriptions posted on the *Understanding* web-site. Our plan is for such postings to become a growing collection of class-room-based descriptions and discussions of what happens when classroom teachers work with English language learners in actual ELT courses. For example, teacher educators who would like to have participants in pre- or in-service courses prepare such descriptions and discussions of language teaching—possibly as part of course requirements—will be able to arrange to have them posted on the website. Participants already serving as in-service teachers might focus their descriptions on a language course they are teaching concurrent with their reading of the book. As illustrated in the coauthored local-perspectives chapters (6, 7, 9, 10, 22, and 23), other par-ticipants may find it more useful to collaborate with a colleague (another teacher) to compose a course description. As editors we ask to be included in discussions of how to carry out such project work to better ensure that the resulting course descriptions make appropriate contributions to the website.

Of course, one does not have to be a student in a teacher-education course to pursue this option. We are particularly interested in working with course descriptions generated by readers who currently serve as English language teachers. In fact, contemporary teachers represent an essential group of potential contributors as we envision the *Understanding* collection's Internet site. We believe this feature of the website to have great potential because it provides a mechanism for readers to contribute to a growing archive of Internet-posted course descriptions that other teachers will be able to read and learn from. As discussed in chapter 3, part of our plan for the collection is to facilitate ways not only for teachers to explore understandings and explanations of how language courses are envisioned and offered but to document, share with others, and receive feedback on their efforts as course instructors, as well. For readers who take advantage of this feature of the Internet site, the possibilities are intriguing since they may begin to tie together role relationships between readers and contributors to the original book. We are very excited about the possibility of extending our work on the *Understanding* collection in such directions through the availability of the World Wide Web.

A theme highlighted in chapter 1 and reintroduced throughout the collection is that *all instances of English language teaching take place within particular settings and sets of circumstances.* With this principle in mind, we look forward to developing more extensive contacts with teachers who work in an even wider range of settings than those represented in the book. We are especially interested in hearing from English language teachers who work in (*a*) non-English-dominant parts of the world, as well as (*b*) elementary, middle, and secondary school settings worldwide. Though ELT courses offered elsewhere are of great interest too, we mention these particular settings because we would like to see wider representation of such areas of expertise in professional resources. There is a pressing need for such contributions to the field of ELT. Currently, large numbers of prospective and current English language teachers come to English-dominant countries from other parts of the world in order to participate in teacher preparation programs. Many such pre- and in-service teachers are international students who plan to return to their home countries to teach English as a foreign language. Teaching EFL in regions of the world such as Africa, Asia, Europe, the Middle East, and South America has direct relevance to their professional preparation, yet too few illustrations of teaching in such settings are available. When teaching EFL in regions such as these, a considerable amount of instruction takes place within public or government-sponsored school systems and programs where the following circumstances may exist.

English classes may be part of traditional school curricula.

English may be taught more as a "school subject" with less clearly recognizable purposes for using the target language beyond the classroom.

Courses may be required to conform to centralized instructional materials and examination systems.

Innovations in instruction sometimes may be discouraged.

Because such settings present language teachers with special challenges, we are very interested in working with course descriptions that illuminate teachers' and learners' efforts in non-English-dominant parts of the world. Of course, there are many other kinds of courses and a wide range of additional instructional settings that would be exciting to learn more about. Some others of great interest include but are not limited to the following: public school courses at various levels of education in English-dominant parts of the world, courses offered through intensive English programs, those offered through private language programs, community-based programs, ESP programs, private tutoring, distance learning, and so forth. Teachers who are interested in contributing original English language course descriptions to the *Understanding* collection's website should (*a*) contact John or Pat so we will be aware of your interest and better prepared to provide guidance, resources, and support; and (*b*) initiate plans to compose a description of a course you teach around the *Understanding* chapter framework featured in chapters 4 and 5 and illustrated throughout the collection in chapters 6 through 23.

At this stage in our journey as editors we have reached the end of our efforts in making the book component of the *Understanding* collection project available. Hopefully, our efforts have only just begun. With the availability of the *Understanding* collection's Internet site, we plan to be involved in projects and other efforts growing out of reader responses to the book for some time to come. With continuing involvement of the editors, chapter contributors, and readers in mind, we would like to close our discussion of local perspectives on English language teaching by returning to an image from Whitman's ([1891] 1992) *Leaves of Grass*. Though alternative interpretations are possible, we celebrate the spirit of Whitman's images as presented throughout this book because we believe the emotional quality they convey is that of a mentor in heartfelt conversation with a friend.

> Not I, nor any one else can travel that road for you,
> You must travel it for yourself.

It is not far, it is within reach,
Perhaps you have been on it since you were born
    and did not know,
Perhaps it is everywhere on water and on land.

—"Song of Myself," lines 14–18

Bibliography

Acton, W. 1979. Second language learning and perception of differences in attitude. Ph.D. diss., University of Michigan.

———. 1984. Changing fossilized pronunciation. *TESOL Quarterly* 18 (1): 71–86.

———. 1997. Direct speaking instruction (and the mora-bound, focal-stress blues). *Language Teacher* 21 (9): 7–12.

———. 1998. The Syllablettes. *Speak Out: IATEFL Pronunciation SIG Newsletter* 17:4–8.

Aebersold, J. A., and M. L. Field. 1997. *From reader to reading teacher.* New York: Cambridge University Press.

Allen, V. 1971. Teaching intonation from theory to practice. *TESOL Quarterly* 5:73– 91.

Allwright, D. 1992. Exploratory teaching: Bringing research and pedagogy together in the language classroom. *Revue de Phonetique Appliquée* 103–4:101–17. Available through Bell and Howell and Sociological Abstracts.

Allwright, D., and K. Bailey. 1991. *Focus on the language classroom: An introduction to classroom research for language teachers.* New York: Cambridge University Press.

American Council on Teaching Foreign Languages (ACTFL). 1986. *ACTFL proficiency guidelines.* Hastings-on-Hudson, NY: ACTFL.

Anderson, N. 1999. *Exploring second language reading: Issues and strategies.* New York: Heinle and Heinle.

Anthony, E. M. 1963. Approach, method, and technique. *English Language Teaching* 17:63–67.

Aquilina, P. 1993. *Timely topics.* Englewood Cliffs, NJ: Prentice-Hall.

Asbjorn, P. C., and J. E. Moe. 1957. *The three billy goats gruff.* New York: Harcourt Brace.

Asher, J. 1996. *Learning another language through actions: The complete teachers' guidebook.* 5th ed. Los Gatos, CA: Sky Oaks Productions.

Atkinson, D. 1999. TESOL and culture. *TESOL Quarterly* 33 (4): 625–54.

Auerbach, E. 1992a. *Making meaning, making change: A guide to participatory curriculum development for adult ESL and family literacy.* McHenry, IL: Center for Applied Linguistics and Delta Systems.

———. 1992b. *Making meaning, making change: Participatory curriculum development for adult ESL literacy.* Washington, DC: Center for Applied Linguistics.

———. 1993. Reexamining English only in the ESL classroom. *TESOL Quarterly* 27 (1): 9–32.

———. 1994. Participatory action research. *TESOL Quarterly* 28 (4): 693–97.

Bailey, K. M. 1983. Competitiveness and anxiety in adult second language learning: Looking at and through the diary studies. In H. Seliger and M. Long, eds., *Classroom oriented research in second language acquisition*, 67–102. Rowley, MA: Newbury House.

Bailey, K. M., and D. Nunan, eds. 1996. *Voices from the language classroom.* New York: Cambridge University Press.

Bailey, K. M., and L. Savage. 1994. *New ways in teaching speaking.* Alexandria, VA: TESOL.

Bandura, A. 1977. *Social learning theory.* Englewood Cliffs, NJ: Prentice-Hall.

Barrera, R., V. Thompson, and M. Dressman. 1997. *Kaleidoscope: A multicultural booklist for grades K–8.* Urbana, IL: NCTE.

Bates, L., J. Lane, and E. Lange. 1993. *Writing clearly: Responding to ESL compositions.* Boston: Heinle and Heinle.

Belfiore, M. E., and B. Burnaby. 1995. *Teaching English in the workplace.* 2d ed. Toronto: Pippin Publishing and OISE Press.

Bell, J. 1995. The relationship between L1 and L2 literacy: Some complicating factors. *TESOL Quarterly* 29 (4): 687–704.

Benesch, S. 1996. Needs analysis and curriculum development in EAP: An example of a critical approach. *TESOL Quarterly* 30:723–38.

Bergen, C. 1984. *Knock wood.* New York: Ballantine Books.

Bernstein, B. 1990. *The structuring of pedagogic discourse.* Vol. 4, *Class, codes, and control.* London: Routledge Kegan Paul.

Blake, W. 1991. *William Blake's Jerusalem: The emanation of the giant albion.* Princeton, NJ: William Blake Trust/Princeton University Press.

Bolinger, D. 1983. Intonation and gesture. *American Speech* 58 (2): 156–74.

———. 1986. *Intonation and its parts.* Stanford: Stanford University Press.

Breen, M. P. 1984. Process syllabuses for the language classroom. In C. J. Brumfit, ed., *General English syllabus design*, 47–60. RLT Document 118. London: Pergamon Press and British Council.

Bridgeman, B., and S. Carlson. 1984. Survey of academic writing tasks required of graduate and undergraduate foreign students. *Written Communication* 1:247–80.

Brinton, D. M. 1991. The use of media in language teaching. In M. Celce-Murcia, ed., *Teaching English as a second or foreign language*, 2d ed., 454–71. Boston: Heinle and Heinle.

Brinton, D. M., J. Goodwin, and L. Ranks. 1994. Helping language minority students read and write analytically: The journey into, through, and beyond. In F. Peitzman and G. Gadda, eds., *With different eyes: Insights into teaching language minority students across the disciplines*, 57–88. White Plains, NY: Longman.

Brinton, D. M., M. A. Snow, and M. B. Wesche. 1989. *Content-based second language instruction.* Boston: Heinle and Heinle.

Brooks, J., and M. Brooks. 1993. *In search of understanding: The case for constructivist classrooms.* Alexandria, VA: Association for Supervision and Curriculum Development.

Brown, G. B., and G. Yule. 1983. *Teaching the spoken language: An approach based on the analysis of conversational English.* Cambridge: Cambridge University Press.

Brown, H. D. (project director). 1992. *Vistas: An interactive course in English* (levels 1–4). Englewood Cliffs, NJ: Prentice-Hall.

———. 1993a. After method: Toward a principled approach to language teaching. In J. E. Alatis, ed., *Proceedings of the Georgetown University roundtable on languages and linguistics,* 509–20. Washington, DC: Georgetown University Press.

———. 1993b. Requiem for methods. *Journal of Intensive English Studies* 7:1–12.

———. 1994a. *Teaching by principles: An interactive approach to language pedagogy.* Englewood Cliffs, NJ: Prentice-Hall Regents.

———. 1994b. *Principles of language learning and teaching.* 3d ed. Englewood Cliffs, NJ: Prentice-Hall Regents.

Brown, J. D. 1995. *The elements of language curriculum: A systematic approach to program development.* Boston: Heinle and Heinle.

Brown, K., and S. Cornish. 1996. *Beach Street 1.* Sydney: New South Wales Adult Migrant English Service.

Brown, R., M. Pressley, P. Van Meter, and T. Schuder. 1996. A quasi-experimental validation of transactional strategies instruction with low-achieving second-grade readers. *Journal of Educational Psychology* 83 (1): 18–37.

Bruner, J. S. 1986. *Actual minds, possible worlds.* Boston: Harvard University Press.

Burns, A. 1991. Action research: Reflecting on practice in the classroom. Paper presented at the Fourth Congress of Latin-American British Cultural Institutes, Santiago, Chile, July.

Burns, A., and H. Joyce. 1998. *Focus on grammar.* Sydney: NCELTR.

Byrd, P. 1995. Issues in the writing and publication of grammar textbooks. In P. Byrd, ed., *Material writer's guide,* 45–63. Boston: Newbury House.

———. 1998. Rethinking grammar at various proficiency levels: Implications of authentic materials for the EAP curriculum. In P. Byrd and J. Reid, eds., *Grammar in the composition classroom: Essays on teaching ESL for college-bound students,* 69–97. Boston: Newbury House.

Byrd, P., A. Forsyth, and R. Sherbahn. 1996. Review of *Life Prints,* edited by JoAnn (Jodi) Crandall and Allene Guss Grognet. *TESOL Journal* 6 (2): 38–40.

Byrd, P., and J. Reid, eds. 1998a. *Grammar in the composition classroom: Essays on teaching ESL for college-bound students.* Boston: Newbury House.

———. 1998b. *Looking ahead: A writing-grammar series at four levels.* Boston: Heinle and Heinle.

Caine, R. N., and G. Caine. 1990. Understanding a brain-based approach to learning and teaching. *Educational Leadership* 48:66–70.

Calkins, L. 1994. *The art of teaching writing.* Portsmouth, NH: Heinemann.

Callaghan, M., and J. Rothery. 1988. *Teaching factual writing: A genre-based approach.* Report of the Disadvantaged Schools Project (DSP) Literacy Project. Sydney: Metropolitan East Region, New South Wales.

Campbell, C., and H. Kryszewska. 1992. *Learner-based teaching.* New York: Oxford University Press.

Canale, M. 1983. From communicative competence to communicative language pedagogy. In J. C. Richards and R. W Schmidt, eds., *Language and communication,* 2–27. London and New York: Longman.

Candlin, C. N. 1984. Syllabus design as a critical process. ELT document 118. In G. Brumfit, ed., *General English syllabus design,* 29–46. London: Pergamon Press and British Council.

———, ed. 1981. *The communicative teaching of English: Principles and an exercise typology.* Burnt Mill, Harlow, UK: Longman.

Carr, E. 1992. Sophie. In S. Norton and N. Waldman, eds., *Canadian content,* 180–83. Toronto: Harcourt Brace.

Carson, J. 1998. Cultural backgrounds: What should we know about multilingual students? *TESOL Quarterly* 32:735–46.

Carson, J., and I. Leki. 1993. *Reading in the composition classroom: Second language perspectives.* Boston: Newbury House.

Carter, R., and M. N. Long. 1991. *Teaching literature.* Burnt Mill, Harlow, UK: Longman.

Casazza, M. E. 1993. Using a model of direct instruction to teach summary writing in a college reading class. *Journal of Reading* 37 (3): 202–8.

Cathcart, R. 1986. Situational differences and the sampling of young children's school language. In R. Day, ed., *Talking to learn: Conversations in second language acquisition,* 118–40. Rowley, MA: Newbury House.

Cazden, C. 1992. *Whole language plus: Essays on literacy in the United States and New Zealand.* New York: Teachers College Press.

Celce-Murcia, M., ed., 1991. *Teaching English as a second or foreign language.* 2d ed. Boston: Heinle and Heinle.

Celce-Murcia, M., D. M. Brinton, and J. Goodwin. 1996. *Teaching pronunciation: A reference for teachers of English to speakers of other languages.* New York: Cambridge University Press.

Celce-Murcia, M., and D. Larsen-Freeman. 1999. *The grammar book: An ESL/EFL teacher's course.* 2d ed. Boston: Heinle and Heinle.

Center for Applied Linguistics. 1989. *Basic English skills test.* Washington, DC: Center for Applied Linguistics.

Chamot, A., and M. O'Malley. 1996. The cognitive academic language learning approach: A model for linguistically diverse classrooms. *Elementary School Journal* 96 (3): 259–73.

Chaudron, C. 1988. *Second language classrooms: Research on teaching and learning.* New York: Cambridge University Press.

———. 1995. Academic listening. In D. Mendelsohn and J. Rubin, eds., *A guide for the teaching of listening,* 74–96. San Diego: Dominie Press.

Chela-Flores, B. 1998. *Teaching English rhythm: From theory to practice.* Caracas, Venezuela: Fondo Editorial Tropykos.

Cherryholmes, C. 1988. *Power and criticism: Poststructuralist investigations in education.* New York: Teachers College Press.

Clarke, A. 1990. Canadian experience. In L. Hutcheon and M. Richmond, eds., *Other Solitudes,* 48–70. Toronto: Oxford University Press.

Clarke, M. A. 1983. (The scope of) approach, (the importance of) method, and (the nature of) technique. In J. E. Alatis, H. H. Stern, and P. Strevens, eds., *Georgetown University roundtable on languages and linguistics,* 106–12. Washington, DC: Georgetown University Press.

———. 1984. On the nature of technique: What do we owe the gurus? *TESOL Quarterly* 18 (4): 577–94.

———. 1994. The dysfunctions of the theory/practice discourse. *TESOL Quarterly* 28 (1): 9–26.

Clemens J., and J. Crawford. 1986. *Lifelines.* Adelaide: NCRC.

Coelho, E. 1994. Social integration of immigrant and refugee children. In F. Genesee, *Educating second language children: The whole child, the whole curriculum, the whole community,* 301–27. New York: Cambridge University Press.

Collie, J., and S. Slater. 1987. *Literature in the language classroom: A resource book of ideas and activities.* Cambridge: Cambridge University Press.

Corder, S. P. 1967. The significance of learners' errors. *International Review of Applied Linguistics* 5:161–70.

Cornish, S. 1996. *Making contact: Your child's school.* Sydney: New South Wales Adult Migrant English Service.

Cornish, S., and S. Hood. 1994. *Troubled waters.* Sydney: New South Wales Adult Migrant English Service.

Corson, D. 1995. *Using English words.* Norwell, MA: Kluwer Academic Publishers.

Costa, V., C. Lockhart, L. Miller, and P. Rogerson-Revell. 1992. *Reading skills: Authentic readings for manufacturing engineering.* Hong Kong: City University of Hong Kong.

Crawley, J. 1991. Gender relations. In L.Tepperman and R. J. Richardson, eds., *The social world: An introduction to sociology,* 288–309. Toronto: McGraw-Hill–Ryerson.

Crookes, G., and C. Chaudron. 1991. Guidelines for classroom language teaching. In M. Celce-Murcia, ed., *Teaching English as a second or foreign language,* 2d ed., 46–67. Boston: Heinle and Heinle.

Cross, D. 1992. *A practical handbook of language teaching.* New York: Prentice-Hall.

Culleton, B. 1992. *In search of April Raintree.* Winnipeg: Peguis.

Cummins, J. 1981. The role of primary language development in promoting education success for language minority students. In Office for Bilingual Bicultural Education, ed., *Schooling and language minority students: A theoretical framework,* 3–49. Los Angeles: Evaluation, Dissemination, and Assessment Center, California State University.

———. 1986. Empowering minority students: A framework for intervention. *Harvard Educational Review* 56:18–36.

———. 1996. *Negotiating identities: Education for empowerment in a diverse society.* Ontario, CA: California Association for Bilingual Education.

D'Agostino, F. 1986. *Chomsky's system of ideas.* New York: Oxford University Press.

Dauer, R. 1993. *Accurate English: A complete course in pronunciation.* Englewood Cliffs, NJ: Prentice-Hall Regents.

Day, R. 1990. Teacher observation in second language teacher education. In J. C. Richards and D. Nunan, eds., *Second language teacher education,* 43–61. New York: Cambridge University Press.

———. 1993. *New ways in teaching reading.* Alexandria, VA: TESOL International.

Day, R., and J. Bamford. 1998. *Extensive reading in the second language classroom.* Cambridge: Cambridge University Press.

DeCarrico, J., and J. R. Nattinger. 1988. Lexical phrases for the comprehension of academic lectures. *English for Specific Purposes* 7 (2): 91–102.

Deegan, J. E. 1996. *Children's friendships in culturally diverse classrooms.* Washington, DC: Falmer Press.

Delaruelle, S. 1997. *Beach Street 2.* Sydney: New South Wales Adult Migrant English Service.

Derrida, J. 1982. *Margins of philosophy.* Translated by A. Bass. Chicago: University of Chicago Press.

DeVillar, R. A. 1994. The rhetoric and practice of cultural diversity in U.S. schools: Socialization, resocialization, and quality schooling. In R. A. DeVillar, C. J. Faltis, and J. Cummins, eds., *Cultural diversity in schools: From rhetoric to practice,* 25–56. New York: State University of New York Press.

———. 1998. Indigenous images and identity in multicultural Mexico: Media as official apologist and catalyst for democratic action. In Y. Zhou and E. T. Trueba, eds., *Ethnic identity and power: Cultural contexts of political action in school and society,* 187–219. New York: State University of New York Press.

DeVillar, R. A., and C. J. Faltis. 1991. *Computers and cultural diversity: Restructuring for school success.* New York: State University of New York Press.

———. 1994. Reconciling cultural diversity and quality schooling: Paradigmatic elements of a socioacademic framework. In R. A. DeVillar, ed., *Cultural diversity in schools: From rhetoric to practice,* 1–22. New York: State University of New York Press.

DeVillar, R. A., C. J. Faltis, and J. Cummins, eds. 1994. *Cultural diversity in schools: From rhetoric to practice.* New York: State University of New York Press.

Diederich, T. 1998. Web use among students continues to rise. *CNN,* August 31. Retrieved January 1, 1999, from the World Wide Web: <http://cnn.com/TECH/computing/9808/31/opstud.idg/index.html>.

Doughty, C. 1991. Second language instruction does make a difference: Evidence from an empirical study of second language relativization. *Studies in Second Language Acquisition* 13 (4): 431–69.

Dowrick, P. 1983. Self-modeling. In P. Dowrick and S. Biggs, eds., *Using video: Psychological and social applications,* 105–24. New York: Wiley.

Dowrick, P., and S. Biggs, eds. 1983. *Using video: Psychological and social applications.* New York: Wiley.

Dunn, W., and J. Lantolf. 1998. Vygotsky's zone of proximal development and Krashen's *i* + 1: Incommensurable constructs; incommensurable theories. *Language Learning* 48 (3): 411–42.

Edelsky, C., B. Altwerger, and B. Flores. 1991. *Whole language: What's the difference?* Portsmouth, NH: Heinemann.

Edge, J. 1994. Comments on Donald Freeman and Jack C. Richards's conceptions of teaching and the education of second language teachers: A reader reacts. *TESOL Quarterly* 28 (2): 395–400.

Eggly, S. 1998. English for medical purposes: International medical graduates. *Language Teacher* 22 (11): 27–31.

Elbow, P. 1973. *Writing without teachers.* New York: Oxford University Press.

Ellis, G. 1996. How culturally appropriate is the communicative approach? *English Language Teaching Journal* 50:213–18.

Ellis, R. (985. *Understanding second language acquisition.* Oxford: Oxford University Press.

———. 1994a. Factors in the incidental acquisition of second language vocabulary from oral input: A review essay. *Applied Language Learning* 5:1–32.

———. 1994b. *The study of second language acquisition.* New York: Oxford University Press.

English Language Services. 1967. *Stress and intonation part 1: Drills and exercises in English pronunciation.* New York: Collier MacMillan International.

Enright, D., and M. L. McCloskey. 1985. Yes, talking! Organizing the classroom to promote second language acquisition. *TESOL Quarterly* 19 (3): 431–53.

———. 1988. *Integrating English: Developing English language and literacy in the multicultural classroom.* Reading, MA: Addison-Wesley.

Erdrich, L. 1994. *Bingo palace.* New York: Harper Perennial Publishers.

Ernst, G. 1994. "Talking circle": Conversation and negotiation in the ESL classroom. *TESOL Quarterly* 28 (2): 293–322.

Fanselow, J. F. 1987. *Breaking rules: Generating and exploring alternatives in language teaching.* New York: Longman.

Ferris, D. 1995a. Student reactions to teacher response in multiple-draft composition classrooms. *TESOL Quarterly* 29:33–53.

———. 1995b. Teaching students to self-edit. *TESOL Journal* 4 (4): 18–22.

———. 1997. The influence of teacher commentary on student revision. *TESOL Quarterly* 31:315–39.

———. 1998. Students' views of academic aural/oral skills: A comparative needs analysis. *TESOL Quarterly* 32:289–318.

———. 1999. The case for grammar correction in L2 writing classes: A response to Truscott (1996). *Journal of Second Language Writing* 8:1–10.

Ferris, D., and J. Hedgcock. 1998. *Teaching ESL composition: Purpose, process, and practice.* Mahway, NJ: Lawrence Erlbaum.

Ferris, D., and T. Tagg. 1996a. Academic oral communication needs of EAP learners: What subject-matter instructors actually require. *TESOL Quarterly* 30 (1): 31–55.

———. 1996b. Academic listening/speaking tasks for ESL students: Problems, suggestions, and implications. *TESOL Quarterly* 30 (2): 297–320.

Flavell, J. H. 1979. Metacognition and cognitive monitoring. *American Psychologist* 34 (10): 906–1. Special issue.

Flores, B., P. T. Cousin, and E. Diaz. 1991. Transforming deficit myths about learning, language, and culture. *Language Arts* 68:369–79.

Flowerdew, J. 1993. Content-based language instruction in a tertiary setting. *English for Specific Purposes* 12:121–38.

———. 1994. *Academic listening: Research perspectives.* New York: Cambridge University Press.

Flowerdew, J., and L. Miller. 1995. On the notion of culture in L2 lectures. *TESOL Quarterly* 29 (2): 345–73.

Fotos, S., and R. Ellis. 1991. Communicating about grammar: A task based approach. *TESOL Quarterly* 25 (4): 605–28.

Frankel, I., and C. Meyers, with E. W. Stevick. 1991. *Crossroads 1 students' book.* New York: Oxford University Press.

Freeman, D. 1998. *Doing teacher research: From inquiry to understanding.* New York: Heinle and Heinle.

Freeman, D., and S. Cornwell, eds. 1993. *New ways in teacher education.* Alexandria, VA: TESOL International.

Freeman, D., and Y. Freeman. 1994. *Between worlds: Access to second language acquisition.* Portsmouth, NH: Heinemann.

Freeman, D., and K. Johnson. 1998. Reconceptualizing the knowledge-base of language teacher education. *TESOL Quarterly* 32 (3): 397–417.

Freeman, D., and J. C. Richards. 1993. Conceptions of teaching and the education of second language teachers. *TESOL Quarterly* 27 (2): 193–216.

Freeman, Y., and D. Freeman. 1998. *ESL/EFL teaching: Principles for success.* Portsmouth, NH: Heinemann.

Freire, P. 1988. *Pedagogy of the oppressed.* New York: Continuum.

———. 1997. *Pedagogy of the oppressed.* 2d ed. New York: Continuum.

Frey, W. H. 1998. The diversity myth. *American Demographics* 20 (June, no. 6): 39–43.

Fried-Booth, D. L. 1986. *Project work: Resource book for teachers.* New York: Oxford University Press.

Frodesen, J. 1991. Grammar in writing. In M. Celce-Murcia, ed., *Teaching English as a second or foreign language,* 2d ed., 264–75. New York: Newbury House/ HarperCollins.

Fuchs, M., and M. Bonner. 1995. *Focus on grammar: A high-intermediate course for reference and practice.* Longman Focus on Grammar Series. White Plains, NY: Addison-Wesley.

Gardner, D., and L. Miller. 1996. *Tasks for independent language learning.* Alexandria, VA: TESOL.

———. 1999. *Establishing self-access: From theory to practice.* Cambridge: Cambridge University Press.

Gartner, J. 1998. Internet will become core of business by 2003. *TechWeb,* October. Retrieved January 1, 1999, from the World Wide Web: <http://www.techweb.com/wire/story/TWB19981014S0014>.

Gebhard, J. 1996. *Teaching English as a foreign or second language: A teacher self-development and methodology guide.* Ann Arbor: University of Michigan Press.

Gebhard, J., and R. Oprandy. 1999. *Language teaching awareness: A guide to exploring beliefs and practices.* New York: Cambridge University Press.

Gebhard, M. 1999. Debates in SLA studies: Redefining classroom SLA as an institutional phenomenon. *TESOL Quarterly* 33 (3): 544–57.

Gerngross, G., and H. Puchta. 1992. *Creative grammar practice.* New York: Longman.

Gianelli, M. 1991. Thematic units: Creating an environment for learning. *TESOL Journal* 1 (1): 13–15.

Gilbert, J. 1993. *Clear speech: Pronunciation and listening comprehension in North American English.* Cambridge: Cambridge University Press.

———. 1994. *Clear speech: Pronunciation and listening comprehension in North American English.* 2d ed. Cambridge: Cambridge University Press.

———. 1995. Intonation: A navigation guide for the listener. In J. Morley, ed., *Pronunciation pedagogy and theory: New views, new directions,* 38–48. Alexandria, VA: TESOL.

Gillepsie, M. K. 1996. *Learning to work in a new land: A review and sourcebook for vocational workplace.* Washington, DC: Center for Applied Linguistics.

Goldstein, L. M., and S. M. Conrad. 1990. Student input and negotiation of meaning in ESL writing conferences. *TESOL Quarterly* 24:443–60.

Goldstein, T. 1997. *Two languages at work: Bilingual life on the production floor.* Hawthorne, NY: Walter de Gruyter.

Goodwin, J. 1997. Getting into the content. In D. M. Brinton and P. Master, eds., *New ways in content-based instruction,* 122–27. Alexandria, VA: TESOL.

Gossard, J. 1987. Using read-around groups to establish criteria for good writing. In C. B. Olson, ed., *Practical ideas for the teaching of writing,* 148–51. Sacramento: California State Department of Education.

Goto, M., and T. Murphey. 1997. Student selected and controlled input and output flooding. Paper presented at TESOL 97, Orlando, Florida, March.

Grabe, W. 1991. Current developments in second language research. *TESOL Quarterly* 25:375–406.

Grabe, W., and R. B. Kaplan. 1996. *Theory and practice of writing.* New York: Longman.

Graddol, D. 1997. *The future of English.* London: British Council.

Graham, J. G. 1994. Four strategies to improve the speech of adult learners. *TESOL Journal* 3 (3): 26–28.

Grant, L. 1993. *Well said: Advanced English pronunciation.* Boston: Heinle and Heinle.

Graves, K. 1996. A framework for the course development process. In K. Graves, ed., *Teachers as course developers,* 12–38. New York: Cambridge University Press.

Greenberg, C. 1997. *Teaching pronunciation through problem posing. College ESL* 7 (1): 62–71.

Grellet, F. 1981. *Developing reading skills: A practical guide to reading comprehension exercises.* New York: Cambridge University Press.

Grenfell, M. 1994. Flexible learning: The teacher's friend? *Modern English Teacher* 3 (4): 7–13.

Grognet, A. G. 1995. Adult education in the workplace. *Literacy, work, and education reform: Summary of a symposium marking the thirty-fifth anniversary of the Center for Applied Linguistics,* 11–12. Washington, DC: Center for Applied Linguistics. ERIC Document Reproduction Service ED 379 970.

———. 1996. *Planning, implementing, and evaluating workplace ESL programs.* Washington, DC: Center for Applied Linguistics, Project in Adult Immigrant Education.

Grosse, C. 1991. The TESOL methods course. *TESOL Quarterly* 25 (1): 29–49.

Gunderson, L. 1991. *ESL literacy instruction: A guidebook to theory and practice.* Englewood Cliffs, NJ: Prentice-Hall Regents.

Hacker, D. 1995. *A writer's reference.* 3d ed. Boston: Bedford Books of St. Martin's Press.

———. 1996. *A Canadian writer's reference.* 2d ed. Toronto: ITP Nelson.

Hahn, L., and W. Dickerson. 1999. *SpeechCraft: Discourse pronunciation for advanced learners.* Ann Arbor: University of Michigan Press.

Halliday, M. A. K. 1994. *An introduction to functional grammar.* 2d ed. London: Arnold.

Hammerly, H. 1991. *Fluency and accuracy.* Cleveland, UK: Multilingual Matters.

Hammond, J., A. Burns, H. Joyce, D. Brosnan, and L. Gerot. 1992. *English for social purposes.* Sydney: NCELTR.

Handman, W., ed. 1978. *Modern American scenes for student actors.* New York: Bantam Books.

Harmer, J. 1991. *The practice of English language teaching.* 2d ed. London: Longman.

Harris, J. 1987. Proofreading: A reading/writing skill. *College Composition and Communication* 38:464–66.

———. 1995. Where is the child's environment? A group socialization theory of development. *Psychological Review* 102 (3): 458–89.

Harris, M. 1986. *Teaching one-to-one: The writing conference.* Urbana, IL: National Council of Teachers of English.

Harris, V., ed. 1992. *Teaching multicultural literature in grades K–8.* Norwood, MA: Christopher Gordon.

Heath, S. B. 1986. Sociocultural contexts of language development. In California

State Department of Education, ed., *Beyond language: Social and cultural factors in schooling language minority students,* 143–86. Los Angeles: Evaluation, Dissemination, and Assessment Center.

———. 1993. Inner city life through drama: Imaging the language classroom. *TESOL Quarterly* 27 (2): 177–92.

Hedge, T. 1988. *Writing: Resource books for teachers.* New York: Oxford University Press.

Heiberger, M. M., and J. M. Vick. 1998. Do I need my own home page? *Chronicle of Higher Education,* August 28. Retrieved January 1, 1999, from the World Wide Web: <http://chronicle.com/jobs/v45/i02/4502talk.htm>.

Helgesen, M. 1997. What one extensive reading program looks like. *Language Teacher (Japan Association of Language Teaching)* 21 (5): 31–33.

Hewings, M., and S. Goldstein. 1998. *Pronunciation plus: Practice through interaction.* New York: Cambridge University Press.

Hinkel, E., ed. 1999. *Culture in second language teaching and learning.* New York: Cambridge University Press.

Hino, N. 1988. Yakudoku: Japan's dominant tradition in foreign language learning. *Language Teacher (Japan Association of Language Teaching)* 10:45–55.

Hofstede, G. 1986. Cultural differences in teaching and learning. *International Journal of Intercultural Relations* 10:301–20.

Holten, C. 1997. Literature: A quintessential content. In M. A. Snow and D. M. Brinton, eds., *The content-based classroom: Perspectives on integrating language and content,* 377–87. White Plains, NY: Longman.

Hopkinson, D. 1993. *Sweet Clara and the freedom quilt.* New York: Alfred A. Knopf.

Hornberger, N. 1994. Ethnography. *TESOL Quarterly* 28 (4): 688–90.

Hornsby, D., and D. Sukarna, with J. Parry. 1986. *Read on: A conference approach to reading.* Portsmouth, NH: Heinemann.

Horowitz, D. M. 1986. What professors actually require: Academic tasks for the ESL classroom. *TESOL Quarterly* 20:445–62.

Howatt, A. P. 1984. *A history of English language teaching.* Oxford: Oxford University Press.

Hruska, B. 1998. Constructing second language learners through the discourses of bilingualism, friendship, and gender. Ph.D. diss., University of Massachusetts at Amherst.

Hudelson, S. 1994. Literacy development of second language children. In F. Genesee, ed., *Educating second language children: The whole child, the whole curriculum, the whole community,* 129–58. New York: Cambridge University Press.

Huizenga, J., and G. Weinstein-Shr. 1996. *Collaborations: English in our lives, beginning I.* Boston: Heinle and Heinle.

Hutchinson, T., and A. Waters. 1987. *English for specific purposes: A learning-centered approach.* Cambridge: Cambridge University Press.

James, C. J., ed. 1985. *The ACTFL foreign language education series: Foreign language proficiency in the classroom and beyond*. Lincolnwood, IL: National Textbook Company.

Janzen, J. 1996. Teaching strategic reading. *TESOL Journal* 6 (1): 6–9.

Janzen, J., and F. L. Stoller. 1998. Integrating strategic reading into L2 instruction. *Reading in a Foreign Language* 12 (1): 251–69.

Johns, A. M. 1981. Necessary English: A faculty survey. *TESOL Quarterly* 15:51–57.

———. 1990. L1 composition theories: Implications for developing theories of L2 composition. In B. Kroll, ed., *Second language writing: Research insights for the classroom*, 24–36. New York: Cambridge University Press.

———. 1991. English for specific purposes (ESP): Its history and contributions. In M. Celce-Murcia, ed., *Teaching English as a second or foreign language*, 67–77. Boston: Heinle and Heinle.

Johnson, D., and R. Johnson. 1987. *Learning together and alone: Cooperation, competition, and individualization*. Englewood Cliffs, NJ: Prentice-Hall.

Johnson, K. 1992. Learning to teach: Instructional actions and decisions of preservice ESL teachers. *TESOL Quarterly* 26 (3): 507–35.

———. 1994. The emerging beliefs and instructional practices of preservice ESL teachers. *Teaching and Teacher Education* 10 (4): 439–52.

———. 1995. *Understanding communication in second language classrooms*. New York: Cambridge University Press.

———. 1996a. Portfolio assessment in second language teacher education. *TESOL Journal* 6 (2): 11–14.

———. 1996b. The role of theory in L2 teacher education. *TESOL Quarterly* 30 (4): 765–71.

———. 1999. *Understanding language teaching: Reasoning in action*. New York: Heinle and Heinle.

Johnston, W. B., and A. H. Packer. 1987. *Workforce 2000: Work and workers for the twenty-first century*. Indianapolis, IN: Hudson Institute. ERIC Document Reproduction Service ED 290 887.

Jones, S. 1985. Problems with monitor use in second language composing. In M. Rose, ed., *When a writer can't write: Studies in writer's block and other composing-process problems*, 96–118. New York: Guilford Press.

Joyce, H. 1998a. *Words for living*. Sydney: NCELTR

———. 1998b. *Words for work*. Sydney: NCELTR.

Kagan, S. 1988. *Cooperative learning resources for teachers*. Laguna Niguel, CA: Resources for Teachers.

Keh, C. L. 1990. Feedback in the writing process: A model and methods for implementation. *English Language Teaching Journal* 44:294–304.

Kelly, L. G. 1969. *Twenty-five centuries of language teaching*. Rowley, MA: Newbury House.

Kessler, C. 1992. *Cooperative language learning: A teacher's resource book*. Englewood Cliffs, NJ: Prentice-Hall Regents.

Klippel, F. 1987. *Keep talking: Communicative fluency activities for language teaching.* New York: Cambridge University Press.

Knowles, M. 1990. *The adult learner: A neglected species.* Houston: Gulf.

Korczak, J. 1967. The child's right to respect. In M. Wolins, ed., *Selected works of Janusz Korczak,* 463–500. Washington, DC: National Science Foundation.

Krashen, S. 1985. *The input hypothesis: Issues and implications.* London: Longman.

———. 1998. Comprehensible output? *System* 26:175–82.

Kroll, B. 1979. A survey of the writing needs of foreign and American college freshmen. *English Language Teaching Journal* 33:219–27.

———. 1990. The rhetoric/syntax split: Designing a curriculum for ESL students. *Journal of Basic Writing* 9 (1): 40–55.

Kumaravadivelu, B. 1993. Maximizing learning potential in the communicative classroom. *English Language Teaching Journal* 47 (1): 98–107.

———. 1994a. The postmethod condition: (E)merging strategies for second/foreign language teaching. *TESOL Quarterly* 28 (1): 27–48.

———. 1994b. Response to D. Liu's comments on "The postmethod condition: (E)merging strategies for second/foreign language teaching." *TESOL Quarterly* 29 (1): 177–80.

Laleman, J. P., and R. Preiss. 1994. *Manufacturing technology.* Bloomington, IL: Meridian Education Corporation. Video recording.

Lane, J., and E. Lange. 1999. *Writing clearly: An editing guide.* 2d ed. Boston: Heinle and Heinle.

Lanham, R. A. 1993. *The electronic word: Democracy, technology, and the arts.* Chicago: University of Chicago Press.

Larsen-Freeman, D. 1986. *Techniques and principles in language teaching.* New York: Oxford University Press.

———. 1987. Comments on Leo van Lier's review of *Techniques and principles in language teaching. TESOL Quarterly* 21 (4): 769–75.

———. 1991. Second language acquisition research: Staking out the territory. *TESOL Quarterly* 25 (2): 315–50.

———. 2000. *Techniques and principles in language teaching.* 2d ed. New York: Oxford University Press.

Larsen-Freeman, D., and M. Long. 1991. *An introduction to second language acquisition research.* London: Longman.

Lazar, G. 1993. *Literature and language teaching: A guide for teachers and trainers.* Cambridge: Cambridge University Press.

Lee, J. F., and B. VanPatten. 1995. *Making communicative language teaching happen.* New York: McGraw-Hill.

Leki, I., and J. C. Carson. 1994. Students' perceptions of EAP writing instruction and writing needs across the disciplines. *TESOL Quarterly* 28 (1): 81–101.

———. 1997. "Completely different worlds": EAP and the writing experiences of ESL students in university courses. *TESOL Quarterly* 31 (1): 39–69.

Lemke, J. L. 1998. Metamedia literacy: Transforming meanings and media. In D. Reinking, M. McKenna, L. Labbo, and R. D. Kieffer, eds., *Handbook of literacy and technology: Transformations in a post-typographic world,* 283–301. Hillsdale, NJ: Lawrence Erlbaum.

Leslie, G. R., and S. K. Korman. 1989. *The family in social context.* 7th ed. New York: Oxford University Press.

Lessac, A. 1967. *The use and training of the human voice.* 2d ed. New York: Drama Book Specialists.

Levis, J. 1999. Intonation in theory and practice, revisited. *TESOL Quarterly* 33 (1): 37–63.

Li, D. 1998. "It's always more difficult than you plan and imagine": Teachers' perceived difficulties in introducing the communicative approach in South Korea. *TESOL Quarterly* 32 (4): 677–703.

Lipson, M., S. Valencia, and C. Peters. 1993. Integration and thematic teaching: Integration to improve teaching and learning. *Language Arts* 70 (4): 252–63.

Littlewood, W. 1981. *Communicative language teaching: An introduction.* Cambridge: Cambridge University Press.

Liu, J. 1998. Review of *Write to be read: Reading, reflection, and writing,* by W. Smalzer. *TESOL Journal* 7 (2): 41.

Long, M. 1983. Does second language instruction make a difference? A review of research. *TESOL Quarterly* 17 (3): 359–82.

Long, M., and G. Crookes. 1992. Three approaches to task-based syllabus design. *TESOL Quarterly* 26 (1): 27–56.

Long, M., and P. A. Porter. 1985. Group work, interlanguage talk, and second language acquisition. *TESOL Quarterly* 19 (2): 207–28.

Long, M., and J. C. Richards, eds. 1987. *Methodology in TESOL: A book of readings.* Boston: Heinle and Heinle.

Long, M., and P. Robinson. 1998. Focus on form: Theory, research, and practice. In C. Doughty and J. Williams, eds., *Focus on form in classroom second language acquisition,* 15–41. Cambridge: Cambridge University Press.

Long, M., and C. Sato. 1983. Classroom foreigner talk discourse: Forms and functions of teachers' questions. In H. Seliger, W. Herbert, and M. Long, eds., *Classroom oriented research in language acquisition,* 268–85. Rowley, MA: Newbury House.

Longman. 1997. *Longman dictionary of American English.* White Plains, NY: Addison-Wesley Longman.

MacGowan-Gilhooly, A. 1991. Fluency first: Reversing the traditional ESL sequence. *Journal of Basic Writing* (spring) (updated in TESL-L Archives, October 1995).

Madraso, J. 1993. Proofreading: The skill we've neglected to teach. *English Journal* 82 (2): 32–41.

Magy, R. 1998. *Working it out.* Boston: Heinle and Heinle.

Manna, A., and C. Brodie, eds. 1992. *Many faces, many voices: Multicultural literacy experiences for youth.* Fort Atkinson, WI: Highsmith Press.

Manning, B., and B. Payne. 1996. *Self-Talk for teachers and students: Metacognitive strategies for personal and classroom use.* Boston: Allyn and Bacon.

Mason, B., and S. Krashen. 1997. Extensive reading in English as a foreign language. *System* 25:91–102.

Matthews, N. 1990. Sociology 1: Introduction to sociology. Course syllabus, Los Angeles, UCLA.

Maurer, J. 1995. *Focus on grammar: An advanced course for reference and practice.* Longman Focus on Grammar Series. White Plains, NY: Addison-Wesley.

McCarthy, M., and R. Carter. 1994. *Language as discourse: Perspectives for language teaching.* London: Longman.

McGroarty, M., and S. Scott. 1993. Workplace ESL instruction: Varieties and constraints. *ERIC Digest.* Washington, DC: National Clearinghouse for ESL Literacy Education.

Mendelsohn, D. 1991–92. Instruments for feedback in oral communication. *TESOL Journal* 1 (2): 25–30.

———. 1992. Making the speaking class a real learning experience: The keys to teaching spoken English. *TESL Canada Journal* 10 (1): 72–89.

———. 1994. *Learning to listen: A strategy-based approach for the teaching of listening comprehension.* San Diego: Dominie Press.

———. 1999. Janusz Korczak. Untunneling our vision: Lessons from a great educator. In D. Mendelsohn, ed., *Expanding our vision: Insights for language teachers,* 174–86. Toronto: Oxford University Press.

Mendelsohn, D., and J. Rubin, eds. 1995. *A guide for the teaching of second language listening.* San Diego: Dominie Press.

Miller, L. 1995. Materials production in EFL: A team process. *FORUM* 33 (4): 31–33.

Miller, S. 2000. *Targeting pronunciation: The intonation, sounds, and rhythm of American English.* Boston: Houghton Mifflin.

Mittan, R. 1989. The peer review process: Harnessing students' communicative power. In D. M. Johnson and D. H. Roen, eds., *Richness in writing: Empowering ESL students,* 207–19. New York: Longman.

Mohan, B. A. 1986. *Language and content.* Reading, MA: Addison-Wesley.

Moll, L. C. 1988. Some key issues in teaching Latino students. *Language Arts* 65 (4): 465–72.

———. 1992. Bilingual classroom studies and community analysis: Some recent trends. *Educational Researcher* 21 (2): 20–24.

Moll, L. C., C. Vélez-Ibáñz, J. Greenberg, K. Whitmore, R. Andrade, J. Tapia, E. Saavedra, J. Dworin, and D. Fry. 1990. *Community knowledge and classroom practice: Combining resources for literacy instruction.* Final Report. Tucson, AZ: University of Arizona, OBEMLA Contract 300-87-0131.

Montgomery, E., and M. Eisenstein. 1985. Real reality revisited: An experimental communicative course in ESL. *TESOL Quarterly* 19 (2): 317–24.

Morgan, B. 1992–93. Teaching the Gulf War in an ESL Classroom. *TESOL Journal* 2 (2): 13–17.

———. 1995–96. Promoting and assessing critical language awareness. *TESOL Journal* 5 (2): 10–14.

———. 1997. Identity and intonation: Linking dynamic processes in an ESL classroom. *TESOL Quarterly* 31 (3): 431–50.

———. 1998. *The ESL classroom: Teaching, critical practice, and community development.* Toronto: University of Toronto Press.

Morley, J. 1994a. Multidimensional curriculum design for speech-pronunciation instruction. In J. Morley, ed., *Pronunciation pedagogy and theory: New views, new directions,* 64–91. Alexandria, VA: TESOL.

———, ed. 1994b. *Pronunciation pedagogy and theory: New views, new directions.* Alexandria, VA: TESOL.

Moskowitz, G. 1979. *Caring and sharing in the foreign language class: A source book on humanistic techniques.* Boston: Heinle and Heinle.

Murphey, T. 1993. Why don't teachers learn what learners learn? Taking the guesswork out with Action Logging. *English Teaching Forum* (January): 6–10. Washington, DC: USIS.

———. 1997. Content-based instruction in an EFL setting: Issues and strategies. In M. A. Snow and D. M. Brinton, eds., *The content-based classroom: Perspectives on integrating language and content,* 117–31. White Plains, NY: Addison-Wesley Longman.

———. 1998a. Motivating with near peer role models. In B. Visgatis, ed., *JALT97 conference proceedings: Trends and transition,* 205–9. Tokyo: Japan Association of Language Teaching.

———. 1998b. *Language hungry!* Tokyo: MacMillan LanguageHouse.

———. 2000a. *Shadowing and summarizing.* Honolulu: University of Hawai'i, Second Language Teaching and Curriculum Center. NFLRC Video 11. <http://www.LLL.hawaii.edu/nflrc>.

———. 2000b. Strategies for zoning in on the ZPD. Paper presented at the American Association of Applied Linguistics conference, Vancouver, Canada, March.

Murphey, T. , and T. Kenny. 1996. *LSEV: Learner self-evaluated videos.* Honolulu: University of Hawai'i, Second Language Teaching and Curriculum Center. NFLRC Video 10. <http://www.LLL.hawaii.edu/nflrc>.

———. 1998. Videoing conversations for self-evaluation. *Japan Association of Language Teaching Journal* 20 (1): 126–40.

Murphey, T., and L. Woo. 1998. Videoing student conversations: Educational video's diamond in the rough. *Language Teacher* 22 (8): 21–24, 30.

Murphy, J. 1991. Oral communication in TESOL: Integrating speaking, listening, and pronunciation. *TESOL Quarterly* 25 (2): 51–76.

———. 1992. Preparing ESL students for the basic speech course: Approach, design, and procedure. *English for Specific Purposes* 11 (1): 51–70.

———. 1993. An ESL oral communication lesson: One teacher's techniques and principles. *Basic Communication Course Annual* 5:157–81.

———. 1994. Principles of second language teacher education: Integrating multiple perspectives. *Prospect: A Journal of Australian TESOL* 9 (1): 7–28.

———. 1996a. Integrating listening and reading instruction in English for academic purposes (EAP) programs. *English for Specific Purposes* 15 (2): 105–20.

———. 1996b. Teaching pronunciation with "The Odd Couple": Using excerpts from plays. In V. Whiteson, ed., *New ways of using drama and literature in language teaching,* 119–22. Alexandria, VA: TESOL.

Nation, P. 1994. *New ways in teaching vocabulary.* Alexandria, VA: TESOL.

Nattinger, J. R., and J. S. DeCarrico. 1992. *Lexical phrases and language teaching.* Oxford: Oxford University Press.

Nelsen, J., L. Lott, and H. S. Glenn. 1986. *Positive discipline in the classroom: How to effectively use class meetings and other positive discipline strategies.* Rocklin, CA: Prima Publishing.

Nelson, G. 1998a. Categorizing, classifying, labeling: A fundamental cognitive process. *TESOL Quarterly* 32 (4): 727–32.

———. 1998b. Intercultural communication and related courses taught in TESOL master's degree programs. *International Journal of Intercultural Relations* 22:17–33.

———. 1995a. Considering culture: Guidelines for ESL/EFL textbook writers. In P. Byrd, ed., *Material Writer's Guide,* 23–42. Boston: Heinle and Heinle.

———. 1995b. Cultural differences in learning styles. In Joy Reid, ed., *Learning styles in the ESL/EFL classroom,* 3–18. Boston: Heinle and Heinle.

Nelson, G., and J. M. Murphy. 1993. Peer response groups: Do L2 writers use peer comments in revising their drafts? *TESOL Quarterly* 27 (1): 135–41.

New South Wales Adult Migrant English Service (NSW AMES). 1997. *Certificates in spoken and written English.* Sydney: New South Wales Adult Migrant English Service.

Nieto, S. 1996. Affirming diversity: The sociopolitical context of multicultural education. White Plains, NY: Longman.

Norton, B. 2000. *Identity and language learning: Gender, ethnicity, and educational change.* London: Longman.

Novey, D. W., and E. C. Cowin. 1991. *Perfect English pronunciation.* Northbrook, IL: Skills International.

Numrich, C. 1995. *Consider the issues.* 2d ed. White Plains, NY: Pearson Education (formerly Addison-Wesley).

———. 1997. *Face the issues.* 2d ed. White Plains, NY: Pearson Education (formerly Addison-Wesley).

———. 1998. *Raise the issues: An integrated approach to critical thinking.* White Plains, NY: Pearson Education (formerly Addison-Wesley).

Nunan, D. 1988. *Syllabus design.* New York: Oxford University Press.

———. 1989a. *Designing tasks for the communicative classroom.* Cambridge: Cambridge University Press.

———. 1989b. *The learner-centered curriculum.* Cambridge: Cambridge University Press.

———. 1989c. *Understanding language classrooms: A guide for teacher-initiated action.* Englewood Cliffs, NJ: Prentice-Hall.

———. 1990. Action research in the language classroom. In J. C. Richards and D. Nunan, eds., *Second language teacher education,* 62–81. New York: Cambridge University Press.

———. 1991a. *Language teaching methodology: A textbook for teachers.* New York: Prentice-Hall.

———. 1991b. Communicative tasks and the language curriculum. *TESOL Quarterly* 25 (2): 279–95.

———. 1995. *Atlas: Learning-centered communication* (levels 1–4). New York: Heinle and Heinle.

———. 1999. *Second language teaching and learning.* Boston: Heinle and Heinle.

———. 2000. *Seven hypotheses about language learning and teaching.* Audiotape 110-1524. Plenary Address, TESOL International Convention, Vancouver, Canada, March.

———, ed. 1992. *Collaborative language learning and teaching.* Cambridge: Cambridge University Press.

Nunan, D., and C. Lamb. 1996. *The self-directed teacher: Managing the learning process.* New York: Cambridge University Press.

Nunan, D., and L. Miller. 1995. *New ways in teaching listening.* Alexandria, VA: TESOL International.

Oller, J. W., and P. A. Richard-Amato. 1983. *Methods that work.* Boston: Heinle and Heinle.

Olsen, J. 1984. *Look again pictures.* Hayward, CA: Alemany Press.

Omaggio, A. C. 1993. *Teaching language in context: Proficiency-oriented instruction.* 2d ed. Boston: Heinle and Heinle.

Oprandy, R. 1999. Jane Jacobs: Eyes on the city. In D. Mendelsohn, ed., *Expanding our vision: Insights for language teachers,* 41–59. Toronto: Oxford University Press.

Orion, G. F. 1996. *Pronouncing American English: Sounds, stress, and intonation.* 2d ed. Boston: Heinle and Heinle.

Ostler, S. 1980. A survey of academic needs for advanced ESL. *TESOL Quarterly* 14:489–502.

Oxford, R. 1990. *Language learning strategies: What every teacher should know.* Boston: Heinle and Heinle.

———. 1992. Who are our students? A synthesis of foreign and second language research on individual differences with implications for instructional practice. *TESL Canada Journal* 9 (2): 30–49.

Paci, F. 1982. *Black madonna.* Toronto: Oberon.

Paley, M., ed. 1991. *William Blake's Jerusalem: The emanation of the giant albion.* Princeton, NJ: William Blake Trust/Princeton University Press.

Pally, M. 1999. Sustaining interest/advancing learning: Theoretical background and rationale. In M. Pally, ed., *Sustained content teaching in academic ESL/EFL,* 1–18. Boston: Houghton Mifflin.

Palmer, H. 1976. Mosaic versus melting pot? Immigration and ethnicity in Canada and the United States (abridged). *International Journal,* summer:488–528.

Palmer, H. E. 1917. *The scientific study and teaching of languages.* Yonkers, NY: World Publishers.

Parry, K. 1996. Culture, literacy, reading. *TESOL Quarterly* 30:665–92.

Pearson, P., and L. Fielding. 1991. Comprehension instruction. In R. Barr, M. Kamil, P. Mosenthal, and P. Pearson, eds., *Handbook of reading research,* vol. 2, 815–60. White Plains, NY: Longman.

Pearson, P., L. R. Roehler, J. A. Dole, and G. G. Duffy. 1992. Developing expertise in reading comprehension. In S. J. Samuels and A. E. Farstrup, eds., *What research has to say about reading instruction,* 145–99. Newark, DE: International Reading Association.

Pease-Alvarez, L., and O. Vasquez. 1994. Language socialization in ethnic minority communities. In F. Genesse, ed., *Educating second language children: The whole child, the whole curriculum, the whole community,* 82–102. New York: Cambridge University Press.

Pennycook, A. 1996. Borrowing others' words: Text, ownership, memory, and plagiarism. *TESOL Quarterly* 30 (2): 201–30.

Peters, A. 1983. *The units of language acquisition.* Cambridge: Cambridge University Press.

Peterson, R. 1992. *Life in a small place: Making a learning community.* Portsmouth, NH: Heinemann.

Pica, T. 1994a. Language learning research: How it can respond to classroom research. In J. D. Macero and V. Chesser, eds., *NYSTESOL student-centered perspectives and practices,* 1–28. New York: NYSTESOL.

———. 1994b. Questions from the language classroom: Research perspectives. *TESOL Quarterly* 28 (1): 49–79.

Plaister, T. 1993. *ESOL case studies.* Englewood Cliffs, NJ: Prentice-Hall.

Politzer, R. L. 1970. Some reflections on "good" and "bad" language teaching behaviors. *Language Learning* 20:31–43.

Powers, T. 1989. *Special effects in the movies.* San Diego: Lucent Books.

Prabhu, N. S. 1990. There is no best method—why? *TESOL Quarterly* 24 (2): 161–76.

———. 1992. The dynamics of the language lesson. *TESOL Quarterly* 26 (2): 225–42.

Pressley, M., and P. Afflerbach. 1995. *Verbal protocols of reading.* Hillsdale, NJ: Lawrence Erlbaum.

Pressley, M., J. Almasi, T. Schuder, J. Bergman, S. Hite, P. El-Dinary, and R. Brown. 1994. Transactional instruction of comprehension strategies: The Montgomery County, Maryland, SAIL program. *Reading and Writing Quarterly* 10 (1): 5–20.

Pressley, M., and V. Woloshyn. 1995. *Cognitive strategy instruction that really improves children's academic performance.* 2d ed. Cambridge, MA: Brookline Books.

Qian, D. 1998. Depth of vocabulary knowledge: Assessing its role in adults' reading comprehension in English as a second language. Ph.D. diss., University of Toronto/OISE.

Raimes, A. 1991. Errors: Windows into the mind. *College ESL* 1 (2): 55–64.

Report of the National Reading Panel. Teaching children to read. National Institute of Child Health and Human Development. Retrieved May 7, 2001, from the World Wide Web: http://www.nichd.nih.gov/publications/nrp/findings.htm.

Reid, J. 1993. *Teaching ESL writing.* Englewood Cliffs, NJ: Prentice-Hall Regents.

———. 1998. "Eye" learners and "ear" learners: Identifying the language needs of international student and U.S. resident writers. In P. Byrd and J. Reid, eds., *Grammar in the composition classroom: Essays on teaching ESL for college-bound students,* 3–17. Boston: Heinle and Heinle.

Richard-Amato, P. 1988. *Making it happen: Interaction in the language classroom from theory to practice.* New York: Longman.

Richards, J. C. 1983. Listening comprehension: Approach, design, procedure. *TESOL Quarterly* 17 (2): 219–39.

———. 1989. Profile of an effective reading teacher. *Prospect* 4 (2): 13–29.

———. 1996. Teachers' maxims in language teaching. *TESOL Quarterly* 30 (2): 281–96.

———, ed. 1998. *Teaching in action: Case studies from second language classrooms.* Alexandria, VA: TESOL.

Richards, J. C., and C. Lockhart. 1994. *Reflective teaching in second language classrooms.* New York: Cambridge University Press.

Richards, J. C., and T. S. Rodgers. 1982. Method: Approach, design, and procedure. *TESOL Quarterly* 16 (2): 153–68.

———. 1985. Method: Approach, design, and procedure. In J. C. Richards, ed., *The context of language teaching,* 16–31. Cambridge: Cambridge University Press.

———. 1986. *Approaches and methods in language teaching: A description and analysis.* New York: Cambridge University Press.

Richards, K. 1994. Teachers' knowledge: From guessing what teachers think to finding out what teachers know: The need for a research agenda. *TESOL Quarterly* 28 (2): 401–4.

Rigg, P. 1991. Whole language in TESOL. *TESOL Quarterly* 25 (3): 521–42.

Rinvolucri, M. 1984. *Grammar games: Cognitive, affective, and drama activities for EFL students.* New York: Cambridge University Press.

Rinvolucri, M., and P. Davis. 1995. *More grammar games: Cognitive, affective, and movement activities for EFL students.* New York: Cambridge University Press.

Robinson, P. 1991. *ESP today: A practitioner's guide.* London: Prentice-Hall.

Routman, R. 1991. *Invitations: Changing as teachers and learners K–12.* Portsmouth, NH: Heinemann.

Rubin, J., and I. Thompson. 1994. *How to be a more successful language learner.* Boston: Heinle and Heinle.

Rudman, M., ed. 1993. *Children's literature: Resource for the classroom.* Norwood, MA: Christopher-Gordon Publishers.

Rueda, R., C. Goldenberg, and R. Gallimore. 1992. *Rating instructional conversations: A guide.* Educational Practice Report 4. Santa Cruz: National Center for Research on Cultural Diversity and Second Language Learning.

Rylant, C. 1985. *The relatives came.* New York: Scholastic.

Samway, K., and G. Whang. 1995. *Literature study circles in a multicultural classroom.* York, ME: Stenhouse.

Sarmiento, A. R., and A. Kay. 1990. *Worker-centered literacy: A union guide to workplace literacy.* Washington, DC: AFL-CIO Human Resources Development Institute. ERIC Document Reproduction Service ED 338 863.

Scarcella, R., and R. Oxford. 1992. *The tapestry of language learning: The individual in the communicative classroom.* Boston: Heinle and Heinle.

Schmidt, R. W., and S. N. Frota. 1986. Developing basic conversation ability in a second language: A case study of an adult learner of Portuguese. In R. Day, ed., *Talking to learn: Conversation in second language acquisition,* 237–326. Rowley, MA: Newbury House.

Schulman, M., and E. Mekler. 1984. *The actor's scenebook.* New York: Bantam Books.

Schumann, J. 1978a. The acculturation model for second language acquisition. In R. C. Gingras, ed., *Second language acquisition and foreign language teaching,* 27–50. Arlington, VA: Center for Applied Linguistics.

———. 1978b. *The pidginization process: A model for second language acquisition.* Rowley, MA: Newbury House.

Science Research Associates (SRA). 1999. New York: McGraw-Hill. <http://www.sra4kids.com/reading/default.html>.

Sears, A. M., and A. S. Hughes. 1996. Citizenship education and current educational reform. *Canadian Journal of Education* 21:123–42.

Secretary's Commission on Achieving Necessary Skills. 1991. *What work requires of schools: A SCANS report for America 2000.* Washington, DC: U.S. Department of Labor. ERIC Document Reproduction Service ED 332 054.

Shaughnessy, M. 1977. *Errors and expectations: A guide for the teacher of basic writing.* New York: Oxford University Press.

Shelly, G., T. J. Cashman, and J. F. Repede. 1998. *Netscape Composer creating web pages.* Cambridge: Course Technology. <http://www.course.com>.

Shetzer, H., and M. Warschauer. 2000. An electronic literacy approach to network-based language teaching. In M. Warschauer and R. Kern, eds., *Network-based language teaching: Concepts and practice,* 171–85. Cambridge: Cambridge University Press.

Shih, M. 1992. Beyond comprehension exercises in the ESL academic reading class. *TESOL Quarterly* 26 (2): 289–318.

———. 1998. ESL writers' grammar editing strategies. *College ESL* 8 (2): 64–86.

Short, K. G., and J. C. Harste, with C. Burke. 1996. *Creating classrooms for authors and inquirers.* Portsmouth, NH: Heinemann.

Silva, T. 1990. Second language composition instruction: Developments, issues, and directions in ESL. In B. Kroll, ed., *Second language writing: Research insights for the classroom,* 11–23. New York: Cambridge University Press.

Silverman, R., and B. Welty. 1992. *Case Studies for faculty development.* New York: Center for Case Studies in Education, Pace University.

Silverstein, S. 1974. Sister for sale. *Where the Sidewalk Ends.* New York: Harper-Collins.

Skehan, P. 1996. A framework for the implementation of task-based instruction. *Applied Linguistics* 17:38–62.

Smalzer, W. 1996. *Write to be read: Reading, reflection, and writing.* New York: Cambridge University Press.

Smith, F. 1978. *Understanding reading.* 2d ed. New York: Holt, Rinehart, and Winston.

———. 1982. *Writing and the writer.* New York: Holt, Rinehart, and Winston.

———. 1983. *Essays into literacy: Selected papers and some afterthoughts.* Portsmouth, NH: Heinemann.

———. 1990. *To think.* New York: Teachers College Press.

Snow, M. A. 1991. Teaching language through content. In M. A. Snow, ed., *Teaching English as a second or foreign language,* 315–28. Boston: Newbury House.

Snow, M. A., and D. M. Brinton, eds. 1997. *The content-based classroom: Perspectives on integrating language and content.* White Plains, NY: Longman.

Spack, R. 1997. The rhetorical construction of multilingual students. *TESOL Quarterly* 31 (4): 765–74.

Spada, N. 1994. Classroom interaction analysis. *TESOL Quarterly* 28 (4): 685–88.

Spanos, G. 1987. On the integration of language and content instruction. *Annual Review of Applied Linguistics* 10:227–40.

Stansfield, C. W. 1992. ACTFL speaking proficiency guidelines. *ERIC Digest.* Washington, DC: ERIC Clearinghouse on Languages and Linguistics. ERIC Document Reproduction Service ED 347 852.

Steckley, J. 1997. Aboriginal peoples. In P. U. Angelini, ed., *Our society: Human diversity in Canada,* 132–58. Toronto: ITP Nelson.

Steptoe, J. 1987. *Mufaro's beautiful daughters: An African tale*. New York: Lothrop, Lee and Shepard Books.

Stern, H. H. 1975. What can we learn from the good language learner? *Canadian Modern Language Review* 31:304–18.

Stevick, E. W. 1976. *Memory, meaning, and method*. Boston: Heinle and Heinle.

———. 1980. *Teaching languages: A way and ways*. Boston: Heinle and Heinle.

Stewart, E. 1995. Parizeau "lacks courage" federalist leaders insist. *Toronto Star*, September 8, p. A12.

Stoller, F. L., and W. Grabe. 1997. A six-T's approach to content-based instruction. In M. A. Snow and D. M Brinton, eds., *The content-based classroom: Perspectives on integrating language and content*, 78–94. White Plains, NY: Longman.

Susser, B., and T. Robb. 1990. EFL extensive reading instruction: Research and procedure. *JALT Journal* 12:161–85. Available at <http://www.kyoto-su.ac.jp/~trobb/sussrobb.html>.

Swain, M. 1985. Communicative competence: Some roles of comprehensible input and comprehensible output in its development. In S. M. Gass and C. G. Madden, eds., *Input in second language acquisition*, 235–53. Rowley, MA: Newbury House.

———. 2000. The output hypothesis and beyond: Mediating acquisition through collaborative dialogue. In J. Lantolf, ed., *Sociocultural theory and second language learning*, 97–124. Oxford: Oxford University Press.

Tarvin, W. L., and A. Yl Al-Arishi. 1991. Rethinking communicative language teaching: Reflection and the EFL classroom. *TESOL Quarterly* 25 (1): 9–27.

Tharp, R., and R. Gallimore. 1991. *The instructional conversation: Teaching and learning in social activity*. Research Report 20. Santa Cruz: National Center for Research on Cultural Diversity and Second Language Learning.

Ting, Y. R. 1987. Foreign language teaching in China: Problems and perspectives. *Canadian and International Education* 16:48–61.

Trahey, M., and L. White. 1993. Positive evidence and preemption in the second language classroom. *Studies in Second Language Acquisition* 15:181–204.

Truscott, J. 1996. The case against grammar correction in L2 writing classes. *Language Learning* 46:327–69.

Tudor, I. 1996. *Learner-centeredness as language education*. Cambridge: Cambridge University Press.

U.S. Department of Education. 1992. *Workplace literacy: Reshaping the American workforce*. Washington, DC: U.S. Department of Education.

Ur, P. 1996. *A course in language teaching: Practice and theory*. New York: Cambridge University Press.

———. 1990. *Grammar practice activities*. New York: Cambridge University Press.

Valdes, A. I., and A. C. Jhones. 1991. Introduction of communicative language teaching in tourism in Cuba. *TESL Canada Journal* 8 (2): 57–63.

van Lier, L. 1987a. Review of *Techniques and principles in language teaching*, by D. Larsen-Freeman. *TESOL Quarterly* 21 (1): 146–52.

————. 1987b. The reviewer responds to "The author reacts." *TESOL Quarterly* 21 (4): 775–77.

————. 1988. *The classroom and the language learner: Ethnography and second-language classroom research.* London: Longman.

Vander Zanden, J. W. 1990. *Sociology: The core.* 2d ed. New York: McGraw-Hill.

Vygotsky, L. [1934] 1962. *Thought and language.* Cambridge: MIT Press.

————. [1934] 1978. *Mind in society: The development of higher psychological processes.* Reprint, Cambridge: Cambridge University Press.

Wajnryb, R. 1992. *Classroom observation tasks.* New York: Cambridge University Press.

Wallace, M. 1998. *Action research for language teachers.* New York: Cambridge University Press.

Warschauer, M. 1996. Motivational aspects of using computers for writing and communication. In M. Warschauer, ed., *Telecollaboration in foreign language learning: Proceedings of the Hawai'i symposium,* 24–46. Honolulu, HI: Second Language Teaching and Curriculum Center, University of Hawai'i.

————. 1999. *Electronic literacies: Language, culture, and power in online education.* Mahwah, NJ: Lawrence Erlbaum.

Watkins, D. A., and J. B. Biggs, eds. 1996. *The Chinese learner: Cultural, psychological, and contextual influences.* Hong Kong: Comparative Education Research Centre.

Weaver, C. 1994. *Reading process and practice.* Portsmouth, NH: Heinemann.

Weedon, C. 1987. *Feminist practice and poststructuralist theory.* New York: Basil Blackwell.

Wenden, A. 1986. Helping language learners think about learning. *English Language Teaching Journal* 40 (1): 3–12.

Wesche, M., and T. S. Paribakht. 1996. Assessing second language vocabulary knowledge: Depth versus breadth. *Canadian Modern Language Review* 53 (1): 13–41.

White, R. V. 1988. *The ELT curriculum: Design, innovation, and management.* Oxford: Basil Blackwell.

Whiteson, V., ed. 1996. *New ways of using drama and literature in language teaching.* Alexandria, VA: TESOL.

Whitman, W. [1891] 1992. Song of myself. *Leaves of grass.* New York: Library of America.

Whitmore, K. F., and C. G. Crowell. 1994. *Inventing a classroom: Life in a bilingual whole language learning community.* York, ME: Stenhouse.

Widdowson, H. 1978. *Teaching language as communication.* London: Oxford University Press.

Wilkins, D. A. 1976. *Notional syllabuses.* Oxford: Oxford University Press.

Willett, J., J. Solsken, and J. Wilson-Keenan. 1998. The (im)possibilities of constructing multicultural language practices in research and pedagogy. *Linguistics and Education* 10:165–218.

Williams, J. 1995. Focus on form in communicative language teaching: Research findings and the classroom teacher. *TESOL Journal* 4 (4): 12–16.

Willing, K. 1988. *Learning styles in adult migrant education.* Sydney: NCELTR, Macquarie University.

———. 1989. *Teaching how to learn: Learning strategies in ESL,* report 8. Sydney: NCELTR.

Wilson-Keenan, J., J. Solsken, and J. Willett. 1999. "Only boys can jump high": Reconstructing gender relations in a first/second grade classroom. In B. Kamler, ed., *Constructing gender and difference: Critical research perspectives on early childhood,* 33–70. Cresskill, NJ: Hampton Press.

Wolfe, P., and R. Brandt. 1998. What do we know from brain research? *Educational Leadership* 5, no. 3 (November): 8–13.

Wong, R. 1987. *Teaching pronunciation: Focus on English rhythm and intonation.* Englewood Cliffs, NJ: Prentice-Hall.

Wong-Fillmore, L. 1989. Language learning in social context: The view from research in second language learning. In R. Dietrich and C. F. Graumann, eds., *Language processing in social context,* 277–302. Amsterdam: Elsevier.

Woods, D. 1989. Studying ESL teachers' decision-making: Rationale, methodological issues, and initial results. *Carleton Papers in Applied Language Studies* 6:107–23.

———. 1996. *Teacher cognition in language teaching: Beliefs, decision-making, and classroom practice.* Cambridge: Cambridge University Press.

Wright, T. 1987. *Roles of teachers and learners.* New York: Oxford University Press.

Yalden, J. 1983. *The communicative syllabus: Evolution, design, and implementation.* Oxford: Pergamon Press.

Yorio, C. 1994. The case for learning. In R. Barach and J. C.Vaughn, eds., *Beyond the monitor model: Comments on current theory and practice in second language acquisition,* 125–37. Boston: Heinle and Heinle.

Zamel, V. 1982. Writing: The process of discovering meaning. *TESOL Quarterly* 16 (2): 195–209.

———. 1985. Responding to student writing. *TESOL Quarterly* 19:79–102.

———. 1992. Writing one's way into reading. *TESOL Quarterly* 26:463–85.

Contributors

William Acton
Nagoya University of Commerce, Japan

Carolyn Armstrong
Goodwill Industries of the Columbia Willamette, Portland

Susan M. Barone
Vanderbilt University, Nashville

Donna M. Brinton
University of California, Los Angeles

Anne Burns
National Centre for English Language Teaching and Research, Macquarie
University, Sydney, Australia

Patricia Byrd
Georgia State University, Atlanta

Robert A. DeVillar
University of Texas at El Paso

Dana R. Ferris
California State University, Sacramento

Janet M. Goodwin
University of California, Los Angeles

Janet G. Graham
Vanderbilt University, Nashville

Joy Janzen
Moorhead State University, Minnesota

Binbin Jiang
University of the Incarnate Word, San Antonio, Texas

Pam McPherson
National Centre for English Language Teaching and Research, Macquarie
University, Sydney, Australia

David J. Mendelsohn
York University of Toronto, Canada

Lindsay Miller
City University of Hong Kong

Brian Morgan
York University of Toronto, Canada

Tim Murphey
Nanzan University, Nagoya, Japan

John Murphy
Georgia State University, Atlanta

Carol Numrich
American Language Program of Columbia University, New York

Thomas N. Robb
Kyoto Sangyo University, Japan

Janice Ruhl
Portland Community College

Heidi Shetzer
University of California, Santa Barbara

May Shih
San Francisco State University

Judith Solsken
University of Massachusetts

Marjorie Terdal
Portland State University

Mark Warschauer
University of California, Irvine

Jerri Willett
University of Massachusetts

Jo-Anne Wilson-Keenan
Springfield, Massachusetts, Public Schools

Author Index

Subject Index